Not Your Average Joe

Not Your Average Joe

A Biography of
Joseph William Hobbs (1891–1963),
Whisky Entrepreneur

TIM SMITH

T

Troubador Publishing Ltd
Unit E2 Airfield Business Park
Harrison Road, Market Harborough
Leicestershire LE16 7UL
Tel: 0116 279 2299
Email: books@troubador.co.uk
Web: www.troubador.co.uk

ISBN 978 1 80514 425 0

British Library Cataloguing in Publication Data.
A catalogue record for this book is available from the British Library.

Printed and bound in Great Britain by 4edge Limited
Typeset in 11pt Minion Pro by Troubador Publishing Ltd, Leicester, UK

Contents

Introduction

In an industry littered with great characters and extraordinary personalities, Joe Hobbs stands out as one of the whisky world's most colourful and interesting entrepreneurs, a man who packed more into each decade of his life than most people manage in a lifetime. Whilst certain episodes and activities from his life are quite well known, often quoted and referred to (not always with the greatest accuracy) in whisky articles, blogs and stories, Joe's fascinating life story has not been told in full before.

A passionate 'whisky nerd' with an interest verging on the obsessional, I was perusing an article on a whisky blog one day in 2020 when my attention was caught by a comment the blogger made. Given Joe Hobbs' varied and colourful career in whisky, the blogger pointed out, it was surprising nobody had written the full story of Joe's life history. This triggered in me the germ of an idea to research and write a thorough and systematic biography of Joe Hobbs, documenting for the first time the whole story of his extraordinary life and achievements.

At the outset, I thought a biography of Joe Hobbs might also be welcomed by others like me with an interest in whisky, keen to know more about Joe's work building a network of seven Scottish distilleries under Associated Scottish Distilleries in the 1930s, and then owning Ben Nevis and Lochside distilleries after

WW2. As I researched and interacted with people who might know something of relevance to Joe's life, I realised interest in Joe Hobbs runs much wider. Nautical and aviation history groups in Canada and the UK wanted to know more about Joe's exploits as one of the first military aviators during World War 1 and his shipping and rum-running activities in Canada in the 1920s-30s. Canadians and especially those with a connection to the stunning city of Vancouver were interested to know more about Joe's leading role in the design, construction and funding of Vancouver's first 'skyscraper', the iconic 'Marine Building'. And those with an interest in the history of the Highlands of Scotland (and in particular, its agricultural history) were intrigued to learn about Joe's pioneering work to transform 10,000 acres of barren upland into Britain's first cattle ranch, drawing on North American concepts of stock rearing with his successful Great Glen Cattle Ranch.

I also realised as I sought to document Joe's eventful life that there would be many general readers for whom the story of how Joe made and lost a fortune in Canada before returning to the land of his birth and making a second fortune would be an exciting read, and could provide some insight into the character, risk-taking and persistence of an impressive entrepreneur. Along the way, the book delves into Joe's character and the drivers of his behaviour to help the reader understand what made Joe Hobbs the person he was. It highlights his bold and energetic entrepreneurship – the failures as well as the successes – his "up and at it" attitude and determination never to give up, his constant challenging of orthodoxy, and ability to bring modern methods and a scientific approach to improve businesses and take advantage of opportunities. In this way, the reader gains insight into Joe's personality, which brings to life the human side of the many events in his most active life.

Joe had an impressive ability to communicate, promote

and build support for his many ideas and initiatives, especially through the media, which together with official historic records has left a rich seam of documentation from which to piece together a detailed timeline of his life. However, this book could not have been written without the strong support and generous sharing of information, stories, photographs and memorabilia of Joe Hobbs and his family by his surviving family members, much of which has not been shared publicly before. In particular, Joe's grandson Joseph Peter Hobbs and his wife Margaret, and his grand-niece Alexandra Anthony (the granddaughter of Joe's sister Alexandra) have contributed substantially, not just with material for the book but also with advice, feedback, suggestions and encouragement, which have done a great deal to give colour to the factual history of Joe's timeline and bring elements of his character to life.

The author has also benefitted from material, input and advice from a wide range of others, including Dr Chris Robinson at the West Highland Museum in Fort William, Scotland; writer and broadcaster Hugh Dan MacLennan, who has researched Joe Hobbs' life and given public talks on the subject; Ralph Palmer, son of the estate Factor on Joe's Inverlochy Estate, who is one of the few people still living with first-hand knowledge of Joe; Paolo and Elspeth Berardelli, who today successfully run Achendaul Farm, the centrepiece of the land that was Joe's Great Glen Cattle Ranch; Col. John Orr, a Royal Canadian Air Force veteran who has researched Joe and his brother Basil's aeronautical exploits; Dominic Sargent, who wrote the official history of Inverlochy Castle Hotel; and whisky writer Iain Russell, who has written excellent profiles of Joe Hobbs and many other whisky characters for the Dictionary of National Biography and www. scotchwhisky.com among other publications.

I am also extremely grateful to Jenny McIlreavy for her work to edit the text, and to my wife Helen and daughter Lilly for taking the time to read numerous chapter drafts and give helpful suggestions for improvement.

Not Your Average Joe has been a labour of love for me as an author, aiming to tell in an interesting way the life story of someone whose activities and achievements I believe should be much better known. If it provides the reader with a fraction of the enjoyment I have had in researching and writing the book, the effort will have been well worth it.

Hong Kong, January 2024.

1

Pioneering Stock

Sometimes, simply by virtue of their success, a successful parent creates expectation for their children. Whether real or imagined, this expectation to live up to the achievements of their parent can weigh heavily on the child. This can be a powerful driver of a person's ambitions and actions, influencing their life and career choices. It can be a source of positive inspiration, but often the desire to show they are 'made of the same stuff' and can achieve success in their own right brings unhelpful pressure to the next generation, driving them to attempt things which may prove – to themselves, to their parents, and to wider society – that they are just as capable.

This was the case in the family of Joseph Hobbs, a very successful farmer and landowner in the rolling downland around Newbury in Berkshire, some 70 miles west of London, towards the end of the 19th century. Joseph's success resulted in his eldest son, Joseph William Hobbs, stepping out on his own in business. An initial period of rapid expansion and positive achievement mirroring his father's successful career unfortunately could not be sustained, resulting in his eventual bankruptcy. The circumstances of his business collapse created a rift in the family that was not resolved in his father's lifetime, and led to Joseph William taking his family and emigrating to Canada.

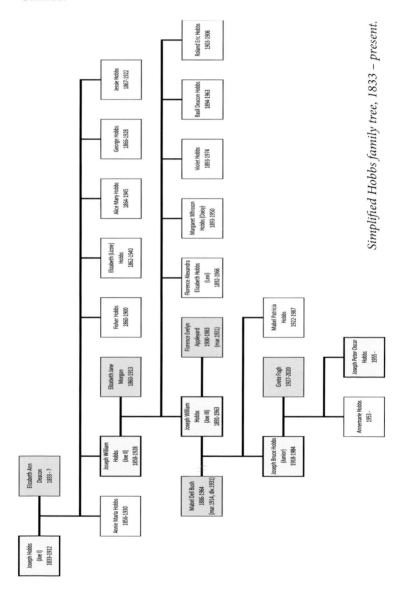

Simplified Hobbs family tree, 1833 – present.

Somewhat confusingly, five generations of older sons all took the name Joseph. The original Joseph Hobbs (born 1834) will here be called Joe I, and his son Joseph William (born in 1859) will be called Joe II. The third-generation Joseph William Hobbs (born in 1891), who is the principal subject of this biography, we will simply call Joe.

Joe's family background sowed the seeds that set his life on its extraordinary trajectory. His father's actions in embarking on an ambitious and high-risk programme of business expansion at a time of agricultural depression ended in financial disaster, and led the family to emigrate to Canada. The background of an entrepreneurial father determined to 'make good' and show what he was capable of, and the consequences for the whole family of his business failure, were strong formative influences on Joe, and contributed significantly to making him the man that he was – a highly driven entrepreneur and businessman with a strong desire for success, a willingness to take risks, and an "up and at it!" philosophy that enabled him to deal with setbacks and persevere, however tough things became. Later influences in Canada also contributed substantially to shape the man who was to become one of the most interesting and colourful figures in the whisky industry and live a life packed full of incident and activity. But Joe's initial years in England, and the actions of his father and grandfather, were clearly formative on his character, and essential to an understanding of what made Joe Hobbs the dynamic and successful person he became in later life.

Of humble origins, Joe I was born in 1833 at Whitley, near Reading, the son of an agricultural labourer. He lived his early years in near poverty, but Joe I had entrepreneurial flair and was to develop a shrewd business sense that enabled him to become a wealthy man, eventually owning and operating four farms extending to over 1,600 acres in total in the area around Thatcham, a historic market town 3 miles to the east of Newbury. This was a significant achievement for someone of his background, especially given the context of agricultural depression and continually increasing competition.

Southern England, showing the location of Newbury, Berkshire.

Not content to follow in his father's footsteps as an agricultural labourer, Joe I initially worked as a butcher in the town of Newbury. He is recorded as a young man of 18 in the 1851 Census, already making his way in the world with his own butcher shop at 118 Market Place, Newbury, and employing a housekeeper, a slaughterman, and an errand boy.

Joe I met Elizabeth Ann Deacon (b.1833 at Cookham, Berkshire) and the couple married in April 1855 at Bradfield, Berkshire. They started a family the following year with the arrival of Annie Maria Hobbs, born in January 1856, whilst the couple were still living at Newbury. Their second child and oldest son Joseph William Hobbs was born on 15th August 1858, by which time Joe I had moved on from his butchery business and was prospering as a cattle dealer living in a substantial Victorian villa at Woodspeen, to the west of Newbury. From here, we can trace the family through the second half of the 19th century from the census returns, which chart Joe I's progressive development from butcher to cattle dealer and then, at the age of just 36, to head of household at Manor Farm, Thatcham, on the eastern side of Newbury. By that time, Joe I and Elizabeth had expanded their family to seven children in total. In addition to employing three domestic servants to take care of the family, Joe I also provided work for 22 people on the 310-acre farm.[1]

Manor Farm, Thatcham, as it looks today.

The extremely challenging environment for domestic farmers in Britain made the success of Joe I all the more extraordinary. During the last quarter of the 19th century, Britain experienced a long decline in its agricultural economy, known as 'the Great Depression of English Agriculture'.[2] The fundamental cause was the 1846 Parliamentary Act to repeal Britain's Corn Laws, which removed the long-standing tariffs on imported grains that had protected England's farming sector for decades, and opened Britain's agricultural economy to the full force of free trade.[a] During this period, Britain became the most industrialised country in the world, and the nation with the smallest share of its economy derived from agriculture. By 1914, Britain relied on imports for 80% of its wheat and 40% of its meat.[3]

Joe I continued to succeed as a farmer and cattle trader through the 1870s-80s despite the agricultural depression, and was able to progressively expand his business by acquiring three additional farms in the area – Garfield Farm, at East Hendred; Snelsmore Farm, at Donnington; and Ashfields Farm near Newbury. All told, by the 1890s Joe I eventually owned and operated four separate farms, totalling over 1,600 acres, and commanding considerable capital. Joe I and his family lived in a separate farmhouse at The Rookery, Henwick, with gardens and surrounding parkland.

---

a   The repeal of the Corn Laws did not give rise to the immediate dramatic fall in grain prices that many farmers feared. However, the opening up of the American Mid-West to cultivation in the 1870s and expansion of lower cost agriculture in many of Britain's colonies (especially in Australia and New Zealand), plus the increasing availability of cheap transportation spurred by expansion of the US railroads and development of global steamship networks, led to a progressive rise in imported agricultural products of all types into the 'old country'. As an example, the cost of transporting a ton of grain from Chicago to Liverpool fell from 37 shillings in 1873, to 21 shillings in 1880, and to only 14 shillings in 1884. Consequently, between 1871–75 and 1896–1900, imports of wheat and flour increased by 90%, those of butter and cheese rose 110%, whilst for meat there was a 300% increase in imports. Whilst the improved availability and lower prices of a wealth of imported products was undoubtedly beneficial for Britain's urban population, and was a spur to Britain's further development and industrialisation, the adverse impact on agriculture and rural communities was profound and prolonged. Agricultural prices in the UK fell continuously from the early 1870s; for example, the price of wheat declined from 56s 0d a quarter on average between 1867–71 to 27s 3d on average between 1894–98, with the low point in 1894–95, when the price of 22s 10d per quarter was the lowest level for 150 years.

The Broadway, Thatcham, Berkshire, in the early 20th century.

In 1897, a local auctioneer gave the following description of Joe I's home at this time: 'It had a good walled-in garden with good aspect, spacious coach-house, and stabling. The former was 42ft. by 14ft and would accommodate 8 carriages. It is currently occupied by four. The stabling comprised two good stalls and two loose boxes. The house itself was in a most lovely situation. The parkland was 39 and ¼ acres in extent, the whole of which was good holding ground.'[4] Together with other property in the area he bought over the years and rented out (e.g. land and buildings he acquired on the Chieveley Estate in 1892),[5] all this in combination made Joe I a substantial land and property owner, and a person of wealth and high standing in the area.

As Joe I's older son, Joe II must have felt considerable pressure to show what he was capable of achieving in his own right. Initially Joe II worked as his father's deputy as they expanded the business together. In 1876, Joe I and Joe II, by then 18 years of age, lost a case to a farmer from Overton in Hampshire who had sued them for selling diseased pigs at market,[6] providing evidence that Joe II was already taking his first steps in dealing in livestock with his father.

But then, as we know from later newspaper articles,[7] in 1885 at the age of 27, Joe II took the decision to step away from helping his father run the family farms and set about building up his own farming business, just as his father had done before him. In January of that year, he moved six miles south to Burghclere, just across the county border into Hampshire, and took a lease on Heatherwold Farm, to begin his own career as a farmer and cattle dealer. Joe I was a tough, demanding and controlling character, so Joe II's move potentially also reflected a desire to have some 'room' of his own, and the freedom to make his own decisions. But, from his subsequent actions, it seems Joe I was not impressed by his older son walking out on the family business. This was the beginning of a rift that persisted through the remainder of Joe I's life, going some way to explain why Joe I did not do more to help Joe II when he later found himself in trouble, and why Joe II received hardly anything from his father's will. As the older son, he probably stood to have inherited the majority of Joe I's estate.

However, following in his father's footsteps, initially Joe II also achieved considerable success. Heatherwold Farm, Joe II's first step in business on his own, was a part of the Earl of Carnarvon's Highclere Estate, centred around the impressive

Heatherwold Farm, Burghclere, where Joseph William Hobbs was born on 28th January 1891. Today it is a successful stud farm.

Highclere Castle, which would later become famous as the setting for the TV series *Downton Abbey*.[b] As was typical at the time, many of the farms and landholdings of the Highclere Estate were let out to tenant farmers to operate, with the estate managed by professional land agents employed by Lord Carnarvon to run it on his behalf. It was a bold move for Joe II to take the lease on one of these farms, and a clear sign of his ambition and confidence. This marked the start of an intense period of expansion and activity for Joe II and his family.

Highclere Castle, Hampshire, in the late 19th century.

---

b   Henry Howard Molyneux Herbert, the 4th Earl of Carnarvon, was a Tory politician who was twice Secretary for the Colonies (where, in an interesting link given the Hobbs family's later links with Canada, he was responsible for the British North America Act of 1867, which established the federation of Canada) and also served as Lord Lieutenant of Ireland. His family estate was at Highclere in Hampshire (where his father the 3rd Earl had been responsible for building the marvellous house subsequently made famous in *Downton Abbey*, completed in 1878) and was a major landowner in the area.

In 1889, Joe II got married, aged 31 – quite late for the times. His wife was Elizabeth Jane Morgan, from London. We do not have information about how she and Joe II met, but from court records we know that she gave testimony at the Old Bailey on 12th September 1881, after her purse was snatched by two men. A cabbie gave chase and apprehended the thief, who was sentenced to five years in prison. Elizabeth comes across from her witness testimony as a plucky and determined woman, capable of sticking up for herself.[8]

The couple wed on 19th June 1889 at St Peter's Church, Berkhamsted, Hertfordshire, the ceremony being conducted by the Rev. Charles Morgan, who was a cousin of Elizabeth's.[9, 10,] In the wedding announcement, Elizabeth's father, the late John Morgan, was said to live at 'the Manor House, Great Berkhamstead' (sic), which gives the impression he was minor gentry or a wealthy rural farmer. However, from Elizabeth's baptism record, John Morgan was shown as a licensed victualler in St Pancras, London – so this is a little misleading, and perhaps indicative of a desire by the couple to show themselves as people of good standing, although we do know from subsequent records that Elizabeth had inherited over £5,000 from her father (equivalent to around £650,000 in today's terms).

Not long after the wedding, Joe II took another big step. On 29th September 1889, he took the lease on a second farm on the Highclere Estate, Ivory Farm.[11] This was in addition to his existing commitments at Heatherwold Farm. The following year, he expanded further again, taking up the lease on a third property, Snelsmore Farm, in the village of Chieveley, some 10 miles north of Highclere on the other side of Newbury. The lease for the new farm was to run for 14 years. The rent agreed was £65 per annum for the first 4 years, and then £131 per annum for the remaining 10 year period. [12] This farm was leased from Joe II's father, which was to have important ramifications later when Joe II fell behind on the rent. In the early 1890s, Joe II also took a lease on a fourth property, Arlington Grange Farm, in the same parish as Snelsmore.[13] So, by the early 1890s, in the space of just a few short years, Joe II had expanded to manage and operate four farmsteads in total, two at Highclere and two 10 miles away at Chieveley, north of Newbury.

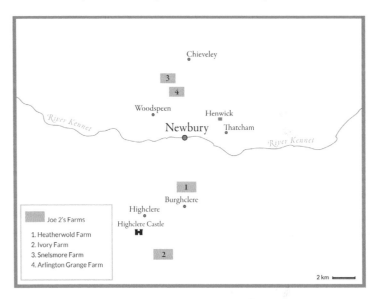

Joe II's farms near Newbury and Burghclere.

It seems highly likely that in doing all this Joe II was trying to prove that he was as capable as his father as a farming entrepreneur. However, against the background of the agricultural depression, with prices that could be achieved for farm products falling year after year, this was extremely risky behaviour. Whilst it is hard to be sure, it is quite likely these additional farms became available to rent because their previous tenants could not make them pay. This was a period when the amount of agricultural land under cultivation in England contracted progressively, a time when there was a steady and substantial flow of people leaving agriculture and the countryside and moving to towns and cities to live and work. Unlike his father, who had slowly built up his estate and owned his land outright, Joe II had expanded his business rapidly, and, as he was renting his farms, needed to be able to keep up regular payments to his landlord. In addition, the agreement for at least one of the farms had substantial rent increases written into the lease, and it was clearly a significant undertaking for a young and relatively inexperienced person like Joe II to manage four separate farm properties simultaneously. The management and organisation challenge alone would be a big stretch even for an experienced businessman, which Joe II most definitely was not. Such a rapid expansion of responsibilities in just a few years was extremely ambitious, and would prove too much for him.

To begin with, however, things went well. On 5th April 1890, Joe II was appointed, together with William Henry Robson, as an 'overseer' for the parish of Burghclere.[14] Under

By the mid-1890s, Joe II had also built up a network of our farms, just like his father. This is a picture of Snelsmore Farm, near Chieveley, Berkshire, today.

England's antiquated Poor Law system (a sort of social safety net to take care of the rural poor), two overseers in each parish were traditionally appointed at Easter each year to administer poor relief to the disadvantaged in the community.[c] The appointment indicates Joe II was a man of good standing in the parish.

Soon after this, Joe II and Elizabeth had their first child. The couple's first son, also named Joseph William Hobbs, was born on 29th January 1891 at Heatherwold Farm, Burghclere, with the birth registered at nearby Kingsclere, Hampshire.[15] Joe's birth certificate confirms he was born in the county of Hampshire, although some sources say he was born in Berkshire – but this is perhaps because Joe himself often stated his place of birth to be 'Newbury' (in Berkshire), probably because people were more likely to know where Newbury was, compared with Burghclere. Joe II was 32 and Elizabeth 31 years old at the time of their first son's arrival. They would have four more children in the following few years, and a sixth child later on, after moving to Canada.

The birth certificate of Joseph William Hobbs, the subject of this book, born 29th January 1891, at Burghclere, Hampshire.

c   The role was a somewhat onerous, but also locally prestigious (unpaid) position. After the 1834 Poor Law, the parish overseer role was abolished in many locations, but continued in some places as a method of collecting the 'poor rate', a tax on each property in the parish that was used to fund assistance for the poor in the district.

The 1891 Census shows Joe II and Elizabeth living at Heatherwold Farm, Burghclere, with two-month-old Joe, Elizabeth's sister Ann Morgan, and two domestic staff.[16] In September 1892 Joe II took the "Reserve Rosette" for best agricultural horse at the Newbury Horse Show,[17] indicating he was doing well with his business and may have been breeding and rearing horses as well as cattle. Then on 19th September 1892 came the birth of their first daughter, Florence Alexandra, known as Lex or Lexi. Exactly one year later, Elizabeth gave birth to twin daughters Marguerite – known as 'Daisy' – and Violet on 19th September 1893.[18]

So far, so very good. Joe's family and business were both expanding rapidly, and he was held in high esteem in his community.

However, soon after this, things took a turn for the worse, at the start of a period that was to be considerably more difficult and challenging for the Hobbs family. It began when Joe II got into a running feud with the agents of Lord Carnarvon's estate, from whom he was leasing two of the four farms he operated, and on which he relied heavily for his income. The trouble started in September 1893, when Lord Carnarvon's agents gave him 12 months' notice to quit the Heatherwold Farm property – the reason is unclear. Joe II duly complied and vacated the farm where four of his children had been born on 29th September 1894. However, after inspecting the farm, Lord Carnarvon's agents claimed that he had not returned it in the condition stipulated in the lease. In particular, the lease required that he should have been growing wheat on some parts of the farm, but he had not done so, and was therefore guilty of 'miscropping'. Moreover, he had not left any wheat straw for the incoming tenant, as was written in the lease. The agents also claimed costs for failing to repair and keep up some parts of the property. Joe II argued that since he had been using the farm entirely for oats and grass and grew no wheat, he could not be expected to leave wheat straw. The matter was sent for arbitration.[19]

Whilst the arbitration progressed, Joe II unwisely became embroiled in two further disputes with Lord Carnarvon's estate managers. First, in an article entitled "The Game Laws: Important to Farmers" the *Berkshire Chronicle* of 3rd November 1894 reported that Joe II lost a case at Burghclere Petty Sessions brought by Lord Carnarvon's agents, which challenged his right to invite friends to shoot on the Heatherwold Farm he rented from Carnarvon.[20] Joe II had a seven-year lease on the farm, and was in the habit of inviting a group of his friends from the village (on this occasion numbering seven people, including the blacksmith, an innkeeper and several other local farmers) to an annual shoot on the land. However, the court clarified that, under the Game Laws, Lord Carnarvon as landlord retained the rights to kill winged game on the property, and that the Ground Game Act meant Joe II only had the right to shoot rabbits and hares, and this right extended only to himself plus one other person. Lord Carnarvon's solicitors successfully argued that Hobbs had no right to invite the shooting party, and that they were all technically trespassers. Mr J A Rutherford (Lord Carnarvon's Estate Manager) and John Fox (Under Keeper) gave evidence for the Earl, whilst Joe II gave evidence for the defence, clarifying that he and his guests only shot rabbits and hares. The Court determined that shooting of game on the property was reserved for Lord Carnarvon and that Hobbs' guests were all trespassing. However, the Court also judged that they had done so innocently, having been invited by Joe II, so no conviction was recorded and the defendants were just required to pay costs – Lord Carnarvon's, plus their own costs to defend the case.

In parallel with this, in what looks very much like a 'tit-for-tat' response, Joe II sued Lord Carnarvon for damages caused to his crops when Carnarvon's keepers and beaters strayed over his land during a shoot. Hobbs sued for £40 compensation. He ended up taking the matter all the way to Newbury County Court, to be heard by a jury. Lord Carnarvon accepted liability, and the issue became one of assessing damages. At the trial on 12th November 1894, the jury awarded Hobbs £10 10s in total for damages. Furthermore, the judge refused Joe II's request that Carnarvon pay his costs in bringing the suit, arguing that since Joe II had made an 'exorbitant' claim, he felt justified in using his discretion, and ordered that each side pay their own costs. Very likely this would have left Joe II substantially out of pocket, and although he won the claim in principle, the wisdom of pursuing such expensive litigation for a matter such as this, as well as of getting into direct dispute with the landlord for the key properties he relied upon for his income, can certainly be questioned.[21]

As some welcome good news in the midst of these battles, Elizabeth gave birth to the couple's second son and fifth child in less than five years, Basil Deacon Hobbs, on 20th December 1894.[22]

However, this was only a brief respite. As the year turned to 1895, developments in the Heatherwold Farm case had been progressing through the arbitration and legal system. Initially the umpire appointed by the arbitrators seems to have tried to make a balanced finding, ordering Hobbs to pay compensation at market prices for the absent wheat straw, but not making any judgement on whether he was guilty of 'miscropping', and also allowing some of Hobbs' claims in the arbitration. The Earl of Carnarvon's Estate Manager Rutherford immediately appealed the decision, which was referred for review by a Judge in court. The Judge ordered the issue be returned to the umpire whom he instructed must take detailed legal advice and provide a ruling on each of the three questions raised by the landlord (cost of repairs; miscropping; compensation for lack of wheat straw). The Judge further ordered that all costs in the arbitration and escalation to the Judge should be paid by Joe II.[23] The outcome of this further referral does not seem to have been reported in the local papers; however, in light of the Judge's instructions it certainly added substantial costs to Joe II's legal and compensation bills.

Then, on 6th April 1895, the *Reading Mercury* reported yet another – this time ultimately decisive – disagreement that Joe II had with Lord Carnarvon's estate, and its litigious agent James Rutherford. This time, the battle was over the Ivory Farm property Joe II rented on the Highclere Estate. Back in February 1892, Joe II had applied for permission to plough up 52 acres of permanent grassland on the farm. Carnarvon's agents agreed, on the condition that he did not take two "white crops" in succession from the land without growing an intervening "green crop", and that he also took steps to manure the land, to ensure the land's fertility was not depleted. Joe II seems to have ignored these conditions, and the land was cropped continuously for corn for three years in a row from 1892 to 1894 (probably, on the basis of subsequent events, because he needed the income from the more valuable 'white' corn crops). As a result of Hobbs not abiding by the conditions they had set, but also quite likely driven by the developing feud between agent and tenant, on 29th September 1894, Carnarvon's agents served Joe II with two years' notice to quit the farm. However, likely spurred on by Joe II's temerity in taking Lord Carnarvon to court for damage caused to his crops by the beaters, on 22nd October Carnarvon's agents used the fact that Joe II had not paid the half-year's rent which was due to "distrain" him (i.e. forcefully take possession of Joe II's property) to obtain payment for the overdue rent. Amongst other things, they seized two wheat ricks, the produce of a very good crop from 20 acres of the farm. Hobbs told Carnarvon's men to thatch the two ricks to protect them from water damage, which they failed to do, and the wheat was left exposed during a period of very heavy rains from October to December, rendering it useless for any purpose. On 8th December, Joe II agreed to give up possession of the farm within 14 days, with all the disputes between him and the estate management referred to arbitration. Both sides made extensive claims for damages; Joe II included claims of £100 for giving up the farm, damages for "malicious distraint" and recovery of his solicitors' costs.

The arbitrator ruled on the issue on 1st March 1895, denying Joe II's specific claims for damages, but awarding him £148 for other costs and compensation. The Landlord had claimed £289, the largest items of which were the unpaid rent and various claims for disrepair, which the umpire adjusted downwards, awarding the landlord £157 in total. The net outcome was Hobbs had to pay Lord Carnarvon £8 15s 10d, with both parties sharing the £32 cost of administrating the award.[24, 25]

Viewed in isolation, the outcome of this complicated and rather petty battle was not too terrible. However, in combination with the underlying loss-making performance of Joe II's business over the preceding few years, and the fact that as a result of his disagreements with Lord Carnarvon's agents Joe II had now been forced to give up two of the four farms he had been operating – and would soon have to give up the other two at Snelsmore and Arlington Grange as well – this was sufficient to push Hobbs over into bankruptcy. In retrospect, it seems obvious that he expanded too fast. He had set out on his own in January 1885 (at age 27) with the lease at Heatherwold Farm and with £1,000 in capital available to support his business. But the rapid expansion, taking on commitments to three further farms over the next four years, whilst also investing substantial sums to expand and upgrade each of them at a time when farm prices were falling and were close to their lowest level in recent history was highly ambitious and risky, and put a huge strain on his financial resources. The poor market for agriculture at that time was clearly a big factor in contributing to his failure despite the huge energy and effort Joe II undoubtedly expended. But his decision-making was poor in relation to leasing and managing the farms, and he subsequently admitted to losing significantly on his cattle dealing trades as well. It also must be said that making enemies of the agents of Lord Carnarvon, on whom he relied as landlord for two of his four farms and therefore for a sizeable part of his income as well as his home, appears extremely unwise, no matter how much he may have felt aggrieved by apparent injustices done to him.[d]

The sad outcome of all this was that, by the end of 1895, Joe II was declared officially bankrupt. The *Reading Mercury*, which had reported on each of the interim stages of his progressive fall from grace, now dutifully informed its readers of this final humiliation. The *Mercury* outlined that Joe II had formally been declared bankrupt on 16th November. Hobbs had total liabilities of £5,566, with assets of just £1,618, of which £286 was owed to preferential creditors for rates, taxes and wages, leaving a net shortfall of £3,280 (equivalent to around £430,000 in contemporary terms).

The article provides further insight into how Joe II got into this situation. In it he admits he used up all £5,000 of his wife's capital and also owed his father more than £3,200 for rent, stock

---

d   How much all of this featured on the Earl of Carnarvon's 'radar' is hard
      to judge; however, the Earl was certainly busy making preparations
      for other priorities at this time. On 26th June 1895 he married Almina
      Wombwell (rumoured to be the illegitimate daughter of millionaire
      banker Alfred de Rothschild) at St Margaret's Church, Westminster
      (and received a massive £500,000 dowry as a result). And on 17th
      December the same year, Carnarvon hosted the Prince of Wales to
      a visit at Highclere Castle. He went on later to fund the exploration
      and be present at the opening of the tomb of King Tutankhamun in
      Luxor, Egypt. Whilst the late 1890s events on the Highclere Estate were
      life-changing for Joe II and his family, the disputes may not even have
      registered with the Earl of Carnarvon.

he had taken, and money borrowed from him. Joe II attributed the causes of his bankruptcy to "agricultural depression, losses on valuations of previous farms, and law costs" (although much of the latter seem to have been self-inflicted). He explained that the excessively dry year of 1893 had forced him to buy feed for his 500 sheep and 200 cattle (these were very sizeable numbers of livestock for the times) and sell them at a loss; he had invested to upgrade drainage and improve Heatherwold and then incurred litigation/arbitration costs around that; at Ivory Farm he had no income from crops, had lost a dispute over the tenancy and been forced to pay a 'valuation' to Lord Carnarvon (i.e. lost a dispute on the level of rent and payments he had to pay to his landlord); and he had spent more than £1,400 improving drainage and buildings across all four farms.[26] In the public examination of his bankruptcy case, Joe II plaintively stated "I consider I have been badly treated by Lord Carnarvon,"[27] which may well have been the case, but he had also clearly contributed a lot to his own demise.

Formal declaration of bankruptcy resulted in all of Joe II's assets, property and income being managed by the Official Receiver for the next few years, with all but a modest amount that he was allowed to keep from his earnings (sufficient for him to house and feed his family) being used to pay back his creditors. This would have been an awful time for Joe II and his young family. Previously relatively prosperous, with comfortable accommodation, domestic servants and a growing business, their world would have changed fundamentally, with every spare penny Joe II earned being taken by the receiver to repay his creditors. One of his principal creditors was his own father, and the fact that Joe I allowed the bankruptcy to happen, rather than writing off what his son owed him, or even contributing to help him repay his debts to others, says something of significance about the state of the relationship between father and son. We do not have correspondence from which to validate it, but it seems highly likely that there was resentment and disagreement between Joe I and Joe II, perhaps stemming from Joe II's decision to step out from the family business. After his son left to establish his own business, Joe I continued to lend him money and materials, which indicates there was still communication and support, but it is conceivable that Joe I's refusal to help with his son's bankruptcy was a deliberate decision to force his eldest son to learn a painful lesson, and perhaps act less impulsively and speculatively going forward. When Joe I passed away on 31st January 1912 he left an estate worth the very substantial sum of £124,816 (equivalent to £14.3m in today's terms).[28] At the time of Joe II's bankruptcy, his father was a wealthy man and could have afforded to settle Joe II's debts if he had wanted to.[e][f]

---

e   Almost all of his Joe I's estate was left to his other children, the only bequest to Joe II was payment of an annuity of £150 per annum, but only "so long as he shall reside out of the United Kingdom. Although £150 per annum (equivalent to around £18,000 in contemporary terms) was probably very useful to Joe II at that time in Canada, it was tiny by comparison to what Joe I provided to his other children. The bulk of his estate was left to Joe II's younger brother George (who inherited most of the farmland and property), whilst third daughter Alice Mary received £1,000 in cash and ownership of farms at Chilton and Harwell, oldest daughter Annie Maria was provided with £20,000 to invest, and youngest daughter Jessie was allowed to live in her father's house at The Rookery for the rest of her life, and receive a very generous annuity of £1,200 p.a. – worth around £145,000 in contemporary terms, which would have allowed her to live very comfortably. It seems the feud between Joe II and his father was not resolved before Joseph's death.

f   The UK descendants of Joe I subsequently donated papers and archives of his life and business to the University of Reading, documenting his rise from butcher to cattle dealer and then to wealthy farmer and landowner with over 1,600 acres in his possession. His younger son George took over running the main farms, doing so successfully until his own death in 1928, when he in his turn left a substantial estate to his children. George remained on good terms with his older brother Joe II, writing and occasionally sending money to him in Canada. Subsequent generations did not do so well with the farms, and at the time of donating the papers to the university in September 1966 most of the farmland had been sold, with the exception of Snelsmore Farm.

Subsequent to the 1869 Bankruptcy Act, which abolished the long-established practice of sending bankrupts to prison, Joe II was not at material threat of going to jail as long as he fully disclosed all his financial information and worked with the bankruptcy trustee to maximise repayments to creditors. However, he and his family were left to endure a very difficult few years under bankruptcy administration. The authorities sold off almost all his assets and possessions to pay his creditors, including his father. Horses, farm equipment and household effects were all sold off to contribute to repaying his debts.[29] Having been evicted from the farms and his family home, Joe II relocated to Reading, taking his family to live in rooms at 17 Russell Street. He went to work trading cattle and pigs to earn what money he could, although without his farm assets his earning potential must have been hugely curtailed.[30] But, in addition to losing all they had worked for, one of the hardest parts to deal with was likely to have been the humiliation. The bankruptcy process was by design a very public event, deliberately intended to destroy reputations. The stigma of bankruptcy would have hurt. And of course, the adverse publicity of Joe II's bankruptcy would hardly have helped his efforts to earn

17 Russell Street, Reading, today, where the Hobbs family rented rooms after Joe II's bankruptcy at the end of the 1890s.

a living, making it far more difficult to obtain loans from a bank or to secure a lease on a new farm, and his trustworthiness would have been publicly called into question.

Eventually however, there was some light at the end of the tunnel, and the Hobbs family were gradually able to put their life on a new trajectory. Two and a half years after being declared bankrupt, on 11th May 1898 a hearing was held to determine whether Joe II's bankruptcy could be discharged. Since he was first declared bankrupt, evaluation had shown Joe II's confirmed debts above his realised assets had increased to £4,844, a full 50% higher than was originally estimated in 1895. Asset sales were only sufficient to pay back a little over 3% of the debt. Including his own initial capital, plus money he had borrowed from his wife and father, Joe II had put capital and investments of over £9,000 (equivalent to about £1.4m in 2024 terms) into his business, which was a very substantial amount to have lost. Joe II estimated he had lost about £1,000 dealing cattle, and the remainder of his losses came from the operation of the four farms. He admitted that he knew he was already bankrupt by 1894, and had continued to trade whilst insolvent in the vain hope he might be able to trade his way out of trouble. He was publicly criticised for many things: for not keeping better records and books of accounts, for continuing to trade whilst knowingly insolvent, for committing to debts without having any reasonable expectation they could be repaid. But it seems that Joe II was suitably remorseful, and was considered to have made a proper effort during the two years of bankruptcy administration to pay back what he could. The judge remarked that recent years had been extremely tough for farmers, with many similar cases, and he could see Joe II "had thoroughly come to the ground" and that "the disaster was pretty complete". He ordered discharge from bankruptcy, but because of Joe's poor performance in not keeping his books up-to-date, continuing to trade for more than a year whilst knowingly insolvent, and only paying back 8d on every pound owed, the judge suspended the discharge for two years.[31, 32] This suspension period meant Joe II would not finally be released from responsibility for his debts under the bankruptcy until 1900, 4 ½ years after initially entering bankruptcy, and consigned the family to living under a cloud of doubt and relative poverty for a further two years.

Moreover, whilst Joe II was eventually released from having his assets run by an administrator, there would be a permanent civil record of his bankruptcy, which would adversely affect his ability to conduct business in future, for example by making it much harder to get a bank loan, or take out leases or tenancy agreements which could have helped him earn new income.

All of these unfortunate developments contributed to Joe II and his family making the decision to emigrate to Canada. At this time, Canada was calling out for fresh immigrants to populate its vast open spaces and exploit its huge resources, offering assisted passages and the promise of free land grants. Canada was especially keen to attract immigrants from the UK, and above all those with farming experience, so Joe II and his family would have been exactly the type of people that the Canadians were looking for. Joe II sent his papers to Canada House in London to apply to emigrate, and they were readily accepted.

Whilst he was just a young boy through all of this drama, the ups and downs of this period must have left their mark on Joe II's son Joe. Joe's earliest memories were probably of relative wealth and prosperity, with good food and living conditions, regular education, and the help of domestic servants. Suddenly that would all have been turned on its head, with the family forced to swap a sizeable home surrounded by acres of farmland for shared rooms in a nearby town. Money would have been scarce, food and drink basic, to say nothing of the impact of the humiliation and stress on his parents.

One thing did not suffer, as Joe II and Elizabeth found ways to continue to provide a good education for their children. They found the resources to send Lexi to a paid kindergarten in Reading. (Surviving school reports show that Lexi was good at writing and her reading was improving, even if her drawing was 'rather weak' and she had 'not much idea' about singing!) In the same way, Joe II and Elizabeth found ways for Joe, as the oldest son, to continue his education satisfactorily at this time. In a subsequent application to join the Canadian Air Force, and from his later entry in *Who's Who in Canada* Joe declared he had been educated at Bedford Priory School during this period.[33, 34] The school in Greyfriars near the centre of the town of Bedford continues to excel as a primary day school for children aged 3–11 to this day, although when Joe attended it was probably a boys-only boarding school.

The seeds of Joe's future life would have been well established during these early years, with strong influences from his bold and entrepreneurial father and grandfather, a background in farming and cattle rearing with which he never lost touch, as well as a precedent for not using resources to look after less prosperous family members. All of these were features which recurred in Joe's later life, although Joe was too big and determined a character to

An indication of what was to come? Joe and his younger brother Basil Hobbs photographed in Reading shortly before the family emigrated to Canada dressed in naval uniforms. Both were to have successful careers as naval airmen.

be constrained by the circumstances of his early upbringing. However, with his father's final discharge from the bankruptcy process completed in May 1900, at the age of nine years old, Joe and the rest of the Hobbs family, like countless thousands of immigrants before and since, were finally free to set out on a journey to start a new life in a foreign country.

2

Formative Years – Canada

The Hobbs family travelled to Liverpool in August 1900 and boarded the Allan Line steamer 'Tunisian' for the passage to Quebec.

The "Tunisian" was a modern, well-equipped and well-run ship, and doubtless would have made for an exciting journey for nine-year-old Joe Hobbs. It was to be the first of many trips across the Atlantic for him, and the start of an enduring fascination and connection with ships and the sea.

The Hobbs party comprised Joe II (42), Elizabeth (40), and their five children: Joe was the oldest at 9 years old, Alexa 8, the twins Daisy and Violet were 6, and younger son Basil was 5 years old. They were far from alone for the journey to Canada – altogether there were 945 passengers on the Tunisian for this trip, the great majority of them immigrants. The Hobbs family travelled in third or 'steerage' class, which would have been very basic in terms of the quality of accommodation and food, but the Tunisian offered third-class passengers their own enclosed berths to sleep in for the first time – previously Allan Line third-class passengers slept in open dormitories. They arrived

The S.S. Tunisian, c. 1900.

in Quebec on 31st August, before heading on to Toronto as their final destination.

The Hobbs family were part of the third 'great wave' of immigration to Canada, which lasted from about 1890 to 1920, peaking with around 400,000 arrivals in 1912. In total, 41,681 immigrants arrived in Canada in the year 1900.[35] At the time, the Canadian prairie states were opening up, and Canada needed farmers. Clifford Sifton, Canada's energetic Minister of the Interior (with responsibilities for immigration) from 1896 to 1905, had a vision of populating the prairies with agricultural immigrants. Sifton was famously quoted as saying, "I think that a stalwart peasant in a sheepskin coat, born to the soil, whose forefathers have been farmers for ten generations, with a stout wife and a half-dozen children, is good quality".[36] He might almost have been describing the Hobbs family, so closely did they fit Sifton's profile of the ideal immigrants. The Canadian government preferred white, English-speaking immigrants from Britain and the British Empire. However, by this time, the drive to attract more people was such that the liberal Laurier government from 1896 had opened up to immigrants from across Europe, as evidenced by the large numbers of

Scandinavians and eastern Europeans also recorded on the passenger list of the Tunisian. Whilst the government wanted immigrants to move into the newly opening 'prairie' states of Manitoba, Saskatchewan and Alberta in the west of Canada to be farmers, many of the arriving immigrants stayed in the cities further east and joined the industrial labour force.

The eastern provinces of Canada were already developing strongly by this time, especially along the shores of the Great Lakes and St Lawrence River system. The eastern part of the country was the most populous, had the best infrastructure, and the most developed economies. Especially from the 1890s onwards, settlers were encouraged to head west. Since the 1867 Dominion Lands Act, settlers to the western part of Canada over the age of 21 could apply to be allocated a standard 'quarter section' plot of 640 acres of land, selected from the over 200 million acres of the three large Prairie Provinces that had been surveyed and mapped out by the Dominion Lands Survey. The land itself was available free of charge: applicants were just required to pay a $10 administration fee. This 'free land' grant was extremely attractive and successful in inducing tens of thousands of new migrants to Canada to settle the country's undeveloped western provinces.

At first sight, it should have been an attractive option for the Hobbs family, given their precarious financial position following the bankruptcy. However, there were challenges with this system. The lands available were 'unbroken', which meant that considerable work would be required to clear, fence and drain the land, and prepare it for cultivation. Moreover, the land sections did not have any habitation, so the first task for most settlers was to construct a dwelling in which to live, and necessarily many of them were very rudimentary. On top of that, most of the land available was in remote locations, distant from even modest centres of population and services, including schools. The land was free, but the life required to develop it was extremely demanding, and in all probability it would take years for settlers to establish a stable and viable business, and even then the rewards were likely to be fairly slim and the lifestyle basic.

Furthermore, the free land was largely in prairie areas which were most suited to the cultivation of arable crops, especially wheat. This was not Joe II's core area of expertise – he was first and foremost a cattle man. Although parts of the prairies were subsequently successfully developed for cattle rearing and ranching, the standard 'quarter section' land units were not really suitable for raising cattle, which needed much larger areas of land. The formidable Canadian winters which often brought prolonged periods of extreme cold weather were also challenging for cattle production, unless the landowner had the ability to provide winter feed and shelter from the conditions. Although they were 'down on their luck', for these reasons the chance to get free land in the remote west was probably relatively unappealing to the Hobbs.

Arriving in Toronto, the Hobbs family's key priorities would have been to find accommodation and work. Joe II seems to have reckoned that his profession as a cattle-rearer and dealer was unlikely to present many opportunities for work in the main urban centres in the eastern part of the country, and neither was the free land in the far west an attractive proposition for the Hobbs. Consequently, with assistance and advice from the immigration agents in Quebec or Toronto, Joe II turned his attention to locations in the mid-west that were suitable for cattle rearing. The family realised that to manage this part of the transition to a new life in Canada they would need to separate for a while, so Joe II found accommodation for Elizabeth and the children in the Junction area of Toronto, romantically named for its proximity to a sizeable railway junction a short distance

Eastern Canada.

to the west of Toronto's central business district, and then went off in search of work.

That year's Canadian Census shows that Elizabeth and the five Hobbs children were all residing in the Junction area, in the York West district of Toronto. Elizabeth was 'living on her own means' (i.e. not working), and doubtless occupied full-time looking after five children aged from 6-10 years old, who were all enrolled in local schools.[37] Joe II, however, was resident in the small city of Sault Ste Marie, which like Toronto is located in the Province of Ontario, but some 675km to the north-west, on the narrows between Lake Huron and Lake Superior. He was living on his own on a lot of 31 acres with one main building and 2 stables or outhouses. He gave his occupation as 'farmer', and many of his neighbours in the same census were also farmers, living in a semi-rural location on the western edge of the town.[38]

Sault Ste Marie (pronounced Soo Sent Ma-REE) is a town at a natural choke point of the Saint Mary's River in Canada, with two cities of the same name straddling the river, the northern one in Canada, the southern settlement in Michigan, USA. The Ojibwe tribe of native Americans had already colonised this area for around 300 years, valuing the area for its access to the upper lakes, its abundant fish and supplies of maple sugar, when French settlers arrived in the late 17th century. A Jesuit mission was established, and a community of fur, fish and other traders developed. The French named the settlement 'sault' which means 'jump' (as in 'somersault'), named after the cataracts and rapids on the Sainte Marie river, where it descends sharply over 6m (20ft) from the height of Lake Superior in the west down to Lake Huron in the east. Settlement was first established here because of the rapids, which required a stop in riverborne navigation, necessitating overland carriage of boats and cargo between the two lakes.

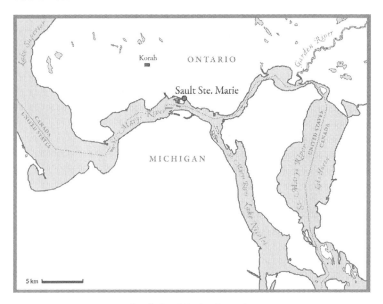

Sault Ste Marie, Ontario.

After the Anglo-US War of 1812, the border between Canada and the USA along the river was closed, impeding north–south trade, and the two cities developed in parallel thereafter. The first rudimentary canal to move boats and canoes past the rapids was built in 1798, with the Americans building a much more substantial canal and a system of 4 large locks in 1855, capable of accommodating lake steamers and ocean ships handling sizeable cargoes of (especially) grain and iron ore, and becoming an integral part of the Great Lakes seaway/navigation system. The American canal was a tremendous success.[g] However, the Americans' refusal in 1870 to let a steamer carrying British Colonel Garnet Wolsey, leading an expedition to quell a rebellion in the Red River area, have permission to transit through their locks at Sault Ste Marie reinforced the need for Canadians to build their own water passage.[39] This eventually resulted in construction of the Canadian Sault Ste Marie Canal, completed in 1895, featuring what at the time was the largest and longest lock in the world.

The new lock enabled an increase in the size of tonnage operable on the western lakes. For many years, the US and Canadian lock systems in combination at Sault were the biggest in the world calculated by number and tonnage of traffic, handling a peak load of 81.9m tons of freight in 1925.

Other transport connections expanded at the same time. A branch line connecting Sault to the Canadian Pacific Railway at Sudbury, Ontario 300km to the east was completed in 1887. The same year also saw the construction of the Sault Ste Marie International Railroad Bridge over the St Mary's River, connecting the Canadian and US sides of the city, and opening up connections to the whole US hinterland again. A road

g   Tonnage passing through the American lock system increased from 14,500 tons in the first year of operation in 1855 to 284,350 tons in 1865 and 1,505,780 in 1875.

bridge connecting the Canadian and US parts of Sault was not constructed until many years later – rudimentary ferry services began operating across the river from the early 1900s, and this was to provide a young Joe Hobbs with his first opportunity in business later in the decade.

All this meant that Sault was booming by the time the Hobbs family arrived in 1901, and that is likely to have been one of the reasons why Joe II brought his family to settle there. The Ontario part of Sault's population grew from 2,400 in 1891 (the year of Joe Hobbs' birth) to 7,200 in 1901 (the year the Hobbs arrived in the town) and then tripled during the years Joe Hobbs lived there, rising to a population of 21,100 by 1921.

Sault's boom during the 1890s owed a great deal to rapid industrialisation and development initiated and driven by the American-born entrepreneur Francis H. Clergue, who arrived in the town in 1894. A lawyer by training, Clergue came to Sault with a plan to develop its cataracts to generate water power to supply the area with energy. His company succeeded with that, and Clergue then drove the business through a phenomenal and rapid expansion over the next 10 years into pulp and paper production, chemicals, nickel and iron ore mining, shipbuilding and railroad construction. In 1900, Clergue started the Algoma Steel Company, for many years afterwards the largest business and leading employer in the area. It is still active today, and continues to be an important contributor to the area's economy.[40]

Clergue's businesses dominated Sault. At its peak in 1902–03, less than 10 years after he came to Sault, the Consolidated Lake Superior Corporation (as the holding company for all Clergue's businesses was named) was valued at C$150 million – a staggering sum for the time. In 1902, the first steel rails were rolled at the new steel mill, and a huge power plant on the Michigan (USA) side of Sault was opened. Clergue spent over $100,000 to mark the occasion, Canada's Prime Minister Laurier was in attendance, and hundreds of invited guests joined a huge celebration dinner, with the entire Sault population invited to watch an impressive fireworks display. Clergue's way of working and method of integrating all his different businesses to support each other were a clear influence on the young Joe Hobbs, whose subsequent career exhibited many parallels with the way Clergue ran his business. Clergue's companies were also to provide Joe Hobbs' first employment when he left school aged 16 in 1907.[h]

The frenetic Clergue-led expansion at Sault was in full flow when Joe II brought his family to the town in 1901-02. Although land in Sault was not 'free' as it would have been if the family settled further west under the Dominion Lands Act scheme, Joe II figured Sault Ste Marie provided a better opportunity that was more fitting to the needs of his family. Land was available to rent or purchase in Sault, and moreover it was already usable. The land around Sault was ideally suited to cattle rearing, and just a year

---

h   Given the extraordinary pace of Clergue's expansion, and the wide range of business ventures he started in just a few years, it is perhaps not surprising that later in 1903 he ran into trouble. A progressive drop in paper prices, and quality problems with initial steel production meant expected revenues did not materialise, precipitating a cash flow crisis. Already over-extended with borrowings, lenders refused to advance further loans, and in September 1903 Consolidated did not have the money to fund its payroll. Unpaid workers rioted, with many of Clergue's buildings and businesses damaged, and rioters seizing firearms from the general store. Sault mayor W.H. Plummer called for support, the state government sending a detachment of militia from Toronto by train to quell the rioting. Reluctantly the Ontario government agreed to provide a C$2 million bailout to the now bankrupt Consolidated. Clergue was ejected from the business (and went on to a number of other ill-starred business ventures elsewhere), but the many businesses in the Consolidated Lake Superior Corporation, some of them later reorganised or under different ownership, continued to form the core of economic activity in Sault for many years. For example, Algoma Steel Inc. and the Algoma Central Railway have survived and continue to contribute substantially to Sault's economy through to the present day.

F. H. Clergue.

prior to Joe II's arrival, importation of live cattle stock to Sault had been made possible by the establishment of a new quarantine station, the L'Anse Michigan Sentinel reporting that "since the station was established a large and gratifying business in the importation of livestock has developed."[41] The booming town of Sault also provided a ready and easily accessible market for meat and dairy products, while access to the CP Railroad and to river steamers also made it easy for cattle to be sent to the stock markets serving the bigger cities further east. In addition, Sault was an emerging town with infrastructure – accommodation could be rented easily and cheaply, and there were schools for the children.

Having established a 'bridge-head' in Sault on his own by mid-1901, Joe II brought the rest of his family up from Toronto soon after. Not long after this, Elizabeth became pregnant again, giving birth to their 6th child and 3rd son, Roland Eric Hobbs, on 24th July 1903, nearly nine years after the arrival of their previous child, Basil. Whilst Joe II made his living rearing cattle using land outside the main built-up area of the town, it seems that the family lived within the urban area of Sault Ste Marie, residing on Bay Street, which was close to the heart of the town at the time (although subsequently it has been redeveloped), and just a stone's throw from the St Mary's River and the famous canal locks.

A photo survives from this time (c.1904), which may be the only one in existence showing Joe II, Elizabeth and all 6 of their children.

The Hobbs family, c.1904. Back row L-to-R: Basil, Alexa, Joseph; Front row L-to-R: Violet, Elizabeth with baby Roland on her lap, Joseph Senior, Daisy.

Tragically, youngest child, Roland Eric, did not survive childhood, dying from meningitis on 20th April 1906, aged only 2 years 9 months.

Joe Hobbs was 10 years old when he came to Sault with his mother and siblings. He attended the Sault-Ste. Marie Public School. His parents set a priority on a good education, as evidenced by their funding of his and his sister Alexa's kindergarten lessons even at the lowest point of the family's financial situation, and they ensured Joe obtained a solid education. Outside of school, around this time (c.1905-06, aged 14–15 years old) Joe sold newspapers as a part-time job, early evidence of his desire to work to earn money and the first fledgling steps in his business career.[42]

During this period, Joe also made some important connections which were to shape his later business career. In a personal letter years later to his niece (and regular correspondent) Barbara Barran, Joe recalls "I well remember the ceremony in 1904 when they celebrated the fifty years…of the opening of the [Sault] Canal. I was 13 years old at the time and went with Judge Johnston and family to see the fireworks set off."[43] His Honor Judge Frederick Wiliam Johnston was a senior judge of the District of Algoma, resident in Sault Ste Marie, and an important local figure. His son F.G. Johnston was a boyhood friend of Joe's in the Sault, with whom Joe later worked closely on the construction of the Marine Building in Vancouver.

After leaving school aged 16 in 1907, Joe joined the Tagona Water & Light Company as a Clerk.[44] TW&LC was a subsidiary of the Lake Superior Corporation, the successor to F.H. Clergue's group of companies. Joe was soon promoted from Clerk to Telephone Inspector, and then in 1909–10 took on the role of Superintendent of the Telephone Department of the overall Lake Superior Corporation. Lake Superior operated a substantial and wide-ranging business in Sault at that time, so performing these roles Joe would have benefitted both from a sound training in telephony, but also from exposure to a wide variety of different industries and processes.

Formal photo of the young Joe Hobbs from around the time he started work in Sault Ste Marie, Ontario.

Joe repairing telephones for the Lake Superior Corporation, Sault Ste Marie, c.1909.

One particular aspect of this period should be noted at this point, because it was to become important in Joe's later career in England during WW2. At the time Joe worked for Lake Superior Corporation in Sault Ste Marie, the Union Carbide company were active in the town, being one of the first users of F.H. Clergue's power generation from 1896. By the time Joe started working on the engineering team for Lake Superior Corp., the Union Carbide plant on the U.S. side of the town was pioneering new experimental Horry furnaces, which made commercial calcium carbide and acetylene production profitable on a large scale for the first time. It is quite likely that this is where Joe first learned about carbide and acetylene production, which was to turn into an important business opportunity with Oxy Ferrolene Ltd in the UK, later in his career during and after WW2. Joe's future brother-in-law Harry Bush was also a foreman at the Union Carbide factory, so Joe got to know all about calcium carbide and acetylene at this time.

By the time of the next Canadian Census in 1911, the remaining members of the Hobbs family were all resident at 192 Woodward Avenue, Sault Ste Marie.[45] This is a smart, although fairly small, woodboard detached house in an avenue of similar dwellings, a little further east from Bay Street, but still very much within the city limits. Whilst not grand, it shows the Hobbs had achieved solid middle-class respectability and a degree of comfort and prosperity in their new lives in Canada.

The 1911 Census shows all of the Hobbs family except mother Elizabeth were working at this time. Joe II's occupation was cattle dealer; the three daughters Alexa (18), Violet and Daisy (both 17) were working for the Arcade Dry Goods and Ladieswear merchandising business. Basil (16) had recently started work as an electrician.

The occupation given in the 1911 Census for Joe himself (by then 20 years of age) is 'launch owner', with the census occupation

Joe's sister Alexa Hobbs (standing centre), in The Arcade Dry Goods and Ladieswear Store, Sault Ste Marie, c.1911.

Joe's sisters Daisy (left) and Violet (right), during the time they lived in Sault Ste Marie.

coding indicating Joe was the owner of a transportation business using boats.[46] That same year of 1911, Joe had left Lake Superior Corp and set out in business on his own for the first time. His new business venture was as a boat owner and ferry service, carrying people across the St Mary's River between the Canadian and U.S. sides of Sault. This was the start of a life-long association with boats, shipping and all things nautical. At that time, although there was a railway bridge across the river after 1887, there was no road bridge connecting the two sides of the city, and people and vehicles had to cross the river by boat. Border inspection services were put in place at both sides from the early 1900s, and it seems Joe saw an opportunity to meet demand for ferry transportation.

His first craft was a small sailing boat. If the craft had a name, it has been lost in the mists of time, but a few photographs have survived in the family's collection.

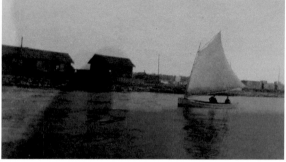

Joe's first boat and first business venture, ferrying passengers across the St Mary's River at Sault Ste Marie, Ontario, Canada, in 1911.

These modest beginnings got Joe started in business and by expanding to offer excursions as well as river crossings, Joe soon earned sufficient money to be able to upgrade his operation. By the spring of 1912, Joe had the financial and technical resources to build a motor launch for himself. This significantly larger and more impressive vessel was named "U-no-me", something of a pre-cursor for other similarly unusual vessel names Joe used later in his shipping career. It was 38 feet long, 9 feet wide and powered by a sizeable 40hp Loew Victor diesel engine. Already demonstrating the marketing and self-promotional flair that became a trademark of his future career, Joe managed to get an article about his new boat into the local 'Sault Star' newspaper, which amongst other things reported that the boat's engine was "one of the finest engines that ever came into the Sault". The vessel had a capacity to carry 30 people for short trips across the river. For longer excursions, it had a range of up to 400 miles, and was equipped with a toilet and sleeping accommodation for six people.[47]

All this fits closely with what we know of Joe from his later life, and is an early example of his energetic entrepreneurship and emerging fascination with boats and ships. Joe studied and passed the examinations to obtain his Master Mariner certification for Inland Waters on 25 April 1913.[48] He continued to operate his launch business until the end of 1913, experiencing some dramas along the way, including nearly losing his ship and passengers when "U-no-me" suffered engine failure and was left drifting for seven hours in violent seas during a heavy gale, whilst transporting two miners to their claims on Parisian Island offshore on Lake Superior.[49] On another occasion, Joe was the rescuer, when another launch hit ice which holed his craft below the waterline on Lake George, 25km to the east of Sault Ste Marie. Joe, bringing a party of hunters back from Echo Lake, arrived just in time to save Harvey Snow, and tow his stricken boat to safety.[50] Perhaps most importantly, however, it was through his launch business that Joe met his future wife Mabel, who lived on the American side of Sault, and who met Joe when she was a passenger on the "U-no-me".[i]

Joe continued to make the local news on several occasions

---

i   Sault Ste Marie had to wait until 1962 before a proper heavy-duty road bridge was constructed to connect the two sides of the city. Today it is the tenth busiest crossing point between Canada and the U.S., and even now it is the only vehicular crossing point between Ontario in Canada and Michigan in the U.S. for 300 miles, so it seems the geographic situation of Sault which supported Joe's idea to run a ferry service between the two sides of the city separated by the St Mary River is still very much a factor even today.

Joe's first motor vessel, the self-constructed "U-no-me" at Sault Ste Marie, Ontario, in 1912.

during this period for performing brave rescues during his work as a boat operator. In the first incident in June 1913, two men leaped into the fast-flowing waters of the St. Mary's River when their launch stalled, and they were about to be run down by the ferry 'Algoma'. Joe witnessed the accident from the dock of the Superior Boat House and, unable to get the attention of a passing launch, threw himself into the river and swam towards the two men, who were struggling to stay afloat. The launch occupants saw Joe throw himself into the water, and turned to collect him, after which Joe directed them to save the struggling men. Both men were picked up in an exhausted condition, but, apart from shock and cold, were in good condition, and made a speedy recovery thanks to Joe's brave efforts.[51] Less than two months later, Joe had taken local doctor James McLurg and his family out for an excursion. After their return to Sault Ste Marie, the party had disembarked and were walking along the dock at the Superior Boat House, when Dr McLurg stumbled and fell into the water. One of the other party members held Joe by the feet as he stretched out to grab Dr McLurg by the collar and drag him ashore. The Sault Star reported that fortunately neither man was "any the worse for the experience".[52]

Elizabeth Jane Hobbs, Joe's mother, at Sault Ste Marie.

Joe's mother Elizabeth passed away on 19th November 1913, aged just 53. The cause of death was a haemorrhage from an ovarian cyst. Plucky to the last, she walked to the hospital on the day she died, but the doctors were unable to save her. She is buried at Greenwood Cemetery, Sault Ste Marie. Today there is a memorial stone at Greenwood in tribute to her life which also features her sons Roland and Basil, but surprisingly there is no memorial there to her husband, Joe II.[j]

Much more happily for Joe, only seven months later, on 30th June 1914, he married Mabel Della (or Dell) Bush, an American born and brought up on the Michigan, USA side of Sault Ste Marie.[53] Mabel was the third of five children of Charles S. and Angelina Bush. Charles Bush was self-employed as a carriage and wagon painter. His daughter Mabel had studied to fourth year of high school, after which she worked initially as a seamstress. She then lived for a few years in Minneapolis, Minnesota, working as a stenographer in a hotel before returning to Sault and finding

---

[j] Basil later put up a memorial to his father Joe II at Christ Church, Korah, Sault Ste Marie. The 1938 edition of the Algoma Missionary News reports: "On every hand in the church are interesting signs and indications of the efforts of faithful workers, who have made gifts to the glory of God and in memory of those gone before. On a front pillar is a plaque, telling of the gift of the electric lights in memory of Daniel and Mary Thompson Everett and John Everett by J. P. Everett. On the opposite pillar a similar plaque bears witness to the gift of the woodwork screen across the chancel by Basil D. Hobbs in memory of his father Joseph W. Hobbs".

Gravestone for Joe's mother Elizabeth and brothers Roland and Basil,
Greenwood Cemetery, Sault Ste Marie.

work in her home town, also as a stenographer. The marriage
registration indicates she was not working at the time of the
wedding. The marriage, witnessed by Joe's brother Basil and
Mabel's sister Lulu, a manicurist, is registered in the Michigan
part of Sault, and it may well be that she and Joe lived in the
US part of the town after marrying. Mabel's birth year is shown
as 1890, which would make her one year older than Joe. In the
following years, Mabel often declared her year of birth on travel
documents as 1890; however, on subsequent official documents
her actual birthdate is stated as 3rd March 1886, and this seems
to be the correct date. So, Mabel was fully four years older than
she declared on her marriage certificate, and was actually aged
28 on her wedding day, and five years older than Joe. Whether
this was known to Joe at the time of the wedding is very much
open to question!

Mabel Dell Bush, the first Mrs Joe Hobbs

Joe's occupation at the time of his marriage was given as "Fourman [sic] Construction Work". In actual fact, after four years working for Lake Superior Corporation, and three years running his first business as a launch operator, Joe sold his boat "U-no-me" to the local government and switched jobs to join the engineering staff of the Sault branch of the Dominion Department of Public Works. This was the government department responsible for procurement, provision of internal services and administration to all branches of government in Canada. A specific responsibility was construction and maintenance of all government buildings, and Joe worked for this government department for two years prior to the start of WW1. Again, this would have been valuable experience for the young Joe Hobbs, giving him property and construction experience to add to his engineering and telephonic training received at Lake Superior Corporation. Although he did not formally get a university degree, his initial nine years of work experience in Sault equipped Joe with a lot of technical and engineering knowledge and expertise.

The 14 years that he spent in Sault Ste Marie from 1901 to 1915 clearly had many strong formative influences on Joe Hobbs. His father's business rearing cattle influenced Joe's successful cattle ranching venture in Scotland after WW2. His schooling and boyhood connection with F.G. Johnston established the basis for their later partnership in the construction of the 'Marine

Building', Vancouver's iconic first skyscraper in the late 1920s. Joe's employment in F.H. Clergue's Lake Superior Corporation provided technical training and a first taste of management, and taught him about acetylene which informed Joe's significant work with Oxy Ferrolene in the UK during WW2. Clergue's method of closely integrating all his businesses to support each other shaped Joe's approach when he developed multiple businesses of his own in later life. His work for the government provided civil engineering and property management experience, which proved highly valuable later when Joe acquired and rebuilt a network of Scottish whisky distilleries with Associated Scottish Distilleries in the 1930s, and subsequently with his ownership of Ben Nevis and Lochside distilleries. And running his own business as a boat operator provided early success as an entrepreneur, and was a first step towards his subsequent shipping, rum-running and naval careers, and the beginning of a lifelong association with ships, boats and all things nautical. In all these ways, Joe's years in booming Sault Ste Marie prior to WW1 had a lasting and significant impact on his subsequent lifestory.

Following the outbreak of World War 1 in Europe, Canada (as a Dominion of the United Kingdom) was officially at war with Germany. In mid-1915, in a move which was to put his life and career on a totally different trajectory, Joe Hobbs volunteered for war service and joined the (British) Royal Naval Air Service, becoming one of the first trainee pilots in the British Royal Navy.

3

A Splendid War

Although Canada, as a British Dominion, was officially at war with Germany from 4th August 1914, there was initially no conscription of servicemen from Canada to fight in Europe. However, many Canadians started to volunteer for the armed forces, and there was strong popular support for the war effort, especially for those in Canada of English descent. In Sault Ste Marie, a local militia which could trace its roots back to the (British) 49th Regiment of Foot stationed in the area from 1802 was reformulated and renamed as the 51st Regiment 'Soo Rifles' in February 1914.[54] After war broke out, it witnessed a surge in local volunteers joining up. Joe Hobbs was among them, seemingly on a part-time basis, with the regiment being deployed mostly on guard duties at sites of strategic value in the area, especially the Sault Ste Marie Canal.[55]

During the second-half of 1914, the Ottawa government organised the Canadian Expeditionary Force (C.E.F.) to go to Europe and contribute troops to Britain's war effort. The C.E.F. was manned on a voluntary basis, and an initial batch of over 35,000 volunteers from across Canada were sent to the army camp at Valcartier in Quebec for induction before sailing to England for further training. About two-thirds of the men that formed the first contingent of the C.E.F. had been born in the United Kingdom, and right through to the end of the war in 1918 around half of Canada's soldiers were actually British born.[56, k]

Given his background, Joe likely felt considerable pressure to join up too, especially when in October 1914 the Soo Rifles sent a company of 125 men to join the 2nd Canadian Infantry Battalion serving in Europe. However, Joe aspired to serve as an airman in the navy, and in mid-1915 signed up for training at the new flight training school being set up at Long Branch, Toronto, by John McCurdy. McCurdy, the first Canadian to be granted a pilot's licence by the International Aeronautical Federation in Paris, had been actively lobbying the Canadian government to set up aircraft manufacturing in Canada and form its own aviation corps to contribute to the war effort through the new discipline of military aviation. Unable to win government support and funding for his proposals from Canadian Prime Minister Robert Borden, McCurdy turned to the private sector instead and in April 1915 took up a role as the first Managing Director of the new Curtiss Aeroplanes and Motors Ltd company, established to build aircraft and train pilots in Canada.[57]

Curtiss was an American aircraft and vehicle manufacturer, whose owner Glenn Curtiss had been recruited by Alexander Graham Bell as one of the founding members of his Aerial Experiment Association in 1907. Curtiss then went on to form his own aircraft company in 1909, and with the advent of war and a rapid rise in demand, Curtiss brought B. Douglas Thomas from British aircraft manufacturer Sopwith to develop a new

---

k   The CEF eventually grew to more than 600,000 men and women by the end of the War, by which time about 425,000 served overseas.

biplane design, which became the very successful JN-3/JN-4 'Jenny' biplane. Curtiss also worked with John Cyril Porte in 1914 to develop a flying boat for the Daily Mail Transatlantic prize. With the commencement of the war, this became the first in a series of highly successful flying boat designs that included the Curtiss H-12 and the Felixstowe F.3 and F.5., which were to be used extensively by the Royal Navy and the Americans during the war. There was strong collaboration between the British, Americans and Canadians around these initiatives, with Curtiss opening a flight training school (to complement their new aircraft production centre) at Long Branch Aerodrome at Port Credit, west of Toronto, on 20th May 1915. In doing so, Long Branch became Canada's first aerodrome. The 100-acre site had a basic corrugated hangar and a grass/dirt strip for take offs and landings.[58]

Following an order from the British Admiralty for 50 Curtiss JN-3 'Jenny' biplane aircraft, Captain William Elder of the Royal Naval Air Service made a visit to North America to inspect production facilities. As part of his visit, Elder agreed arrangements with Canadian Prime Minister Borden to recruit

Long Branch Aerodrome, Toronto, 1917.

trainee pilots for the R.N.A.S (and later also the Royal Flying Corps) at the Curtiss Aviation School at Long Branch. The Royal Naval Air Service was the British Royal Navy's air arm, under the direction of the Air Department of the Admiralty. It existed from 1st July 1914 until 1st April 1918, when it was merged with the British Army's Royal Flying Corps to form the new Royal Air Force.[59]

As a consequence, a recruitment campaign was organised, calling for "young alert men of fair education aged 18-30 years old" to sign-up for training. Volunteers had to be British subjects, and pass an interview and a medical, which put particular emphasis on quality of eyesight. Once accepted, volunteers had to pay for their own training, at a cost of C$400 (which is the equivalent of about $11,750 in contemporary terms in 2024), albeit successful recruits that completed their training and were then accepted into the R.N.A.S. received a gratuity of $365, enabling them to recover most of their training costs. Recruits also received a payment of $1.10 per day during their training.[60]

Joe Hobbs was one of the first to volunteer and successfully pass his interview and medical to join this programme.[61] Joe and Mabel were able to take advantage of an opportunity for a brief holiday in New York, staying with friends in the north of Manhattan[62] before Joe began his military training. And then, in July 1915, Joe presented himself at the Curtiss Aviation School in Toronto, to begin his training to become one of the first naval pilots.

The training was organised and examined to standards set by the Royal Aero Club of the United Kingdom. Joe's $400 fee entitled him to 400 minutes of flying time, supplemented with extensive classroom training on aeronautics, navigation etc. The first 200 minutes of flight training was done on 2-seater Curtiss Model F flying boats, with the instructor sitting alongside the trainee, from a base at a beach rented at Hanlan's Point from the City Government for a fee of $1. This was then followed by a further 200 minutes training on a landplane, the Curtiss JN-3 'Jenny' Biplane trainer. The 'Jenny' was the primary WW1 training aircraft used by the British in Canada (and in fact across North America it was estimated that 95% of all WW1 pilots were trained on the 'Jenny'). It was a tandem-seat, dual-control biplane, where the student sat in front of the instructor. It had a 90hp engine giving a top speed of 75mph and a service ceiling of 6,500 feet. Over 6,800 aircraft were produced in various configurations.

At the end of the training and to be awarded their pilot's licence, students had to make three solo flights – the first time they were required to fly unaccompanied. For the first two solo flights, students had to fly in a 'figure-of-eight' pattern around posts 500 metres apart for a distance of at least 5 kilometres. At the end of each test, students had to land the within 50 metres

After completing his flight training Joe was awarded his Aviator's Certificate by the Royal Aero Club of the United Kingdom in October 1915.

of a specified point. For the final test students had to switch off their engines at a height of 100 metres and glide their aircraft in to land without power.

Joe successfully completed his training and the solo test flights, obtaining his aviator's certificate on 13th October 1915. He was the 44th pilot to graduate from the Curtiss Aviation School, making him one of the first Canadian military aviators, being part of the first batch of 129 pilots trained at Long Branch before the Royal Flying Corps took over direct responsibility for training Canadian airmen in 1917. On completion of his training, Joe was formally accepted into the R.N.A.S., and accorded the rank of Temporary Probationary Flight Sub-Lieutenant on 31st October 1915.[63] The term 'temporary' was applied to officers that were recruited into the services in wartime and given 'war duration' commissions in the military, to differentiate them from the regular commissioned officers of the armed forces for whom working in the military was a career appointment that pre-dated the war. His rank was 'probationary' until he completed further flight training in the UK (at Calshot and Eastbourne) to be officially rated as a Naval pilot.

Whilst there was undoubted glamour in being one of the first military airmen, Joe with typical boldness had also chosen an incredibly dangerous way to serve his country. Of course, active service in World War 1 resulted in huge numbers of fatalities and injuries across the whole spectrum of military activity, but military flying was amongst the most dangerous: aviation was a very new science; moreover, aircraft technology and design was extremely basic. Aircraft were flimsy affairs typically made of wood and canvas, and totally exposed to the elements, with airmen having to deal with cold and low levels of oxygen with altitude, and without protection from enemy fire. Airmen flew without parachutes, and had no means of communication except for hand signals. All this meant that just surviving training was already a significant achievement – 8,000 Royal Flying Corps airmen died during the course of the war before they could even finish their flight training.[64] Once operational, the risks were clearly far higher, especially during the early years of the war, when the R.N.A.S. and R.F.C. crews were up against German pilots who were substantially better equipped and armed, especially once the Germans were the first to develop the technology of mounting machine guns timed to fire in the gaps between the rotating aircraft propellors. All told, average life expectancy for the R.F.C. fliers in World War 1 was just 18 flying hours.[65]

After completion of his initial flight training in Canada, Joe and Mabel travelled to England together in November 1915. In December 1915, Joe's younger brother Basil completed his own flight training course at the Wright Flying School at Dayton, Ohio, paid for with $500 he had saved up from his work as an electrician. He followed in his brother's footsteps by also joining the R.N.A.S. as a Flight Sub-Lieutenant on 27th December 1915. Joe and Basil were showing exceptional bravery in choosing this most challenging and dangerous way to serve. Basil went on to be one of Canada's most successful and decorated aviators,

Flight Lieutenant Joseph Hobbs in front of a Curtiss JN-4 'Jenny' biplane during WW1.

earning the Distinguished Service Order, the Distinguished Service Cross and Bar (for subsequent acts of bravery) and an O.B.E. Among other things, he is credited with shooting down Zeppelin airship L-43, and sinking 2 German U-boat submarines. After the war, he completed the Halifax to Winnipeg leg of Canada's first trans continental flight in 1920 and did pioneering work in Canada's aerial survey. Basil also served as a Group Captain during WW2, and was posthumously inducted into Canada's Aviation Hall of Fame.[66, 67]

In England, from December 1915 until August 1916, Joe was deployed on flight operations over the North Sea and English Channel.[68] Initially based at Eastbourne on the south coast, Joe transferred to Calshot in Hampshire on the west side of the Solent near Southampton, and undertook 2 months of training on seaplanes. Whilst at Calshot, he also passed his aerial gunnery course. Following this, Joe was posted to Yarmouth on the east coast, and from April to October 1916 saw active service operating seaplanes on North Sea Patrol work. Most pilots did not last a month in active service; the ones that did rapidly acquired experience that equipped them to survive longer

Joe Hobbs whilst on active service as a naval airman based in England during WW1.

Contact! As a military pilot Joe Hobbs had chosen statistically one of the most dangerous ways to serve his country during WW1. This photo from Joe's collection was taken from a plane overflying a German biplane, although we do not know for sure that Joe was actually in it at the time!

after that. So, by surviving this first 7-month tour of duty it can certainly be concluded that Joe was one of the more capable and experienced pilots, as well maybe as one of the luckier ones.

Both Joe's wife Mabel and his brother Basil's wife Helen were allowed to accompany their husbands during their wartime service in the U.K. As wives of serving officers posted overseas, it is likely Mabel and Helen kept themselves busy in support of their husband's units and local initiatives assisting the overall war effort.

Having completed an extensive first tour of duty, on 7th September 1916, Joe was admitted to the Naval Hospital at Chatham in Kent and diagnosed with 'morbus corbis functionalis' – heart disease.[69] The term "functionalis" indicates the doctors believed this was a 'functional' rather than 'structural' problem with Joe's heart, possibly inflammation of the heart, and that it therefore was potentially treatable and temporary. But it was the first diagnosis of a problem with his heart that (many years later) would debilitate Joe and eventually contribute to his death. As a result of the diagnosis, he was not fit to fly, and was granted home leave. Mabel had already travelled back from Liverpool to New York in August 1916;[70] Joe followed in November.

On completion of their home leave, Joe and Mabel travelled back to the UK together to commence a second tour of duty, arriving on 16th January 1917.[71] Initially after his return, he performed some non-flying duties. He was posted to Windermere in the Lake District of north-west England for 3 months, where he supervised the dismantling and relocation of an air station, which presumably made good practical use of his civil engineering skills. Then, having been passed fit to resume flying duties again on 19th April 1917, Joe was posted to the Royal Naval Air Station at Newlyn in Cornwall, and from May 1917 until February 1918 was deployed flying seaplanes on Channel patrol duties from both Newlyn and also from the Cattewater air station near Plymouth. On 30th June 1917 he was promoted to Flight Lieutenant.

Unlike his younger brother Basil, whose wartime gallantry resulted in a number of awards and recognition which mean details of his exploits were documented and are known to us today, Joe's work flying seaplanes on patrol duties, scouting for submarines and escorting shipping convoys on the UK western approaches was not 'mentioned in despatches'. However, his military records show that much of Joe's flying from this time was on various types of flying boat, including the Curtiss Flying Boat H12, and its British-enhanced successor the Felixstowe F-2A, which was equipped with more powerful engines and a more aerodynamic hull; the Shorts 225 Flying Boat; and the

Sopwith Schneider Floatplane. He flew these various flying boats in multiple roles during the remainder of the War and beyond.[72, 73] These types of operations were oriented towards patrol, reconnaissance and convoy support activities. However, the seaplanes Joe was flying still saw combat action, were equipped with machine guns, and carried bombs – and later torpedoes – which were used to attack submarines and ships, and flying them would have required a rare blend of airmanship, navigation skills, and mental and physical toughness. Flying over the North Sea or Atlantic in an open cockpit in all weathers, and without modern navigation and communication aids such as radios would have required guts, resilience and determination, as well as an ability to keep a cool head and think logically during times of danger or challenging physical conditions. Doubtless, these experiences toughened Joe up, and added considerably to his formidable array of skills and capabilities.

Joe's military records do give one detailed account of his flying exploits at this time, when on 25th July 1917 the Short Seaplane (B9092) that he was piloting crashed on landing at Cattewater, resulting in the total wreck of the aircraft. The exact circumstances of the accident are not recorded – possibly the aircraft had been damaged or the landing was made difficult by

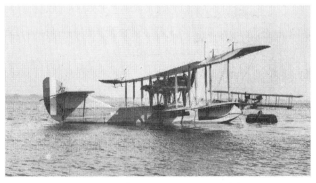

Curtiss H-12 Flying Boat in R.N.A.S livery.

bad weather – but his commanding officer wrote in his official military record that Joe had "made a very skilful landing on the ground. No blame is attributable to the pilot."[74] Despite the write-off of the aircraft, Joe seems fortunate to have walked away from the incident relatively unharmed, and after a short period of ground duties, he was soon passed fit to fly again.

Resuming flying duties, from October 1917 Joe took on a bigger role, leading a 'flight' of 3 or 4 planes operating together. He was responsible for management, both in the air and administratively, of the more junior officers or 'wingmen' that flew the other aircraft in the flight and reported to him. Joe was promoted again to the rank of Flight Commander on 12th February 1918.[75] For the duration of his active service in England until June 1918, Joe served as 2nd-in-Command of the Cattewater air station at Plymouth, where he was responsible for two squadrons of aircraft – one operating active patrols in the Channel, the other a training squadron.[76]

On 1st April 1918, the British authorities merged the Royal Naval Air Service (the air arm of the British Navy) and the Royal Flying Corps (the air arm of the British Army) to form the Royal Air Force. At this point, Joe was appointed to the rank of Captain in the Royal Air Force. As the war in Europe ground towards a conclusion in 1918, Joe and Mabel returned to Canada, but Joe's military service was far from over.[77]

Joe was sent back to Canada along with a number of ex-RNAS officers, now members of the RAF. Their mission was to assist with the establishment of the Royal Canadian Naval Air Service. Britain had warned Canada that upgrades in the U-boat fleet meant Germany now had the capability to launch raids on shipping along North America's Atlantic seaboard. Aircraft had proven effective against submarine operations by forcing them to keep submerged, and the R.C.N.A.S. was formed in 1918 with an initial focus to provide air cover for

Atlantic shipping convoys off Canada's east coast.[78, 79] Because in 1918 the R.C.N.A.S. was not yet fully operational, the U.S. Navy deployed aircraft to Nova Scotia (Halifax and North Sydney) to conduct aerial anti-submarine patrols until the R.C.N.A.S. could gear up to take over the responsibilities themselves. During the autumn of 1918, Joe took on the role of Liaison Officer in the R.C.N.A.S. mission which supervised construction of the new naval air station at Sydney, Nova Scotia in the far east of Canada.

At that time, Sydney Harbour was used extensively as a safe haven for merchant ships waiting to form up into convoys heading to resupply the United Kingdom, and was the patrol base for naval operations in the Gulf of St Lawrence. Joe's role as Liaison Officer required him to co-ordinate communications between the local Canadian naval authorities and the US Naval Air Force personnel located in North Sydney. Once again, Joe's

Map of Sydney and Halifax in Nova Scotia; Labrador and Newfoundland.

Merchant shipping waiting to form transatlantic convoys in Sydney Harbour, Nova Scotia c.1918.

organisational skills came to the fore as he supervised the construction of the new naval air station as well as co-ordinating operational deployments. Local historians have researched the history of these bases, and correspondence has survived showing Joe hard at work obtaining a hydraulic dredger for construction work, arranging tents as initial accommodation for men billeted on site during the construction phase, and chasing up freight agents and the railroad company for the delivery of goods.[80]

The new Sydney and Halifax bases became operational in the autumn of 1918, and operated with Curtiss HS-2L Flying Boats on coastal and anti-submarine operations along the eastern seaboard. Both stations operated with six flying boats by the end of the war, with each plane able to remain airborne for four hours at a time, armed with 2 x 230lb depth charges and a flexible 0.30 inch Lewis machine gun, and between them clocking up an impressive number of flying hours on convoy protection and coastal surveillance work searching for U-boats.[81]

It was as a result of this posting that Joe and Mabel's first child, Joseph Bruce Hobbs (hereafter Joe Junior), came to be born at Sydney, Nova Scotia, on 14th September 1918. Joe Junior can be said to have been born in Canada but conceived in England. He grew up and went to school in Canada, but subsequently followed his father back to the old country and played an active part in supporting Joe's later career there from the 1940s.

Having completed his work with the commission of the new air station at North Sydney, Joe was then tasked with undertaking

COMDR. BARBER, DR. GRENFELL, CAPT. HOBBS, on board STADACONA

H.M.C.S STADACONA   LABRADOR   NOV. 9/18

Joe Hobbs was serving on 'HMCS Stadacona' in Labrador and Newfoundland at the time of the armistice which ended WW1 in November 1918. It was his first acquaintance with a ship he was subsequently to own.

the survey work to extend the network of flying boat bases on the east coast of Canada, Newfoundland and Labrador. Initially he visited Cape North, on the northern tip of Nova Scotia, then he was authorised to make two survey cruises on the Canadian naval vessel 'HMCS Stadacona' to assess possible locations for air stations in Labrador and Newfoundland.[82] This was Joe's first acquaintance with the ship 'HMCS Stadacona', a vessel that he was subsequently to buy and operate as part of his successful post-war shipping business. As a result, on Armistice Day, 11th November 1918, Joe was on board 'Stadacona' off the Newfoundland coast, scouting sites for seaplane bases in the Strait of Belle Isle.[83] After this, Joe spent some time at the end of 1918 and early part of 1919 in the USA, visiting Washington and Hampton Roads to consult with US naval authorities and inspect new aircraft under development.[84] Joe was evolving from a seasoned and experienced pilot to broader management and leadership roles, trusted with important projects and missions, and representing Canada's interests in its engagements with the British and the Americans.

Despite the end of hostilities in WW1, Joe was not finished with military service. In the spring of 1919 he, Mabel and Joe Junior were posted back across the Atlantic again for five months while Joe was attached to the staff of the General Officer Commanding R.A.F. Dublin in southern Ireland.[85, 86] Joe's role in Dublin was to act as liaison officer between the RAF and the U.S. Naval Air Service in Ireland, presumably building on his track record of successfully working with the Americans in Nova Scotia and Washington.

After that, Joe was still needed for further interesting and dangerous active service, when from May to September 1919 he was posted on HMS Pegasus to the Archangel campaign in north-west Russia.[87] This rather confusing codicil to WW1 in Europe had started after the Russian revolution had led the new

Bolshevik government to negotiate the Treaty of Brest-Litovsk with the Germans on 3rd March 1918, formalising Russian withdrawal from WW1. The British, French and American Allies were concerned that this took pressure off the Germans on their eastern flank, enabling them to concentrate all their effort on the western front. Their fears were compounded when in April 1918 a brigade of German troops entered Finland, raising the prospect that they would capture the Murmansk–Petrograd railway and seize the large stockpiles of military stores and equipment the Allies had dumped in north-west Russia, and especially the naval bases at Murmansk and Archangel.

Consequently, the British proposed a plan to send a force to the Russian north-west to secure the extensive stocks of military equipment, and work with Russian volunteers to reorganise the eastern theatre and keep Germany engaged and stretched on two fronts.[88]

Joe's role in this uninspiring conclusion to the war was in command of seaplane operations from HMS Pegasus. Pegasus was one of two prototype aircraft carriers used in the Archangel campaign, among the first experiments attempting to combine naval and air power. It was fitted with a 'flying-off deck' at the front of the ship, capable of launching the five Sopwith Camel fighters stored in the ship's forward hangar. Aft of the bridge a larger hangar accommodated four seaplanes. Two cranes at the back of the ship could lower the seaplanes into the water while the vessel was steaming at up to 19 knots, and recover them again after operations whilst moving at up to 6 knots.

Within Russia, the situation had deteriorated after 1917, and civil war was raging between the Red Army of the new communist government and the White forces opposed to the Bolshevik takeover. The Allies supported the Whites in a campaign that lasted from the summer of 1918 to the autumn of 1919. However, after initial progress, the Allied

HMS *Pegasus in WW1 'dazzle' camouflage.*

expeditionary force became spread out over a long front, giving the Bolsheviks (who had an advantage in artillery) the opportunity to attack the exposed flanks of the Allied forces. With awful Russian winter conditions and regular mutinies amongst the White Russian forces, the Allies became bogged down. Conditions were so bad the British called for help from polar explorer Sir Ernest Shackleton, who, together with some of his team from the 1917 Endurance expedition to Antarctica, advised on winter equipment, clothing, sledges and the use of dogs to help the army operate in the extreme frozen tundra conditions.[89] For Joe and his team of naval fliers, coping with the extreme cold in exposed, open-cockpit aircraft at altitude must have been an incredible challenge, requiring exceptional fortitude and resilience.

With the armies bogged down and little progress being made, once the Armistice that ended WW1 was signed in November 1918, the rationale for an Allied anti-German campaign in Russia disappeared, and public opinion in Britain and America turned strongly against maintaining the Russian campaign. The Daily Express newspaper famously paraphrased Bismarck in saying "the frozen plains of Eastern Europe are not worth the bones of a single grenadier." Eventually, the decision was taken to withdraw – one of the last decisions made at the Paris Peace Conference in June 1919 that resulted in the Treaty of Versailles imposing war reparations on Germany was agreement to withdraw all Allied forces from Russia.[90, 91]

With the withdrawal of British forces in September and October 1919, Joe's active war duties were finally over almost a year after the formal end of WW1. Joe had not only survived four years' service in one of the most dangerous disciplines in the armed forces; he had served with distinction in a wide range of roles, shown considerable bravery, adaptability and leadership, and contributed to the development and application of the new concept of aerial warfare. Joe, Mabel and Joe Junior were able to return to Canada, arriving by steamship on 8th November 1919.[92]

Although the war was over and Joe was finally demobilised, his association with the navy and with flying was far from finished. On 12th November 1919, Joe transferred to work for the

L–R: Joe, Helen (Basil's wife), Mabel, and Basil Hobbs together after the end of WW1. The occasion is the homecoming parade organised for Basil by the town of Sault Ste Marie.

Operations Department of the newly formed Canadian Air Board (Joe's younger brother Basil also joined the Air Board shortly afterwards). The Air Board had been created by act of Parliament on 6th June 1919 as Canada's first governing body for aviation. It had three main roles: the air defence of Canada; the regulation of civil aviation; and the conduct of government air operations.

In a civil extension of his war work in Nova Scotia, one of Joe's first assignments for the Air Board was to scout locations to use for air stations. In December 1919 Joe, now aged 28, visited Vancouver and British Columbia (B.C.) for the first time, gaining his first experience of the place that he would make his home for more than a decade. Joe's mission was to stimulate civil aviation in B.C., where aviation was seen to have multiple new practical applications supporting lands and forestry patrol, fire protection, transport of mail, and support for police, public works, surveying, marine and fisheries activities.

The Vancouver Sun and Victoria Daily Times both carried stories of Capt. Hobbs' visit. He spent a month in Victoria collecting data and preparing a report for the government in Ottawa.[93, 94] Later in the month, Joe is mentioned by the Calgary Herald as returning to Vancouver on 16th December after a survey cruise up the B.C. coast, again making use of the Canadian navy ship 'HMCS Stadacona', which had now been transferred to the Pacific coast. Joe was researching a government report on how and where to set up a sea plane base in Vancouver, with refuelling stations to be established at various locations up the coast, taking advantage of good natural water landing areas which could boost aviation without the need to build expensive airstrips.[95] Whilst Joe's activities would have been of interest to the general public, the fact that these stories made the newspapers indicates that Joe was starting to develop his media communication skills, which were to be a trademark of his business career subsequently.

His report recommended a site which was developed into the Jericho Beach Air Station in Vancouver, opening in 1920, the first of several along the B.C. coast. The stations were used by government departments for anti-smuggling, fishery and forestry management operations, and for transportation to remote communities. The Royal Canadian Air Force took over Jericho Beach as a base for flying boats and seaplanes in 1924, and it continued in military use until returned to the city in 1969. All the hangars were demolished in 1996 and it is now Jericho Beach Park.[96, 97]

After moving to Vancouver in the spring of 1920, Joe continued to dabble occasionally in aviation matters, but his interest and attention turned to whisky and shipping, which were to provide him with his first fortune. He had survived the war unscathed, which, given the nature of his service, is remarkable in itself. The range of his war experiences undoubtedly helped develop his toughness, resilience and determination, his leadership, management and communication skills, and equipped Joe for his very successful post-war career as a businessman and entrepreneur. Several post-war newspaper articles described Joe as having had "a splendid record during the war."[98] That this phrase was used more than once and typically in connection with Joe's self-promotion initiatives could indicate that it had been coined by Joe himself. But whilst it is hard to use the description "splendid" in connection with an international conflagration that resulted in so much pain and suffering, Joe's war experience undoubtedly further developed his skills, capabilities and reputation, setting him up for the enormous success he achieved in his business career after the war.

4

Boom Years

Although aviation was his initial interest and focus after demobilising from the air force at the end of 1919, Joe explored a number of different business opportunities over the next few years before focusing his attention on shipping and whisky, which were to provide his first fortune, and which became enduring features of the rest of his life.

Having travelled extensively during the war years, Joe decided to settle permanently with his family in Vancouver. In April 1920, Joe is reported by the Vancouver Daily World as having arrived in Vancouver to make it his home. The article said that Capt. Hobbs "was so much impressed by the attractions of this city (Vancouver)" during his visit for the Air Board that he had decided to live there.[99] Vancouver was developing rapidly. The city had been growing fast since the arrival of the Canadian Pacific transcontinental railway in 1887, and the opening of the Panama Canal in 1914 was a major spur to Vancouver's growth by opening a cost-competitive sea route to and from Europe, to complement Vancouver port's existing good situation as a gateway for trade to and from Asia. Its mild climate and the opening of the University of British Columbia in 1915 also contributed to continued growth for Vancouver, which after WW1 overtook Winnipeg to become the largest and most important city in western Canada. It would have presented an attractive location to live and a multitude of opportunities for Joe as he set out in business after the war.

In May 1920, Joe was elected as the new vice president of the Air Service Association (A.S.A.) in Vancouver.[100] At the time, there were Air Service Associations in each of the main provinces of Canada. They developed initially as associations to promote the interests of returning air servicemen after the war, organising social events and promoting employment and welfare initiatives for members. Later merging into a single national organisation, the Air Service Associations took on a more formal role in Canada's evolving civil aviation administration, providing skilled and experienced airmen to participate in industry regulation under Canada's Air Board, e.g. as members of Air Board committees on licensing and standards. Joe's involvement with the A.S.A. does not appear to have lasted very long, as his attention soon switched to new areas of business. Joe's brother, now Major Basil Hobbs, also came to reside in Vancouver at this time, having been appointed to represent the government appointed Air Board of Canada in the west.[101]

In early 1921, Joe and Mabel helped to organise a dance held by the Vancouver Flying Club at the Navy League Auditorium in Vancouver.[102] After this, although Joe kept an interest in aviation and briefly returned to the field at the end of the 1920s, he ceased to be active in aviation issues.

It is interesting to speculate about why Joe turned away from aviation as a career at this time. He had only recently completed a very successful period as a flier during WW1, and his reputation as an aviation leader was clearly very good, as evidenced by the increasing responsibilities with which he was entrusted.

At that time, aviation was an exciting new industry which was receiving a huge amount of attention and expanding very fast as the potential civil applications were explored for new aviation technologies developed during the war. In a large country like Canada, aviation clearly had an exciting future and presented many opportunities. But instead of continuing in aviation, Joe turned to ships and whisky, which at first sight might be thought to have presented less attractive possibilities.

There were probably a number of different factors which contributed to Joe's thinking on this. Firstly, Joe had an enduring passion for ships and boats, a theme which sustained throughout his life. Since he did not grow up by the sea, his interest in ships must have been triggered later, conceivably first sparked by the exciting transatlantic journey on the 'Tunisian' that brought his family to Canada, perhaps reinforced by proximity to the many ships Joe would have seen every day as a young man passing through the world's busiest canal system at Sault Ste Marie, and given tangible expression in his early entrepreneurial role running a ferry service across the St Mary River at Sault. He might also have been inspired by the colourful and charismatic F.H. Clergue, who kept a stylish and glamorous yacht named 'Siesta' moored at Sault for boating trips on Lakes Superior and Huron. In addition, even after ceasing active service as a naval airman after the end of WW1, Joe maintained strong ties with the Navy, which was something he put great effort into sustaining for the remainder his life, and on both sides of the Atlantic. Joe continued in the Naval Reserve in Vancouver in the early 1920s, and was appointed to set up and lead the new Royal Canadian Navy Volunteer Reserve in Vancouver in 1924.

A second driving factor is likely to have been the potential to make money, and lots of it, trading in whisky, especially in the unique environment of Canada at that time. The western part of Canada constituted a decent-sized market in its own right for the import of alcoholic drinks, and Joe was able to successfully acquire the 'agencies' to import and represent a number of leading brands of whisky. However, with the advent of Prohibition in the USA from 1919, a huge and highly lucrative trade developed to bring alcohol into Canada for subsequent re-export to supply America, where the demand could not be met by direct imports, as this had been banned by Prohibition. Although importing alcohol into the USA was illegal during this period, there were no Canadian laws preventing export of alcohols which subsequently were brought to the USA. Demand for alcohol in Canada at this time was huge, mostly driven by demands for the re-export trade, and the profit margins exceptionally high for entrepreneurs like Joe able to secure supplies of whisky from the network he would build up in the U.K.

A third stream of influence could have been sibling rivalry, or a pragmatic decision for Joe and Basil to explore different opportunities rather than 'fish in the same pond.' As the elder brother, Joe had been the first to get involved in flying and had achieved great success with it during the war. But, undeniably, Basil was extraordinarily talented as an aviator and had outshone his older brother, winning multiple decorations and later being awarded an O.B.E. After the war, Basil was promoted to Major in the Air Force and secured a leading role in Canada's Air Board, the new governing body for aviation in Canada, whilst Joe was now only involved in the less influential Air Service Association. As the older brother, Joe may have decided it was better to let his extremely talented younger brother take the lead on the aviation side, whilst he would focus on maritime activities. If so, that was to prove a good decision, with both brothers going on to excel in their respective areas of focus (whilst also collaborating successfully on the whisky importing business).

It took a little while for Joe to settle on shipping and whisky as the two key focus areas of his business career after WW1, which drove the accumulation of his first fortune. First, he dabbled in ranching, an experience which would prove extremely valuable to him years later in Scotland when he developed the Great Glen Cattle Ranch in the 1950s. In a much later newspaper article in The Province from 1955 Joe said he "came to the Olds district of Alberta as a rancher in 1920-22" and then "followed this with ranching in the Cariboo country of B.C." Olds is on flat prairie land just to the east of the Rockies in Alberta, 100km due north from Calgary, whilst the Cariboo area is 700km north of Vancouver. These are both big centres of cattle ranching in Canada which developed in the 1880s with the coming of the railways. Ranching in the Cariboo was given a further boost in the early 20th century, when a railway-building frenzy saw the construction of no fewer than three major railroads in the area – the Grand Trunk, Canadian Northern and Canadian Pacific railroads. These railways employed huge crews of men to undertake their construction, all of whom needed feeding. The ranchers of the British Columbia interior were in a perfect position to supply cattle to each of these markets. Between 1910 and 1912, about 12,000 head of cattle were purchased and driven to the Grand Trunk Pacific railway crews alone. Ranching in British Columbia received a significant boost and the cattle industry there became well established.

After WW1, the ranches in the Cariboo reoriented, evolving from a preponderance of small ranch units into larger holdings. Although consolidation of holdings had occurred for several decades, and most of the very large ranches had taken shape before the war, there was an increased trend toward the establishment of medium and large ranches after the war. By the 1930s, a typical ranch in the British Columbia interior comprised about 3,000 acres and ran around 500 head of cattle. We do not have records to prove it, but it seems likely Joe was involved as an investor in some of these ranch consolidations. In typical Joe Hobbs style, he seems to have adopted a 'hands-on' approach and gained first-hand experience of ranch operations. Along the way, he probably spent time in the saddle, honing the horse-riding skills he first acquired on his father's farm in the Sault, and developing into a first-class horseman.

However, whilst this was useful experience for the fledgling entrepreneur, Joe's involvement in ranching did not sustain as he searched for the best opportunities to develop his business career. In a somewhat fanciful explanation given in an interview much later with the Liverpool Echo in 1954, Joe said of this time "I put my war gratuity into property, bought myself more property, and got myself an interest in shipping and banking."[103] Whilst shipping, property development and finance were to feature prominently in his post-WW1 career, at this time in the early 1920s Joe most commonly described himself as a 'broker'. Joe was actively searching for and exploring multiple business opportunities, and the description 'broker' can be applied to many buying/selling transactions involving a middleman. It is possible that Joe 'brokered' multiple commodities and cargoes (for example grain and packed meat, which were voluminous exports from Vancouver and British Columbia), and that his involvement in movement of these cargoes evolved into his role as an owner and operator of ships. However, the core of his brokerage activities was in buying and selling whisky, and in the early part of the 1920s, whisky trading became the central component of his business and the most substantial contributor to his income. It has been conjectured that Joe visited Scotland during WW1, making initial connections that got him started in the whisky business, and this now became the central part of the business he built up in Vancouver from the early 1920s.

Between 5th August and 30th September 1921 Joe went on his first business trip to the UK.[104] He stated his occupation on the ship's manifest as 'broker' and his UK address as Chilton

House, Chilton, the address of his 'uncle' W.J. Harris, married to his aunt Alice Mary (his father's younger sister), who farmed Chilton Farm, Chilton, in Berkshire. Joe regularly used his extended English family's various homes as his UK contact address on his early visits back to the old country, which also demonstrates that, whilst Joe's father and grandfather never resolved their differences, relations with the rest of the family remained cordial. There are no records stating definitively what Joe got up to on this trip, but in all probability, this was the first time that he went to meet face-to-face with suppliers in the whisky trade, negotiating commitments for supplies of whisky from Scotland to Canada (and maybe also for onward sale to the USA).[105] For this first business trip, Joe travelled second class (in contrast to his later travels, which were almost always in first class), indicating that his business was not yet established enough to justify premium class travel.

Joe started as an agent for Peter Dawson Distillers in the early 1920s.[106] Peter Dawson had owned Auchnaghie distillery near Pitlochry, in the heart of the Scottish Highlands in the 1880s, and, then in partnership with a group of Glasgow-based blenders, he built the Convalmore distillery in Dufftown, and three years later also built the Towiemore distillery nearby. In 1910, Capt. Robert Falcon Scott chose Towiemore malt whisky to take as the expedition whisky for his ill-fated attempt to be the first to reach the South Pole.[107] By the early 1920s, Dawson's were better known for their blended whiskies, Peter Dawson Special, Extra Special and Old Curio. Certainly, Peter Dawson's whiskies were popular in Canada and the USA at that time, the Montreal Gazette reporting that "Peter Dawson Scotch is one of the most popular brands of whisky imported into the Dominion and has an excellent reputation for quality".[108] This popularity only increased after H.R.H. The Prince of Wales asked to be supplied with Peter Dawson whisky during his visit

Advertisement for Peter Dawson 'bramble and dimple' bottled whisky, 1924.

to Canada in 1908: "With the world's best to choose from, His Royal Highness selected Peter Dawson Scotch as the best".[109] The popularity of Dawson's was boosted again in 1924 following the launch in Canada of their famous 'brambles and dimples' bottles, which as well as being an attractive design was also introduced as an initiative to prevent counterfeiting, a major challenge in the industry.

Whether Joe was actually formally appointed as the agent for Dawson's is less clear. In documents released in connection with a Canadian Government procurement investigation a few years later, Peter Dawson himself was quoted as saying he "had no agent in British Columbia" at that time, although he was open to having one.[110] But from 1923 Joe was claiming in correspondence to represent Peter Dawson in British Columbia, and he certainly traded Dawson's whiskies, albeit possibly not on an exclusive basis. In 1925, Dawson's were amalgamated into the UK's largest whisky producer, the Distiller's Company Limited (DCL), as part of an ongoing process of industry consolidation, with Dawson joining the DCL board. Since the DCL already had an agreement with another Canadian whisky baron, Sam Bronfman, who set up a business (the Distillers Company – Seagrams Limited) in the 1920s to distribute DCL's whisky in North America, it is likely this spelled the end of Joe's business importing the Dawson brands into Canada, and maybe also marked the start of Joe's subsequent mistrust of and competition with the DCL.

In addition to Dawson's, we also know that Joe started working with the famous UK wine and spirit merchant W.&A. Gilbey from at least 1923, from which year advertisements in the Canadian press indicated Joe was working as Gilbey's agent in western Canada. The firm had been founded in 1857 by brothers Walter and Alfred Gilbey. The business specialised in wines from South Africa that they bottled and sold under their own Gilbey's 'house' label. Starting from premises near Oxford Street in London, the good quality-to-price value proposition of these 'house' wines was attractive to an emerging middle-class of drinkers, and by 1861 Gilbey's were already the third-largest wine importer in the UK. They diversified into producing spirits in 1872, going on to become very well known for their brand of London dry gin, and also expanded into whisky, opening branches in Dublin and Edinburgh, building a warehouse in Edinburgh and – as with the wines – purchasing whiskies to retail under their own brand name.

Gilbey's acquired a string of distilleries in the Speyside region in order to secure supplies for their blends, starting in 1887 with the purchase of Glen Spey distillery in Rothes, then

Gilbey's whisky advertisement, Vancouver Daily Mail, December 1924.

Strathmill in Keith in 1895, and Knockando in the Moray village of the same name in 1903. In 1905, Gilbey's took a further step with the acquisition of Aberdeen-based blending company James Catto & Co., in partnership with another London wine and spirit merchant, Corney & Barrow. As one of the main players in the industry with access to substantial stocks, Gilbey's would have been a very strong partner for Joe and his developing whisky brokerage business in Canada. His connections with Gilbey's would prove of value later, enabling Joe's subsequent introduction to his important business partner National Distillers of America.[111]

In his entry in the 1931 edition of *Who's Who in Canada*, Joe was also reported to be a director of the firm of W.H. Holt & Sons Ltd.[112] Holt's were a Manchester brewing company which, between the years of 1921–45, were owners of the Aberlour Distillery in the village of the same name in the Speyside area of Banffshire, Scotland. Holt's produced a brand of whisky marketed as "Mountain Cream", with whisky from Aberlour Distillery as a principal constituent, which enjoyed some success in the UK and Canada in the 1920s-30s. Given his involvement with Holt's, Joe would have been importing Mountain Cream into Canada at this time, although the brand's profile seems relatively weak in Joe's home state of British Columbia, selling better in Montreal and Winnipeg.[1]

After returning from his first UK business trip in the summer of 1921 (likely to negotiate contracts for the supply of whisky from Peter Dawson, W.&A. Gilbey and others), Joe took

---

1   W.H. Holt & Sons subsequently got into financial difficulties in the challenging market conditions during World War 2 and went bankrupt. Their principal asset, Aberlour Distillery, passed to the firm of S. Campbell & Sons Distillers Ltd, in a very murky transaction associated with some possibly fraudulent trading to avoid responsibility for wartime excess profit tax levied on whisky traders. There is no evidence Joe Hobbs was still involved with the company by that time.

Advert for Holt's "Mountain Cream" whisky, a brand based on whisky from the Aberlour Distillery in Speyside, Scotland. Joe Hobbs was a director of Holts in the 1920s.

up residence at 3256, 3rd Avenue West, Vancouver, B.C. together with his wife Mabel and son Joseph junior. 3rd Avenue West is a pleasant avenue of modest detached houses, an indication that Joe was already solidly prosperous.[113]

In January 1922, Mabel gave birth to the Hobbs' second child, a daughter, in Vancouver. Continuing the Hobbs tradition of naming children after their parents, the new arrival was named Mabel Patricia Hobbs – called Patricia hereafter in this book. Joe was aged 31 and Mabel Dell 36 at the time of their daughter's arrival.

In 1922, Joe took some steps to establish the second key focus of his life during this period, relating to sailing and shipping. Joe was to become a very active member of the Royal Vancouver Yacht Club, where he was able to indulge his love of sailing and boats, and which was also to prove very valuable to him in social and business networking aspects, since many of Vancouver and British Columbia's leading lights in the 1920s and early 1930s were involved in the club. The same year, he also joined the Vancouver Automobile Club,[114] further evidence of his rising wealth, and was fined $45 together with a Mr J. Wright for speeding when racing their cars on Kingsway, Vancouver.[115]

But, in the spring of 1922, Joe took a big step when he successfully acquired his first yacht, the ex-Canadian Navy training vessel 'HMCS Naden'. The 2-masted schooner Naden

RVYC Point Grey Clubhouse Vancouver under construction 1927.

was originally built as a government survey ship in 1913. After WW1, it became part of the fleet of the fledgling Canadian navy, based at Esquimalt Naval College on Vancouver Island and used as a training ship. She was decommissioned in 1922 and Joe bought her, changing the name to Mabel Dell in honour of his wife. At 80 feet long and 91 tons, the Mabel Dell became the largest sailing boat in the R.V.Y.C.. Joe raced Mabel Dell in R.V.Y.C. regattas, and used her for entertaining, but also deployed her in connection with his work as founding commanding officer of the Vancouver company of the Royal Canadian Navy Volunteer Reserve, using the yacht as a training vessel for naval cadets. In 1925, Joe refitted and upgraded the Mabel Dell, installing a bigger (220hp) engine, and then remasted her and put in extra sails in 1926.[116]

The acquisition of Mabel Dell says a great deal about Joe's growing status and resources. While it was probably through Joe's naval connections that he had the opportunity to buy Mabel Dell, yachting is a rich man's pastime and the fact he could afford to buy, maintain and crew her indicates his business was already doing extremely well and he had substantial funds available for a prestige hobby. That he was now, at the age of just 31, the owner

Joe's first yacht, Mabel Dell.

Joe and Mabel at the helm of the Mabel Dell.

of the largest yacht in R.V.Y.C. would certainly also have done a great deal for his social standing.

In the second quarter of 1923, in a further sign of Joe's rapidly rising reputation, Joe and Mabel (without the children) made an extended visit to the UK from 5th May–17th July. Joe participated as one of a 27-member delegation from the Vancouver Board of Trade to the UK. While Joe was clearly working, the purpose declared on Mabel's immigration form was 'on holiday'!

The party went first to Montreal, arriving on 10th May, and were hosted at events put on by the Montreal Board of Trade, before travelling on to the UK on Canadian Pacific's steamer 'Empress of Scotland', leaving from Quebec on 12th May. In the UK, the delegation toured from 23rd May to 15th June, visiting a number of industrial plants, attending a ceremony at

VANCOUVER BOARD OF TRADE delegation to Great Britain, May 23-June 15, 1923. Left to right —Willie Dalton, A. L. McLennan, F. C. Wade, K.C., (B.C. Agent-General), R. W. Brown, J. B. Thomson, president Vancouver Board of Trade, J. W. deB. Farris, K.C., Nicol Thompson, Hugo Ray, H. W. White, sr., Percy White, jr., Earl McNair, W. E. Payne, secretary Vancouver Board of Trade, O. B. Allan, J. B. Johnson, Capt. J. W. Hobbs, Jonathan Rogers, Harry Nansen, Judge J. N. Ellis. The delegation toured the United Kingdom, visiting many of the great industrial plants, attended a ceremony at the grave of Captain George Vancouver and was entertained widely by the Empire's leading business and commercial organizations. The photograph was taken in the City of London.

Vancouver Board of Trade delegation to Great Britain 23rd May-15th June 1923. Joe Hobbs standing fourth from right.

the grave of Capt. George Vancouver, the founder of Vancouver city in B.C., and being entertained by many leading business and commercial organisations.

Roy W. Brown, Editorial Manager of the Vancouver daily newspaper 'The Province' was also part of the delegation, an association which seems likely to have assisted Joe's positive media profile in Vancouver thereafter.

The Hobbs then had several weeks on their own, including a stay at the Russell Hotel in London before returning home in July 1923. Only four years after his demobilisation from military service and at just 32 years of age, clearly Joe's business was flourishing, and the fact he was able to participate in such a prestigious delegation indicates he was already of considerable standing in the business community. Joe continued to describe his occupation as a 'broker' during his participation in this delegation. He and Mabel travelled both ways first class, which was to become their habit in the years ahead.[117, 118]

By July of 1923, the Hobbs were now living at 3315, 26th Avenue West, Vancouver. This is a quiet leafy avenue of medium-sized detached houses. Whilst not as palatial as some of his subsequent homes, it was a further step up from his previous residence at 3rd Avenue West.[119]

On 15th April 1924, Joe was appointed as Acting Lieutenant in the Royal Canadian Navy Volunteer Reserve (R.C.N.V.R.) and authorised to form the Vancouver "Half Company" of the new R.C.N.V.R. In Vancouver, an informal volunteer reserve of the Canadian navy had existed since shortly after the end of WW1, formed by 87 volunteer members of the Royal Vancouver Yacht Club. However, it took until 1923 for the R.C.N.V.R. to be formally inaugurated with approval and funding from the Canadian government, when Rear-Admiral Walter Hose was authorised to establish a nationwide naval reserve force for the Royal Canadian Navy. The purpose was to recruit and train a reserve force that could be called up to the Canadian Navy in time of need. Initially, the R.C.N.V.R. was established with a strength of 1,000 men of all ranks across Canada, with Naval Reserve Divisions set up in every major Canadian city, 15 in all. Most of these were established at "Half-Company" strength (comprising 50 men of all ranks), with three cities (Toronto, Montreal and Winnipeg) ordered to set up "Full-Company" strength operations, comprising 100 men of all ranks.

There has been some speculation that the authorities hesitated over Joe's appointment to lead the R.C.N.V.R. in Vancouver, because part of his nautical experience was rumoured to be associated with rum running. Joe's appointment in Vancouver came later than similar appointments elsewhere in Canada (e.g. appointments to lead HMS Chippawa, the R.C.N.V.R. company in Winnipeg, had already been made in the spring of 1923). However, Joe's strong naval connections and commitment to training seafarers seems to have won the day, and his appointment was eventually confirmed.

Joe took his R.C.N.V.R. duties seriously, and was active in the Vancouver branch's management, often making his yachts available for training purposes and joining the volunteers on training trips. The R.C.N.V.R. became important to Canada as a cost-effective way of training men in naval skills and having them ready and available in time of need, and as a feeder into the main Navy. Its value was demonstrated at the onset of World War 2, when the R.C.N.V.R. was used as a vehicle to rapidly recruit and train a substantial body of men for war service. By the end of WW2, Canada had the third largest navy in the world, with a complement of nearly 100,000, many of whom had been trained through the R.C.N.V.R. [120, m]

In 1924, Joe had the opportunity to buy another ex-naval ship, the HMCS Stadacona, and took his first steps into business as a ship owner. Joe already had quite an association with the historic steam yacht Stadacona, as he had been on board her both in Newfoundland when still serving with the Navy at the end of WW1, and in British Columbia in 1919, when conducting his survey of possible airstrips and seaplane bases for the Canadian Air Board. The Stadacona was a 168-foot-long steam yacht of nearly 800 gross tons. Although Joe's existing yacht Mabel Dell was the largest yacht in the Royal Vancouver Yacht Club, there is no evidence Joe ever used Mabel Dell to carry cargoes for business – Stadacona was different, and, whilst Joe appreciated her history and graceful lines, she was bought and operated as a working cargo ship. Originally built in 1893

---

m   Footnote: the site allocated to the R.C.N.V.R. in Vancouver on
    Deadman's Island (just next to the RVYC Coal Harbour clubhouse)
    is still in use by the Canadian armed forces to this day as the training
    station HMCS Discovery.

Joe Hobbs supervising Royal Canadian Navy Volunteer Reserve training on board his yacht Mabel Dell, Vancouver, c.1925.

in America for J. Harvey Ladew, an executive for the Singer Sewing Machine company, the ship had been used by the US Navy in the Spanish-American War in the Philippines under the name Wasp, and fought in the Battle of Manila Bay in 1898. In use again after that as a private yacht named Columbia, in 1915 she was purchased for the Canadian navy, renamed HMCS Stadacona, and served as the Admiral's flagship on the Atlantic coast during WW1, when Joe first had contact with the ship. After the end of the war, Stadacona transferred to the Pacific coast, where she was used for hydrographic survey work and fisheries protection duties, and again Joe travelled on the vessel for his seaplane base survey work in British Columbia.

Continuing his phenomenal post-war wave of commercial expansion and success, on 29th September 1924 Joe announced that he was building a mansion on Laurier Avenue in the fashionable and highly prestigious Shaughnessy Heights area of west Vancouver. This is an area of exclusive houses and mansions which, since it was first mapped out by famed landscape architect Frederick Gage Todd on 'garden city' principles with spacious plots of minimum 10,000 square feet, has been home to many

Stadacona, Joe's first commercial ship, whilst still in military service.

of 'the great and the good' of Vancouver. Quite apart from the utility and comfort that such a grand house would provide to Joe and his family, as with the purchase of the yacht Mabel Dell, this was another very public statement of Joe's rising wealth and active presence amongst Vancouver's elite.[121, n]

In the spring of 1925, Joe, Mabel and Joe Junior (but seemingly not daughter Patricia, who stayed at home) made a trip to the U.K. They travelled out to Liverpool in February 1925, and returned to Quebec in May 1925. This was a whisky-buying trip. Joe recorded his intended address in the UK as 37 Hope Street, Glasgow. Then as now, this was the site of a hotel nearby Glasgow Central station. However, it is also literally around the corner from the Glasgow headquarters of Train & MacIntyre,

---

n   The mansion Joe built at 1656 Laurier still exists today in the still highly
     desirable Shaughnessy district. Whilst there has been considerable price
     inflation in Vancouver's property market in recent years, the house
     fetched a staggering C$15m when it last changed hands in October
     2020, after an extensive renovation.

The mansion that Joe Hobbs had built at 1656 Laurier Avenue, Shaughnessy Heights, Vancouver under construction in 1925.

who later became the U.K. arm of the American company National Distillers Products Corp., with whom Joe was to work extensively in the 1930s as together they built up their portfolio of Scottish distilleries in Associated Scottish Distilleries, and close by many other established companies in the whisky trade. On the same trip, Joe had meetings with Gilbey's at their headquarters in London, recording on the returning ship's manifest he had stayed at "W.A.Gibbey [sic], The Pantheon, Oxford Street, London" before returning home.[122, 123]

After their return to Canada, the Hobbs moved into the mansion Joe had been building at 1656 Laurier Avenue, Vancouver.

At just 34 years of age, and after a remarkably short period of time, Joe had become a very wealthy man and acquired all the outward symbols of success – a mansion, a yacht, cars, he was a member of Vancouver's Board of Trade and leading member of the Royal Vancouver Yacht Club, and a prominent figure in the business community, pre-eminently through the Merchant's Exchange. His whisky and shipping business was clearly booming.

Contemporary photograph of Joe's mansion at 1656 Laurier Avenue,
Vancouver, in the prestigious Shaughnessy Heights district.

In early 1926, Joe took the step of incorporating his fast-developing whisky and shipping businesses into a new company, 'Hobbs Brothers Limited', in partnership with his brother Basil, and their mutual friend Colonel O.F. Brothers. The company name is a neat play on the fact that the owners comprised the two Hobbs brothers, who were in partnership with Colonel Brothers. Whatever the shareholding however, there was no doubt that Joe Hobbs was the driving force behind the company's business success. Hobbs Brothers was used as the entity for all Joe's trading and shipping activities thereafter. While Basil continued to be active in aviation matters, from this time onwards he worked much more closely with Joe on the whisky trading and shipping businesses. Joe and Basil made a trip to the UK together in April 1926, the brothers both listing their occupations as 'brokers'. This seems to have been the first time Basil travelled to the U.K. in relation to the whisky trading business, something he was to do many more times in the decades ahead, in furtherance of the successful spirits retailing business he continued to run in Canada long after his older brother Joe turned his attention to new opportunities in the U.K.[124, o]

It is extremely interesting to note that Joe's future wife Evelyn Appleyard and her son John (aged 5) were also on the same ship that Joe and Basil took to England in April 1926. This is too much of a coincidence, and implies that Joe and Eve were already a couple and were discreetly travelling together. The three adults all travelled back to Canada in June 1926. There is no record of Eve's son John, who seems to have been left behind in England.[125]

Who was Evelyn Appleyard? We do not know when and where exactly Joe and Eve first met, only that it was in Vancouver at some stage between 1923 and 1925. Eve had been born in Bawtry, near Doncaster in Yorkshire, in 1900, the elder of two daughters of George Henry (Harry) Snow, a coachman, and his wife Flora. The family relocated to London before the time of the 1911 Census, with Harry still working as a coachman, and living at 7 Blithfield Street, Kensington. At some stage towards the end of WW1, Eve had met Frederick Appleyard, a Lieutenant in the 38th Battalion of the Canadian Expeditionary Force. Frederick had served as a machine gunner in France, and been evacuated back to the UK after being wounded in November 1916. For the rest of the war Frederick served as a Lewis gun instructor at the

---

o   Although it was Joe Hobbs that first got into the whisky importing business in Canada, Basil continued to be successful as a liquor importer long after Joe returned to the UK in the early 1930s. After he resigned from the Royal Canadian Air Force in 1925, Basil established his own business, Basil D. Hobbs and Sons, Wine & Spirit Merchants, in Montreal. He was successful in winning the agencies to represent a number of leading liquor brands in Canada, including Cutty Sark whisky and Mumm Champagne. Subsequently merged with another leading player in the industry, the firm is now named Charton Hobbs, still in Basil's family ownership, and one of the largest and most successful liquor businesses in Canada, with representations in all major regions of the country.

Canadian military training school at Seaford, on England's south coast. Eve and Frederick got married at the Kensington Registry Office in west London on 9th May 1919, where Eve seems to have lied about her age, claiming to be 21 years old so that she could marry without parental consent, being in reality only 19 years old at the time. Shortly afterwards, Frederick was repatriated to Canada, travelling to Quebec, and being honourably discharged from the Canadian forces at Ottawa on 20th September. Eve was able to travel with him; however, she was only able to spend a month in Canada before returning to the UK in October. On her immigration form, Eve stated her reasons for leaving Canada to be "urgent family affairs", and back in Kensington she gave birth to a son John Henry Appleyard in April 1920.

It is not clear why Eve returned to the UK to have her son; however, over the next few years she travelled back and forth across the Atlantic to Canada on a regular basis. At the end of October 1920, she travelled to Canada again with John Henry, moving to Sudbury, Ontario, to be with her husband Frederick. Sudbury is a mining town, and it seems Frederick had found work as a mining engineer. However, 18 months later, she and John Henry went back to England again, this time citing "health reasons" as the reason for her departure. Mother and son remained in the UK for around a year on this occasion, before once again returning to Canada in May 1923, this time travelling to Montreal to join her husband at Bruce Mines, Ontario. Bruce Mines was the site of Canada's first copper mine. On the shores of Lake Huron, it is only 70km east of Sault Ste Marie; however, Joe Hobbs was already living in Vancouver by that time, and it was there that Eve met Joe.

The next time we have records of Eve Appleyard is in April 1926, when she travelled to the UK from Canada on the same ship as Joe and Basil Hobbs. This clear evidence that Joe and Eve were already together at this point is reinforced by the fact that soon afterwards, Joe's first wife Mabel made a lengthy trip to Hawaii on her own. Mabel travelled to Honolulu in July 1926, and only returned to Vancouver in September. Something was clearly wrong with her marriage to Joe.

With the turn of the year to 1927, on 19th January Joe was nominated to the Executive Committee of the R.V.Y.C., a further reinforcement of his position and influence amongst Vancouver's social elite.[126]

1927 was probably the peak year for Joe and Hobbs Brothers' shipping activities. A summary of the fleet they owned and operated in the 1920s is as follows:

Vessel Name	Type	Tonnage	Length	Owned	
				From	To
Mabel Dell	Yacht (schooner)	91	90ft	1922	1927
Stadacona/Lady Stimson	Steam yacht	798	168ft	1924	1929
Lillehorn	Motor freighter	504	207ft	1926	1927
Hurry On	Motor freighter	638	173ft	1926	1931
Vencedor	Motor Yacht	382	146ft	1927	1930
Oaxaca	Motor Yacht/freighter	1690	254ft	1928	1931

During 1927, Joe traded up his already impressive personal yacht. On 28th April, The Province reported that he had sold his yacht Mabel Dell to American film actor John Gilbert, who relocated it to Los Angeles. Joe later told the story that John Gilbert wanted the yacht as part of his efforts to court Greta Garbo – he renamed the yacht 'The Temptress', the name of the film Garbo was making at the time. (Gilbert's strategy of using the yacht to pursue Garbo seems to have paid dividends: the pair embarked on a high-profile romance and went on to make several films together.) For Joe, it seems that his decision to get rid of the yacht Mabel Dell was also symptomatic of the fact his marriage to the real-life Mabel Dell had broken down.[127, 128]

The replacement was, in true Joe Hobbs style, a vessel with plenty of history and character. In London, the Metropolitan Asylums Board was responsible for administering relief and

Greta Garbo and John Gilbert together in the film "A Woman of Affairs", 1928

On LAND or SEA

The two homes of John Gilbert. On land, Mr. Gilbert lives on one of the highest of the Beverly Hills. When he's at sea, his home is his yacht, The yacht is called "The Temptress." Do we hear a faint chorus of "Ah, theres?"

Late 1920s postcard showing John Gilbert's "Two Homes" – his house in Beverly Hills and his yacht The Temptress – ex-Mabel Dell.

assistance to the poor across greater London, providing hospitals and other forms of support across a wide range of activities to the needy. Since 1875, the board had used ex-Navy sailing ships to give naval training to boys aged 13 to 16, many of whom went on to join the Merchant or Royal Navies. In 1913, the board had commissioned the Exmouth 2, a 146ft, 382-ton, three-masted schooner, to a design by famous marine architect J.H. Biles to continue this training work. During a visit to the UK in 1927, Joe discovered it was for sale, and bought it. He had it refitted in England, removing the central mast and installing a new diesel engine, renamed her Vencedor (which means "winner" in

Joe's second luxury yacht, Vencedor.

Portuguese), and had the ship sailed out to Vancouver. Once in B.C., Joe had roomy and handsome saloons and cabins fitted at the shipyard at Esquimalt, and used it regularly for cruising in the waters around Vancouver.[129, 130, 131]

Joe had bought the Vencedor during his now-annual trip to the UK in the spring of 1927, and arrived back at Quebec on 17th June. On this voyage, he listed his home address as "c/o Mrs J Hobbs, 54 Ponsard Avenue, Montreal".[132] This gives an indication that he and Mabel had now split up, with Mabel living in the Laurier mansion in Vancouver. Whether for this reason, or just to supervise the refit of his new yacht, very soon afterwards Joe made another trip back to the UK, travelling to Southampton on 2nd August 1927, his occupation now listed as 'ship owner'.[133]

Joe spent two months in the UK, but was back in Canada for the end of the year, returning on 8th October 1927.[134] This time he listed 'Belle Irving Building' (sic) in Vancouver as his address, which again gives the impression that he was somewhat homeless at this time, with Mabel occupying the Laurier mansion with Joe Junior and Patricia, and Joe living and travelling elsewhere. Henry Bell Irving was a prominent and successful businessman, focused particularly in salmon canning, insurance and real estate. He constructed the Bell Irving Building at 300 Burrard Street in 1926, just across from the future site of what was to become Marine Building at 355 Burrard Street. Bell Irving was also commodore of the Vancouver Yacht Club in the early 1920s, and perhaps Joe prevailed upon Irving to help him out by putting him up during a difficult time. It was not until 23rd February 1931 that Joe and Mabel finalised their divorce, but certainly from the end of 1927 the marriage was on the rocks.

Despite these troubles in his family life, Joe's business, viewed from the evidence of the extravagant life he was leading with yachts, mansions, cars and extensive first class travel, clearly boomed throughout the 1920s, the time during which Joe accumulated his first fortune. So where did the money for this flamboyant lifestyle come from? Joe had only been de-mobbed from the air force at the end of 1919, and did not come from a wealthy family. Although he would have received a war gratuity (which he later said he had invested well in property), this would not have been a huge sum and could not have generated a large enough return to pay for the biggest yacht in the Royal Vancouver Yacht Club within two years. Whilst Joe was to repeatedly prove he was an exceptional entrepreneur and businessman, the extraordinarily rapid and sustained increase in his wealth during his 'boom years' in the 1920s indicates Joe had developed some unusually profitable businesses. The source of these profits will be explored in more depth in the next chapter.

5

Rum Runner

Throughout his life Joe showed proved himself repeatedly to be a highly successful entrepreneur, and his business savvy would undoubtedly have enabled him to make a living as a whisky broker in almost any circumstances. But the period of Prohibition in the United States from 1919 to 1933 certainly added considerable tailwinds to support Joe's raw talent, which significantly accelerated the accumulation of his first fortune. Joe benefitted from increased demand and prices for his products. But also, for a period of time, he was able to 'supercharge' his earnings by participating as an active 'rum runner' supplying liquor to the USA. A deep analysis of Prohibition is beyond the scope of this book, but it is important to Joe Hobbs' story to know something about how Prohibition in the USA impacted on trade in alcohol in Canada, because it substantially shaped the way Joe's businesses in whisky and shipping developed.

Prohibition had its roots in earlier movements in the 19th century towards religious revival, temperance and the abolition of slavery. A number of individual states had passed their own legislation prohibiting or restricting sale of alcohol, and by the turn of the 20th century there were many temperance societies active in cities and states across America. The pressure was not just from religious groups – there was a strong feminist component to the movement: for example, the Women's Christian Temperance Union cited alcohol as contributing to a broad range of social problems including violence and mistreatment of women and families, divorce, crime, debt and poverty. There was also support from business leaders who favoured Prohibition as a means to increase productivity and reduce absenteeism and accidents in industry. The Anti Saloon League that came to spearhead lobbying for Prohibition can be seen as one of the most effective political pressure groups in US history, eventually succeeding in getting the US Constitution amended.[135]

Following an initial wartime alcohol ban to reserve grain supplies for use as a foodstuff, in 1917 Congress submitted proposals for the 18th Amendment to the US Constitution, which outlawed the manufacture, transport and sale of alcohol. These proposals had to be ratified by three-quarters of individual states before they could become law – in practice, 33 states enacted their own Prohibition legislation as soon as 16th January 1919. Congress passed the National Prohibition Act in

October 1919 to bring the national legislation formally into effect. The Act was formally proposed by Representative Andrew Volstead of

Andrew Volstead (Republican, Representative for Minnesota, Chairman of the House Judiciary Committee 1919–23) who sponsored and championed the Prohibition legislation.

*"By Jing, the old ceiling leaks!"
Political cartoon by Morris
in The Literary Digest, 30th
October 1920, graphically
representing Canada's role in
supplying illicit alcohol to the
USA during Prohibition.*

Minnesota, chairman of the
House Judiciary Committee,
and consequently the
legislation is often known as the Volstead Act. Later, President
Herbert Hoover famously called it a "great social and economic
experiment, noble in motive and far reaching in purpose."[136]

Right from the start, authorities struggled to enforce the
Act. Even though many voices had been raised in support of
Prohibition, there was still a large demand for alcohol, and a
sizeable, diverse and well-organised industry developed to keep
American drinkers supplied. While the US had laws prohibiting
the importation of alcohol (except with a government permit),
there were no Canadian laws preventing Canadians from selling
or supplying alcohol to the USA. Canada consequently became
a major conduit supplying alcohol to the US market during
Prohibition, including Canadian-produced drinks (such as
beer and whisky) as well as international products imported
to Canada and then re-exported to the US. Because of the US
restrictions and the illicit nature of the trade, prices shot up, and
although there were costs and risks for suppliers, margins were
very high. It was said that a case of liquor which cost $25 or $30
in Canada often retailed for $50–60 once across the border in
the USA, and profits were large for suppliers able to operate at
scale.

Canada shared a long land border with the USA, which

alongside the Great Lakes provided many opportunities to move liquor into the United States. In addition, a substantial seaborne trade via "rum runner" ships also developed along both the eastern and western seaboards. In western Canada, in the months after Prohibition was first introduced, it was relatively easy for smugglers to move alcohol into the USA overland across the land border between British Columbia and Washington state. As the USA geared up and became more effective at policing its borders, a trade by sea grew up from Vancouver and, especially, Victoria, which was just a short distance across the Strait of Georgia and Salish Sea to US landfalls around Seattle and northern Washington state. Because distances were short, this trade could be serviced by launch and smaller local boats, and

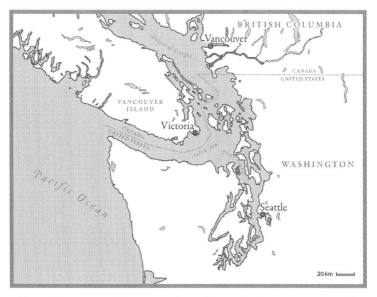

Map of Vancouver / Victoria and north-west Washington state. In the early years of Prohibition, small rum runner vessels left Vancouver and Victoria on a daily basis to ferry alcohol across the Straight of Georgia and Salish sea to landfalls in the north-west USA.

regular (and surprisingly overt) rum-runner boats left Victoria and Vancouver every day in the early 1920s, disrupted from time-to-time by US raids.[137]

As time went on, the trade became increasingly sophisticated. Larger 'mother ships' operated in the Haro Strait east of Victoria near D'Arcy Island, where they were met by fast launches which ferried the booze ashore to quiet landings across Washington state. However, there were progressively more examples of fighting and theft between operators in the illicit trade, so the rum-running vessel operators and crews armed themselves and there were frequent incidents.[138] Sensing opportunity, organised crime began to get involved, and piracy and theft started to become the norm in the 'short-sea' trade around B.C. and northwest Washington state.

In response to this, the trade evolved again. A 'transhipment' trade developed whereby ocean-going ships loaded with crates of alcohol sailed from Vancouver and other B.C. ports to Mexico, with their cargoes of alcohol discharged there and then carried overland to US markets.

A further evolution of the modus operandi, adopted by around 60 vessels operated from Vancouver and southern British Columbia at various times during the 13 years of US Prohibition, was for 'depot' ships of various sizes to load up with thousands of cases of liquor and barrels of beer, and head out perfectly legally from Canada, ostensibly on a voyage to a port in Mexico or some country on the west coast of Central America. However, in practice the ships hardly, if ever, reached their stated destination, with the liquor sold in transit and off-loaded onto small boats and launches to be landed at some quiet spot along the west coast of the USA. In practice, these rum-running depot ships often spent weeks drifting in the area, which came to be known as 'Rum Row' in international waters at least 12 miles off the west coast of California. Here they

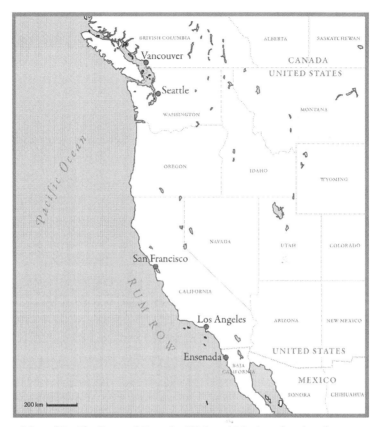

Map of Pacific Coast of Canada, USA and Mexico, showing the area of the coast of California ubiquitously known as 'Rum Row' during the Prohibition era.

acted as 'floating warehouses' of alcohol, conducting nightly rendezvous with launches and coastal craft that came out to meet them to pick up specific orders, typically of 50–200 cases at a time, before dodging the US Coastguard cutters to make their deliveries at remote landfalls along the U.S. west coast. Operators developed elaborate code systems to communicate orders, meeting locations and timings. Many ships sailed from Vancouver ostensibly destined for Ensenada, the first major port on the west coast of Mexico south of the US border at San Diego, or other ports along the west coast of Central America, although in practice little or none of the cargo made it that far. Customs officers in Ensenada were bribed to provide landing certificates to be filed back in Vancouver as 'proof' their liquid cargoes had been delivered. American efforts to have Canada prosecute those filing forged landing certificates fell foul of the fact that Canada had no witness treaty with Mexico.

Because the rum runners were not doing anything illegal in Canada, they made no effort to disguise their activities, which were well-documented in frequent newspaper articles at the time. Agents and buyers for the US interest would meet with Canadian suppliers, often in Vancouver, but also in some cases in the USA to negotiate orders and arrange payment.

Ships of many different types were used. Of the approximately 60 main craft involved in the trade during the Prohibition years, the six-masted wooden sailing schooner 'Malahat' was probably the most famous, capable of carrying 75,000 or so cases of liquor at a time. At first sight, it may seem strange that the rum runners used sailing ships and yachts like the Malahat or the Little Maid II for their business. The reason was that in their role as 'depot ships' they acted like a floating warehouse for every sort of liquor and drink. These ships needed to stay out for weeks, floating in international waters, and running out of fuel was a regular problem. Joe's ship Stadacona suffered this problem in 1925, and had to hurriedly dispose of all her liquor cargo before being allowed to limp into San Francisco for emergency refuelling. Being able to sail was a big advantage. Furthermore, as the Malahat captain at the time, John Vosper, has explained, when rum runners were being shadowed or observed by coastguard vessels, they could not unload their cargo to the launches. In such situations, the Malahat would just put up its sails and head out to sea – the

The Rum Runner 'Malahat' at dock.

coastguard could not follow for long without running out of fuel, so they would often give up, and Malahat would be able to circle round and come back for another drop a short time later. Because these depot ships had to remain at sea until all their cargoes had been offloaded, it was often necessary to resupply them with fuel, food and even mail for their crews – coded messages were sent by wireless back to the ships' owners, who sent supply vessels out to keep the mother ships operational.

As time went on, rum runners in Vancouver and B.C. even went as far as buying ship-loads of liquor from Scotland, and shipping it all the way across the Atlantic through the Panama Canal, or even via the Suez Canal and the Pacific to avoid the US-controlled Panama Canal, and then, whilst the vessels were still at sea off the coast of Mexico or California, transloading the cargoes onto a fleet of smaller craft for delivery ashore. The mother vessel then proceeded to Vancouver, declaring that all cargoes had been sold in transit.[139]

Rum-running operations like these were organised along all the main US coasts as well as over America's land borders throughout the period of Prohibition. For example, it is probably not a surprise that Chicago became a centre of illicit alcohol during Prohibition, given the ease of access to

Canadian supplies across the Great Lakes. And in the early 1920s, it was said 9 out of every 10 people in the town of Windsor, Ontario, were involved in the trade of illicit liquor into neighbouring Detroit across the Detroit River. Elsewhere regular supply routes operated bringing alcohol into Florida from the Bahamas and Caribbean, and into the East Coast and the Jersey Shore from off shore motherships, using a variety of tonnage including even on one occasion a fishing trawler. But there was a particularly active community of rum runners working in the Vancouver area, and certainly within Canada their actions were surprisingly overt and carried out in full public view. Many of the ships they used were known to be operating as 'rum runners' and the B.C. newspapers seem remarkably well-informed about the size, deployment and activities of the rum-running fleet and were happy to publicise this information on their pages throughout the 1920s.

Although relatively disorganised at the start of Prohibition, the Americans did progressively gear up and worked actively to prevent this trade, with more regular raids, stepped up coastal patrols, and efforts to catch and prosecute those involved in the trade. Over 200 new 75-foot 'Six Bitter' patrol craft capable of 15 knots and armed with one-pound cannons entered service between 1924 and 1925, to which was added 33 larger, faster (diesel-powered) and well-armed 125-foot 'Buck-and-a-Quarter' cutters from 1927. The US Coast Guard was expanded from 4,000 to over 10,000 personnel during Prohibition, and more and ever-faster patrol craft were added to the fleet right through to the end of Prohibition in 1933. There were armed gunfights, and shots (usually across the bow of a fleeing rum runner to induce it to stop) from larger artillery pieces mounted on US Coastguard cutters. By the latter part of the 1920s, rum running down the west coast of the USA was not a business for the fainthearted. In time, the Americans went even further, and started intercepting suspected rum runners not just in US waters, but also in international waters, such as in the 'Rum Row' area far out to sea off the US west coast.

This became something of a political minefield for the UK and Canadian governments dealing with the US, who had to balance their own citizens' rights to do business and long-held principles of free trade against increasing demands from the Americans to take action to stop British and Canadian citizens conniving to break US laws. The issue became even more sensitive as the US became more aggressive in policing, and started intercepting and seizing suspected rum-running vessels in international waters.

In June 1924, Canada made a treaty with the USA aimed at suppressing smuggling between Canada and the USA, a result of years of US pressure to clamp down on rampant smuggling of alcohol into their country. The treaty provided that "each government shall notify the other government of all clearances and transportation of goods starting from one country into the other where such goods are dutiable". It also stipulated that clearances would not be given to boats containing liquor cargoes heading for a distant or foreign country where it was evident from the size of the boat that it would not be able to make the voyage or weather the seas. Although not a complete solution (after the Canadians notified the Americans that a liquor ship was cleared for export, the Americans still had to find the ship and stop it), this was an important step in efforts to prevent rum running.

Although some leading voices in the UK were not sympathetic at all to Prohibition (Winston Churchill thought that Prohibition was "an affront to the whole history of mankind"), around the same time the Americans made progress negotiating with the British government too. In May 1924, the UK entered into an agreement with the USA known as 'The Liquor Treaty'[p] aimed at preventing smuggling of liquor into the USA.[140, 141] This provided that the American government had authority to board any British vessel suspected of an attempt to smuggle liquor into the United States, and to examine that vessel, provided the ship was within one hour's sailing distance of the American coast. If evidence was found of an attempt to smuggle liquor into the United States, the treaty allowed the American authorities to seize the vessel and take it into an American port to be dealt with according to American law. Since Canadian ships mostly operated under the British flag, many Canadian ships were also bound by this treaty.

From about 1925 onwards, US authorities further tightened the net on Canadian-origin liquor smuggling by "going after the money" and targeting Canadian alcohol suppliers for taxes and duties on alcohol brought into the USA illegally. For example, in June 1925 Prohibition agents forced open a safe deposit box in a San Francisco bank used by James Woitt of the Northwestern Brokerage Co. Ltd. of Vancouver, to discover forged liquor customs clearance papers.[142] Similarly on 17th December 1926 the Seattle Revenue Collector seized $75,807 which was to have been wired to Consolidated Exporters in Canada, holding it as partial payment for income tax the US was now demanding from Consolidated for their facilitation of illegal rum running into the USA.[143, 144]

Whilst rum running and supply of liquor from Canada into the USA continued right through until the eventual repeal of Prohibition in 1933, risks gradually became much higher for the rum runners: the risk of having ships and valuable stocks of liquor seized and impounded; the risk that cash and funds

p   More formally the agreement was titled: "The Convention between the United States and Great Britain – Prevention of Smuggling of Intoxicating Liquors", published on 22nd May 1924.

in America (also from legitimate business) could be seized; the risk of arrest if rum runners visited the USA; and also the reputational risk of being caught in an illicit trade. Whilst there were many articles in the Canadian press which spoke about rum running and its prospects from season to season as if it was a perfectly legitimate industry, and public opinion in Canada never seems entirely sympathetic to the US position, serious businessmen in Canada craved respectability, and association with this colourful and sometimes downright criminal trade did not sit well with that. This meant that, as the 1920s went on, legitimate businessmen like Joe Hobbs would have been giving serious thought to the wisdom of being involved in rum running, despite the obvious financial attractions it offered.

All of this provides context for how Joe developed his whisky trading, ship operating and (for at least some of the time) rum-running businesses during the 1920s. With respect to Joe's entirely legitimate business importing whisky from Scotland and Ireland for sale in Canada, he benefitted from the strong demand in Canada for whisky which was ultimately destined for the Prohibition-era United States. Unable to import whisky directly, high demand from American importers and intermediaries trying to work around the Prohibition laws pushed prices and profit margins up, and meant Canadian liquor importers like Joe who had the contacts in Britain to obtain reliable supplies of whisky could benefit from strong demand and high prices.

But Joe would also have been well aware that for those willing to go a step beyond merely supplying whisky for consumption in Canada, who were prepared to take on the challenge and risk of organising the delivery of alcohol to customers in the USA, the profits were even greater. In Vancouver and British Columbia at that time, there were many individuals and businesses that were attracted by these high margins and a whole industry grew up to keep America supplied with alcohol despite Prohibition laws. Prohibition in the US had already started when Joe began his career as a whisky trader, and the high profit margins to be made quite likely were part of what attracted him to the business in the first place.

Initially in the early 1920s, Joe appeared not to want to take on the risk of arranging distribution to the USA himself, being content to supply whisky to the community of rum runners in Vancouver. However, possibly lured by the extremely high profit margins, from around 1924 Joe started a commercial shipping business, and began to use his ships for rum running alongside legitimate shipping activities. We know that the operators of the small boats and launches that ran the liquor ashore from 'mother ship' supply vessels charged $1–2 per case for their work, whilst the local boats which transported the liquor from Vancouver to the US shores typically charged $10–11/case in the first part of the 1920s. By moving into shipping, Joe was doing what modern-day business schools call 'vertically integrating' – enabling him to retain the profit on the transportation as well as his margin as a whisky trader (the difference between what it cost him to buy the whisky from Scotland, and what he could sell it for). Even after paying Canadian export duty at $10/ case, by delivering the liquor close to market in international waters off the US Coast, rum runners could easily make a 100% margin on a case of whisky bought from Scottish suppliers for $17–20 per case. With the size of ships Joe began operating, the total profit became really sizeable. Following acquisition of the Stadacona, Joe was able to organise regular voyages transporting 12,000 cases per trip down to 'Rum Row', which could earn a gross margin of over $200,000 per trip, equivalent to around $3m in modern terms. Joe would have had substantial costs to purchase and operate the ships – for example, the crews willing to take on this dangerous work were extremely well paid – and each voyage could take months. But, whilst the move into ship-owning and rum running certainly brought much higher risks, it also offered the potential to operate at a different level, and by the middle of the decade Joe was using ships for rum running on a sizeable scale. In this way, initially through legitimate trade, and then subsequently via rum running, Joe took advantage of the specific situation of Vancouver during US Prohibition to build a highly successful business trading whisky in the early 1920s, and quickly became very wealthy as a result.

Joe's own transition from simple whisky trader to active rum runner centred around his acquisition of the ship Stadacona. After the end of WW1, Stadacona had been retired from government service and was acquired by the Central America Shipping Agency. This company had deployed Stadacona on rum-running operations, and prior to Joe's acquisition the ship already had quite a reputation as a 'rum runner'. Joe had been supplying Central America Shipping Agency with whisky, and they owed him the sizeable sum of $75,000 (equivalent to over $1m today). It seems they could not pay their due, and Joe converted the debt into a formal loan, with Stadacona quite likely used to provide security for what was owed. Quite soon afterwards, perhaps foreclosing on the loan, Joe took the ship over fully in 1924, and entered directly into ship operations himself for the first time. Joe used Stadacona for at least one voyage to and from the UK to collect liquor, in an operation he was to repeat several times subsequently with other vessel acquisitions, after which in 1925 he sent the ship for a refit to be converted for use as a rum runner depot ship.

With her prior history and also during the time Joe Hobbs owned and operated the Stadacona, the ship was one of the most well-known rum runners, and was extensively involved in drama and incidents. Given her notoriety, the US Coastguard cutters took to shadowing Stadacona as soon as she left Canadian waters. In March 1925, the Coastguard cutter 'Snohomish'

*Stadacona when owned by Joe Hobbs
in the 1920s.*

doggedly trailed Stadacona down the US west coast. Despite Stadacona doing everything possible to shake off her escort, making multiple zig-zags and turns, the Snohomish stubbornly stuck in position about 300 yards behind Stadacona's stern. In the end, Stadacona turned and steamed straight out to sea for 30 miles before proceeding south and eventually shaking off her tail. While not always successful, the US Coastguard deployed this tactic with some success to disrupt Joe and the other rum runners' operations. Seattle Coastguard Commander F.G. Dodge was quoted in the Canadian newspapers as saying "We

*US Coast Guard cutter Snohomish, which played cat and mouse with
Joe Hobbs' rum-running ship Stadacona in 1925.*

are going to trail every big liquor cargo to its destination. If they clear for Mexico, to Mexico they go."[145]

Not long afterwards, in May of 1925, the Stadacona was fined $800 for submitting a false customs declaration, when the Americans were able to prove that, despite declaring it had entered the Mexican port of Ensenada to discharge its cargo of liquor, port records proved it had never been there.[146]

Probably in response to Stadacona's high profile and notoriety, at the time of the ship's refit in 1925 Joe decided to rename her, and chose the very unusual new name 'Kuyakuzmt'. The story was that Joe looked on the map of British Columbia for a name not previously used on the Ship Registry, and spotted Kuyakuz Mountain in the Cariboo area of B.C. (an area known to him from his involvement in cattle ranching immediately after the war). However, when Joe wired the shipyard to rename the vessel 'Kuyakuz Mt' it seems the yard workers literally painted 'Kuyakuzmt' on the bow and stern. It was said the new name confused her captain and crew, but, since it would then also probably confuse the US Coastguard, it seems Joe decided to stick with it. A wonderful article in The Province newspaper commented "If all the vessels engaged in the liquor trade south from Vancouver follow the precedent established by the Stadacona, a conversation among the United States prohibition protection fleet officers will soon sound like an influenza epidemic."[147]

Usually, the larger rum-running vessels rarely risked coming ashore or entering US coastal waters to avoid the risk of being impounded by the US Coastguard or excisemen. However, a dramatic incident in June 1925 involving a mystery ship, which was rumoured to be the Stadacona/Kuyakuzmt, indicates that was not always the case. Acting on a tip off, Sheriff Oyer of the Monterey, California, police, positioned his men in hiding around Pebble Beach golf course, when a large steam yacht emerged out of the fog into Carmel Bay. Light signals from the yacht were answered from the shore, and the police observed six cars come down onto the beach. Working with the ship's crew, they started ferrying cases of liquor ashore. The police surprised the rum runners and called on them to surrender. In the darkness, all but three of the smugglers were able to escape, whilst the yacht rapidly weighed anchor and headed back to sea. The officers fired on the ship, which disappeared into the fog. One of the ship's crew fell overboard during the daring escape, and had to be pulled aboard by his crewmates using a lifeline. Several newspapers conjectured about the identity of the mystery ship. The Province newspaper pointed out that the Kuyakuzmt/Stadacona was in the area at the time, and suggested that "the description of the mystery vessel of Monterey might apply to the Stadacona."[148]

Years later, stories taken from the diaries of the Stadacona's wireless operator in 1925, referred to only by his Christian name, "Ronnie", provide a lot of colour about the modus operandi of the ship during the time when it was owned and operated by Joe Hobbs. Ronnie's diaries tell us that the ship would load up with 12,000 cases of liquor and 50 barrels of beer on each trip, and then head out from Vancouver or Victoria and travel south, remaining for weeks at a time in international waters off the Californian coast, rarely going closer than 50 miles to the shore. It would make multiple rendezvous, offloading consignments of a few dozen cases at a time to small high-speed craft who would try to dodge the Coastguard patrols on their way back to shore. The Stadacona crew repacked the liquor bottles from their wooden crates into hessian or canvas sacks, which made them easier to transfer at sea and in an emergency would sink instantly when thrown overboard, where a wooden crate might float for hours. Ronnie's job as a wireless operator was somewhat intermittent – Stadacona maintained almost total radio silence, only communicating on the captain's orders, with all messages sent in code (e.g. to confirm arrangements for when and where to meet to deliver the next consignment). The codes used by the rum runners were surprisingly elaborate and sophisticated, to the extent the US Treasury department actually deployed trained code breakers to decipher them, with some success.[149, 150]

The crews of these vessels came from all walks of life, attracted by the excellent pay. At a time when Canada's biggest steamship operator Canadian Pacific's ship captains earned around C$250/ month, the rum runner skippers earned C$1000/month, First Officers/Chief Engineers C$750, whilst deck hands got C$3-400 (compared to the C$60–65 per month they could earn in regular seafaring jobs). There was some glamour and excitement in this life as well, matching wits with the Coastguard cutters, and playing games of cat-and-mouse to avoid them and still be able to make planned rendezvous to offload their cargoes. Ronnie, the wireless operator on the Stadacona, told of when he and his crewmates fixed a lamp to a pole on a buoy whilst being observed by a US Coastguard vessel, and then extinguished all the Stadacona's lights to enable them to slip away in darkness. There was some danger and occasional high-octane bursts of excitement, especially later in the 1920s as the Americans took more aggressive action to disrupt the rum runners, sometimes firing on the smugglers. The launches used to run ashore were armed, but usually just to protect against hijackers. But, for the most part, the boredom and the long days away from home were probably bigger downsides of the job than the danger. Ronnie summed up the view of quite a few of the Canadian sailors who worked on the rum-running ships in the 1920–30s: "Most of us had our photographs on U.S. post office walls for a considerable time for, after all, we were law breakers. But in my opinion Rum Row was a good, hard practical training ground for some of the men who became top quality Royal Canadian Naval officers during World War II."[151]

It is interesting to speculate whether Joe ever directly participated on board his ships in their rum-running activities. He was a keen sailor and qualified master mariner, and from what we know of his character it is easy to believe he would have loved the thrill of skippering his ships and trying to outwit the US Coastguard. But, because rum running was illegal in the US, Joe would have wanted to avoid any record of his direct participation, and, whilst officers and crew members of several rum-running ships did subsequently record memoirs of their activities, Joe never did. As records from his appearance at a subsequent investigation into Canadian Customs in 1927 show, it was an important part of Joe's defence to be able to claim he was just a ship owner, and not directly involved in anything which was illegal. From around 1927, Joe took steps to move his businesses firmly towards legitimacy, and worked hard to manage the transition to respectable businessman – as such, he did not want any association with illicit activities to be recorded or remembered. So, while it is not impossible he was aboard the rum runners, particularly Stadacona, there is no firm evidence, and it is unlikely Joe was actively involved in physical operations.

In the spring of the following year, on 18th March 1926, Joe formally incorporated Hobbs Brothers Ltd as a shipping company, with registered capital of $250,000 ($3.6m in 2024 terms). Joe was managing director and had 1750 shares, his brother Basil was a director and had 1000 shares, with their friend and partner Col. O.F. Brothers acting as company secretary and owning 1000 shares. Joe already owned the vessels Kuyakuzmt and Mabel Dell (until it was sold in 1927) in his own right, but Hobbs Brothers Ltd was to be the vehicle for further expansion in ship owning and operating, which was to continue even after Joe withdrew from active participation in rum running. Col.

Brothers featured frequently in the Vancouver press at this time. He was the aide to General Sir Arthur Currie, commander of Canadian forces during WW1, and was awarded a DSO and an OBE.[152, 153]

After incorporating Hobbs Brothers, Joe used the company for the acquisition of two additional ships during the course of 1926, both of which had unusual features in common. We know about this because in January 1927 Joe was called to give evidence to the Commission of Enquiry into the Customs Department, and had to explain the circumstances of two voyages of the ships 'Lillehorn' and 'Hurry On'. Joe had bought both ships in Europe, and admitted to the enquiry that they had been used to carry liquor, although Joe took care to portray himself as an entirely innocent ship owner, who had no interest in the liquor cargoes themselves.

With respect to the 'Lillehorn', Joe had bought the ship in Europe for use on the British Columbia coastal trades. For the positioning voyage to Canada from the UK, the ship had been chartered to the Scottish Shipping Agency for a voyage from Leith (the port of Edinburgh and an important whisky trading centre) to Vancouver. The ship was loaded there with liquor

The motor-freighter Lillehorn.

(by repute the cargo was 13,000 cases of Teacher's whisky) and proceeded to Antwerp, where the cargo was discharged and carted through the streets to a second wharf in the free port area where it was reloaded – this was done in order to release the British excise bond, and collect the rebate of 3d per case in excise duty. Hobbs told the enquiry this was all done by the charterers; he only knew of it "by report".

The ship left Antwerp heading for Vancouver or Victoria, with a permit from the US consul in Antwerp to pass through the Panama Canal. After a stop in the Azores, she passed through the Panama Canal with another stop at Balboa. En route north, Joe told the enquiry her cargo had been sold to a third party off the coast of Mexico, and transferred while on the high seas. On arrival at Vancouver, declaration was made that the cargo had been sold en route.

The 'Hurry On' case was almost identical: the vessel was acquired from Schroder's Bank in Europe, before picking up a cargo of whisky in Antwerp and proceeding to Canada via Panama, with all the whisky sold en route.

The motor-freighter 'Hurry On'.

Hobbs also gave evidence he was a supplier to Central American Shipping Agency (in fact he was a creditor, being owed $75,000 by them); and also that as agent for 'Scottish Distillers' he had business with R.R. Fidelity Company, a syndicate of Americans who purchased liquor and shipped it in transit through Vancouver. Joe told the enquiry that the vessels 'Prince Albert' and 'Kuyakuzmt' (Joe did not mention he owned this ship) were two ships used by R.R. Fidelity for shipments from Scotland to Mexico that Hobbs was aware of, and on which he admitted he had provided advice to R.R. Fidelity.[154]

From a purely economic perspective, these positioning voyages of the 'Lillehorn' and 'Hurry On' were brilliant business. While there would have been costs for fuel, the crew, and port costs on the journey out, the sale of the liquor would have made Hobbs Brothers a gross profit of around $325,000 (equivalent to just under $5m in current terms) on each voyage. After the voyage, the ships were positioned to Canada ready for use in Hobbs Brothers' entirely legitimate coastal shipping business. But, from the evidence to the customs enquiry, we can see Joe had an intimate knowledge of the rum-running business that was being conducted by Canadians in Vancouver at the time. Although he claims to have been just an innocent ship owner who was not actively involved in trading liquor to the USA, his ownership and operation of 'Stadacona', 'Lillehorn' and 'Hurry On' during the period when there is so much evidence that, they were actively deployed in liquor trading demonstrates conclusively that at least during the period 1925–27, Joe Hobbs was a rum runner.

However, against the backdrop of progressively more aggressive counter-measures from US authorities, towards the end of 1927 Joe clearly switched tack and started to distance himself from rum running, concentrating his efforts on legitimate business. This was likely because the risks both financial and reputational of rum running were getting too high, and because there were increasingly attractive alternatives open to Joe from entirely legal activities. His call to give evidence to the customs enquiry and publicly explain his involvement in potentially illicit whisky trading may also have been a 'wake up' call which caused Joe to reconsider his approach. In an act which was to bring down the curtain on this particular part of Joe's career, in November 1927 he sold the 'Lillehorn' to Atlantic and Pacific Navigation Co., a company owned by the Reifel brothers of Vancouver, high-profile and flamboyant liquor smugglers. In truth, 'Lillehorn' had been deployed on more legitimate shipping business for most of the time she had been operated by the Hobbs Brothers in Canada after the infamous first journey from Scotland – during the summer months of both 1926 and 1927 the ship was chartered out to Canadian National for use on their north-west coastal service to the Queen Charlotte Islands.[155] And at the time of her sale, the 'Lillehorn' was en route to the UK with a full cargo of 1,400 tons of British Columbian grain, again demonstrating that Hobbs Brothers made good use of the ship for entirely legitimate shipping business. The sale price was $125,000 (about $2.2m today).[156] In selling 'Lillehorn' Joe disposed of an asset that very publicly connected him to the liquor-running business, to players who intended to stay in that business.[q]

It was a clear sign that he was pulling out of rum running and 'going legitimate'. While Joe continued to be active as a ship-owner and ship operator for most of the remainder of his time in Canada until 1931, and indeed added to his fleet in 1928 with

---

q   The Reifels continued to use 'Lillehorn' as a coastal 'mother ship' for liquor smuggling to the USA for some years, e.g. it featured in evidence held before US Commissioner David Head in Los Angeles on 3rd January 1930, where 'Lillehorn' was anchored 75 miles off the coast of California whilst fast launches like the 'Chiquita' were used to bring the contraband ashore at various points on the Californian coast.

the acquisition of his biggest ship to date, the 'Oaxaca', it seems that after the end of 1927 with the exception of 'Kuyakuzmt', which continued to make occasional voyages as a depot ship to Rum Row, his remaining vessels were largely deployed for regular shipping business along the west coast of Canada and the USA, and for cargoes other than liquor. Certainly, the environment for rum running was getting much tougher at this time. In addition to new regulations and firmer enforcement, new treaties allowing the US to stop and search suspect vessels in international waters, as well as the provision of an increased number of faster and better-equipped coastguard cutters, the US authorities proved determined to pursue the money trail of the rum runners, starting to access bank accounts, seize assets, and pursue the trade's organisers through the courts – something they continued to pursue vigorously even after the end of Prohibition.[r] Rum running continued up until the end of Prohibition in 1933, but it became much more difficult, and the rising risks probably influenced Joe's decision to get out of the business.

At the same time, new opportunities were starting to open up for Joe in other areas of business, and there is a clear sense of 'turning the page' as Joe switched focus from shipping and rum running to property development. From around November 1927, Joe started to work with the finance and development company G.A. Stimson and Co, who marketed themselves as "Canada's oldest bond company", with Joe taking over management of their West Coast activities and property development. Stimson's managing director Col. F.G. Johnston was a boyhood friend of Joe's from Sault Ste Marie.[157] It is likely Joe's new business

---

r   The best evidence for this is probably the US government's pursuit of
     the Reifel brothers themselves, who were hit with a civil suit seeking
     repayment of an enormous $17.25m in 1934. They subsequently settled
     out-of-court for $500,000 plus forfeiture of their $200,000 bail bonds.

partners in Stimsons, for whom a good name and reputation was critical to their ability to maintain investor confidence and secure new funds for investment, also encouraged Joe to distance himself from rum running.

In October 1928, Joe bought the freighter/yacht 'Oaxaca' from millionaire plantation owner Capt. Allan Hancock. Typically for one of Joe's ship acquisitions, the vessel was an ex-Navy ship with some history. Originally built in 1918 by the Admiralty, it served during WW1 as HMS Pelargonium, one of a series of Q-ships (sometimes called 'Mystery Ships'), which were heavily armed vessels that had their weapons concealed, with the ships made to look like ordinary merchantmen. The strategy was developed to lure German U-boats to surface assuming the Q-ship was an easy target, at which point the Q-ship revealed its weaponry and engaged in a fight.[s] After the war, the ship was operated by Clan Line in trades to and from Mexico, before in 1921 it was bought by the Mexican national line Compania Naviera de Los Estados de Mexico, who renamed her 'Oaxaca' and used her for passenger and freight service between Mexico and California. Captain Hancock bought the ship in 1927 and fitted her for use as his personal yacht, and also as a transporter between California and his plantation estates in Mexico and Central America.[158]

The ship had run aground in the Wrangell Narrows, in northern British Columbia, in July 1928 when being used by Hancock for a pleasure cruise with friends.[159] After nearly a month of efforts, the ship was salvaged and refloated, then towed to Vancouver for repairs. The engine room and boiler room had been flooded and there were holes in the bottom which would require 28 steel plates to repair. The cost of repair was estimated

---

s   Over 100 Q-ships were built or converted during WW1, and in 150 engagements 14 U-boats were sunk and 60 damaged, at a cost of 27 Q-ships lost.

Joe Hobbs' last and largest commercial ship was the motor-freighter Oaxaca. This is a photo of HMS Harebell, a sister ship to Oaxaca, built as part of the same order for 21 Anchusa class ships by the Royal Navy.

at $60,000, which Hancock considered "out of proportion to the value of the ship", and he indicated that he intended to dispose of her. Joe inspected the ship and found it less damaged than originally thought. He bought it on 9th October, reportedly with the intention for the ship to "enter coastwise trading."[160, 161] The largest ship in their fleet, Hobbs Brothers successfully operated 'Oaxaca' for a number of years in various trades, including being chartered out to Frank C. Hill of Los Angeles for use running between his fish processing factory in Magdalena Bay, Baja California, and San Francisco. Hobbs Brothers eventually sold the ship in 1931, after which she went on trading in a number of different guises before sinking after being bombed by German aircraft off the Greek coast in April 1941.

Meanwhile, the 'Hurry On', having been operated for 7 months on the lumber trade from Canada to Maracaibo in

Venezuela and Curacao in the Caribbean, was subsequently chartered out to Canadian National for use on their northern Canada coastal services.[162] The charter was extended again in the autumn of 1928. The ship was then chartered out to the Los Angeles firm of E.H. Hansen Corporation, carrying tomatoes from Mexican farms to California. Then, in August 1931, Hobbs Bros sold the 'Hurry On' to a new company, McGhie Transportation, who (with advice from Joe it seems) planned a new west Vancouver Island to US service.[t]

With the sale of the three ships, the bulk of Joe's commercial fleet was disposed by the end of 1931. His private yachts were to go the same way. He had already sold his first recreational yacht Mabel Dell back in 1927. Then, in 1929, Joe took the decision to sell Mabel Dell's even grander replacement, 'Vencedor', and to reconvert 'Kuyakuzmt' back from a cargo ship to a private yacht. Joe sold 'Vencedor' to the Lt. Governor of the province of British Columbia, Hon. Eric Hamber, to be used as his flagship during the period he was Commodore of the Royal Vancouver Yacht Club between 1931 and 1935. In spring of 1929, Joe sent 'Kuyakuzmt' to the shipyard at Coal Harbour, Vancouver, to be converted back into a private yacht, after which the vessel's name was changed to 'Lady Stimson'.[163]

Joe made extensive use of the yacht in support of his new property business ventures with Stimsons, for example entertaining Vancouver mayor W.H. Malkin and his new boss F.G. Johnston, the Managing Director of Stimsons, in August 1929.[164] In further evidence of Joe's exceptional media savvy and skills in promotion and communication, he twice during

---

t   McGhie Transportation operated 'Hurry On' until she was sold on to Unus Shipping of Halifax, and transferred to work on the North Atlantic. Sadly in September 1935 the ship sank off Nova Scotia with the loss of 5 lives after her cargo of corn shifted in a gale and the ship turned over.

1929 entertained parties of journalists on weekend cruises on the 'Lady Stimson'. For the second of these trips, The Vancouver Sun reported Joe and 'Mrs Hobbs' (despite their rocky marriage situation, it seems this was Mabel, as Eve was in the UK with her young son John Henry at this time) entertained 70 journalists on an excursion to Indian River, north-east of Vancouver, on board his "palatial yacht", generating favourable media coverage, as well, presumably, as plenty of goodwill.[165]

However, the situation was not to last, and on 30th October 1929 Joe sold the Lady Stimson to Willis P. Dewees, a theatrical entrepreneur, owner of Vancouver's Strand Theatre, and a long-standing member of R.V.Y.C.[166] At first sight it could look like this was a real 'firesale', as it was transacted on the day following the Great Wall Street Crash, but a more likely explanation is that Joe had already realised that he and Stimsons would need more money to complete their ambitious Marine Building office construction project in Vancouver, and that the 'Lady Stimson' was a valuable asset that needed to be cashed in to provide more liquid funds. Dewees renamed the yacht 'Moonlight Maid' and used her for more than 10 years before she was sold to Armour Salvage and Towing Company in 1941 and saw out her final days as a towboat in north Canadian and Alaskan waters.

Consequently, by the end of 1929, Joe no longer owned a yacht, and by the end of 1931 was out of commercial shipping altogether. However, his shipping, whisky trading and rum-running businesses had made him his first fortune, and propelled him into the upper echelons of society in Vancouver and British Columbia. Whilst Joe's business career did not return to shipping after this time, he retained his love of yachts and sailing for the rest of his life, and was to own yachts again once he had made his second fortune after World War 2.

It is reasonable to ask, looking back on all this, whether by engaging in 'rum running' Joe was acting illegally or unethically, and also to wonder why this was not in conflict with Joe's rising social standing.

First and foremost, whilst importing alcohol into the United States was illegal under US law, Canadians involved in the liquor trades were not doing anything illegal under Canadian law. The rum runners paid the Canadian government $10 duty on every case exported, and from the Canadian perspective the exports were above board and the duties were paid.[167] But if it was not strictly illegal, was it at least unethical ? And was it morally right, even if no Canadian laws were broken, for Canadian brokers and middlemen to supply alcohol to people knowing they were going to import it into the USA, in direct contravention of US laws?

There were certainly many people in Canada and America at that time who were strongly opposed to the sale and consumption of alcohol and adopted strong pro-temperance views – for them the rum runners work would definitely have been wrong in principle. But amongst those who did not support temperance in Canadian society at the time, rum running was seen by many as a legitimate business, and moreover, one that contributed a lot to the economy and brought money and jobs to Vancouver and British Columbia. Ron Riter, in the Centenary Edition of the Vancouver Sun in July 1971, comments that for over 13 years "many B.C. distillers, brewers and exporters made fortunes and many otherwise ordinary citizens reaped excellent pay and high adventure in running the goods to slake the Volstead-inspired American drought".[168] It is also a little-remembered fact that British Columbia had conducted its own short-lived experiment with the prohibition of alcohol – from 1st October 1917 until 2nd April 1921, the province had banned the sale of alcohol for local consumption in almost literally a dry run for what the Americans did nationwide later. During this period, it was still perfectly legal for businesses in B.C. to import, manufacture and export alcoholic drinks, and a flourishing industry grew up to do so. Moreover, in a prelude of what was to come in the USA, illegal distilling and bootlegging flourished in B.C. during the Prohibition period, so to again quote Riter "by the time of repeal [of prohibition in B.C.], bootlegging was an institution; flouting liquor laws was an accepted way of life. British Columbians then turned their full energies to flouting the U.S. liquor laws."[169] So, while the rum runners' activities may have looked questionable to some, for many others it was perfectly acceptable, and was part of a well-established industry and way of working, involving many businesses and providing many jobs. And, at least on the Canadian side of the border, the rum runners' activities were all conducted in full public view, and participation in the trade was no impediment to social advancement.

However, it does seem that a desire for 'respectability' was at least part of Joe's motivation for giving up rum running, even if with both his illicit whisky trading and his subsequent property dealings, Joe seems to have been a master at building and protecting his good reputation despite his close association with some decidedly murky goings-on!

6

The Best Art Deco Office Building in the World

Joe started to get involved with the firm of G.A. Stimson & Co Ltd in the late 1920s. A well-known business in Canada during the 1920s, the firm had been founded in Toronto in 1883 by George A. Stimson as a brokerage dealing in the sale of government and municipal bonds. The business prospered and, especially in the years after WW1, found a ready market with investors across Canada willing to buy bonds (interest bearing notes), which Stimson issued to fund investments, especially in property development.[170]

After the death of George Stimson in 1919, Lt. Col. Frederick Graham Johnston, MC, joined the firm in 1920 as Assistant Manager, becoming Vice President and Director soon after, once George Stimson's heirs were bought out of the business. Johnston was an old friend of Joe Hobbs. He was born in 1891 (the same year as Joe) in Sault Ste Marie, the son of His Honor Frederick Johnston, senior judge of the District of Algoma. Joe later recalled in a letter to his niece Barbara Barran: "I well remember the ceremony in 1904 when they celebrated the fifty years (anniversary of the opening of the Sault Canal). I was 13 years old at the time and went with Judge Johnston and family to see the fireworks set off".[171]

F.G. Johnston was educated at Trinity College School in Port Hope, Ontario, and Upper Canada College, a prestigious fee-paying school for boys in Toronto. He started work as a bank clerk at the Imperial Bank of Canada in Sault Ste Marie in 1908, and served in the 9th Battalion Canadian Field Artillery in Europe during WW1, rising to the rank of Captain, and earning the Military Cross and Bar. He was promoted to Lieutenant Colonel in Canada's post-war military reserve. Having become Vice President and Director in 1920, Johnston took over as Stimson President in 1925. He was instrumental in Stimson's evolution from its initial core business as a broker of low-risk government and municipal bonds, into a company that issued its own interest paying bonds, using the proceeds to fund more speculative investments in other projects, especially property development. Johnston was the driving force behind the decision to invest and build the Commerce and Transportation Building in Toronto.[172]

Stimson had built up, over 40 years, a reputation for soundness, proudly advertising that "every bond issue recommended and sold by G.A. Stimson & Co Ltd has paid interest and principal when due."[173] This reputation became less justified as, under Johnston's leadership, Stimson became involved in riskier investments and, especially after 1926, engaged in some decidedly dubious business practices. The company expanded considerably during the 1920s, building a network of 14 offices across Canada. As they expanded, Stimson developed a sales force that evolved from selling relatively low-risk municipal bonds, which were backed by the governments of Canada's large cities, and so likely to be repaid, to actively pushing Stimson's own bond issues, to raise funds for the construction and letting of Stimson's own property investments. These Stimson bonds had a simple and appealing premise to investors: Stimson would pay back the amount invested (principal) on a specified future date, and, in the interim, Stimson would pay the bond-holders a monthly interest payment, usually pitched at a decent rate (typically in the range of 5–7.5% per annum). The impression presented was that money provided by investors who bought Stimson bonds was 'secured' against the value of the properties being developed, so that if there were any problems the bond-holders should in theory have been able to get their principal money back by selling the property. However, that was not always true in practice. As the 1920s went on, Stimson progressed to building large-scale commercial office buildings, often in pre-eminent locations in the major cities. This brought involvement in some high-profile projects such as the Commerce and Transportation Building in Toronto, but also – which may have been less obvious

The Commerce and Transportation Building in Toronto, one of Stimson's flagship commercial developments in the 1920s.

to their many small investor clients across Canada – brought a considerably higher level of risk.

Prior to Joe's involvement, Stimson did not really have a presence on the west coast of Canada. Joe and F.G. Johnston had known each other as children in Sault Ste Marie, and Joe was now a high-profile and well-respected member of Vancouver's business elite, so it was natural that Johnston should reconnect with Joe when Stimson sought to establish and expand their business in Vancouver in the late 1920s. For his part, with increasing constraints and risks in the rum-running business, Joe was looking to diversify into new business areas which could offer a good return, but also manage his transition into more 'legitimate' activities. Joe also wanted to contribute positively to the growth and development of Vancouver, which gelled with Johnston's plans for Stimson to play a major role constructing the building stock of Canada's main cities.

There was a mutual advantage for Joe and F.G. Johnston to work together, and from 1927, about the time he started selling his ships and scaling back his rum running, Joe began to work in partnership with Stimson as their 'ambassador' in western Canada. Initially, this was an informal partnership, although later Joe became a salaried officer of the company. Their first business move together came on 4th November 1927, when they teamed

As a member of Vancouver's business elite, by the late 1920s Joe Hobbs was seeking more 'legitimate' and respectable avenues for his entrepreneurial capabilities in Vancouver.

129

up to buy the Merchants Exchange Building, on the corner of Hastings and Howe Streets in central Vancouver. The seller was high-profile Vancouver businessman A.M. Dollar, a fellow ship owner and friend of Joe's from the Royal Vancouver Yacht Club. The amount paid was $400,000 ($6.1m 2024 equivalent value).[174,] [u] The Merchants Exchange was a very well-known and influential business forum in Vancouver, a sort of 'working club' where all the city's traders, merchants, financiers and ship owners met to negotiate and administrate buying, selling and transportation of goods and commodities. Joe was a prominent and active member of the exchange, and the Merchants Exchange Building itself was a well-known institution and landmark in the city.

Joe and Stimson, however, had not bought the property just to earn money from rent. They swiftly announced a plan to demolish the relatively low-rise building and construct a new 18-storey building on the site at a cost of $2m (more than $30m today). Some tenants of the building had leases which ran until

The Merchants Exchange Building, Vancouver.

u   All dollar figures in this chapter are in Canadian Dollars (C$).

1930, which needed to be 'adjusted', and the tenants vacated from the building before work could start on demolition of the old site and its reconstruction.[175]

This was a bold and ambitious move, and, whilst Stimson had experience with this sort of large property development, it was a huge step up in terms of scale and ambition for Joe. The concept itself was a good one – Merchants Exchange Building was well-situated in the heart of the city's business district, but was only a few storeys high. Many other North American cities had seen a wave of skyscraper construction in the 1920s, but Vancouver was at the time still a rather low-rise city. Building Vancouver's first high-rise office building on a site that could provide prestige accommodation and trading space for the merchant exchange and the city's established trading firms was, like so many of Joe's plans, visionary, but also practical and feasible. Buying a well-located but relatively low-cost building and upgrading it to a much larger, more modern and impressive tower was a business model successfully followed by property developers the world over, but it was the first time this had been attempted in Vancouver, and aroused huge attention in the city, made the news across Canada.

On 22nd December 1927, G.A. Stimson & Co announced they were opening a branch in Vancouver, to be situated within the Merchants Exchange Building they had just acquired. F.G. Johnston planned to visit Vancouver shortly after Christmas to progress his plans to expand in the city, stating he was "convinced that the next 10-15 years will bring to Vancouver a measure of prosperity and growth that will make the city outstanding among Canadian centres".[176]

Despite all the work being done on the new property development business, Joe still found time in the spring to make his annual business trip to England, but he was back by mid-April.[177] This was Joe's yearly trip to the UK to maintain his contacts and negotiate ongoing supplies of whisky. However, on this occasion it was also something of a 'calm before the storm' moment at the start of what became a very hectic and challenging phase of Joe's life.

In April 1928, Stimson issued a new bond to raise $300,000, secured against the value of the Merchants Exchange Building. Investors could buy bonds denominated at $100, $500 or $1000, and receive 6% p.a. interest until redeeming their principal in 1948. The bond was 'secured' by the mortgage Stimson had on the building, which had been valued at $440,000 by A.E. Austin & Co real estate agents.[178]

Then on 3rd May 1928, Joe's father passed away at Algoma, Ontario, aged 69. The cause of death was a cardiac arrest. Joe II had continued to work rearing cattle and farming, living at his farmstead in Korah Township, Algoma, a short distance to the north-west of Sault Ste Marie town, for 15 years prior to his death.[179] Towards the end of his life, Joe II had married again, which seems to have caused a rift in the family.

In 1924, Joe II (by that time 65 years of age) took a final trip back to the UK, staying from January to July. He travelled with his daughter Violet, giving as his U.K. address the home of his older sister Annie Maria, who was by then widowed and living on the inheritance from her father's estate. This was the first time Joe II had been back to the U.K. since he took his family and emigrated to Canada in 1900. At first sight, it seemed like the 'last visit' of an ageing man, keen to see the land of his birth and meet with family and friends in his old age, but, in an interesting twist, Joe II got married for the second time during his visit. He and Violet had been staying at the White Hart Hotel, Newbury, and were scheduled to return to Canada on 27th June. However, they postponed their return by a month, and then on 12th July 1924 Joe II was married to Mary Moon, at Newbury Parish Church. Mary was 51, and had been living at

Breach Farm, St Mary Bourne, Hampshire prior to the wedding. St. Mary Bourne is only 10 miles from Highclere, where Joe II had been a farmer, prior to leaving for Canada, so it seems likely that Joe II knew Mary from his time in the area before he left the U.K. However, with no surviving correspondence, we do not know if their relationship from that earlier time was just a friendship or something more serious. Nor is it clear if Joe II had returned to England with the specific intention of marrying Mary, or if this was a 'spur of the moment' decision, although the fact Joe II and Violet postponed their return voyage would imply the latter. Mary had lived a quiet and relatively poor life as a dressmaker, taking care of her elderly mother in her final years, before marrying William Moon, a low-paid draper's assistant 15 years her senior, at the age of 43 in 1916. William passed away less than three year's later in 1919, leaving an estate of only £870 (the equivalent of £46,000 in today's money), which would not have been sufficient to live on.

Joe II's decision to remarry and to leave most of his estate to his new wife seems to have caused some shock and bad feeling amongst the children from his first marriage to Elizabeth. Following her new husband to Canada, Mary was only married to Joe II for a little under four years before her husband pre-deceased her. Apart from a few mementoes and keepsakes, Joe II left his house, farm and most of his belongings to his second wife. Particularly for his daughters Alexa, Violet and Daisy, who were not at all well-off and would have benefitted considerably from a share in their father's inheritance, that seemed a little strange. Alexa, who had married Frederick Wilkes and had four children with a fifth on the way, was not wealthy, and additional income would probably have been welcome, but she was tough and determined, and had the resources to get by. But for the twins Violet and Daisy, who never married and struggled to make a living as artists and painters living in a tiny cottage in the small rural community of Bala, near Lake Muskoka 200km north of Toronto, it may have seemed like a betrayal. Joe II was buried in Greenwood Cemetery, Sault Ste. Marie, but is not remembered on the family gravestone there. His son Basil did later donate a wooden screen across the chancel at Christ Church, Korah, Sault Ste Marie, and dedicate it to his father's memory.

After Joe II passed away, his son Joe came and took some of the furniture and other belongings from his father's house at Korah, without discussing it with his brothers or sisters, or asking if they wished to have anything from the house. Whilst Joe was the elder son and was bequeathed these items in Joe II's will, he was also by far the most economically successful of his siblings, and could have easily afforded to share some or all of these items. This led to something of a feud with his sister Alexa, who did not speak to Joe for some years afterwards. When, later, Alexa's son Rowley visited Joe in England, Joe had clearly forgotten the cause of their disagreement – the family's view is that this was typical of Joe, who had a tendency to focus on what was important to him at the time, and could 'box off' things that were less important or that he did not wish to discuss. This does seem to be consistent with what we know of Joe's character – while he could be loving and affectionate to those he was close to, he also had a determined and ruthless streak and a thick skin. On many occasions he displayed his generosity to others by sharing his resources, but Joe was not moved to help his siblings out financially after their father's death, despite their poor situation.

Back in 1928, the timing of Joe II's passing was rather inconvenient for Joe, who had commitments to a number of activities to promote his new business with Stimson in Vancouver. Just two days after Joe II's death, it was announced that Joe was to join G.A. Stimson & Co as Vice President. The Vancouver Province newspaper states Joe was a lifelong friend of Col. Frederick Johnston, who as Stimson President had personally invited Joe "to superintend the development planned by the company in the port of Vancouver". Up until this point, Joe had been operating as an independent partner to Stimson, but now he was on the payroll and formally assumed an executive position in charge of the company's West Coast operations and developments.[180]

At some stage during the course of 1928, Joe and Stimson changed their plans for the Merchant Exchange Building, deciding to postpone the redevelopment and focus on another opportunity instead. The reasons seem to be a combination of factors. Firstly, it proved more difficult to 'adjust' the lease terminations of some of the existing Merchants Exchange Building tenants than had been expected. On the other hand, it seems the partners realised the steady rent they earned from tenants in the Merchants Exchange Building was a good business in its own right. They also risked losing all the existing Merchants Exchange Building tenants after the original building was demolished before the new replacement building could be constructed, and the smooth functioning of the Exchange would also have been disrupted. Then, an opportunity emerged to buy an alternative, equally well-situated plot, which did not have all the complications of existing tenants or demolishing substantial existing buildings. The new site was perfect, located near the waterfront, close to the Customs House and the Canadian Pacific and Canadian National steamship terminals, and near the existing focus of the city's maritime and trading businesses that were members of the Merchant's Exchange. So, following visits to Vancouver from F.G. Johnston and his number two, L.E. Clark (Stimson First Vice President), the partners developed a plan to buy the new site at the corner of Burrard and Hastings Streets in central Vancouver, and develop it into what became known as the Marine Building. They adjusted their timeline, prioritising development of Marine Building first, still planning to redevelop Merchants Exchange Building later, anticipating that some existing Merchants Exchange Building tenants might be persuaded to move to the new Marine Building when it was finished.

The new site was acquired on 11th November 1928 from the Winnipeg grain company James Richardson & Sons. The price was initially reported in some newspapers as a very modest $30,000 – in fact it was $300,000, although the previous owners ended up having to sue Stimson in 1931 to get the money they were owed for the site.[181]

The vision for the development was spectacular, with Stimson announcing that a new 18-storey skyscraper, by far the tallest in Vancouver and one of the tallest in Canada, would be built on the site at a cost of $1,500,000, to a design by local Vancouver architects McCarter and Nairne. The plan for the design and fit-out of the new building was also impressive, the intricacy and quality still marvelled at today. The news was covered for months in all the main B.C. and Canadian papers, and was received very positively as a huge sign of confidence in Vancouver.[182] Stimson let it be known that they intended to build a similarly impressive building on the site of the Merchants Exchange Building later, which generated further interest and praise, although it was less clear where the funding would come from for all this, and it seems some or all of the monies raised under the Merchants Exchange Building bonds Stimson had sold were in practice used to help fund the construction cost of Marine Building.

However, it was certainly true that Vancouver was booming at this time, and a wave of optimism for its future brought much interest and speculation, and also quite some actual investment. The newspapers of the day were full of stories of new companies setting up in the city, and the port regularly achieving new records for volumes of cargoes handled. Joe and Stimson were instrumental in communicating a vision for the development of Vancouver, exploiting its strategic location as the largest and best port in the north-west of the American continent, situated at the western end of two transcontinental railways, making it the perfect gateway for cargoes and people moving to and from 'the Orient' and, since the opening of the Panama Canal, also well connected to Europe. Vancouver was well positioned to lead the development of the whole western part of Canada, with its great agricultural and mineral resources. Joe and Stimson set out their vision for a rapidly expanding commercial metropolis, with the Marine Building at the centre, strategically located in the heart of the business district, in a prominent position overlooking Vancouver Harbour, with access to the waterfront and in close proximity to the financial district. The Marine Building would also provide new and expanded premises for the Merchants Exchange, and accommodation for all the Vancouver firms involved in import and export trades, shipping, insurance and the port.[183]

Joe, Stimson, and the local architects McCarter and Nairne went to town on the design and fit-out of Marine Building, which was to win plaudits for years to come. UK Poet Laureate (and passionate advocate for good architecture) Sir John Betjeman described it as "the best Art Deco office building in the world."[184] McCarter and Nairne jumped at the chance to design their first skyscraper, and seem to have been inspired by New York's Chrysler Building, the art deco skyscraper then under construction that was to become the world's tallest building when completed in May 1930. They worked closely with Joe on the Marine Building blueprints, creating an art deco masterpiece, the design including many features which visually referenced the various maritime, shipping, and trade businesses that were planned to occupy its premises.[185] As usual with Joe

Hobbs, this was bold and visionary thinking, and his energy, drive and persistence was essential to the successful conclusion of the project, overcoming enormous challenges after the Great Crash of October 1929 and the subsequent bankruptcy of Stimson.

But that was all still in the future. On 6th December 1929, Joe stepped down as Commander of the Vancouver company of the R.C.N.V.R. in order to devote more time to his business interests, principally to the Marine Building development.[186]

Early in the new year of 1929, Joe made his annual visit to England, a shorter trip than usual, arriving in January and returning in February.[187] Joe again stayed at Hope Street in Glasgow, close by the headquarters of Train & McIntyre, who were to become Joe's close partners in the 1930s. Although he was clearly prioritising Marine Building, Joe still made the time to maintain and develop his whisky business and connections, which would pay considerable dividends for him later.

In January 1929, Stimson and Hobbs announced that the small house known as the 'old Mahon residence' on the Marine Building site was to be demolished, with the E.J. Ryan Construction Co. starting work to clear the site. They further announced that the architects McCarter and Nairne were in Toronto at Stimson's head office finalising the designs for Marine Building. Moreover, it was reported that F.G. Johnston would return to Vancouver in early February to finalise with Joe the placement of the construction contracts for building Vancouver's first skyscraper. Excavation of the site post-demolition was planned to begin in late February.[188]

Then, on 13th March 1929, to much fanfare and publicity, construction work on Marine Building got underway.[189, 190] Newspapers across Canada reported that Vancouver mayor W.H. Malkin blew a golden whistle to get the work started at a ceremony with other worthies present, including W.C. Woodward (President of the Board of Trade) and G.V. Holt (President of the Merchants Exchange, who were also announced as being the first tenants for the new building). The construction cost was estimated at $1.5m. The build was planned to be extremely fast, scheduled for a little over 12 months. This was the second-largest construction contract to date in Vancouver, eclipsed only by the $6m Canadian National Hotel project – whose construction by Canada National railways was in practice to be delayed by 10 years because of the Great Depression, and only concluded in 1939.[v]

A steady stream of newspaper reports documented progress on the Marine Building construction, which mostly moved smoothly and extremely quickly.[191] Despite the frantic pace of the Marine Building, Joe still found time to pursue other business opportunities and engagements. In July 1929 he was

Vancouver mayor W.H. Malkin (fourth from left, front row) blows a golden whistle to start construction work on the Marine Building, 13th March 1929.

---

v   Today this building is the Fairmount Vancouver Hotel.

appointed 'surveyor of aircraft' for western Canada for the British Register of Shipping and Aircraft. This was one of the UK classification societies that surveyed and certified construction and maintenance standards of aircraft and ships.[192] In August, Joe was in the papers again, donating an impressive silver cup to the B.C. High Schools' Olympiad, with the cup to be presented to the best overall team from the 30 schools competing from around the province.[193]

Keeping up the tide of positive publicity, on 17th August Stimson published a glossy promotional booklet on Vancouver, 'The Tide of Commerce and the Port of Vancouver,' demonstrating Vancouver's accelerating growth and future potential as a leading city on the west coast of North America.[194] In September, Joe and 'Mrs Hobbs' (this was Mabel, since Evelyn was in the UK at this time) entertained 70 journalists on an excursion on Joe's yacht 'Lady Stimson' to the Indian River area north-east of Vancouver. This was the second occasion in 1929 Joe had arranged an event like this for the media, demonstrating the effort he was making to promote his ideas for the Marine Building and the development of Vancouver.[195]

In October, following completion of the steel frame of Marine Building, Joe was able to announce the award of $855,000 of contracts to fit out the interior of the building. At that point, Joe estimated that construction would be completed in March 1930 and the building would welcome its first tenants in May of the same year.[196]

However, at the end of that month, on 29th October 1929, came the Great Wall Street Crash, giving rise to the period of economic slump known as 'The Great Depression'.

The very next day, on 30th October 1929, it was announced that Joe had sold his yacht the Lady Stimson. It is probable that Joe had already decided to sell Lady Stimson before the Crash, and the timing of the sale the day afterwards was more of a

Marine Building under construction, Vancouver, 1930.

coincidence.[197] However, it is also reasonable to postulate that Joe had realised more funds would be needed to complete the ambitious Marine Building project, and possibly also began to have some insight into the real state of Stimson's finances. Given Joe's passion for yachting, it is unlikely he would have wanted to give Lady Stimson up, so this could be an indication that he took a hard decision to sell a prized asset to help the strained funding of Marine Building, and his personal financial exposure to the project increased substantially.

Between 26th November 1929 and 4th January 1930, Joe made his annual visit to the UK. He again stayed at Hope Street, Glasgow. The fact that he travelled out via New York and visited Glasgow is further evidence he was already working closely with National Distillers of America, whose head office was in New York, and their UK subsidiary Train & MacIntyre.[198]

By the time he returned to Canada after this trip, he was facing a very different outlook for his property development projects in Vancouver. In some respects, Canada did quite well in managing the fallout of the Great Wall Street Crash. For example, whilst over 9,000 banks in the USA failed during the

Great Depression from 1930 to 1935, not even one Canadian bank went bankrupt at this time.[199] However, the appetite for investment changed overnight. Investors, especially smaller ones, were keen to secure and recover their capital from investments already made and reluctant to invest new money, especially for riskier projects. On top of that, the overall economic slowdown meant businesses generally reduced their activities and cut costs, rather than expanding. For Stimson, the growth market that had fuelled their rise and substantial expansion through the 1920s changed dramatically. The broad market of small and medium-sized investors that they relied on to buy their bonds dried up, while the value of the bonds Stimson issued to fund their property developments declined. The slowing economy meant there were fewer tenants for their buildings, and that rental income from their existing property assets was lower than expected. On top of all this, Stimson were still committed to funding large-scale building construction – not least the Marine Building – with substantial payments required in advance for land and construction costs, with no income received until some time later. In combination, this meant Stimson income and value of assets went down, while they were still committed to substantial costs and outgoings – this resulted in cash in the business drying up fast.

With the benefit of hindsight, it also seems distinctly possible that Stimson's leaders 'believed their own propaganda' and for too long failed to see that the risk of a changing market was an existential threat to their business. The storm clouds were darkening appreciably over the operators of "Canada's oldest bond house" who proudly claimed never to have missed a payment of interest or principal when it was due.

Despite the worsening situation, Joe did his best to put on a brave face and continued to demonstrate confidence in the Marine Building project. He reported to The Province newspaper that work on Marine Building was proceeding well and the building would be ready for its first tenants in the summer.[200]

On 25th February, Joe provided another update, emphasising that despite the financial crash there was no delay to Marine Building's progress. Joe advised that 300 workers would be deployed from the following week as warmer weather allowed work to be accelerated, and that they were aiming for an opening in late June. Stimson planned to take occupancy of their unit in the building on 1st May, and Bank of Montreal would move in on 1st June. [201]

William A. Starrett Jr.

However, by 9th April 1930, the first hard evidence starts to emerge that Stimson's financial situation was worsening and this was having an adverse impact on the Marine Building project. Joe announced that the Starrett Investment Corporation of New York had agreed to underwrite $1m of Stimson Marine Building securities, providing the funding to complete the construction. Starrett's President, William Aiken Starrett Jr, was a pioneering architect and builder of skyscrapers, most notably the Empire State Building in New York. Marine Building was Starrett Corp.'s first Canadian investment. Explaining the move, Joe said they had originally intended to fund the building completely from within Canada; however, following the financial crisis some Canadian investors who had contracted to buy Marine Building securities could not make payments, and so he had to look elsewhere for funding. He added that formal opening of the building, originally planned for May 1930 and then postponed to 1st June, was now going to be on 1st July 1930.[202, 203]

On 30th April, the Vancouver Sun printed a long article

summarising Joe's vision for Marine Building and for the wider development of Vancouver, indicating Joe was still working hard to maintain confidence and momentum in the project, and putting continued effort into talking up the long-term potential of Vancouver.[204]

Through May and June 1930, Joe continued to feature in the news in a positive light. On 12th May it was reported that he had been nominated as a director of Associated Property Owners of Vancouver, the industry association and leading lobbying organisation in the city for property owners and developers.[205] And then, on 15th June, it was announced that Joe had been promoted to the rank of Lieutenant-Commander, permitted to retire from active service in the British Royal Navy and transferred to the Royal Canadian Naval Reserve.[206] The Province newspaper described Joe as a "financier and yachtsman" with a "splendid record during the war" in aerial, naval and engineering branches of the services.[207] He was also not too busy to pen an extended essay on the pleasures of yachting around Vancouver and the British Columbia coast, and making the case that in that part of Canada at least, yachting was a hobby that could be enjoyed "at very moderate cost."[208]

However, the pressures on Joe continued to mount over the summer of 1930 as Stimson's financial situation deteriorate. On 4th September more substantial evidence emerged that they were getting into financial trouble. An article in the National Post stated that the outlook for Stimson's Canadian Development Corporation (SCDC, the entity used to fund and build the Commerce and Transportation Building in Toronto and Marine Building in Vancouver) was "decidedly uncertain". After the Crash, Stimson sales of debentures and bonds declined appreciably to the point they did not have funds to complete Marine Building, pay the workers and complete payment for the land. Only an estimated $50,000 of the agreed

$300,000 purchase price for the land had been paid. This was why Stimson had contracted with Starrett Corporation from New York to contribute $800,000 in cash to ensure funds were available to complete the construction, secured on a mortgage on the building. This had proved insufficient, and Starrett had to advance another $500,000, which was secured by liens on other Stimson properties. This new funding was good in that it meant money was available to finish the building, but it also meant Starrett 'leapfrogged' the other investors in terms of security, leaving the owners of the SCDC debentures and stock with no secured assets. If there was a problem, the SCDC stockholders would only be fourth in line, after payment of the remaining $250,000 owed for the land purchase, plus the $800,000 and $500,000 to be returned to Starrett Corporation for the funds they had provided to pay for the remaining construction costs. Whilst Marine Building was a high-quality building with good long-term rental possibilities, it was starting to look like the original individual investors in SCDC were at high risk of not getting all that they were owed on the Stimson bonds they had bought.[209] Another consequence was that the need to obtain additional sources of financing had taken some time, which resulted in a further delay in the finalisation of construction, which was now put back to the autumn.

Joe himself was far from immune to these challenges, being forced to sell a property he owned on Marguerite Street, Vancouver, for $9,000. His business partner Col. Brothers also sold his primary residence in Point Grey for $10,000 at the same time. The reason for the sales is likely to have been to contribute to the funding of the Marine Building, or to pay for investment losses following the Great Crash.[210]

Despite the gathering storm clouds, Stimson continued to put out favourable publicity about themselves in Vancouver. A full page 'advertorial' in the Sunday Province newspaper on

5th October talked at length about the company's history and achievements, their role creating employment, training industry leaders, and providing a safe return for investors for over 45 years. As Joe was a Vice President of Stimson and responsible for their business in Vancouver, it is hard to believe this could have been issued without his knowledge and approval. Since there was now glaring evidence of serious problems with Stimson finances, this seems at best misleading and possibly deliberately deceptive – no matter the importance from a Stimson perspective of maintaining the confidence of their investors to avoid even further trouble.[211]

Finally, however, Joe's passion and persistence (especially his work to arrange refinancing from Starrett so that funds were available to complete the building) paid off when on 7th October 1930 construction of the Marine Building was completed. Despite the delays, the building had been finished in a little over 18 months. However, the total cost of construction, originally estimated at $1.5m, finally came in around $2.3m, and with the Great Depression exerting a stranglehold on economic development, the market value of the building at the time of completion was far less than the cost of construction.

The Vancouver Sun published a special 'Marine Building Supplement' to celebrate the occasion.[212] On the following day, Monday, 8th October, the official opening ceremony was held, with the great and the good of Vancouver society on parade to celebrate the opening of the city's first skyscraper. Mayor W.H. Malkin formally declared the building open, accepting a 'golden key' to the building from the architect J.Y. McCarter and symbolically presenting it to Joe. The Lieutenant Governor of the Province of British Columbia Randolph Bruce gave a toast, saying that "the whole of British Columbia is proud of this magnificent building." Mayor Malkin heaped praise on Joe and Stimson, paying "warm tribute to the courage and initiative of

Marine Building shortly after its opening.

Lieut. Commander Hobbs and G.A. Stimson & Co in building such a structure, worthy in every way of the city and of the name 'Marine Building.'" He declared "the building symbolises a new epoch" for Vancouver, and that the completed building was substantially due "to [Commander Hobbs'] vision, courage and initiative." Joe expressed his own pride in the building, thanking the architect and contractors for their work, but also declaring that, with the completion of Marine Building, Stimson had "planted its house in the West," which appears frankly disingenuous in light of subsequent events with Stimson which were very soon to play out. Interestingly, F.G. Johnston and other senior leaders of Stimson are notable by their absence, in retrospect a sure sign that there were major difficulties behind the scenes.[213]

The public were invited to inspect the building on the opening day, and what they witnessed really was magnificent. McCarter and Nairne had designed the building to look like "some great crag rising from the sea, clinging with sea flora and fauna, tinted in sea-green, touched with gold."[214]

Amongst the many extraordinary features of the building were that:

• The builders used 2,000 tons of steel, one million cubic yards of brick, 72,000 sacks of cement, 1,046,000 feet of lumber, 172,000 sq. ft. of hollow tile, 75 miles of wiring

The impressive outline of the completed Marine Building stood out as the first 'skyscraper' on Vancouver's skyline after its opening in 1930.

in the elevators and 54 miles of wiring in the rest of the building, plus 950 windows and 2,100 panes of glass in the construction.

- The exterior is studded with stonework flora and fauna, tinted in sea-green and touched with gold.
- The main entranceway pays tribute to Captain George Vancouver, featuring a stained-glass depiction of Vancouver's ship on the horizon framed by a rising sun.
- The Grand Concourse lobby is 27 metres long, filled with stained glass and modelled on a Mayan temple.
- There are depictions of a huge variety of marine life on many of the walls, including sea snails, skate, crabs, turtles, carp, scallops, seaweed and sea horses.
- In addition, there are terracotta cameos of famous explorers and mariners such as Captain Cook and Captain Drake, and a separate terracotta transport theme featuring trains,

biplanes and zeppelins (possibly a nod to Joe's brother Basil and his wartime exploits).

- Inside the brass-doored elevators the walls are inlaid with 12 different varieties of hardwoods.
- The elevators themselves operated at 700 feet per minute when the average at that time was only around 150 feet per minute.

Unfortunately, Joe's moment of glory did not last long, and indeed his achievement seems better understood and recognised today than it was in the aftermath of Stimson's disastrous implosion, the company's finances unravelling soon after the opening, bringing widespread losses and recriminations. The painful crash was to cost Joe his entire fortune (all bar £1,000), but

The stunning and intricate features of the Marine Building in Vancouver are as impressive today as when the building first opened.

somehow he seems to have been able to avoid taking the blame for the disaster, and also avoided criminal liability – not the case for three of the other senior leaders of Stimson. From the high point of the Marine Building opening in October 1930, the next two years was a rapid downhill slide for Joe Hobbs.

Only a month and a half after the Marine Building opened, real signs of strain started to show in the Stimson empire. They wrote to their investors in Commerce and Transportation Building offering those who were owed interest or dividends an alternative in the form of a new short-term 'promissory note' payable just a few months later on 1st April 1931, with the option of a bonus of 10% on the face value at the time it was paid back, or interest at 20% per annum.[215] The short-term nature of the offer perhaps indicates Stimson management still thought their cash flow challenges were temporary, and if they could just bring in some additional short-term cash, they might still trade their way out of trouble.

But, in a further sign of the radical actions being taken to free up cash in December, an investor in another Stimson business, Dominion Timbers Ltd, Col. P.C. McGillivray alleged "fraud, misfeasance and breach of fiduciary capacity" against Stimson, F.G. Johnston and L.E. Clark. Dominion Timbers had apparently sold significant quantities of their stocks of British Columbian fir at a price of $24 per 1,000 board feet, compared with the open market price of $44 and the actual cost to the company of $41. McGillivray obtained a court order preventing Dominion from disbursing the proceeds until the matter had gone to trial at court.[216]

On 24th December 1930, Stimson still had sufficient funds to be able to publish newspaper advertisements wishing their customers a happy Christmas.[217] There were then three weeks without news about Stimson in the papers, before the story crashed in mid-January 1931 that the company was bankrupt. On 14th January 1931 media across Canada carried the explosive news that four subsidiary companies of G.A. Stimson & Co Ltd group had entered voluntary assignment, i.e., had been handed over to an insolvency professional to be liquidated. The four were:

1. National Debenture Corporation Ltd: assets $836,000, liabilities $974,000.
2. Toronto Bond Exchange: assets $166,000, liabilities $300,000.
3. Stimson Building and Investment Corporation Ltd: no separate breakdown of assets and liabilities given.
4. Stimson Canadian Development Company Ltd: assets only $700, liabilities $1.46m (debenture owners were liable for $1.30m of this). This was the main entity used to develop Marine Building.

G.T. Clarkson was appointed custodian, an independent professional to manage the bankruptcy process. [218]

Stimson explained that the situation had arisen because their supply of new funds had almost completely dried up. Two years prior, they had hundreds of bond salesmen in 14 offices across Canada selling bonds and securities to investors of all sizes, generating steady incoming cash flows. Following the Crash, this source of income almost entirely disappeared and they did not have the funds to pay the cost of constructing the buildings they had committed to and also make the interest payments to investors and creditors. It may have been a deliberate misrepresentation, but a company spokesman gave the impression that, whilst these four specific subsidiaries were in trouble, the parent company G.A. Stimson & Co Ltd was still viable, stating it had total assets of $6.3m and liabilities of $6.0m. [219]

In its coverage of the bankruptcy, the Vancouver Sun newspaper – a long-time supporter of Joe – reported that, whilst Joe had been in charge of construction of Marine Building, his contract with Stimson had expired with completion of the building and he was "no longer associated with the firm". Commander Hobbs was stated now to be engaged in his own business as a financial agent. This sounds very convenient! Prior to this story, there had been no hint from the normally publicity-hungry Joe Hobbs after completion of Marine Building that he had parted ways with Stimson. The reality was more likely that when Joe realised Stimson was in serious trouble he resigned his employment with them to try to distance himself from responsibility.[220]

In addition to providing more information on the four bankrupt subsidiaries, The National Post said the 'voluntary' assignments had arisen directly as a result of some petitions filed by creditors on 13th January, and moreover that the Stimson parent company had also ceased to meet liabilities coming due and given notice to some creditors that it had stopped payment of debts. F.G. Johnston met the press and issued a statement, saying that "we believe our clients … will eventually receive the return of the full par value of your investment and the full face value of your treasury notes". The management still maintained that the company's valuable property assets, in particular Commerce and Transportation Building in Toronto and Marine Building in Vancouver, would cover all the liabilities provided the properties were kept intact.[221, 222] Whilst Stimson were clearly doing all they could to stave off bankruptcy and buy time to 'trade their way out of trouble', this statement seems downright misleading. For example, whilst Marine Building still had reasonable prospects for lease rental income in the years ahead, if it had to be sold to cover Stimson liabilities, substantial losses would be realised – the building had cost over $2.3m to construct, but was worth less than $1.0m at market prices prevailing by the time it was finished.

On 19th January, the Vancouver Sun ran the story that the Stimson offices had been raided by police and many of their books of account taken away for analysis.[223] They followed up two days later with another article claiming "Marine Building out of Stimson Probe" which seems to indicate officers had already determined there were no illegalities in how finance was raised for Marine Building, but given the short period since news of the bankruptcy had emerged it seems extremely premature to have been able to reach such a conclusion.[224]

On 22nd January, the financial pages of The National Post – who for some time had been one of the few voices speaking out against Stimson's increasingly dubious business practices – broke the news that four Stimson executives (F.G. Johnston, President; L.E. Clark, Vice President; W.J. Dow, Secretary/Treasurer; and H.H. Thomas, Sales Manager) were to face criminal charges over the company's bankruptcy. The Post ran extensive stories over two pages revealing years of suspect practices. In particular, they highlighted that Stimson repeatedly sold new bonds, mostly to small investors, to raise finance for their building developments without making it clear that there were already loans and mortgages in place on the buildings, which would have priority for repayment in case of any problem. In addition, Stimson had on multiple occasions encouraged investors to exchange their shares in existing funds for new bonds in larger funds, without providing transparency on the financial status of the new funds, making it very hard for investors to keep track of what they actually owned, and the relative degree of risk of their investments. Stimson had also established a series of cross-shareholdings between their various funds and subsidiaries, so that in many cases the principal assets of one Stimson subsidiary were shares in another Stimson company. It took the administrator weeks to unravel this complex mess, and when he finally did so it unsurprisingly emerged that the valueless shares of the four initially bankrupt Stimson entities then meant the assets of the other business units were worth much less than investors might have imagined. In total, The Post estimated 5–10,000 investors would lose out, with net losses of more than $5m expected (today equivalent to around $87m).[225]

How much of this chicanery was known (or should have been known) by Joe Hobbs is hard to know. Joe was initially involved with Stimson only as an external, arms-length business partner in Vancouver, only officially becoming a Vice President of the company in May 1928. From the Post's analysis, Stimson had been engaging in progressively more dubious financial practices since at least 1926, but the full extent of the deception senior managers in Toronto were orchestrating was probably known only to a few high-level insiders around F.G. Johnston himself. However, Joe was criticised in the Post article, that amongst all the pomp and celebration at the "delightful ceremony" for the opening of Marine Building nothing was revealed of the true state of the company's finances, deceiving the many Canadian investors "who still remained under the delusion that they owned a well-financed building."[226] This was one of the few times that Joe was publicly criticised in the aftermath of the Stimson collapse, and overall, he seems to have fared remarkably well to have kept out of the firing line and avoided any responsibility for the financial mismanagement.

On 23rd January, F.G. Johnston and L.E. Clark appeared in court in Toronto and were bailed in the amount of $50,000 until the next hearing.[227] A third Stimson executive charged over the affair, sales manager H.H. Thomas, had temporarily absconded. A reward of $2,000 was offered by Ontario state police for his capture, before Thomas gave himself up to authorities on the Canadian side of the border with the USA at Niagara Falls in February.[228] William Dow, the Secretary-Treasurer of Stimson, who was also arrested, was soon released and became a material witness for the prosecution, helping investigators unravel the complex web of transactions in the case.

By February, it had become clear that all of the Stimson group and its 14 subsidiaries were in bankruptcy and that there were no major assets to pay debts, but since the affairs of the various companies were so interwoven it would take weeks to make a full statement of net assets and liabilities.[229]

In the midst of all this turmoil, Joe's divorce from his first wife, Mabel Dell, was finalised on 23rd February 1931, when Justice D.A. McDonald issued a decree absolute at the Supreme Court of British Columbia. Neither of them was present in court, with the judge confirming the divorce on the grounds of Joe's adultery with Eve. Mabel was granted custody of both children. The decree says nothing about ongoing support or alimony from Joe to Mabel, but it seems that Joe continued to support Mabel and Patricia for the rest of their lives, whilst Joe Junior came to live and work with his father in the UK once he had finished his schooling in Canada.[230]

In March and April 1931, a number of creditors meetings held by the trustee G.T. Clarkson presented a more complete picture of the Stimson collapse. The Marine Building itself was around 40% rented out, and the administrator estimated it was likely to generate $150–175,000 per annum profit after tax and depreciation. This was actually not a bad performance in the post-Great Crash depression environment.[w] But across the

---

w   As part of efforts to salvage some value from the Stimson crash, in March 1931, news seeped out that the Starrett Corporation had proposed that Vancouver City Council lease space in Marine Building as an alternative to continuing in the council's current premises in the Holden Building, which were too small. Starrett suggested the City take up 50,000 square feet of space over 6 floors in the lower part of Marine Building, with an option to buy the whole property for $2m. It subsequently became clear the true market value of the building was much less than this, only around half what Starrett asked the City to pay to acquire it; moreover, if the city had $2m available to spend on accommodation for the council, it could be better spent on a purpose-built Civic Centre, and so the proposal was dropped.

whole group of companies, although there were a few substantial building assets (Commerce and Transportation Building, Toronto; Marine Building, Vancouver; a property on University Avenue, Toronto; Grand Central Market, Toronto), prior claims by mortgage holders and lenders with security would take up most of the proceeds from sale of these properties. Since most of the other "assets" of the various companies were shares and promissory notes between the different Stimson entities which were worthless, other tangible assets whose value would find its way back to investors only amounted to $200,000–300,000, against a face value of more than $6m. It was clear that the liquidation of Stimson's assets would be woefully insufficient to repay the many millions of dollars Stimson had invested on behalf of their Canadian clients under F.G. Johnston's leadership.

The previous owner of the Marine Building land, James Richardson of Winnipeg, successfully sued in the Supreme Court to recover the $250,000 of the purchase price that he was still owed for the land on which Marine Building was constructed. After paying Richardson, this left Starrett Corp, as the Marine Building's owners, holding a mortgage of $1.4m on the building.[231] As secured creditors, Richardson and Starrett recovered what they were owed. But when the whole Stimson mess was finally unwound, small investors ended up getting just 2–3 cents back for every dollar they had invested.[232, x]

On 2nd June after a 5-day trial, the three senior Stimson executives arrested for malpractice over the company bankruptcy were found guilty by the jury at the Assize Court in Toronto

---

x   There is also a (possibly apocryphal) story that, given the bankruptcy and shortage of funds to get the Marine Building construction finished, the architects McCarter and Nairne did not receive their fee. However, the story goes that once Joe had re-established his personal fortune later in the 1930s, he ensured they were paid in cash for the work they had done on Marine Building.

of publishing false prospectuses. However, they were found not guilty of the more serious charge of conspiring to defraud the public, which was punishable by up to 7 years in prison. Mr Justice Sedgewick said "there was evidence of conspiracy between the three men" and "willful misstatement of fact." Johnston was sentenced to 3 years in Portsmouth Penitentiary, which meant he would only earn his release in the latter part of 1934. Clark received a sentence of 2 and a half years, whilst Thomas was given a sentence of 2 years less 1 day. Five further charges of theft and two of falsifying balance sheets against Johnston were deferred for consideration at the Fall Assizes to be held in September.[233]

At the end of September, the appeal of the three Stimson executives against their convictions failed, a panel of judges at the Ontario Court finding 4 to 1 against their appeal. [234]

But there was no mention in all this of Joe Hobbs. Why? He had officially been a Vice President of Stimson, and had actively and very publicly promoted the Marine Building. It certainly seems with the benefit of hindsight that the authorities were reluctant to act against a wide number of players in the Stimson case, preferring to limit charges to the small circle immediately around F.G. Johnston. Certainly, the scale and complexity of the cross-ownership and increasingly desperate deals made by the central leadership team to keep the whole house of cards standing does indicate a higher degree of culpability by Johnston, Clark and Thomas. But there are also quite a few newspaper editorials of the time questioning why the Attorney General and government were not acting with more energy against leaders in large corporate bankruptcies which deprived thousands of ordinary investors of considerable sums. In his defence, Joe is likely to have argued that, as a large investor in Stimson funds himself, especially in relation to Marine Building, he would hardly have done anything to 'defraud himself'. He will certainly have maintained that he acted in good faith throughout and was a victim just like the many other investors who lost out when the Stimson edifice crashed. Today, as a director of a company that allowed the business to continue to trade whilst knowing it to be insolvent, Joe would certainly be held liable for the consequences. However, the regulatory regime in 1930s Canada was not so clear, and Joe was never charged with any wrongdoing in the affair.

During this period, Joe maintained an unusually low public profile. It can be conjectured that his good personal standing and relations with the media especially in Vancouver worked to his advantage at this time, and there are no stories in the press criticising Joe for his role in the Stimson crash. For most of May of 1931, he made an extended visit to California, researching potential new business opportunities in film-making.

Then, on 27th May 1931 in Vancouver, Joe married for the second time, formalising his relationship with Florence Appleyard (Evelyn).[235] Despite the earlier evidence that she had an affair with Joe in 1926, Eve seems to have made the decision to return to the UK in 1927 to live with her son John Henry and raise him there. They lived with Eve's mother in Barnes, south-west London. Sadly, John Henry contracted appendicitis in the autumn of 1929, dying from a burst appendix aged only 9 years old, on 4th March 1929 at Northwood Cottage Hospital, in Middlesex, west of London, one of over 2,000 such deaths in the UK that year. Eve was with her son when he passed away.[236]

Eve remained in the UK for more than a year after her son's passing. But in May 1930 she journeyed to Vancouver. That she travelled first class despite her relative lack of means may indicate Joe paid for the ticket, and the fact that she went to live with Joe's close friend and business partner Colonel O.F. Brothers and his wife in Vancouver indicates that she was coming back to Canada to be with Joe.[237] Later that year, Eve made a trip to California, by which time she declared her status had changed to 'divorced,' and after which she went to live with another friend, Beatrice Raymond, in Vancouver, at an address which Joe had used following his separation from Mabel. [238, 239] With Joe's own divorce from Mabel finalised in February 1931, the couple were free to wed.

As would probably be expected given the carnage of the Stimson collapse going on at this time, their wedding seems to have been very low-key and does not appear to have been reported by any of the local papers – this is notable given Joe's high profile and regular appearances in the Vancouver media. However, the fact that Eve took the step of formalising her marriage to Joe when his circumstances and finances were at such a low ebb says a lot about the strength of their relationship and indicates that Eve was motivated by much more than Joe's money and lifestyle. It perhaps also says something about Joe's need for support from Eve at an extremely difficult and stressful time. Eve was a huge source of support and marrying her at this time doubtless provided Joe with increased strength and determination to rebuild his fortunes.

Whilst Joe was clearly keen to move forward with his new relationship, the divorce was hard on Mabel and the two children Joe Junior (then aged 12) and Patricia (9). In the aftermath of the Stimson disaster, money was very tight, and Mabel and her children struggled for a few years in Vancouver alone after Joe and Eve relocated back to the UK. Joe's grandson Joseph Peter tells the story that, at one point, Mabel sent her son Joe Junior across the U.S. border to Seattle to pawn a valuable ring to make ends meet. The pawn broker was concerned about how Joe Junior had come by the valuable item, and called the police on the suspicion he had stolen it. Joe Junior was only released after his mother came down to Seattle to vouch for him.[240] While their situation improved after Joe was gradually able to rebuild his business and his fortunes, Joe Junior never warmed to Eve, always seeing her as a 'gold digger' and as the cause of the break-up of his family. This resulted in some strain in family relations, and negative feelings about Eve which were passed on to Joe Junior's own children.

Over the next 18 months Joe was forced to sell almost everything he had, and relocate almost penniless to the UK to start over. The parallels between Joe's father's rapid rise, crash and intercontinental relocation and, 30 years later, Joe's own boom, over-extension and bust, creating the necessity to migrate back across the Atlantic, are extraordinary. This genuinely was a case of history directly repeating itself, the ironies of which would certainly not have been lost on Joe himself.

Following the Stimson bankruptcy, Starrett Corporation ended up selling Marine Building to British Pacific Properties Ltd for just $900,000 in 1933, a fraction of the $2.3m it was estimated had been expended on its construction.[241] The managing director of British Pacific Properties, A.J.T. Taylor, moved into the Marine Building's penthouse with his wife. Apparently Mrs Taylor did not like the remoteness of living atop a tall building that was largely empty at night, so they did not live there long.[242] But British Pacific contributed a huge amount to the development of Vancouver in the following decades, making substantial profits for their owners/investors, pre-eminent amongst whom were the Guinness family from Ireland.[y]

---

y   Taylor's involvement with Marine Building was a component of his vision to develop the whole fabric of the city, in which he (like Joe Hobbs) saw enormous potential. The background was that, ever since 1890 when speculator George Mackay first proposed it, Vancouver had been discussing schemes to build a bridge over the harbour narrows. In 1927 the idea of building a bridge was put to a plebiscite (vote) in the city, but was defeated. A.J.T. Taylor saw the potential and worked hard to overcome local opposition, and was able to convince the Guinness family (the family that owned the famous Irish stout beer company

Despite the rocky start to the it's life, Marine Building would eventually prove itself commercially successful. Murray Foster in his article in 'The Great Vancouver Book' documents that "early tenants included the Vancouver Merchants' Exchange-which had contracted for a minimum of 10 years tenancy, the Vancouver Board of Trade, the Bank of Montreal and others. The architects (McCarter and Nairne) themselves moved in, and were tenants for many years."[243] It is still today an iconic component of Vancouver's building infrastructure, even though it no longer dominates the skyline. At 321 feet tall and 22 storeys high, Marine Building was the tallest building in Vancouver when built, and for more than a decade was the tallest building in the British Commonwealth. Joe Hobbs was instrumental in

---

of the same name) to invest in land on the north shore. In 1931 they acquired 1,900 hectares (4,700 acres) through British Pacific Properties Ltd. The purchase price was only $75,000, but with a commitment to spend $1m in infrastructure improvements within the following 5 years.

On 13th December 1933, Vancouver held a second vote on building a bridge, and this time it passed with 70% in favour. After considerable negotiation with the Federal government, approval to proceed was obtained on the condition everything possible was done to maximise local employment (since this was the middle of the Great Depression).

Construction began on the impressive single-span suspension bridge on 31st March 1937 to a design by the Montreal firm of Montsarrat and Pratley. The bridge cost $5.9m to build and opened to traffic on 14th November 1938. It was officially opened by King George VI and Queen Elizabeth during their visit to Canada on 29th May 1939. The bridge opened the way to accelerated development of the whole north shore area of Vancouver, making the lands to the north of the bridge that Taylor and the Guinness family had acquired in 1931 highly desirable and significantly more valuable. The prosperity of their north shore land bank was a considerable source of wealth for the Guinnesses for decades to come.

The Guinness family sold the bridge back to the city in 1955 for exactly the same sum it had cost to build it. Apparently British Pacific Properties continues to own and develop the British Properties residential area of West Vancouver between Capilano River and Horseshoe Bay to this day.

envisioning and then bringing to fruition what was for a long time the most famous, and still in the eyes of many, the most beautiful building in Vancouver.

7

Whisky Baron: Associated Scottish Distilleries

In 1931–32, Joe spent two difficult years in Vancouver, trying to untangle the mess of the collapse of Stimsons and the sale of Marine Building in Vancouver for a fraction of what it had cost to build. He was forced to sell almost all his assets, including his ships and yachts, and his mansion at 1656 Laurier Avenue.[244,z] He was almost bankrupted.

His new wife, Eve, was 10 years his junior, and they would enjoy a happy marriage for most of the rest of Joe's life. Whilst Eve did not come from a privileged background, she was able to fully engage as Joe's equal in an active social and community life as Joe rebuilt his fortunes and standing in the U.K. in the 1930s–50s. A confident and energetic woman with her own interests and hobbies, Eve went on to become a county councillor when the couple lived in Inverness-shire, Scotland, in later life, and make a sustained and valuable contribution

---

z   The buyer was G.W. Dawson, the retired owner of a successful salmon cannery business.

to the community as a social worker, particularly focusing on working with the elderly and youth of the district. In the short term, despite the economic fallout from the Stimsons affair, Joe and Eve continued to participate in Vancouver social life (e.g. when Joe participated and won a prize in the Vancouver Riding and Driving Club jumping event in February 1932),[245] although, having sold all his yachts, he was no longer part of the Royal Vancouver Yacht Club.

Joe spent 1932 trying to develop new businesses. The most promising opportunity, and the idea to which he devoted most effort to develop, was an initiative to establish the motion picture film industry in Vancouver. In the summer of 1932 Joe went to California for two months as the guest of Henry MacRae, Director General of Universal Studios, studying the US film production process, and assessing opportunities for a possible entry into the world of film-making. He was particularly impressed by Universal's attention to costing and budgeting.[246] It is not clear how Joe knew Henry MacRae; possibly he was trading on their both being Canadian and leveraged his network of contacts to earn himself an introduction, but the fact that Joe spent two months with Universal and was given unusual access to their business indicates that Joe's reputation and status was not totally in tatters following the Stimsons disaster, and that he was still seen as a credible businessman and potential business partner in Canada for one of the biggest Hollywood studios.

In August 1932, Joe announced the formation of a syndicate led by him, and including architect J.Y. McCarter (one of the architects of Marine Building) and R.H. Williams (an electrical engineer) to buy the Ontario government moving picture studios at Trenton, Ontario. The studios had been making silent educational films for some time. Joe's idea was to develop the studios to make 'talkies' in Vancouver to compete with Hollywood, retaining at home some of the C\$50m Canadians spent on American films every year, and potentially creating several thousand jobs in Canada. With the advent of sound in films and usage of enclosed stages for filming, California's sunny climate was not the advantage for film production it had once been, and Vancouver could potentially compete. Moreover, a quota system introduced by the British government to promote the British film industry meant Hollywood producers had a problem getting enough 'British content' to be able to show their films in Britain and her dominions. With Vancouver and British Columbia only a few hours up the coast from Hollywood and in the same time zone, the opportunities for the Californian studios to make an alliance with Canadian companies and make 'British' films in B.C. were realistic. Joe quoted the example of similar studios opening in Melbourne, Australia and Cape Town, South Africa, and made the case for a Canadian equivalent. He said several Hollywood studios were considering options to buy all the output of a new Canadian studio in Vancouver, the cost of developing which he estimated at $250,000 plus land costs.[247]

The announcements made the front pages of several Vancouver daily newspapers. However, whilst Joe received support for his proposals, the idea did not take hold. The concept was pitched towards retaining value for Canada in competition with Hollywood, and the fact that Universal were not mentioned anywhere shows that Joe had not been successful in getting their backing. The absence of heavyweight financial support for the proposals was likely fatal in Depression-era British Columbia. Not for the first time, Joe had the kernel of a brilliant idea here: from the 1970s onwards, British Columbia did develop a vibrant and lucrative film and media sector, earning Vancouver the nickname "the Hollywood of the North", and today the film, media and creative sector contributes to the B.C. economy on a par with traditional mainstays such as forestry and mining.[248] Disappointing as it is that we did not see Joe's creativity and flair given free rein as a film mogul, he seems to have realised the idea would not gain traction and eventually to have given it up.

It gradually dawned on Joe that it was going to be very difficult for him to rebuild his business career in Vancouver. He had done well to avoid legal responsibility for the Stimsons debacle, and kept his name largely out of the media in the wave of criticism that followed. However, just like his father before him in similar circumstances, his reputation suffered badly, and Stimsons' bankruptcy made it extremely difficult for him to win new business as a financial agent or property developer. In an uncanny parallel of the situation his father had experienced in the 1890s, Joe learned painfully that losing virtually all he had and trying to start from scratch in the same place is very hard. People were reluctant to do business with him and, even if he was not a social outcast, it was difficult to get traction on new projects. And of course, he had totally lost his asset base and had no money of his own to fund new investments. At a time of economic depression, it would have been virtually impossible to raise new finance or get approval for new bank loans. Like his father before him, Joe spent a largely fruitless year or two trying to rebuild what he had, before deciding (seemingly with quite some prompting from Eve) to quit Vancouver and relocate to the U.K. for a fresh start back in the country of his birth.[aa]

In the space of just a few short years, Joe had gone from millionaire ship owner and property developer to almost penniless. According to his later obituary in The Times, Joe had less than £1,000 to his name when he returned to the UK in 1933 to start over again. Some parts of this sequence of events may have been romanticised or embellished by Joe and others – the story of how he built a fortune from nothing, lost it all, and

---

aa   It is interesting to speculate whether plucky Elizabeth Hobbs, Joe's mother, had played a similar role encouraging J.W.H. Senior's emigration to Canada in 1900.

then rebuilt it again is certainly dramatic and colourful, and Joe proved throughout his life that he was adept at self-publicity, and may have deliberately added to the 'folklore' of his lifestory later on. But without a doubt, the insolvency of Marine Building and Stimsons cost Joe dearly. Estimates of what he lost vary, but The Vancouver Sun and Joe himself have been quoted as saying it was US$250,000 (US$5.2m today); others estimated it was US$400,000 ($8.25m today).[249] The reality was that it took around two years for Joe to untangle himself from the fallout of the Stimsons insolvency and realise it was not going to be possible to rebuild what he had achieved previously in Vancouver before he took the decision to come back to the UK and start again.

Joe later said that it was the persuasiveness of Eve pushing him repeatedly to take her back to England that finally convinced him to travel back to the land of his birth and make a fresh start, and indeed Eve was certainly influential on Joe – he told one interviewer that he had "married an English girl who insisted on coming back to Britain."[250] And so, early in 1933, Joe and Eve finally sailed back to the "old country".

Joe was one of a number of entrepreneurs to see opportunities at this time from the expected end of Prohibition in the USA, and the inevitable surge in demand for legal alcoholic drinks that would be sure to follow. During Prohibition, the American bourbon industry had declined propitiously, with legal production of alcohol restricted to what was required for medical distillates and industrial alcohols. The consequence was that, when Prohibition finished at the end of 1933, there was little capacity within the US to supply increasing demand, and stocks of mature whisky had to be sourced internationally. This would prove very much to the benefit of 'traditional' sources of supply of whisky in Scotland and Ireland. Moreover, despite the restrictions, successful marketing during Prohibition meant that the US had developed a taste for 'light' blended versions of Scotch whisky (for example the famous "Cutty Sark" blend),[ab] which entrepreneurs like Joe Hobbs now sought to exploit.

On 5th December 1933, Utah became the 36th state to ratify the Twenty-first Amendment, which repealed the Volstead Act and restored control of alcohol laws back to the individual states, effectively ending Prohibition at the national level. In the USA, one of the companies that foresaw these developments and acted to try to address the opportunity was the National Distillers Products Corporation. National Distillers, a long-established business dating back to 1887 had come to prominence as an amalgamation of 65 distilleries across southern and mid-western USA which had gone on to develop a business owning almost 200 brands of bourbon. However, the company had been forced to change its business model at the outset of WW1 when whiskey production was halted by government regulations to conserve supplies of grain and glass for the war effort. The onset of Prohibition meant they could no longer distil alcohol for consumption, and so in 1919 the company changed its name to the U.S. Food Products Company, and started dealing in yeast, vinegar and cereal products to try to survive.

In 1921 the market for these products was fiercely competitive, and U.S. Food Products went into receivership. The banks that were lending it money brought in assistance from an engineering firm called Sanderson & Porter to help assess whether the company should be recapitalised or dismantled. The decision was taken to refocus the business and try to continue operations, with Sanderson & Porter's junior partner Seton Porter installed as the new President. Porter started a long period at the helm of the company by changing the name again

---

ab   Interestingly, Joe's brother Basil Hobbs later acquired the agency to market 'Cutty Sark' whisky in Canada, a flagship brand which helped propel his subsequent success as a wine and liquor merchant.

to National Distillers Products Corporation and switching its focus to production of medicinal and industrial alcohol, yeasts and maraschino cherries to steer it through the Prohibition era. Ten years later, with the end of Prohibition in sight, Porter saw the opportunity to get back into whiskey production and retailing, and repositioned National Distillers again to benefit from the expected reopening of the legitimate whiskey market in the USA. They started by buying up stocks of available whiskies in the USA and were successful in acquiring 9 million US gallons, almost half of all the pre-Prohibition stocks of whiskey still remaining in the country, making National the largest owner of aged whiskey stocks. Together with the 200 bourbon brand names owned by the company and ownership of three of the seven legal distilleries in the country, National were well placed to exploit the expected boom in demand.[251]

However, Porter understood that once Prohibition ended and legal distillation of bourbon could be resumed, there would

Newspaper headline celebrating the end of Prohibition, 5th December 1933.

National Distiller's President Seton Porter, on the cover of Time *Magazine the same week.*

be a three to four-year time lag before any newly distilled whiskey would be mature enough for sale. And at that point, the company would also face a choice, either to 'blend' its stocks of aged whiskey with younger production and sell it cheaply, or take a longer-term view and sell its aged whiskey 'straight' at premium prices, and work to gradually replace it over time by building up stocks of mature whiskey, aiming for quality over quantity. Porter chose the latter course, and positioned National to be a major player in the high-quality "bonded" whiskey market. In the USA, bottled "in-bond" whiskey and bourbon is a kind of quality control designation that mandates minimum standards: the spirit must be aged for at least four years and bottled at precisely 100-proof (50% alcohol by volume). It must be made by one distiller at a single distillery in one season, then aged in a bonded warehouse.

Consequently, even though the company earned $15 million

of sales in December 1933 alone, the month that Prohibition finally ended, Porter was already hard at work to secure new supplies of whiskey to sustain National Distillers' position in the market for the longer term. In 1935, National expanded by acquiring the Old Overholt and Old Crow distilleries in Frankfort, Kentucky, and then the Old Taylor distillery at Glenn's Creek, nearby the same town. By securing aged whiskey stocks and distillery capacity in this way, Porter firmly placed National as one of the leaders in the quality "bonded" market for the longer term. In 1936, he went a step further and showed he was thinking internationally and also about drinks other than US-made bourbon when he negotiated a 50:50 joint venture with the long-established Dutch company of de Kuyper, makers of cherry brandy, gin and genever, to market their products in the USA. During the mid-1930s, National Distillers grew to be one of the major players in the US bourbon and whiskey markets, and whilst National were not the largest, they were one of the most profitable.[252]

It was against this background that Porter and National Distillers came into partnership with Joe Hobbs. National wanted to secure supplies of good quality whiskies to meet burgeoning demand with the end of Prohibition and build a long-term position as a premium player in the US spirits business. As part of the plan, National were looking to source whisky reliably from Scotland, in particular to develop their own blended Scotch whisky brands to complement their home-produced bourbons, and meet the US market's developing taste for 'lighter' blended Scotch whisky. At the same time Joe, newly returned to England in 1933 and looking to use his old contacts in the Scotch whisky industry to rebuild his career, realised the potential to sell into the booming American market. Joe knew that the Scottish whisky industry had laboured through years of hard times in the 1920s, with chronic overcapacity that had led to significant consolidation in the industry and closure or mothballing of many distilleries, and that this presented an opportunity to acquire good quality distillery assets on the cheap.

The year 1932 was the low point for the whisky industry in Scotland, the biggest slump in its history, when the Pot Still Malt Distillers Association took unprecedented action to close 79 of its members' distilleries for the entire 1932–33 distilling season in a desperate effort to balance supply to demand.[253, 254] However, with America imminently likely to become 'wet' again after the end of Prohibition, 1933 saw much brighter prospects so that, from the nadir in 1932 when only 41 of Scotland's 134 distilleries were operational, 90 were back in business by the autumn of 1933.[255] During this period, there were unique opportunities to acquire distilleries and production capacity at the 'bottom of the market', at prices reflecting the weak demand and industry overcapacity of the lean years since WW1. It was this opportunity that Joe came together with National Distillers of America to address, going on to execute one of the fastest and largest buying sprees in the industry's history, and building a combined force that was ranked second only to the industry's clear leader, the mighty Distillers Company Limited (DCL), in terms of scale and capability.

Initially, Joe collaborated with National Distillers simply by resuscitating his old career as a whisky broker, helping to source Scotch whiskies for them for export to the USA. However, the partners evolved a bold plan to buy up a network of 7 closed and mothballed distilleries across Scotland, refurbish and re-equip them, and put them back into operation to provide a guaranteed supply of Scotch to meet National's growing US demand. Their vision included acquisition of both malt whisky distilleries and also a grain distillery, so that National could reliably produce their own blended whiskies, without having to buy in grain

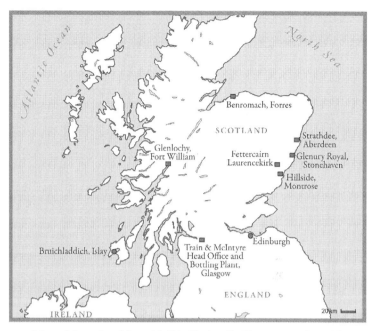

Map of Associated Scottish Distilleries distillery network, 1939.

whiskies from other manufacturers, who were likely to be competitors. Joe used his experience and contacts, as well as his proven negotiating skills, to identify suitable distilleries and negotiate their acquisition for the new business.

Joe would then use his engineering and organisational skills to refurbish and modernise the distilleries he purchased, hire staff to run them, and bring them back into production. Eventually, all the distilleries and production facilities that were acquired in the years ahead would be transferred to National Distillers' UK subsidiary, the old Glasgow firm of merchants and blenders Train and Macintyre (T&M). But since Joe's role and expertise were so vital to the partners' ability to execute the plan, Joe registered a new company called Associated Scottish Distilleries (hereafter referred to as ASD), in which he held a substantial shareholding as the legal entity which owned the distilleries acquired between 1936-1938. Demonstrating that he had lost none of his ability to negotiate highly lucrative business deals, this approach enabled Joe to benefit from two rounds of profit-taking: first, he bought the distilleries very cheaply from their previous owners, and sold them on soon afterwards for considerably larger sums to ASD (which was owned partly by him, and partly by T&M). Then, later on, Joe was able to sell his shares in ASD back to T&M, making a second profit on the same assets, which once they were back in operation and feeding regular orders from the USA were considerably more valuable than at the time ASD acquired them. In combination, Joe's business dealings with ASD enabled him to substantially rebuild his fortune in just a few years.[ac]

When Joe and Eve first returned to England in 1933, they lived initially with Eve's mother at her modest semi-detached house at 62 Lowther Road, Barnes, London SW13, a far cry from his previous mansion in Vancouver. In later life, Joe referred to his occupation after returning to the UK as 'whisky salesman'.[256] In practice, Joe's role was what would now more likely be referred to as a 'whisky broker' or 'whisky trader', buying whisky from

---

ac   Train & McIntyre were an established and quite sizeable player in the Scottish whisky industry, formed in 1898 from the merger of Thomas Train & Co. (itself dating back to 1845), and John McIntyre & Co. T&M owned shares in the North British grain distillery in Edinburgh, Ardgowan distillery in Greenock and in Bulloch Lade, another old Scottish whisky company that had been active in the ownership of Caol Ila, Lossit, Benmore and Tamdhu distilleries in the past. T&M were also a shareholder (since 1919) in West Highland Distilleries Ltd, which owned 6 distilleries in Scotland's then 'whisky capital' of Campbeltown, on the Kintyre peninsula. T&M also had the marketing rights to sell the whiskies made at Glenburgie distillery on Speyside through most of the U.K. On the blending side, T&M's main brands were 'Old Angus' and 'Train's Grey Label', with a blending and bottling operation in Glasgow that focused on export markets.

Train & McIntyre's Headquarters was at Baltic Chambers, 60 Wellington Street, Glasgow.

distilleries and other traders, and selling them on to blenders and retailers. Most of Joe's work at this time was to supply whisky to buyers in North America, and he travelled back and forth several times across the Atlantic in these years, mostly for business meetings with his main customer, National Distillers, at their headquarters in New York.

Before firmly committing to the opportunity to build a network of whisky distilleries across Scotland in an incredible burst of activity with Associated Scottish Distilleries, Joe, ever the entrepreneur, dabbled with one other potentially revolutionary project. In 1934–35, he became the UK sales agent for Aviation Diesel Engine Company Limited of Los Angeles, who were amongst the leaders of a small group of companies aiming to build a viable diesel-powered aviation engine.

Diesel was attractive as an aviation fuel because of its lower fire risk and greater economy. Diesel engines operate at a lower temperature than gasoline-fuelled engines, and benefit from a higher flash point, which makes an engine fire far less likely. In addition, with a diesel engine it is highly unlikely that the fuel would burst into flames after a crash, and bullets could pass through a diesel fuel tank without sparking ignition, which was attractive for military applications. Diesel fuel was also far cheaper and much more widely available than aviation gasoline, and diesel engines were robust and reliable, all of which made the development of a viable diesel aero engine highly interesting for both commercial and military operation.

The concept had been proven in the USA by Hewlett Packard, who flew the first flight powered by a diesel engine in September 1928.[257] In the early 1930s, a number of companies in the USA and Europe competed to develop an effective and viable diesel aircraft engine design. In the USA, there were three pioneering companies at this time, including the Aviation Diesel Engine Company Limited.[258]

As an entrepreneur, engineer and aviator, Joe was well aware of these developments, and witnessed operation of Aviation Diesel Engine Company's test engine whilst on one of his trips to the USA. Impressed by what he saw, Joe entered into negotiations and in December 1934 was appointed as ADE's sales representative in the British Isles. Doubtless, he saw an opportunity to leverage his British aviation and naval contacts, actively pursued and maintained since his participation in the Vancouver Board of Trade's mission to the UK in 1923, to pursue sales of ADE's engines to the UK Forces. A letter dated 3rd December 1934 signed by John H. Suter (Vice President), the engine's designer, and W.S. Noblitt (ADE Secretary) formally authorised Joe to negotiate contracts with potential customers and entitled him to a royalty payment of 20 cents per horsepower on any engine sales.[259]

John H. Suter, Swiss engine inventor and designer, with his innovative diesel-powered radial aircraft engine, c.1934.

In subsequent correspondence, Joe requested independently verified test data on the engine's performance, and had questions about patents on the design. Although performance of ADE's engine was good, in common with many other contemporary diesel engine designs, the engine was too heavy to be commercially viable. Noblitt, the ADE secretary, wrote to advise ADE were working to reduce the weight of key components to get overall engine weight down (e.g. Suter had a planned improved design for a new piston which could reduce the engine's total weight to a much more competitive 900lbs). However, clearly ADE had problems obtaining financial backing for their plans, and Noblitt explains several times that lack of finance was the key issue holding them back. Noblitt stated his belief that the ADE engine was the only practically available diesel aero engine in the USA at that time (which was probably correct, although in Europe the Germans seem to have been substantially ahead with developments of variants of Junkers Jumo engines, over 900 of which were eventually produced, powering a succession of civil and military aircraft from the mid-1930s and through WW2). But ADE did not have the $5,000 (2024: about US$115,000) that they needed to build the new lower-weight prototype incorporating Suter's design improvements, which Noblitt bewailed was "comparatively darn small when you think of the big stakes at hand." ADE were clearly hoping Joe would help them by investing to bring the new prototype to fruition – Noblitt wrote: "I think when you witnessed its [the engine's] ability to operate and accelerate and were amazed at its unusual flexibility and saw the black marine diesel oil we were using that we actually have something that will sooner or later revolutionise the aviation world, both commercially and as well from a military standpoint."[260]

However, Joe seemingly did not take the bait. Joe was well-connected with both naval and air force decision-makers since his war service with the Royal Naval Air Service, connections he had invested time and effort to sustain. And Joe had been visiting aircraft manufacturers and others in the industry throughout the 1920s, since the time of his visit with the Vancouver Board of Trade in 1924. So, he undoubtedly had the contacts to propose Suter's diesel aero engines to the right decision-makers in the UK, and, from his correspondence with ADE's Noblitt, was active as an intermediary between ADE and potential purchasers in the UK. But, despite seeming interest in Suter's designs, this did not translate into any firm orders. Even if Joe thought the technology had potential, his own fortunes had not recovered sufficiently at that stage to fund construction of ADE's new, lighter-weight prototype engine.

The reality was that diesel engines always suffered from a lower power-to-weight ratio than gasoline-powered engines, and had many other shortcomings besides. Diesel engine designs required fuel injection, a gearbox, and turbo-charging to compete with the power performance of petrol engines, all of which increased the complexity and cost of production and maintenance, making them unable to compete with aviation gasoline-powered aero engines. Especially after WW2, the development of advanced turboprops and then jet engines, and reductions in the cost of aviation gas, resulted in a near total loss of interest globally in diesel engines for aviation, and for all these reasons their development almost totally ceased after WW2. Back in 1935, Joe seemed to realise this particular idea was unlikely to prove commercially successful in the short term, and from the end of that year dropped the idea, switching his full focus to his evolving collaboration with National Distillers in the whisky industry.[ad]

Joe's opportunities in whisky seemed much more attractive and viable, especially after the industry low point in 1932. By this time, Joe was already thinking beyond simply trading in whisky, to a time when he could buy his own distillery and produce whisky as well. This was hinted at with the registration of a new company Joe founded on 29th August 1933, MacNab Distilleries Limited, with a nominal share capital of just £100. The only registered directors at founding were Joe himself and an 'Incorporated Accountant', William R. Sharp. In common with many companies at that time, the registered 'objects' or purposes of MacNab Distilleries were very broad, but someone has underlined the term 'general distillers' on the registration document, which probably gives a hint as to the specific intent Joe had in mind. Almost certainly this was the time when Joe conceived plans to buy up Scottish distilleries on the cheap at the low point in the market, put them back into operation, and use them to supply whisky for the booming US market. However, for various reasons, Joe was not able to proceed with his own plans for distillery ownership under MacNab Distilleries immediately, although he came back to this later on, in the 1950s, when he

---

ad   Interestingly, in the 21st century, increases in the cost of aviation gasoline, and its relative unavailability compared with diesel in remote locations has led to some development of diesel aero engines again, especially for light general aviation. Typically, diesel-powered aircraft have a lower payload because of the heavier engines, but this is partly compensated by a longer range at maximum payload. So, some 80 years after Joe was first interested in the concept, commercially viable diesel engines are now being produced for the aviation industry.

had the time and financial resources required to develop the project himself.

In the short term, though, he was quickly successful in his business dealings as a whisky broker, and his circumstances improved rapidly. Joe and Eve were able to resume travelling in first class on the leading ships of the day on regular transatlantic crossings,[261] and were soon able to move out of Eve's mother's house and upgrade their accommodation to a smart west-end address at Aldford House, Park Lane, London.[262] From about this time, Joe began to list his occupation as 'company director', which was correct, at least for MacNab's Distillers, and it is evident his situation was 'on the up' once again.

Although Joe was working closely with National Distillers as his biggest customer, this was far from an exclusive arrangement, and throughout the coming years Joe kept a close eye on opportunities to enhance his own business interests, as well as those of National. Equally, National Distillers took some time before deciding to commit to work exclusively with Joe Hobbs, and during the mid-1930s were in active discussion with the Distillers Company Ltd (the DCL, the largest Scotch whisky company). As a shrewd businessman, Joe had clearly already identified the potential to acquire Scottish distilleries cheaply at the low point in the market in the early 1930s. However, having lost all his assets, Joe initially had no capital with which to seize the opportunity. Consequently, Joe started to work with two other partners who were able to provide the financial backing Joe needed to release his undoubted entrepreneurial talents.

The first, Hatim Attari, was a wealthy Indian businessman, born in 1900, who had previously run his own company in Mumbai, but who by the 1930s was living and working in London, which was to remain his home for the rest of his life. Attari's main business activities were as a financier and investor, but he also described himself as an entrepreneur and company director. By the time he worked with Joe Hobbs he was already well established in London, living in an expensive apartment in Berkeley Square, and seemingly extremely well-connected with the great-and-the-good of London's social scene. His involvement with Joe seems to have been rather transient, where he provided funding for some of the initial distillery acquisitions that were later transferred into Associated Scottish Distilleries, but thereafter they went their separate ways.[263]

The second was Alexander Tolmie. A Canadian of Scottish descent, by profession Tolmie was an accountant, the son of John Tolmie, a Liberal politician who served as MP for Bruce County, Ontario in Canada's parliament for over 20 years. Alexander served as Canada's Exhibition Commissioner for the 1924-25 British Empire Exhibition in London, where the Canadian stand received great accolades and praise.[264, 265] It is likely Joe knew Tolmie from Canada, and it could even be that Joe's wife Eve made the introductions, as she had lived at Bruce Mines, Ontario, with her first husband, who was a mine engineer. As with Hatim Attari, Joe's partnership with Tolmie in the mid-1930s seems to have been very practical but relatively short-lived. Attari and Tolmie provided Joe with seed capital sufficient to get him started in the whisky distillery business, and make the three of them a quick and clean profit from the purchase and resale of some of the distilleries that were injected into Associated Scottish Distilleries (ASD). Once Joe was 'liquid' again financially in his own right, it seems he preferred to fund his projects himself and did not work with Attari and Tolmie on later investments.

When partnership negotiations between National Distillers and the DCL broke down at the end of 1934,[266] the opportunity opened for Joe to press National with his plan for a partnership to buy Scottish distilleries together. During 1935–36, Joe had extensive discussions with National to firm up his plan of approach, making multiple visits to North America, on at least one occasion in company with Alexander Tolmie.[267] Negotiations took some time, but, once Hobbs and Tolmie were back in the UK after their American visit in August 1936, things moved very fast, and Joe embarked on a buying spree of Scottish distillery assets that, within three years, would cement Joe Hobbs and National Distillers as major players in the Scottish whisky industry.

The first move was on Glenury Royal distillery in 1936. There had been a distillery on the Ury estate at Stonehaven, Kincardineshire, on the east coast of Scotland south of Aberdeen since 1825, two years after the 1823 Excise Act paved the way to legitimise whisky distilling in Scotland. Captain Robert Barclay, then the Laird of Ury, had built his own distillery, retaining ownership until 1858, when he sold it to William Ritchie, whose descendants ran it for the next 70 years or so.

In 1925, Glenury distillery had been put in mothballs due to the downturn in the industry. Serge Valentin in his profile of the distillery tells us the official explanation at the time was that the distillery was being closed for "spring cleaning and plant renewal,"[268] but the depression in the industry was severe and Glenury was to remain 'quiet' for most of the next 12 years, distilling at most for only a few weeks a year during the period 1927–29,[269] before closing fully in 1929 (some reports say 1931). The situation was so bad that at some stage in the following years the Ritchie family sold the distillery to local laird Lord Stonehaven (who had been Governor-General of Australia before returning home in 1930, and was a leading politician and Chairman of the Conservative Party).

It is likely Lord Stonehaven saw himself as a 'caretaker' owner of Glenury Royal, supporting an important local business and employer that had fallen on hard times. So when Joe, with backing from Hatim Attari, made contact proposing to buy the

John Baird, 3rd Laird of Ury and 1st Viscount Stonehaven.

distillery and reopen it, it was doubtless seen very positively by Stonehaven. The price agreed was a very modest £7,500 (2024: £665,000). Joe had ambitious plans for the distillery. Joe Hobbs and Hatim Attari formed a new company with the name of 'Glenury Distillery Company' to take the business forward.[270] Joe employed 30 men to refurbish the buildings, built new access roads and landscaped the site, and upgraded housing for distillery workers. Drawing on his engineering knowledge, Joe spent thousands re-equipping the distillery with modern plant, including a new wort refrigerator, the first time such technology had been used in a Scottish distillery. It reopened on 16th September 1937 with a capacity of 3,000 gallons a week, and a planned first-year production of 130,000 gallons. In 1938, the new owners invested further to convert to oil-powered stills, the first distillery in Scotland to do so, and further increased production to 4,000 gallons per week.[271]

Given the depressed economic situation, this investment and confidence would have been extremely welcome in the area, with the creation of 20 new permanent jobs to run the distillery, and renewed demand for local Mearns-grown barley, which were a significant boost to the nearby economy. Doubtless all this endeared Joe to the local community, which was reinforced when he and Eve went to live at the distillery, throwing themselves into local activities. Joe went on to make

Glenury Royal distillery, Stonehaven, in the early 1900s.

The distillery workforce in 1939, when ASD owned the distillery and Joe and Eve Hobbs lived on site.

Glenury Royal distillery closed down in 1985, and was subsequently demolished, with the site being redeveloped as a housing estate.

Today, none of the original buildings survive, although the bottom of the chimney stack (which can clearly be seen in the 1939 picture above) has been preserved with a plaque to commemorate the site's former use as a distillery.

Glenury the headquarters of ASD, and, ever experimenting, also set up a laboratory and made Glenury the centre of innovation for ASD, including installing a pair of miniature pot stills which were used for all kinds of experiments and improvement ideas.

Following this bold move for Glenury, the next distillery to come into the sights of Joe and his partners was Benromach, one of the smaller Scottish distilleries, located near the town of Forres, west of Elgin on Speyside. Benromach dates from 1898. It was built to a design by famous distillery architect Charles Doig by Duncan Macallum, owner of the Glen Nevis distillery in Campbeltown, and F.W. Brickman, a spirit merchant from Leith, with help from the energetic Alexander Edward (who also was an owner and instrumental in the development of a number of other Scottish distilleries including Benrinnes, Craigellachie, Oban and Aultmore). The site chosen was on land rented at the edge of Alexander Edward's estate at Sanquhar, near Forres. Brickman was caught up in the Pattison crash and went bankrupt in 1899, so, once constructed, the distillery was not immediately able to commence operations. In 1907, Macallum, working alone, managed to use the premises to distil some whisky sold under the name Forres, but only until 1910, when it was forced to close again until after WW1. The London-based firm of Harvey McNair & Co bought the distillery in 1911 but were unable to recommence operations before 1919, by which time John Joseph Calder obtained ownership and transferred it to an entity called the Benromach Distillery Ltd, who finally were able to reopen the distillery in 1920. Struggling through years of hard times, by the time Joe became interested in acquiring it the distillery had been mothballed since 1931.

Against this background, and flushed with success from Glenury, Joe approached the owners of Benromach with a proposal to take over the distillery, reopen it and operate it to make spirits targeting the US market. Joe started by negotiating

Benromach distillery, in the 1930s and today – regrettably now without its pagoda-roofed malt kiln.

a five-year lease to operate Benromach. It must have been made clear to the owners that Joe was working in close partnership with American interests – The Scotsman announced the news on the last day of 1936, where the new leaseholder was described as "an American firm…which trades under the name of J.W.Hobbs."[272]

Subsequently, Joe and his partners seem to have been

successful in persuading the Benromach Distillery Ltd shareholders to sell the whole distillery to Joe in 1938, who then soon afterwards transferred ownership to ASD. The new grouping now had a Speyside distillery to add to their east coast asset at Glenury.

Next in line for the Joe Hobbs treatment was Glenlochy distillery, which, together with the Ben Nevis and Nevis distilleries, was one of three distilleries operating at that time in the city of Fort William in the western Highlands. Whilst Glenlochy was said to be one of the best-equipped distilleries in the West of Scotland, like many others it had fallen on hard times and (as with Glenury and Benromach) had not been operated for some time – in this case since 1926. The trading situation was so poor that its previous owners had sold it for the paltry sum of £850 to Thomas L. Rankin, of Rankin Bros., general contractors from Chryston in Lanarkshire, towards the end of 1934. The original cost of building and equipping the distillery back in 1901 was around £15,000, giving an indication of the poor state of the industry when Joe went on the offensive to buy up distilleries. Rankin was in the business of buying properties for demolition, having recently transacted a similar operation on the Gartloch distillery in Chryston, which probably also contributed to the very low price of the sale, with the seller likely assuming the distillery and equipment would be scrapped.[273] However, Rankin said he had not made a decision about the future of Glenlochy, and might try to sell it as an operational distillery. In 1935, Rankin almost sold Glenlochy to British Aluminium Company, who wanted to use the site as part of their plans to develop water power in the area, but opposition from local people to the plans meant that the deal did not go through. This cleared the way for Joe to acquire the property for £3,500 in 1937. Although this was still a decent profit for Rankin, it was less than a quarter of what the distillery had cost

Glenlochy Distillery today, now converted to flats.

to build and a pitifully small amount to pay for a well-equipped distillery – £3,500 in 1937 equates to less than £300,000 at 2024 prices.[274]

Following the acquisition, Joe made plans to restart production. The Daily Record carried news that workmen had been deployed to renovate Glenlochy and install new plant, aiming for an early start to distilling operations. The distillery was said to have been idle for 10 years.[275] In a burst of economic activity that must have been very encouraging for the civic leaders in Fort William, in March 1937 the town council was informed of plans by the British Aluminium Company to build 150 new houses at their plant to the east of the town, and also that the Glenlochy Distillery Company was requesting a supply of 40,000 gallons of water a week to restart distillery operations. The Burgh Surveyor was quoted as advising that the water catchment area had ample capability to meet the requirement, but that additional filters would be needed.[276] Joe soon had the distillery up and running again, where its renewed output was entirely used to contribute to blends which especially were targeted towards the US market.

In 1937, Bruichladdich on the isle of Islay off Scotland's west coast was the next distillery targeted by Joe Hobbs and his partners. Bruichladdich was yet another distillery that had fallen on hard times. It had not been operational since 1929, and although production recommenced in 1935, when William Harvey, one of three brothers who had founded the distillery back in 1881, passed away in 1936, the other members of the Harvey family seemed to prefer to sell out rather than battle on. This enabled Joe, in partnership with both Hatim Attari and Alexander Tolmie, to acquire the distillery for only £8,000 (2024: £680,000). While it may look somewhat questionable today, Hobbs, Attari and Tolmie were very quickly able to resell Bruichladdich on to ASD a short time later for £23,000, nearly three times what they had paid for it, netting the trio a profit of £15,000 (over £1.25m today!) in just a few months.[277]

In common with the earlier acquisitions, ASD (in which National Distillers/T&M were part owners) immediately invested to refurbish Bruichladdich in 1938. This indicates ASD knew what they were paying for and why, and were keen to press on and get the distillery back into operation. In those days, the peaty whiskies made by the distilleries on Islay were valued more for the powerful flavour contribution they could make to a good blend rather than for sale as a single malt in their own right, and it was in order to secure stocks of peated whisky for production of their own blends that ASD acquired Bruichladdich. This was part of a carefully considered strategic plan orchestrated by Joe to enable ASD to obtain control of all the different components required to make their own blends without having to rely on purchasing from other suppliers, who were potential competitors.

So, in just over a year, from October 1936 to the end of 1937, Joe and his partners had secured operational control of no fewer than four distilleries. But he was far from finished, and as the year turned to 1938, and against a backdrop of rapidly increasing demand for the whisky industry overall, Joe continued on the acquisition trail. The next purchase was Fettercairn, another distillery in the Mearns district of north-east Scotland.

One of Scotland's older distilleries, dating from 1824, Fettercairn was founded by Sir Alexander Ramsey, who owned the Fasque Estate on which Fettercairn is situated, 25 miles south-west of Aberdeen, in an area long used by illicit distillers and smugglers. Soon after the 1823 Excise Act opened the way to legalised distilling in the U.K., Ramsey converted a former corn mill at Nethermill on the outskirts of Fettercairn village and agreed a tenancy with James Stewart (who had a reputation for producing high-quality illicit spirit) to lease and operate it. When circumstances forced Ramsey to sell the Fasque Estate in 1829 (for £80,000), the new owner was John Gladstone, a Scottish merchant who had made his fortune in Liverpool. The distillery and estate was owned for a long time by the Gladstone family,[ae]

[ae] John's second son, William Ewart Gladstone, was one of Britain's longest-serving prime ministers. As Prime Minister, Gladstone did a lot for the whisky industry, repealing taxes on malt and on the Angel's Share, and allowing retail of whisky in bottles (not just in casks).

and the distillery overall fared well through the 19th century, especially when John Gladstone's son William Ewart Gladstone served 4 terms as British Prime Minister. A disastrous fire in 1888 destroyed half of the buildings and forced closure for 2 years. After rebuilding, Fettercairn was in demand during the 1890s boom years as an ingredient for famous blends, especially Johnnie Walker and Buchanans. However, it struggled after the Pattison crash at the end of the 19th century and through WW1, and was forced to close for 13 years from 1926, during which time thought was given to demolishing it.

Joe had expressed an interest in acquiring the Fettercairn distillery as early as October 1936 at the start of his distillery buying spree, when he approached James Mann, the Fasque Estate factor, with a proposal to purchase the distillery, but it took more than two years for the sale to be confirmed and completed. Fettercairn was not far from Glenury Royal, which ASD already had under their belt, and Joe apparently informed Mann he wished to buy "another one in this vicinity".[278] The negotiations progressed very slowly – probably because Joe was playing 'hardball' in offering a very low price –and it was not until 27th January 1938 that Mann wrote to Joe offering the distillery for £5,000 (2024: £420,000). Joe accepted, and the sale was eventually concluded, bringing to an end more than 100 years of Gladstone family ownership of the distillery.

As with all the previous acquisitions, Joe and his partners had acquired a distillery which had been in mothballs for years, and was successfully purchased at a rock-bottom price. The new owners had ambitious plans and were ready to invest to modernise and upgrade their new asset. At Fettercairn, The Scotsman was among a number of newspapers carrying stories in March 1938 that work to install new plant would begin before the end of March, so that distillation could recommence at the start of the next distilling season in September. Fifteen

Fettercairn distillery as it looked in the late 1930s shortly prior to Joe Hobbs' renovations.

How Fettercairn looks today, from close to the same spot.

men would be employed to operate the distillery, and additional labour contracted to renovate the buildings.[279, 280] In practice, however, the renovations at Fettercairn were more like a complete rebuilding, the Aberdeen Press and Journal reporting that "Only the shell of the building will... remain,"[281] while the interiors would all be modernised and new plant and equipment installed sufficient to produce 3,000 gallons of spirit a week. Work was given to over 100 men during the reconstruction, which was completed so that the distillery could recommence production in November 1938, having been idle since 1926.

As with the other acquisitions, the reinvestment would have been extremely welcome to communities in the area after the hardships of the long depression years, and were a significant boost to the local economy. In the same article, it was also reported that "Associated Scottish Distillers have given a pledge to farmers in the Mearns that, as far as possible, Scots barley will be used for malting. This means that farmers as well as distillery workers will benefit from the resumption at Fettercairn". The article also remarked on the rapidly improving industry conditions generally, and that access to sufficient warehousing capacity was likely to be the next problem for the reopening distilleries.[282]

The final piece in the jigsaw, and critical to the plan to supply high-quality blended whiskies for the North American market, was the acquisition of some grain distilling capacity. Having acquired five malt distilleries, Joe and his partners now needed to secure supplies of grain whiskies for their blends, so that they would not have to rely on the industry majors that dominated grain whisky production, and who were ASD's main competitors. The approach taken was very consistent with the model the partners had executed so well with their previous acquisitions. The target this time was Hillside, located on Kinnaber Road, Montrose, not far from Glenury and Fettercairn. It had originally been a flax mill and had also operated as a factory to produce bleach, but, with the late 1890s whisky boom, Dundee wine merchant James Isles converted it into a distillery in 1897 under the name Highland Esk. Isles passed it on to his business partner, the wonderfully named Septimus Parsonage, but only for a couple of years before Parsonage hit cash flow problems and J.F. Caille Heddle took over and renamed it North Esk in 1899. At this time, it was one of the largest distilleries in Scotland. Silent during WW1 it then suffered a fire, and, although the firm of Thomas Bernard saw enough potential to acquire it in 1919, when they reopened it was only for use as a maltings, with no distilling having taken place for nearly 20 years by the time Joe closed in.

In the late summer of 1938, a number of local newspapers reported with some excitement that ASD had successfully acquired the Hillside distillery. ASD moved quickly to re-equip Hillside and put it back into operation. The Brechin Advertiser reported that the buildings were to be converted to a grain distillery employing about 30 workers. The Montrose Review said that considerable alterations would be made to the premises and that the new machinery and equipment required for operation had already been ordered.[283, 284, 285]

It was not reported what price was paid for Hillside; however, on this occasion it seems the distillery was acquired from Bernards directly by ASD, unlike other acquisitions, which were bought initially by Joe (sometimes in partnership with Attari and Tolmie) before selling them on to ASD at a significantly higher price.

On 17th October 1938, ASD reopened Hillside distillery maltings for the production of malted barley, with a first new consignment of 520 tons of barley arriving from Denmark two days later. The distillery announced that after recommencing operations in the maltings they intended to move on to equip the distillery for production of pure grain whisky, expected to be completed in June 1939. One hundred men were to be employed on the construction, and, once completed, 40–50 permanent staff would be employed to operate it.[286] The Aberdeen Evening Express reported that ASD "are responsible for a big new venture" at Hillside, generating substantial employment in a depressed part of the country.[287, 288] Local newspapers reported the facility would be renamed Montrose Distillery.[289]

At that time, consumption of Scotch whisky as a single malt was comparatively rare, at least outside the regions of production in Scotland. By far the majority of whisky consumed in the UK

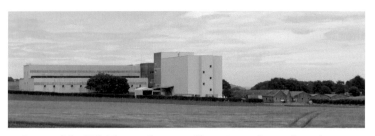

Some of the Hillside warehouses still survive today and can be seen on the right of the photograph as part of Boortmalt's modern Glenesk maltings facility.

and overseas was blended, a combination of different types of single malt whiskies made in small batches using traditional pot stills (usually making up 30–40% of the blend) mixed together with cheaper grain whiskies, produced in Coffey or continuous stills (typically comprising the majority 60–70% of the blend). The advantage of grain whisky production was that it could be done at larger scale, using cheaper raw ingredients, and therefore at considerably lower cost than production of single malts. Grain whisky production is an industrial process, producing far greater quantities than the 'small batch' process required for malt whisky production.

However, then as now, there are relatively few large grain distilleries in existence. Joe and his partners seemed concerned whether they would be able to secure adequate supplies of grain whiskies (and at attractive prices) from the established grain distilleries, most if not all of whom would be competitors to National Distillers and ASD. The innovative solution was to use one of the portfolio of distilleries ASD was acquiring and convert it to produce their own grain whiskies, thereby securing supplies to fuel their own blends, without having to rely on buying in from outside. This line of thinking was to become a common theme with Joe (he took the same approach when he subsequently purchased Ben Nevis and Lochside distilleries after WW2). Joe's willingness to compete with and take on the industry majors was also evident later when he took a leading role in the formation of the Independent Scotch Whisky Association in the early 1950s.[af]

Back in Montrose during the months immediately prior to WW2, the conversion work at Hillside/Montrose was held up by a dispute with the council over waste water, an issue which was to become a recurring problem for Joe's attempts to revive mothballed distilleries after the war. ASD wanted to discharge the distillery waste water into the local sewage system. However, the local Fishery Board had written to ASD warning them not to discharge effluent water into the nearby River North Esk. Meanwhile the District Council were worried that the sewage system in the Hillside area was already overloaded and prone to overspill, whilst some councillors were concerned about the health effects if there were chemicals in the waste water. ASD advised they were planning to invest £50,000 in the new plant (2024: £4.0m), but needed council approval to discharge 30,000 gallons of waste water into the sewage system three times per week to allow their development to go ahead.[290]

The council were conflicted – they wanted the investment, new jobs and worker housing ASD were promising, but were concerned that the Fishery Board were against it, and some

---

af   It is also interesting to speculate whether Joe's thinking and practice at Hillside/Montrose, Ben Nevis, and later on at Lochside to produce malt and grain whiskies within the same distillery was influential on other distillers subsequently. For example, the Japanese distilling giant Nikka (part of the Asahi brewing group) were a long-time customer of whiskies bought in bulk from Ben Nevis and went on to acquire the distillery after Joe's death. In Japan they set up and operated their distillery at Miyagikyo for both malt and grain production, very much along the same lines as Joe had practised at Ben Nevis, as well as experimenting with distilling malted barley in continuous stills.

members, worried about what was in the water, thought that a report should be obtained from the Board of Health. ASD confirmed that no chemicals were involved, it was normal water, only with a low oxygen content. There was a suggestion Joe might have to wait until a whole new sewage system connecting the north part of Montrose town, the Montrose aerodrome and Hillside could be constructed, but a majority on the council did not want to lose ASD's investment in Hillside waiting for an uncertain plan that could take years and might not even happen at all. Eventually, Hillside's request to discharge effluent water into the local drainage system was approved.[291]

With the sewage issue resolved, the rebuilding work was quickly progressed, and ASD were able to commence operations in September 1939.[292]

With the acquisition of Hillside, Joe and his partners brought to a conclusion an extraordinary period of expansion, during which five malt whisky distilleries and one grain whisky distillery had been bought up at bargain basement prices, re-equipped and modernised into a formidable portfolio. In order to manage all these acquisitions, Joe together with National Distillers undertook some administrative housekeeping.

Firstly, on 25th June 1938, Joe registered a new company, Associated Scottish Distilleries Ltd (ASD), with an initial share capital of £100, and a registered address of 33A Gordon Street, Glasgow.[293] ASD was owned jointly by Joe Hobbs and Train & McIntyre, who were in turn owned by Seton Porter's National Distillers Products Corporation.

ASD was set up to be the entity within T&M that owned all the distilleries that Joe had been acquiring, and would be used as the distillery operating arm of National Distillers Scottish businesses. So once Joe had set up the new entity, during the remainder of 1938, all six distilleries that had been acquired since the end of 1936 were transferred into ASD. As a result, before the

33 Gordon Street, Glasgow, was the registered office of Associated Scottish Distilleries when Joe Hobbs set it up in June 1938.

end of the year in 1938, all of these acquisitions were consolidated under the direct ownership of ASD, transforming it into one of the major players in the Scottish whisky industry – the second-largest distillery grouping after the Distillers Company Limited (DCL), who were the clear industry leaders. ASD now owned six distilleries: Glenury Royal, Benromach, Glenlochy, Bruichladdich, Fettercairn and Hillside/Montrose. With this combination, T&M had secured access to reliable supplies of whisky for their blends, and covered all the bases in terms of flavour combinations required to make a good blend, having distilleries in the Western Highlands, Eastern Highlands, Speyside and on Islay, together with their own source of grain whisky.

There was one final piece in the jigsaw: Strathdee, located on the Great Western Road, in Aberdeen had been built in 1821 and operated for almost a century before Robertson & Co (one of the predecessor companies of another industry giant, Edrington, subsequently owners of Macallan and Highland Park) bought it in 1920. Prior to Joe's involvement, T&M had purchased Strathdee in 1925, and, although spirit was no longer distilled at the site, it continued to function as a bonded warehousing facility. With the rapid expansion of production at this time, storage of the finished whisky became a big bottleneck for ASD. Once produced and put in barrels, the new make spirit needed to mature for a minimum of three years before it could be sold as whisky, and for a minimum of four years if it was to be sold to the USA. Bonded warehouse capacity, where the maturing whisky could be stored under customs supervision without having to pay duty to the government until it was ready to be bottled and sold, was required to provide additional space to store the thousands of casks produced by ASD's six distilleries. Strathdee provided very valuable storage space to mature the rising output of the ASD distilleries. In 1938, Strathdee was also transferred into ASD, so that all of the 'operating' parts of National Distillers and T&M's businesses were held together in one legal entity and under one management.

The Strathdee site today, now converted into flats.

What this all provided in combination was an outstanding portfolio of whisky-producing facilities, giving T&M the ability to use 'in-house' stocks to provide the backbone of quality blended whiskies. It was the common practice of distillers in Scotland (perhaps at that time more so than today) for the makers of blended whisky to trade casks so as to secure the exact combination of ages and flavour profiles to meet the 'recipe' for specific blends. Whilst T&M's strong footprint of owned distilleries gave them all the main flavour constituents from distilleries around Scotland necessary to make quality blended whiskies, T&M's trading team would also have been able to trade casks of their single malts and grains with other producers, to obtain supplies of exactly the whiskies required for specific recipes of blended whisky. This meant T&M were enviably positioned to exploit booming North American demand for blended Scotch, which they aimed to target using their two main brands of blended whisky, 'Old Angus' and 'Train's Grey Label'. T&M's unique position is epitomised by an advertisement campaign run in the autumn of 1939 advertising their 'Old Angus' blended whisky, which demonstrated T&M's product offering with a map showing all seven of the ASD distilleries under ownership and direction of Train & McIntyre. The supporting script stresses the advantages that National Distillers now had through being able to control its supplies of whisky and provide assurance against any interruption in supply.[ag]

---

ag T&M had some other Scotch whisky businesses and assets in addition, which were run separately from ASD, comprising their shareholdings in North British grain distillery in Edinburgh, Ardgowan distillery at Greenock (by then only in operation to make industrial alcohol and subsequently almost totally destroyed in the blitz of 7th May 1941), plus the Campbell and Clark blending and bottling business. T&M's previous shareholding in West Highland Malt Distilleries Ltd, a consortium led by Robertson and Baxter, and owner of 5 distilleries in Campbeltown, had already been eliminated with the closure of all 5 distilleries during the period of massive industry over capacity in the 1920s.

National Distillers advertisement for Old Angus blended whisky in the USA, 1939.

However, timing is everything, and the well-thought-through and well-executed plans developed and implemented by Joe Hobbs were unfortunately to be thwarted by events on a bigger stage. Joe had positioned ASD with all the components it needed to produce high-quality blended Scotch whisky to meet the strong growth in demand in the North American markets. However, the onset of WW2 (Great Britain declared war on

Germany on 1st September 1939) totally undermined Joe and National's plans, without which they could quite conceivably have gone on to be a major player in the whisky industry, both in Scotland and in North America, for years to come.

Despite having put so much effort into building up this impressive portfolio of whisky distilleries, Joe decided at this time to sell his entire shareholding in the company back to T&M. With the onset of war, Joe realised the whisky industry would be severely disrupted and subject to government regulation and restrictions for years to come, and consequently the ambitious plans he and National Distillers had evolved for the ASD portfolio would be impossible to achieve. In a post-war interview with The Liverpool Echo, Joe was quoted as saying "It looked as if it was going to be a 10-year war." Moreover, with new opportunities opening up for some of his other business interests, it is likely that Joe saw a chance to cash in his shares with ASD and realise a substantial profit, before the impact from the war devalued them too much, and refocus his attention on new activities that had greater short-term potential.

Certainly, Joe did very well out of these transactions. In 1940, he sold his shares in ASD back to T&M and National Distillers for £38,000 in cash (2024: £2.7m), plus an option to buy whisky stocks for £250,000 (2024: £17.5m). As the founder of ASD, Joe had a major shareholding, for which his initial investment was very modest (the original share capital was only £100), so a large proportion of the proceeds from the sale of his shares in 1940 would have been profit. There were also the profits he had taken (some of which had been shared at least in part with Hatim Attari and Alexander Tolmie) from the acquisition and resale of the distilleries that were injected into ASD, where he very broadly doubled his money from £24,000 invested to £50,000 returned, a gain for Joe in excess of £2m in current terms (see Table 1).

Table 1: Joe Hobbs' profits from his involvement in Associated Scottish Distilleries

	1. Profits from Purchase and Re-sale of ASD Distilleries						
	Distillery	Bought	Price	Sold	Price	Gain	Notes
1	Glenury Royal	1936	£7,500	1938	£18,500	£11,000	With Hatim Attari
2	Benromach	1936	?	1938	?	£0	Leased in 1936, subsequently purchased.
3	Glenlochy	1937	£3,500	1938	£3,500	£0	With Hatim Attari
4	Bruichladdich	1937	£8,000	1938	£23,000	£15,000	With Hatim Attari and Alexander Tolmie
5	Hillside/Glenesk	1938	?	1938	?	£0	Purchased by ASD directly
6	Fettercairn	1938	£5,000	1938	£5,000	£0	Assumed re-sold at least at same level as purchase price
	Total		£24,000		£50,000	£26,000	£26,000 in 1938 is worth £2.2m at 2024 prices
	2. Purchase and Re-sale of Shares in ASD						
	Purchase and sale of ASD shares	1938	£100	1940	£38,000	£37,900	£37,900 in 1938 is worth £3.2m at 2024 prices
	3. Gross Profit from Involvement in ASD:						
	Total Gain		£24,100		£88,000	£63,900	Equivalent to £5.4m at 2024 prices

In combination, and estimating conservatively, Joe made around £5m profit from his direct involvement in ASD (calculated at 2024 price levels). Given he certainly also made money from his whisky trading activities, in addition, it is clear that in the years after returning to the UK, Joe very successfully rebuilt the fortune he had lost with the collapse of his businesses in Canada a decade earlier.

It is interesting to speculate about the ethics of Joe's buying and selling of the distilleries that were injected into ASD, and his subsequent sale of shares in ASD back to National Distillers/ T&M. Joe made substantial profits from buying e.g. Glenury Royal and Bruichladdich, and very soon afterwards 'flipping' them to ASD for a much higher price. Today, this might look like a dubious practice. However, the deals were freely entered into by National/T&M, who were led by experienced businessmen, so it is very probable that Seton Porter and the management of National Distillers felt they were paying a fair price for the distillery assets they were acquiring. Certainly, the prices paid by T&M for the distilleries Joe acquired for them were very low in historic terms, and National probably calculated that Joe was entitled to earn a decent reward for the outstanding work he had done to identify, negotiate and conclude acquisition of an impressive industry-leading portfolio of distilleries in less than three years, and for all the time and effort he put into managing their refurbishment and putting them all back into production. National could not have achieved this without Joe's vision, contacts, experience and drive. The sale of Joe's shares meant the company he had started (ASD) now became a fully owned subsidiary of Train & McIntyre. In this regard, it is also conceivable that National were taking a longer-term view, calculating that they would be better off acquiring Joe's stake in ASD at a time when the value of the shares was relatively low because of the war uncertainty, and that this would position

National to reap a bigger reward after the war was over, when they would be 100% in control of the enterprise. A sale always requires agreement between a buyer and a seller, and it is safe to conclude that both parties got something they wanted from this transaction.

The fact that the deal also included an option for Joe to buy whisky stocks valued at a very substantial £250,000 (more than £17.5m today) certainly implies both that the parties were comfortable in principle to continue to work together in future, and also that Joe was not intending to sever all connections with the whisky industry, even if with the onset of war he saw opportunities in other areas of business as a more attractive focus for his undoubted energy and skills. Indeed, almost immediately there was evidence of Joe's continued interest in the whisky business when he made an unsuccessful attempt to negotiate the lease of Kinnaber Mills near Montrose for use as a distillery, although it is not impossible that this initiative was started on behalf of ASD before Joe sold his shares and stepped back from management of the company. And it would not be very long – only 1944 – before Joe took further substantial steps in the whisky industry, with T&M once again playing a significant role buying the Nevis/Lochaber distillery from him. All this indicates the partners parted company on good terms and Joe's efforts to build ASD created substantial value for National Distillers and T&M.

Joe and Eve were very active in the community in and around Stonehaven during the ASD period. The couple lived at Glenury House, adjacent to the distillery, and were many times mentioned in the local papers engaged in shooting with Lord Stonehaven,[ah] handing out prizes at flower shows, organising the

---

ah   Joe formed a close relationship with Lord Stonehaven, whose agreement to sell him Glenury Royal was the first important step in the whole ASD adventure. Lord Stonehaven died in 1941, and unfortunately his home

parish sale, holding a dance attended by over 300 participants at the Glenury grain loft, and many other activities. Even though they had only been in the area a few years, the couple were seen to have contributed a great deal to the community when Joe left in mid-1940 after resigning from ASD, while Eve continued to live for some while longer at Glenury. Among others, the Brechin Advertiser commended them both for "much excellent work (done) in the county".[295]

Nevertheless, with the sale of ASD in 1940, Joe's period of activity in Stonehaven came to an end, and, with the onset of WW2 dramatically changing the economic environment, Joe moved south to Leicester in the English Midlands to address his next business opportunity, and once again 'do his bit' for his country in time of war.

Ury House had to be sold in 1946 to pay the death duties. The house subsequently fell into ruin, although today is happily being restored as part of a large housing and leisure development, including a new golf course designed by Jack Nicklaus.

8

Duty Calls Again

Joe's extraordinary burst of activity in the late 1930s working with National Distillers of America had been derailed by forces even someone as dynamic and determined as Joe Hobbs could not control. The onset of the Second World War forced a re-think and, ever the pragmatist, Joe moved quickly and unemotionally to sell his stake in ASD and turn his focus to activities more appropriate to the radically altered world situation. Having already served his country with distinction as a young airman during WW1, Joe was able to use his accumulated knowledge and expertise in a very different, but arguably even more valuable, way during the second global conflict.

Despite the frantic pace of ASD's expansion in the whisky business, Joe still somehow found time in the late 1930s to get involved in a new and totally unrelated business venture that was to have great importance for the war effort. The core of Joe's business focus during WW2 was around a company he owned called Oxy Ferrolene Ltd, based in Leicester. Through Oxy Ferrolene, Joe developed and marketed technologies in welding and cutting metals that were highly valuable to war time Britain's needs.

Joe had first registered Oxy Ferrolene as a company in 1934, in the days after his return to the UK when he was exploring new business opportunities to rebuild his career after his near bankruptcy in Canada. The technology which Oxy Ferrolene exploited had started to be developed in the mid-1930s, as part of a wider trend of developing the industrial use of gases. Gas was increasingly being used as a clean fuel source for industry, demonstrating many advantages over coal and oil in powering furnaces, in particular because gas enabled more precise control of heat and maintenance of exact temperatures in a number of industrial processes. Better understanding of the combustion process had enabled improved burner technology, and addition of secondary air supplies contributed to greater economy. These advances opened up a wide range of new applications both in traditional heavy industries like ship building and the metal trades, but also in emerging applications like the automobile, aircraft and electrical industries.

The area Joe focused on was the use of gas as a fuel for welding and cutting metals. The established fuel used in metal welding and cutting torches was compressed oxy-acetylene gas in cylinders. However, it had been discovered that adding certain types of liquids to normal coal gas (the gas which at that time was in common use to power domestic ovens and gas ring hobs for cooking) could provide a better alternative than acetylene as a fuel for industrial and military applications. Joe's company developed a liquid called 'Ferrolene', which when added to coal gas in a torch or burner lowered the temperature at which the torch ignited, and also proved able to cut metal faster and more effectively. The coal gas and Ferrolene combination was also considerably more economic, costing only around half of what it took to produce acetylene. In addition, when used in cutting (rather than welding) mode, torches powered with Ferrolene and coal gas improved the cutting action, enabling 'cleaner' and more precise cuts, and less metal wastage.

Articles in the trade and general press from 1935[296, 297] demonstrate that the base technology behind this was understood and increasingly being employed in practice. Joe set up the small Oxy Ferrolene Ltd company, at Oadby near Leicester in the English Midlands, a location Joe thought ideal for its central location and ability to supply all the main industrial centres in the UK quickly and cost effectively. When the onset of WW2 put an end to Joe's whisky making ambitions with Associated Scottish Distilleries, Joe was quick to pivot his attentions to Oxy Ferrolene's potential to assist the war effort. He spent most of the war years developing Oxy Ferrolene for the manufacture and supply of practical applications of 'Ferrolene' and 'Ferrogas' for use in welding torches and burners. Joe's company had taken out its first patents in October 1939, for designs to improve the torch apparatus for burning and applying gaseous fuels in welding, but under Joe's active leadership a wide range of enhancements, improvements and new patents followed over the succeeding years.

Whilst the technology had considerable general potential for application in a broad range of industries, as usual with Joe, timing was everything, and developments in the wider world were to give a specific boost to Ferrolene's importance.[298] In the spring of 1940, the Germans had invaded Norway, whose fall during the second quarter of the year meant that after June 1940 the UK unexpectedly lost access to three factories which were its main sources for the supply of calcium carbide. Calcium carbide was used in production of fertilisers and other industrial processes, but was also the key component used to manufacture acetylene, which (in a properly designed torch) could be burned at a very high temperature (>3,000 degrees Celsius). As a consequence, oxy-acetylene torches had become vitally important as the main method for welding and cutting metals, especially steel. Britain had long been an investor in, and buyer of, carbide manufactured in Norway, especially from the Odda factory in western Norway, which had been the largest carbide plant in the world in the years after WW1. With the German occupation, Britain's supply was abruptly cut off.

With the loss of supply from Norway, and war raging across Europe, the UK's only viable alternative source of calcium carbide was the United States. With burgeoning wartime demand, the UK needed 200,000 tons of calcium carbide a year. Transporting it from the USA was dangerous as it is highly inflammable, and subject to attack and disruption by German U-boats across the Atlantic Ocean. The U-boats caused havoc with Britain's supply chains of vital imports, especially in the early years of the war, on a scale which threatened the country's ability to sustain the war effort. In total during WW2, more than 3,500 Allied merchant ships were sunk, the vast majority on the Atlantic.[299] After the war, Churchill wrote: "The only thing that really frightened me during the war was the U-boat peril. I was even more anxious about this battle than I had been about the glorious air fight called the 'Battle of Britain.'"[300]

The freighter Konprinsen after being hit by a torpedo from German U-boat U432 whilst carrying a cargo of calcium carbide from the USA to the UK in June 1942.

Joe knew all about calcium carbide and acetylene from his youth growing up in Sault Ste Marie in Canada, where his employer F.H. Clergue's Consolidated Lake Superior Corporation provided the power which drove the Union Carbide company factory producing calcium carbide. Joe worked on the engineering team for Lake Superior Corp. for three years from 1909, at the same time as the Union Carbide plant on the US side of the town was pioneering new experimental Horry furnaces, which made commercial calcium carbide and acetylene production profitable on a large scale for the first time. In addition, Joe's brother-in-law Harry Bush (the older brother of Joe's first wife Mabel Bush) was a foreman at the Union Carbide plant. The knowledge he acquired during this time, coupled with Joe's technical mindset and lifelong talent for understanding how to apply engineering and scientific principles to drive improvements in industry, enabled Joe to see the potential to use Ferrolene to provide a practical alternative to acetylene in welding and cutting metals, and in the process

Horry furnaces in use to make calcium carbide by Lake Superior Carbide Company, Sault Ste Marie.

help solve Britain's wartime problem obtaining reliable supplies of calcium carbide.

Evidence that Joe took some of his inspiration at this time from youthful memories of Sault Ste Marie is supported by his nephew Rowly Wilkes' memoir of his uncle's time with Oxy Ferrolene during WW2. Rowly recalled that Joe told him he had rented a school house (there was a school right across the road from the Oxy Ferrolene headquarters and factory at Oadby, Leicester) and hired a team of engineers and scientists to 'hot house' ways to improve the application of Ferrolene for welding and cutting of metals. Joe provided the team with food and board, and asked them to stay in the school house, working intensively without external distractions until they had come up with new applications. In this way, Joe was able to develop new solutions which enabled welding and repair of steel underwater, which was especially valuable in wartime, and new designs for gas nozzles and burner torches. Interestingly, this is exactly how F.H. Clergue was said to have worked when he drove his Lake Superior Corporation through its extraordinary and rapid expansion in the 1890s. Clergue put together teams of scientists and engineers and set them to work intensively to develop new ways of making first mechanical, and then chemical, paper pulp; to recover sulphur from nickel ore refining; and to produce new alloys of nickel and steel. Clergue's methods were instrumental to Lake Superior Corp's phenomenal expansion and success, and were apocryphal in Sault Ste Marie, and Joe would certainly have known of them.

When Joe took over the Leicester premises that became Oxy Ferrolene's home in the spring of 1940, they were – in the words of Joe's grandson Joseph Peter – "defunct". But, with the changed situation caused by Nazi Germany's invasion of Norway, Joe saw the huge potential of the business. He recruited a team who worked with him to develop the technology which could easily be adopted and used in a wide variety of industrial applications, substantially contributing to the war effort. Joe's formula for "Ferrogas" was mixed with normal coal gas and supplied via a compressor to burning nozzles to cut and weld metal. The nozzles were designed also to draw in air so that oxygen from the atmosphere improved their burning efficiency. Joe's team did tests and gave presentations which showed their burners could cut through a six-inch diameter steel bar in only four seconds, which (with due regard for wartime security concerns) Joe made sure was widely publicised, including in national newspapers like the Daily Express.[301]

In addition to saving the import of large quantities of hard-to-obtain and dangerous-to-transport calcium carbide, Joe's technology contributed to genuine improvements in cutting and welding of steel, aluminium and other metals for industrial processes. Cutting speeds 15% faster than with traditional acetylene burners were reported,[302] and fuel efficiency was higher by over 30%.[303] A subsidiary benefit was that use of thousands of tons of steel needed to make heavy cylinders to contain pressurised acetylene gas could be avoided. Joe's team manufactured and distributed a simple and easy-to-use apparatus to deploy his technology in industrial premises "consisting of a storage tank for Ferrolene, a compressor...a mixer, and [connector to] a supply of coal gas. After compression...the gas is passed through the mixing device to the cutting appliances."[304] Oxy Ferrolene made no charge to supply the equipment and plant, but just earned their income from the sale of Ferrogas paid for on a consumption basis.

Joe used his naval and military connections to get his technology approved by the Ministry of Aircraft Production, who endorsed its application for cutting and welding aluminium and steel in aircraft factories. Whilst the exact formula of Ferrolene was kept secret during the war years, the technology was rapidly exploited with full support from the government, and by 1943 Oxy Ferrolene's equipment was in use in over 200 war factories across the UK.[305] The technology was also broadly applied in a number of more general applications for cutting, welding and recycling steel and other metals, in a wide variety of industries.[306] By the spring of 1944, Joe wrote to his friend A.S. Seggie in Aberdeen, advising him "The business we are engaged in has extended greatly since we took it over in 1940, and we are rendering good service to the nation with our gas flame cutting process, which is a substitute for imported carbide, acetylene, etc."[307]

Joe worked closely with his son Joe Junior in the development of Oxy Ferrolene Ltd, and running the company was to become a central part of Joe Junior's business career for the rest of his life. Joe Junior had come to the UK from Vancouver in May 1937 as an 18-year-old student to complete his education in Aberdeen, when Joe and Eve were living at nearby Glenury in Stonehaven during Joe's ASD days. He later spent time at ASD's Fettercairn distillery at Laurencekirk, working as a chemist. However, from the early 1940s, he relocated to Leicester and lived in a flat above the Oxy Ferrolene offices. Working closely together, Joe and Joe Junior put continued effort into researching and developing their technology during the early years of WW2, enabling them to file a string of new patents in 1943, for example for fuel gas mixing, body belts to be used by welders, and welding torch burner nozzle designs. They also experimented with using welding torches to apply powdered and coloured metals to a surface.[308] The technology and patents they developed continued to support Oxy Ferrolene's commercial success for many years after the War.

As a successful entrepreneur, Joe doubtless appreciated how important it was to invest time and effort to improve the usefulness and applications of the technology he owned.

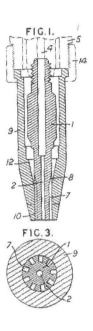

One of Joe Hobbs' patents for Oxy Ferrolene during WW2. This one was for improvements in nozzles for metal-cutting torches.

But his own inclination for constant experimentation and trying new things was definitely also a factor. Eve was quoted at the time as saying "My husband…has a kink for experiments. He is forever trying out something new, learning from his failures, and starting afresh."[309] Taking out the patents was a sensible step to ensure Joe could control development of technology that had considerable practical application, but during the war years Joe did not exploit the situation for his own ends, working closely with the authorities, and receiving strong government support. Years later, Joe's nephew Rowly Wilkes said that Joe licensed the marketing and application of Ferrolene technology to the War Ministry for just £1, so that it could be used to the maximum extent possible to support the war effort[310] (although obviously Joe's firm benefitted directly from sales of the product).

Typically for Joe, his strategic vision had enabled him to identify a specific need or opportunity, and then move boldly and quickly to exploit it and develop something of great value. Acetylene technology was a relatively obscure aspect of industrial production, but Joe's unique experience and knowledge, coupled with his entrepreneurial capabilities, put him in a position to contribute significantly to his country's strategic need in wartime by providing a solution to the critical shortage of carbide. Use of Ferrolene was estimated to save a shipload of priority imports to the UK every month, extremely valuable amidst constant German submarine attacks.

WW2-era photos of the Oxy Ferrolene factory at Oadby, Leicestershire.

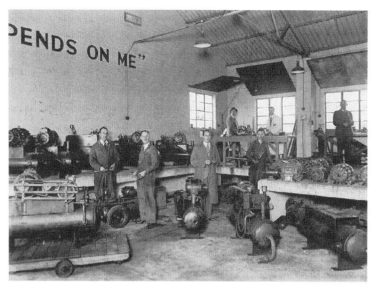

Operating the Gaz compressors (Joe Junior standing in the centre of the picture), overlooked by the wartime "It All Depends on Me" slogan.

Manufacturing brass nozzles using lathes.

Joe played an active dual role in Oxy Ferrolene's success. As the MD of the company, he saw the 'big picture' opportunity for Ferrolene and his company's welding and cutting equipment in the wartime situation, and had the scientific mind and practical engineering training to understand the technology his company was developing, as well as the contacts in the military to explain their value and get official backing for what he was doing. But he was also directly involved with product development, putting effort into hiring a small team of scientists and engineers to work under his direct supervision, and it was this process that enabled Oxy Ferrolene to file a string of successful new product patents. Joe found the right balance between strategic direction of the company and 'hands on' support of the product development process, building on his habit of constant experimentation and tinkering, with frequent interaction with the Oxy Ferrolene engineers on specific design improvements. He was instrumental in Oxy Ferrolene's success.

Joe, Eve and Joe Junior all moved to live in Leicestershire during this period, with Joe and Eve taking up residence at a substantial farmhouse at Carlton Curlieu Manor, situated in the countryside about ten miles south-east of Leicester. Joe Junior lived 'above the shop' in a flat over the Oxy Ferrolene company offices on the corner of Harborough Road and New Street, Oadby, about six miles from his father. Ironically, given Joe's success as a whisky trader and distiller, the building Joe chose as Oxy Ferrolene's base had been constructed in 1932 as a temperance hotel named the 'Oadby Knight'. Joe renamed it 'Oxy Ferrolene House' and made it the registered address for the company. The premises comprised ground-floor offices and a first floor flat where Joe Junior, his second wife, Grete Fogh, and their children Annemarie and Joseph Peter lived right through until 1964. The site also included a production factory and warehousing for storage. There were also stables which Joe used to renew his passion for riding, where Joe Junior kept three horses and taught his own children to ride, and even a small swimming pool – an unusual feature for that time. After the war, Joe Junior kept Joe's treasured western saddle, a superb piece of leather saddlery he brought over from Canada, in the stables, until it was unfortunately stolen and never recovered.

Joe and Joe Junior were substantially aided in their work by Gilbert Saunders, a faithful employee recruited by Joe who eventually took over responsibility for daily management of the company after the War. While the company's work was quite technical, the business also had some characterful employees including a blacksmith named Bill Smith, whom Joe's grandchildren remember always wore jodhpurs over his bandy legs, and although he had no teeth could crunch through an apple with his hardened gums.[311] Joe's grandson Joseph Peter Hobbs also remembers his father accumulating the brass filings which were waste from the nozzle manufacturing process and storing them in an air raid shelter to be sold off for recycling.

As with their time in north-east Scotland during the years of ASD's expansion, Joe and Eve were active contributors to

Manor Farm House, Carlton Curlieu, Leicestershire, where Joe and Eve Hobbs lived for much of World War 2.

Oxy Ferrolene House as it looks today, now functioning as a pre-school.

the local community in Leicester during the war years. After Joe had relocated to the Midlands in the spring of 1940,[312] Eve had remained in Stonehaven for a time, moving out of Glenury House after Joe sold his shares in ASD, and relocating to Carronbank House closer to the centre of the town. However, Eve later moved south to join her husband, and got involved in full-time war work in Leicestershire with the Women's Voluntary Service, amongst other things running two war-time canteens.[313] She and Joe also found time to ride with the local Fernie Hunt, helpful in embedding the couple in the local social scene.

Joe returned briefly to Scotland in August 1941 for the funeral of Lord Stonehaven. That he should have made the trip despite wartime travel challenges indicates the strength of connection he had formed with Viscount Stonehaven, who had sold him the Glenury Royal distillery, and which was the first step in the whole ASD adventure. Lord Stonehaven was a strong supporter of the work Joe and ASD did in reviving distilling and stimulating development in Stonehaven and across Scotland, and Joe and Eve had become regular and welcome visitors to Ury House.[314] Amongst many other activities, Lord Stonehaven was an active supporter of the Red Cross and St John's organisations, and it could well be his enthusiasm that influenced Joe's own involvement, culminating in his enrolment as a Commander of the Order of St John in 1950.

In this way, Joe made a substantial contribution to the war effort. In recognition of his work and its support for Britain's military and industrial production, Joe was inducted into the Worshipful Company of Shipwrights in 1946 – an honour he shared with Sir Winston Churchill among others.

After the war, Joe went back to whisky distilling in Scotland, and Joe Junior took the lead in running Oxy Ferrolene from his base in Leicester. The firm continued to develop enhancements and took out a string of further patents for fuels and delivery mechanisms for welding equipment, filed through the war years and on into the late 1950s, sustaining the firm's commercial viability for some time after the war.

In this way, father and son built a business which had some longevity and proved to be successful over almost 50 years. Joe Junior ran the Ferrolene business from Leicester right up until his death in 1984, shortly after which the family sold Oxy Ferrolene Ltd and Ferrolene House.

9

Ben Nevis

Joe had first become involved with distilleries in Fort William, the place that was to be his home from 1945 onwards, during the late 1930s, as part of the buying spree that saw him build up a portfolio of Scottish distilleries through ASD. At that time, he successfully acquired Glenlochy Distillery, one of three distilleries then operational in the town, for ASD.

By the end of that decade, with war looming, he sold all his shares in ASD back to National Distillers, but this was far from the end of Joe's involvement in the whisky business, and also not the last of his dealings with National Distillers and Train & McIntyre. In selling his shares in ASD, Joe had also negotiated the option to buy the sizeable quantity of 500,000 gallons of whisky stocks, indicating that he was fully intending to continue in the whisky trading business, a business in which he had been active for over 20 years up to this point.

Further evidence that Joe never really intended to get out of the whisky business came soon after T&M bought out his shares in ASD. On 6th February 1940, an article in the Brechin Advertiser reported that Joe had retired from active involvement in the management of ASD, and was relocating to the Midlands to take an important executive post in a "gun shop and shell factory" (this was actually Oxy Ferrolene), but that Eve intended to continue to live in Stonehaven, and commended them both for their contribution during the time they had been members of the community in Stonehaven.[315] However, only a month later, on 15th March, the Montrose Standard reported that negotiations were going on between Joe and the Montrose Town Council for the lease of Kinnaber Mill and grounds, for conversion to use as a whisky distillery.[316]

Shortly afterwards, the leader on the Montrose Standard front page was an article quoting a letter from David Ross, Chairman of ASD (and director of T&M) to the town council, denying that ASD was in negotiation or dialogue with the Montrose Town Council to lease Kinnaber Mill. It seems everyone had assumed that Joe's discussions with the council to lease the facilities at the mill were on behalf of ASD. Ross rather tetchily made clear such discussions had nothing to do with ASD and moreover that Joe no longer represented the company: "No negotiations are taking place in any form whatsoever between representatives of this company and Commander Hobbs or the sub-committee of the Town Council". In a follow up letter on 29th March, Ross went on to explain: "The facts are that it was Mr Hobbs as an individual who negotiated with the Montrose Town Council for the lease of Kinnaber Mill and lands. The name of Associated Scottish Distilleries Ltd should not have been linked with Mr. Hobbs' activities in this connection."[317]

This hints at Ross' displeasure that, less than a month after leaving ASD, Joe was already thinking about another foray into the whisky industry on his own account. Ross could understandably be irritated that, having sold out of ASD, Joe would contemplate an immediate return in competition with them, and in their own back yard in Montrose as well. The Kinnaber Mill negotiations fell through, and the mill ended up being demolished. But even if thwarted on this particular occasion, Joe clearly had no plans of giving up his activities in the whisky industry just yet.

Soon afterwards, Joe relocated to his new home at Carlton Curlieu Manor in Leicestershire and focused on his wartime work with Oxy Ferrolene. However, three years later, Joe took a major step back into the whisky business when in December 1943 he acquired the lease on the Ben Nevis distillery, at Fort William in Inverness-shire.

Joe's opportunity arose following the death in 1939 of Colonel Archibald W. Macdonald, who had been the senior partner in the firm of D.P. Macdonald and Sons, which owned the Ben Nevis distillery.[318] Macdonald was a prominent local figure, Chairman of the Lochaber District Council, a member of the Inverness-shire County Council and a Deputy Lieutenant of Inverness-shire. He was a descendant of the famous 'Long John Macdonald' who had done much to establish Ben Nevis

Ben Nevis Distillery, Fort William.

distillery's reputation after he took it over in 1830 from his cousin Angus McDonnell (who founded it in 1825).

Whilst certainly not the prettiest of Scotland's distilleries, there is no denying Ben Nevis distillery's spectacular setting, occupying an impressive site at the foot of the mountain of the same name, the highest peak in the British Isles.

Ben Nevis was the first legal distillery in Lochaber district after its founding. Its name was made by 'Long' John Macdonald of Keppoch (1798-1856), who was a descendant of the Macdonalds that fought with Bonnie Prince Charlie at the battle of Culloden in the culmination of the Jacobite rebellion of 1745. This John Macdonald was known as "Long John" on account of his stature (he was 6 feet, 5 inches tall), and after whom the famous Long John whisky blend was named. He was only 32 when he took over running the distillery at Ben Nevis, having borrowed £1,200 to buy into the ownership. The scale of operation was relatively modest at first, producing around 200 gallons of spirit per week. It was well situated, not just because of its spectacular setting, but also with good access via steamers on Loch Linnhe for import of raw materials and export of finished products.

Availability of extremely good water from the slopes of Ben Nevis mountain itself had been a key factor in the decision to build the distillery on this site in 1825, with Long John writing that he "…was fortunate to find a constant and consistent source of pure clean water in two small lochans", the Coire Leis and Coire na'Ciste, whose waters were extracted for use at the distillery.[319] Writing more than 60 years later, Alfred Barnard who visited all the whisky distilleries in the UK in 1886 for his famous book 'The Whisky Distilleries of the United Kingdom' quoted from a scientific analysis of this water by Dr Stevenson Macadam, who advised that "it is of the very best quality; cannot be surpassed, and is very seldom equalled in quality."[320] Macdonald's main

THE PRINCE OF WALES'S WHISKY.—We understand that Mr Macdonald, distiller, Ben Nevis (better known as "Long John"), has received the Queen's permission, dated on board the royal yacht off Campbeltown, to present the Prince of Wales with a cask of whisky, to be kept at Buckingham Palace till his Royal Highness is of age.

How one newspaper covered the story of "Long John" Macdonald's gift of whisky to Queen Victoria.

product "Long John's Dew of Ben Nevis" became very popular, especially after Queen Victoria visited Scotland in 1847 with her 6-year-old son Albert, the Prince of Wales (who was later to become Edward VII). Long John presented a cask of his whisky to the Queen, which was transported to Buckingham Palace, and was apparently subsequently opened when the Prince turned 21 years of age.[321] Long John's shrewd advertising further contributed to growth in demand for Ben Nevis' products, with the distillery expanding to produce a substantial 3,000 gallons of spirit per week by the 1860s.

Long John Macdonald died in 1856 and ownership of the distillery was inherited by his son Donald P. Macdonald, who rebuilt and expanded Ben Nevis distillery between 1863-65, and then built a second distillery in 1878 called "Nevis Distillery" on a site in a bend in the River Nevis approximately two miles closer to Fort William town from the original Ben Nevis site. The new distillery, which was "as modern in style and construction as any in Scotland",[322] used the same water source as the original Ben Nevis Distillery. By 1886, Nevis was producing 5,000 gallons of spirit a week (in addition to the 3,000 gallons produced at the original Ben Nevis Distillery).[323] D.P. Macdonald also constructed new concrete piers on the shores of Loch Linnhe to handle the steamers serving the distilleries. By 1889, the combined operation was one of the largest in the industry, producing nearly 250,000 proof gallons of spirit a year, deploying the largest maltings facility in Scotland, with storage of over 10,000 casks on site, and employing more than 200 people.[324] Operations were further assisted by the completion of the West Highland Railway, which reached Fort William in 1894, facilitating the delivery of coal and despatch of mature casks via the distillery's own rail siding.

D.P. Macdonald died on 1st November 1891, leaving an estate valued at over £110,000 (2024: £17.5m), handing the business over to his sons John and Archibald. John went to live in South Africa, resulting in second son Archibald Macdonald, after a military career that saw him reach the rank of Colonel and serve in the Lovat Scouts, going on to run the distillery and serve as senior partner in the family business.

However, in an industry plagued by repeated 'boom and bust' cycles, and having performed very well for more than seven

Advertising Hoarding for Long John's Dew of Ben Nevis – the whisky that made Ben Nevis Distillery famous.

Ben Nevis distillery c.1900, with the mountain behind it.

decades, the turn of the century brought much tougher trading conditions, and Ben Nevis was unable to ride out the whisky industry crash that followed the boom years of the 1890s. The many years of chronic oversupply that followed the crash forced change at Ben Nevis, and the Macdonalds took the decision to merge their two distilleries into a single operation in 1908.[325] Thereafter, the Nevis site, which was closer to the town and to the loch piers for the import of barley, was used mostly for malting barley and as a bonded storage and warehousing facility, while distilling activities were concentrated at the original Ben Nevis site. The first part of the 20th century was tough for the whole whisky industry, and Ben Nevis was no exception, having to close on several occasions in the years leading up to WW2. In 1921, the decision was taken to sell the 'Long John' trade name to London wine and spirit merchants W.H. Chaplin.[326, ai] The

---

ai   Chaplins were later absorbed into Seager Evans (a company that grew to

fame of the 'Long John' brand was able to bring the Macdonalds some vital income during very tough times, so it was sold to bring in much-needed cash; but the distillery itself was retained, and remained in the Macdonald family until 1943. Tragically, Colonel Archibald's son had died in France just days before the end of WW1, so, with no male heir, when Archibald Macdonald himself passed away in 1939, just after the outbreak of WW2, and with the Ben Nevis distillery shut down as part of wartime restrictions on distilling, there was considerable uncertainty over the future of the distillery.

War had brought immediate restrictions; there was no barley to distil, and little likelihood the distillery could operate normally or make any money for years ahead. With his excellent contacts, whisky industry knowledge, and nose for a deal, Joe would have been well aware of the opportunity that Ben Nevis presented. From the autumn of 1943, Joe was clearly starting to think about and prepare for post-war opportunities, and searching for ways to re-enter the whisky distilling business, as evidenced by his move to inject £9,900 of additional capital into his distilling company MacNab Distillers. Joe saw the potential of Ben Nevis distillery, and negotiated with the Macdonald family, agreeing to purchase the lease on the distillery for £20,000 on 1st December 1943 (2024: £1.1m).[327, 328, 329] The land on which the distillery was built was originally part of Lord Abinger's Inverlochy Estate, but the freehold had been sold to the British Aluminium Company in 1924. So, when Joe bought the lease to Ben Nevis, British Aluminium effectively became his landlord.

The sale included Lochaber maltings and warehousing (the old 'Nevis' distillery), and in a 'wheeler dealer' manoeuvre

---

become quite a force in the industry, building Strathclyde grain distillery in Glasgow, operating Laphroaig distillery on Islay and Glenugie distillery near Aberdeen, and commissioning Tormore distillery on Speyside).

Ben Nevis Distillery, Fort William. The still house block on the left was built by Joe Hobbs. The accommodation and storage block to the right has since been demolished.

typical of Joe, he sold the Lochaber facilities (17 bonded warehouses and the barley maltings) to his old partners at Train & MacIntyre, for the exact same amount of £20,000 he had paid the Macdonalds. T&M were keen to augment the limited malting capacity and storage facilities they had at nearby Glenlochy (the distillery which had originally been purchased for them by Joe back in 1937). So, for T&M, acquiring the Nevis facilities, often referred to as 'Lochaber' to differentiate it from the original Ben Nevis distillery, clearly made good business sense. However, it is interesting to speculate whether they realised Joe had only paid £20,000 for the *combined* Ben Nevis *and* Lochaber distilleries in total, and that by selling Lochaber for the same price Joe had effectively acquired Ben Nevis for nothing! At the very least, it was further evidence of Joe's eye for the main chance, and ability to use his market intelligence and negotiating skills to realise substantial profits from buying and selling distillery assets.

Somehow, during the short period between buying and selling Lochaber, Joe found the time to move the imposing cast iron front gates and their supporting stone gate posts from Lochaber over to the original Ben Nevis distillery site.[330] The ornate gates remained at Ben Nevis until 2020. Whilst impressive to look at, the gates were entirely ornamental because, having

Nevis Distillery and maltings.

been designed for another site, they were too narrow to cross the full width of the entry road. Following a rebranding exercise, the distillery's current owners, Nikka of Japan, agreed to sell the old gates to Angus Macdonald, a local Fort William entrepreneur and descendant of the family of 'Long John' Macdonald, and he relocated the gates to his property at Roshven, near Glenuig, on the coast 30 miles to the west of Fort William, where they stand resplendent framing the view out to Rhum, Eigg and Skye.

The ex-Nevis and Ben Nevis distillery gates, when still onsite at the distillery.

The old gates, now sited at Angus Macdonald's property at Roshven, 30 miles west of Fort William.

Wartime restrictions meant that the distillery, which had not operated since 1942, remained closed for some time, so, although Joe now owned the lease on Ben Nevis, he could not immediately recommence business. Joe set up a new company, 'Ben Nevis Distillery (Fort William) Ltd', to own and operate the business, with Joe and Joe Junior as the two directors, on 10th January 1944. In February 1944, Joe injected some money into the new Ben Nevis company, which was funded by 1000 shares of £1 each nominal capital.

In a letter to his correspondent A.S. Seggie in Aberdeen at the time Joe wrote, "As soon as possible after the War, I intend to enlarge the distillery and make it a model place."[331] However, unfortunately, years of restrictions and shortages during and after the war prevented him from operating Ben Nevis normally

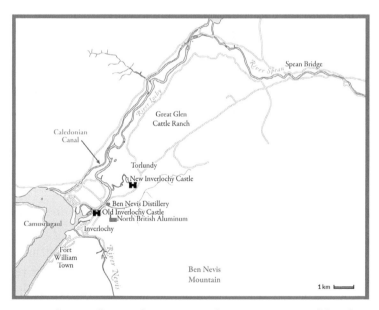

Map of Fort William and Ben Nevis. In the 1940s, Joe acquired first the Ben Nevis distillery at Fort William, and subsequently the large Inverlochy Estate, on which he went on to create the Great Glen Cattle Ranch.

for quite some time. To the frustration of the whole industry and to consumers, government-imposed rationing and restrictions continued for nearly a decade after the end of the war, restricting Joe's efforts to put Ben Nevis back into full-time operation.

Faced with substantial war debts and repeated currency crises for the pound sterling, the post-war government prioritised development of hard currency-earning exports, and especially those with a high value-to-volume ratio where Britain had a unique ability to supply – Scotch whisky was at or near the top of the government's list of priority industries to support and develop. However, strong official government support of whisky production for export could not initially overcome the dire shortages of barley and grains which Britain continued to experience as a legacy of the war years. In 1946, Minister of Food Sir Ben Smith announced a 'Food Before Whisky' policy and publicly stated that "Not one grain more" of barley would go to the distillers because scarce cereals needed to be prioritised to feed people and livestock.[332]

The government imposed nationwide restrictions on distilling, with an annual quota allocating the maximum amount of barley that could be used by distillers for the production of whisky. Each year this barley quota was insufficient to allow all the distilleries in Scotland to work full-time, and, once the quota had been used, there was little choice but to close down operations and lay off or redeploy staff. Obtaining experienced workers was another issue: an article published in the Daily Record in August 1945 reporting on the reopening at Ben Nevis explained that whilst the distillery's pre-war staff complement was 30 people, only 13 people were available at the time of re-opening, including a number of boys, with even the office-girl pressed into service to help rolling barrels in the warehouse.[333] It would take quite some years for materials and labour to be available sufficiently reliably for the distillery to come back into full production. Joe seems at the time to have been frustratingly aware that could be the case: another article in the same week in the Aberdeen Press and Journal quotes an un-named 'prominent Highland distiller' as saying "There will be an all-round shortage of whisky for at least eight years".[334] There are good reasons to suppose the un-named distiller was Joe Hobbs, given the only distillery mentioned by the writer of the article was Ben Nevis. It was a remarkably accurate prediction – it took fully eight years before Ben Nevis was back in full production.

Having not distilled since 1942, an article in The Scotsman newspaper on 13th January 1945 announced that Ben Nevis would soon go back into operation. Building repairs were done and staff taken on to allow recommencement of distilling from mid-February, with initial production around 3–4,000 gallons of spirit per week. Joe is quoted as saying Ben Nevis was likely to complete its quota, which was only one-third of the amount of barley which the distillery had used in 1938, within 10 weeks of operation. "We hope by that time the quota will be increased," he said.[335]

In actual fact, the distillery completed use of its quota in July 1945, and had to close again – being the first of the Highland Distilleries to do so that distilling season. By that time, 45,000 gallons had been produced, a little more than Joe had estimated, and around 36% of the amount produced in the last pre-war year of production in 1938. An article in The Scotsman dated 23rd August indicated Ben Nevis had been given a new quota for the 1945–46 distilling season, which was increased to 50% of the 1938 level, and which would allow around 62,500 gallons to be produced. The article commented rather wryly that, even if production was allowed at 100% of 1938 levels, there would still be serious shortages of whisky for the coming five years.[336]

Unfortunately, the barley shortage did not ease quickly after the end of the war, and this process of quotas and restrictions was to continue into the early 1950s.

Table 2: Post-WW2 Scotch whisky production. (Source: data extracted from 'The Making of Scotch Whisky', by John R. Hume and Michael S. Moss, 2000 edition.)

Year	Operating Distilleries	Malt Whisky Production (m gallons)	Grain Whisky Production (m gallons)	Total Whisky Production (m gallons)	Export Volume (m gallons)	Export Value (£ m)
1938-39	92	10.67	27.10	37.77		
1939-40	93	7.26	6.40	13.66		
1940-41	72	3.24	4.75	7.99		
1941-42	44	1.85	0.27	2.12		
1942-43	33	1.39	-	1.39		
1943-44	1	-	-	-		
1944-45	57	3.69	6.01	9.70		
1945-46	80	5.85	8.50	14.35	5.88	£10.86
1946-47	82	3.52	5.66	9.18	6.77	£13.57
1947-48	88	8.33	12.59	20.92	7.90	£16.20
1948-49	91	11.33	16.34	27.67	8.52	£18.74
1949-50	95	12.79	16.73	29.52	9.69	£26.27
1950-51	97	12.32	16.18	28.50	10.63	£29.59
1951-52	97	12.73	18.79	31.52	11.52	£33.03
1952-53	97	12.43	14.94	27.37	13.20	£37.77
1953-54	96	13.75	20.47	34.22	13.69	£39.05
1954-55	95	15.14	25.25	40.39	15.36	£43.67
1955-56	95	15.86	27.09	42.95	16.44	£47.80
1956-57	97	18.22	31.42	49.64	17.91	£52.14
1957-58	100	20.55	33.69	54.24	19.32	£56.03
1958-59	101	22.41	36.59	59.00	21.69	£61.85
1959-60	106	25.07	44.64	69.71	23.15	£65.56
1960-61	106	26.50	49.36	75.86	26.82	£74.43
1961-62	105	27.11	56.99	84.10	30.07	£80.86
1962-63	107	28.88	65.20	94.08	31.77	£84.83

As the table above shows, for the industry overall, it took until 1955 before total production of whisky in Scotland grew to exceed the last pre-war year of production in 1938. In some ways, for Ben Nevis this was no bad thing. In common with the Inverlochy House and Estate that Joe bought in the area not long after acquiring Ben Nevis, and which was to become Joe's home for the rest of his life, the distillery was substantially run down at this time, after years without new investment to replace or upgrade equipment. Joe later described Ben Nevis as being virtually "a derelict distillery" at this time.[337] But he held back from his usual practice of immediately investing in new equipment and deploying labour to refurbish the distillery, bringing the distillery right up to date and enabling it to operate and compete effectively. Part of the reason for that in Ben Nevis' case was certainly due to the barley and labour constraints that applied in the years after WW2 – there was no point in investing to upgrade the distillery if he would only be able to run at half-capacity or less. But it was also because Joe leased, rather than owned Ben Nevis outright, and the terms of the lease with regular break clauses and potential risk of substantial rent increases meant Joe could not be certain he would get a good payback on any investments he made to improve the distillery at that time.

Of the two causes, it was really the barley quota problems that most constrained the business in the immediate post-war years. For the 1945–46 distilling season, Ben Nevis had used its barley as early as 15th February 1946, and was forced to close again. Joe was again active with the press, saying Ben Nevis had expected further quotas to be released, but when that did not happen he had taken the decision to operate at much-reduced capacity to eke out available barley stocks and keep his men in work. This also enabled him to continue to provide a limited supply of animal feed for dairy herds in the area (including especially his own cattle)! Staff were set to maintenance work to make good use of time that could not be used making whisky.[338]

The situation got worse before it got better. No new supplies of barley were forthcoming for the remainder of 1946, and Joe redeployed his men to work on the Inverlochy estate and also to the Torlundy lime quarries, which was becoming another keen object of interest for him. Ben Nevis had to wait almost a full year until February 1947 to get its next allocation of barley, when the Ministry of Food allocated around only one-sixth of that which had been used in 1938, enough for just 18,000 gallons of production.[339] By 17th June 1947 the distillery was closed again, having used up its quota. The 25 men employed

Joe Hobbs at Fort William in May 1946.

at the distillery were once again redeployed on other tasks.[340]

With help from the industry to prioritise exports and restrict whisky sales in the UK home market, some progress with the government's whisky export objective was achieved, with small increases in the volume and value of whisky exported achieved in 1946 and 1947. However, this was unsustainable without allocating more grain for distillation, also allowing for the minimum three-year lead time after distillation before new make spirit was old enough to be sold as whisky. When new Minister of Food John Strachey took over in 1947, the decision was taken to make more grain available to distillers, on the condition that the industry would prioritise overseas exports, especially to the United States.

Consequently, 1948 was a slightly better year for Ben Nevis. In July of that year, the Ministry of Food allocated another 250,000 tons of malt to distillers across Scotland, with Ben Nevis receiving enough to operate through to December. However, in January 1949, unable to obtain a permit to buy more barley, Ben Nevis shut down yet again. Joe was once more active in the newspapers deploring the situation, pointing out that 25 men would now lose their jobs, and the supply of feedstock to local cattle would dry up mid-way through the winter. Joe complained "I wrote to the Ministry of Food pointing out that, on the understanding a second allocation was due and that distilling would be continuous, I imported 250 head of Irish cattle to add to my stock on my farm on the Inverlochy estate." The Ministry replied "While fully appreciating the position outlined in your letter, we regret we are unable to accede to your request. To do so would mean exceeding the total barley which the industry is permitted to use during the current year."[341]

In parallel with these developments, Joe became involved in a protracted dispute with North British Aluminium Limited (NBAL), who owned the land on which Ben Nevis distillery sat. The dispute with NBAL was the second factor, in addition to shortages of barley, that prevented Joe from investing to upgrade Ben Nevis distillery after WW2.[aj]

The dispute arose because Joe, acting both as M.D. of Ben Nevis distillery and as proprietor of the Inverlochy Estate, claimed that noxious fumes from the NBAL plant were damaging vegetation and animal stock on his properties,

---

aj   Inverlochy and the foothills of Ben Nevis were chosen as the site for an extraordinary development between 1921 and 1929 comprising the construction of a hydro-electric power station by the Lochaber Power Company and a huge aluminium smelter by North British Aluminium Ltd. The scheme involved damming the headwaters of the rivers Treig and Spean, and funnelling their water through 24km long, 5m diameter tunnels to the lower slopes of Ben Nevis mountain – until 1970 these were the longest water-carrying tunnels in the world. Emerging from the side of the mountain just above Ben Nevis distillery, the water was channelled down 5 massive penstocks (sluice tunnels) to a hydro-electric power station located on the same site as the new North British Aluminium smelter, for which it provided the power. The villages of Inverlochy and Kinlochleven were built to provide housing for workers for the construction and subsequent operations of the power station and smelter. As part of the development, North British took over ownership of a large parcel of land (including the land on which Ben Nevis distillery was located) which had previously been part of the Inverlochy Estate owned by Lord Abinger. The Lochaber hydro power station and aluminium smelter are still in operation today, the latter is now the only aluminium producing facility in the UK, still turning out 40,000 tonnes of aluminium ingots a year.

and reducing the milk yield of his dairy herd. Joe first raised this as an issue soon after he purchased the Inverlochy Estate in August 1945. Noticing that some trees on the estate were dead, and others suffered with blighted branches and a lack of leaves, Joe consulted the District Forestry Officer, who was of the opinion the trees were being poisoned by noxious fumes from the aluminium smelters. A report was commissioned from a forestry consultant in September 1946, Robert Cowal Smith confirming the diagnosis that the aluminium plant was the cause of the problem: "I felt the weight of evidence was overwhelming that the damage was caused by fumes from the… factory."[342] Another expert opinion was obtained to investigate the falling yields of his herd of Ayrshire dairy cattle, which also blamed emissions from the aluminium plant. Joe raised his complaint with NBAL, who agreed to investigate the situation and issue a report on potential fluorine damage, which they submitted towards the end of 1946. Between 1946 and 1948, both parties engaged in negotiations to try to find an out-of-court settlement to the dispute. NBAL agreed to replace their furnaces and upgrade equipment (fitting 'scrubbers' to capture the noxious fumes) at a cost of more than £500,000, which they said would solve the problem. However, it also seems that NBAL took their time implementing this agreement, with the upgrade and replacement of their smelters only scheduled to take place gradually with final completion in 1950, in order to avoid closing down a large part of the plant's capacity. Given the dispute started whilst WW2 was still in full swing, it is perhaps understandable initially that the war economy's need for aluminium was prioritised over the emissions issue.

But the slow pace of progress resulted in Joe going to court in the spring of 1948 to try to force NBAL to speed up their corrective action. His patience wearing thin, Joe escalated the issue by taking NBAL to the Court of Session in Edinburgh, petitioning the court to 'interdict' (forbid) NBAL from producing aluminium in any way that allowed noxious vapours to pass over his land – potentially this could have closed the whole plant down if Joe's demand was agreed by the Court. At a first hearing in March 1948 the scale of the issue became clear when NBAL stated that, if Joe's petition was successful, 72% of the entire output of aluminium in the U.K. would be suspended, with a cost to the U.K. Exchequer of £1,750,000 annually.[343] (Later, when the case came to court, NBAL stated if the Lochaber smelter was forced to close down the UK would have to import aluminium from the USA and Canada at a cost of US$7–8,000,000 a year at then current prices).[344] In May 1948, the Judge hearing the case found that there was a case to be answered, and that Joe and the Inverlochy Estate did indeed seem to be suffering damage from the fumes emitted by the aluminium smelters.[345]

As part of the slow and long-drawn-out legal process, Joe himself took the stand, requiring lengthy spells in the witness box. Joe told the court that the Ben Nevis distillery leased its land for a rent of £640 p.a., with NBAL also providing free electricity for the plant and estate. The lease ran until 1966, with break clauses every five years. Joe explained how he had witnessed damage to trees on the estate, and suffered from low yields from his dairy herd. He asserted that NBAL were mainly upgrading their smelters in order to benefit themselves from higher production capability, and that they were not interested in eliminating the emissions.[346] Both sides presented expert witnesses on the extent of the damage. Professor George Boddie, Professor of Medicine at the Royal Veterinary College provided evidence on damage to the jaw bones and teeth of cattle on Joe's estate caused by fluorine poisoning, compared with healthy cattle.[347] NBAL called on forestry consultant Thomas Dalgleish, who gave evidence that the Inverlochy estate had not had any proper forestry management for 40–50 years, attributing the damage to "bad forest management, disease and fire."[348]

Lord Birnam gave his decision on 11th March 1949, coming to the conclusion that Joe had "a very substantial cause for complaint with regard to the effect of the fumes from the [aluminium] factory on...Inverlochy Estate." The Judge "did not think there was any room for doubt that the fumes from the factory constituted a serious interference with the rights of the petitioners [Joe Hobbs] in the natural use of their property."[349] However, he also had to balance the national interest to allow NBAL to continue producing aluminium, and it was for that reason only that he decided not to issue immediately the 'interdict' order (that would force NBAL to cease operations whilst they sorted out the emissions problem). He therefore decided to give NBAL more time to put remedial actions in place. However, the Judge was very critical of NBAL, pointing out they had had several years to implement what they now proposed to do to solve the case, had wasted a great deal of time, and paid too little attention to solving the nuisance which Joe had been complaining about since 1946. He made this decision on the understanding and having received an assurance from NBAL that they would take remedial action to resolve the problem "with the utmost possible expediency".[350]

This was a substantial victory for Joe, with the court also deciding that NBAL should pay his legal costs and expenses in bringing the case. However, in addition to the strong legal backing for Joe's case, one of the more interesting issues to emerge from the dispute concerns the argument about the Ben Nevis distillery lease, and it was this that was to provide real and lasting benefit to Joe. NBAL had alleged in court that improving the terms of the Ben Nevis distillery lease was the real underlying reason why Joe had raised the dispute and taken it to court – and with the benefit of hindsight, it seems they could well have been right.

1949 aerial photograph showing the North British Aluminium plant at Lochaber, and its close proximity to Ben Nevis distillery (the buildings to the bottom right of the photograph).

NBAL's control of the lease on the land on which Ben Nevis distillery operated meant there was always a risk Joe could be turfed out at any one of the break points in the lease (as Joe in fact alleged NBAL had threatened during his legal testimony), and/or have to pay substantial increases in rent. This would also have been a major problem discouraging Joe from investing to upgrade and renew Ben Nevis – it would have been too risky to invest in refurbishing the distillery and purchasing a lot of expensive new equipment with the possibility his lease could be terminated before the investment had time to pay off. In evidence at the court case, Joe was recorded as saying "I felt very insecure at the distillery on account of a break in the lease in 1951."[351]

One element of a proposed agreement which was discussed between the parties out-of-court was that NBAL might offer Joe a new 21-year lease, giving him greater security of tenure. Commodore R.G.H. Linzee, British Aluminium's Director of Establishments (responsible for personnel and estates), said in court that his recollection of the out-of-court discussions ended with Joe giving an ultimatum that it was "the distillery or a lawsuit". Linzee said that the impression he formed was that the principal reason for Joe's complaint was to try to obtain security of tenure and control over the distillery's land. Joe denied this assertion in court, stating that he had tried for a long time to get NBAL to deal with the fumes nuisance and the damage it was having to his trees and cattle, and that it was in fact only after NBAL sent a letter threatening to cancel his lease that Joe decided to institute legal proceedings against them.[352]

But evidence supporting a supposition that Linzee might have been correct in his thinking on this comes from the very fact that Ben Nevis distillery was party to the dispute at all: by far the biggest impact of the fluorine was on the cattle, trees and grassland of the Inverlochy estate and farms – the distillery itself would have been much less affected. By including Ben Nevis as a party to the dispute, Joe cleverly ensured that his distillery business could

directly benefit from any settlement.

The lease issue was certainly not the whole story however. Evidence published in 1947 and 1948 by the Committee of the Medical Research Council (C.M.R.C.) from investigations done at Fort William

Commodore R.G.H. Linzee, C.B., C.B.E., R.N. (Retd), Joe Hobbs' principal protagonist in the British Aluminium 'Fumes Case' with Ben Nevis.

showed that emissions of fluorine had indeed had a major impact on sheep and cattle farming in the area, and moreover that there could be human health consequences. Joe's reasons for bringing the case were legitimate and well-founded, and the issue was serious enough for Lord Stonehaven to raise questions in the House of Lords about the issue in December 1948 and request full publication of the C.M.R.C. report. NBAL did not rush to implement the remedial actions they had promised in the previous negotiations, with only 18 of 148 furnaces at the Lochaber plant replaced in the year after Joe first proved the damage he was suffering, fully justifying Joe's decision to go to court to have the matter expedited.

With the strong legal backing from the court findings behind him, Joe was able to negotiate from a position of strength, and obtained an outstandingly good settlement. The case was fully resolved on 11th January 1950, when it was reported that Joe had withdrawn his petition, a mutual agreement having finally been successfully agreed between the parties.[353] By this time, the Ministry of Supply were also involved, doubtless concerned to ensure that NBAL could continue to produce aluminium. Records show that with NBAL supplying over 70% of the UK's aluminium, the Ministry of Supply had intervened in the case twice in support of the company. However, with the Court ruling in Joe's favour, and Joe having proved the damage the fluorine was causing, it can certainly be supposed that the government added their pressure on NBAL to find a way to appease Joe without disrupting aluminium production.

However, appease him they certainly did, and it was a huge victory for Joe. The key feature of the settlement was that Joe was awarded a 99-year lease on the Ben Nevis distillery, at a rent of just £1 a year. Originally, the lease was subject to renewal every five years, with final expiry in 1966. Now Joe had secured tenure for far longer, and at a purely nominal rent to boot – previously, he had been paying rent of £640 per annum, escalating every five years. Whether in taking NBAL to court Joe was always aiming at achieving security of tenure for his distillery operations at Ben Nevis, as Commodore Linzee of British Aluminium alleged, is very hard to say with certainty. But it is tempting to interpret all this as Joe Hobbs the hard-nosed, calculating and toughened businessman deliberately taking on one of the largest corporations in the country and the might of the Ministry of Supply in order to secure his distillery's future. Either way, security of tenure for a peppercorn rent certainly paved the way for Joe to redevelop and then successfully operate the distillery for the remainder of his life and (via his family) for some time afterwards.

However, even though the legal dispute was now resolved, the frustrating constraints and rationing of the post-war years were to drag on for some time longer, with the government only fully relaxing the restrictions on use of grains for distilling in mid-1953. This was a factor in why it took so long before Ben Nevis went back into full operation, which was not finally achieved until 1955. However, with the lease issue resolved and providing more certainty that an adequate return could be achieved on new investment, Joe used the period from 1953 to 1955 to substantially re-equip the distillery in preparation for a return to full production. In typical Joe Hobbs style, he brought in a raft of innovations and changes. New pot stills, faithful to the design of those installed at the time of the 1865 refit, were installed in 1955. Joe built a whole new still-house to accommodate them, and also built a new office and administration block. New washbacks were installed, with an innovative square shape, and unusually made of concrete. A new malt hammer mill was fitted, and new electrical control systems installed throughout. The distillery was unusual for the time also in being 100% electrically powered.

Construction of the new still-house at Ben Nevis distillery built by Joe Hobbs in 1954–55.

But, from the viewpoint of whisky history, his most interesting innovation at that time was to source and install a Coffey still (also known as a continuous, column or patent still) to the operation, the first one installed in a malt whisky distillery after WW2. Coffey stills are large pieces of industrial equipment used for distilling grain whisky at scale. They are operated very differently from the smaller pot stills traditionally used to make malt whisky, which operate on a 'batch' basis. Because of their size and scale, Coffey stills are usually operated on large, industrial sites dedicated to the production of grain whisky.

Joe seems to have been thinking along lines similar to those he deployed pre-war with ASD: in those days, blended Scotch whisky was the big seller; there was only a very limited market for what has become known as 'single malt' whiskies from individual distilleries like Ben Nevis. To meet consumer

Ben Nevis distillery today, showing the still-house (above) and administration block (below) built by Joe Hobbs in the 1950s still in operation today.

demand, Joe needed to produce blended whisky, and the key to blended whisky production was access to a reliable supply of grain whisky at a competitive price. Consolidation of the industry meant supply of grain whiskies was controlled by a small number of large players.

As earlier with ASD, Joe was working on the principle that he needed to control his own supply of grain whisky in order to produce his blends. Once again this demonstrates Joe's bold thinking: patent stills are large pieces of capital equipment, expensive to buy, requiring large-scale inputs of grains as well as supporting equipment and infrastructure to operate. Patent still operation was also more technical and advanced than malt whisky distillation – more of a scientific process and less of an art. This is also typical of Joe's mindset, applying modern methods and a scientific approach to 'upgrade' industrial capabilities, but it was unusual for the times, and ambitious given the poor economic conditions and slow recovery of markets after the hiatus of the war. Joe clearly still believed in his business model of controlling the means of producing good blends, and using them to exploit high-paying demand in the export markets, especially in North America.

The Coffey still was sourced from John Dore & Co Ltd, of Bow in London, which was the successor company to that originally set up by Aeneas Coffey himself to market and manufacture his invention. It was installed in a newly constructed building immediately behind the new still-house Joe built to accommodate the four new pot stills. Unfortunately, distillery records have not survived to provide information about how much the new continuous still cost or how it was used. Because it had a much higher capacity than the pot stills, it would certainly have required a significant upgrade in the whole production process, starting from sourcing more grain, obtaining many more wooden casks to take the output form the still, and expanding warehouses for storage. It would have been a complex challenge for distillery management to balance this operation together with that for operating the pot stills. But as a result of the Coffey still, for a period between 1955 and 1971 Ben Nevis was one of the very few Scottish distilleries capable of producing both malts and grains, and its own 'single blends', all from the same site.

Joe also made other innovations at this time. He installed new washbacks (the vessels which are used to ferment the malted barley into the rich beer called 'wash' ready for distillation), made from concrete. Up until that time, washbacks in the Scottish whisky industry were almost always made of wood, and it was typical of Joe that he should experiment with a more 'modern' material like concrete. (Joe also made innovative use of concrete as a building material on his Great Glen Cattle Ranch, using lime from the Torlundy Lime Quarries for the raw materials – all these developments were interrelated, and it was characteristic of Joe

New electrical equipment installed by Joe Hobbs at Ben Nevis distillery in 1955 to operate the new Coffey still.

to use assets from one part of his business to support operations on another.) While much of the new investment and expansion at Ben Nevis during Joe's time was for the good, the concrete washbacks were not a very successful innovation. Ralph Palmer, son of Joe's factor on the Inverlochy Estate Charlie Palmer, worked as an exciseman at Ben Nevis distillery at this time. He remembers the washbacks beings installed and was involved in 'gauging' (measuring and certifying) the quantities of wash they produced prior to distillation. They were square-shaped (rather than round, as is the case with traditional wooden washbacks), and did not have 'switchers' (rotating blades) at the top to help dispel the carbon dioxide and 'froth' which builds up during the fermentation process. And because concrete as a material was not good at conducting the heat which is produced in the fermentation process, the new washbacks gave inconsistent results in making the wash, with a tendency to overheat and overflow the washback itself. They were also difficult to clean. For all these reasons, this particular experiment was not a success, and the concrete washbacks were subsequently replaced with a more traditional wooden design. But, as Ralph Palmer says, "there is a theme here of constantly pushing boundaries and innovation. [With Joe Hobbs] the establishment were constantly taken out of their Comfort Zone!"[354]

Joe also experimented with different types of casks and barrels for maturing his Ben Nevis whisky, and was the pioneer of a concept he termed 'blended from birth', where malt and grain whiskies were filled into the same casks for maturation. In the 1950s–60s, distilleries in Scotland usually filled their whisky into casks against specific orders received from blenders. As David Daiches explains in his seminal work 'Scotch Whisky: Its Past and Present', "for the most part [a distillery] fills casks sent to it by the blenders, who keep the whisky maturing in the distillery until they want it."[355] The blenders then called forward the stock when they needed it, which was transported to a blending and bottling plant, where all the whiskies (both malts and grains) were emptied from their barrels into a large blending vat. After a period resting in these vats to allow all the whiskies and flavours to 'marry' together, the blended whisky was bottled. Joe, however, innovated to put the malt and grain whiskies together in the same wooden cask as soon as they were made, with the whiskies already blended in the barrel, ready to be bottled directly once they were mature. This 'Blended from Birth' concept became something of a Joe Hobbs trademark: he had pioneered the idea at Hillside (Montrose) back in ASD days before WW2, and was to repeat the same approach again at Lochside in the 1950s. Joe also experimented at this time with different types of casks for maturation of the finished whisky, in particular by trialling use of barrels which had previously been used to store and mature beer, predating industry trends which became widespread later.

Ben Nevis was also unusual at this time in being one of the first distilleries to use electric power for all its fuel needs, enabling the distillery to do without coal totally. Power came from the Lochaber Power Company's generating plant at Inverlochy, less than half a mile from the distillery.

Joe re-equipped Ben Nevis very well for the period of expansion that followed once the brakes were finally released in the mid-1950s, allowing the distillery to significantly expand its production. In a letter to his niece Barbara Barran in Canada in May 1954, Joe said "The Distillery is going well and the new plant I installed last Summer is giving great results."[356]

Whilst in 1955 Joe was the first post-WW2 distillery owner to develop the capability to produce both single malt and grain whisky at the same distillery, he was not alone in his thinking. Several other distilleries, including Invergordon (producing Ben Wyvis malt whisky at their huge grain distillery in Alness between 1965 and 1977), Inver House (producing Glen Flagler, Killyloch and Islebrae malt whiskies at the Moffat grain distillery in Glasgow between 1965 and 1970) and William Grant & Sons (producing Ladyburn malt whisky at the Girvan grain distillery in Ayrshire from 1966 and 1975), subsequently equipped themselves to produce both types of whisky. [ak] These other large distillers seemingly followed Joe's thinking that it was valuable to control some supply of both malt and grain whiskies for their own blended whiskies, as well as to provide stocks that could be traded with other distillers to obtain a variety of flavour profiles which typically comprise a successful blended whisky.

All of these other examples of malt and grain whisky production within the same distillery started from the other end of the spectrum from Joe Hobbs – Joe added a Coffey still to produce grain whisky at Ben Nevis distillery to supplement his existing malt whisky production capability, whereas Invergordon, Inver House and Grants all installed pot stills to make malt whisky within their existing (much larger) grain whisky-producing distilleries. But the thinking was very similar. Probably the owners of these distilleries also figured that they would get some economies of scale from these initiatives – they already had the distillery sites, skilled labour, supplies of barrels and storage capacity, so adding another production line to produce a slightly different type of whisky could be done relatively easily and cost effectively.

It is not certain that the management of Invergordon, Inver House and Grants were influenced by Joe Hobbs' thinking on this. But Joe was certainly the first to go down this route after WW2, and show that it could be done successfully – in that

---

ak   The William Grant & Sons distillery at Girvan was itself constructed in 1963 as a response by the then head of WG&S Charles Grant Gordon to being unable to secure reliable stocks of grain whisky for their blends from industry leader the Distillers Company Limited.

A very rare bottle of Ben Nevis 1962 'blended at birth' whisky, bottled from stock put into cask when Joe Hobbs still owned and ran the distillery.

sense, it could well be that Joe's initiative had a role in prompting development of these so-called 'integrated' distilleries, for the flexibility and independence they brought to their owners to develop their own blends. None of these integrated distilleries producing malt and grain on the same site sustained in the long run, with all of them reverting to being specialist distilleries of either malt or grain whisky during the 1970s, although, interestingly, Grants have more recently given the approach a second try, producing Ailsa Bay malt whisky within the Girvan facility. Joe's thinking and innovation on this in context seems now to be a response to the industry situation at the time, rather than the start of a sustained industry trend. But arguably Joe's influence had a hand in giving rise (in the form of Ben Wyvis, Glen Flagler and Ladyburn malt whiskies, as well as Ben Nevis single blend whisky) to some of the rarest and most sought-after whisky collectibles!

At Ben Nevis, production figures from the period during which Joe owned and operated the distillery have not survived. However, with all the impediments to production removed, it is clear Joe was able to ramp up production substantially from 1955 until the year of his death in 1963, and fully contribute to the post-war boom in Scottish whisky production and exports. As Table 2 above makes clear, it took until 1955 before production of whisky in Scotland recovered and exceeded the level of the last pre-war year of production in 1938. However, once the brakes came off in the mid-1950s, production was rapidly expanded year-by-year, more than doubling by 1963 (the year of Joe's death) as the industry geared up to meet latent demand. During this period, the volume and value of whisky exported from Scotland also increased dramatically, driven by incredible growth in demand from the USA in particular.

When, in 1947, the decision was taken to make more grain available to distillers, the condition was that the industry would prioritise overseas exports, especially to the United States. To back this up the government decreed that sales of whisky to the UK domestic market were to be rationed to a volume that equated to 25% of domestic sales in 1938. Chancellor Hugh Dalton further reinforced this approach by raising duty on domestic sales of whisky by 21% in his autumn 1947 budget.[357] The following year, Stafford Cripps added another 10% to whisky duty, raising it to £1.23 per bottle (at a time when the retail price of a bottle of whisky was 33s 4d, or £1.67 in the metric system, and when average working wages were around £2 per week), and further limiting home sales to only 20% of the 1938 level.[358] This had the desired effect, with export sales exceeding the government's target of 10 million gallons for the first time in 1950–51, of which more than half was destined for the USA. In fact, growth in consumption of Scotch whisky in the US market was nothing less than phenomenal over the coming years, with US Scotch imports growing from 5.28m gallons in 1950, to 12m gallons by 1960, and to more than 33m gallons by 1968. This incredible growth in US demand was exactly what Joe had foreseen – although, because of WW2 and subsequent rationing, it took 15 years for his prediction to become reality.

In the late 1940s and early 1950s, this regulation of the UK domestic whisky market gave rise to a flourishing black market. Traders, brokers and speculators got involved supplying illicit whisky to those that could afford it, making windfall profits selling whisky at prices considerably higher than set in the government-controlled trade, and also selling whisky for export to markets which were not able to secure supplies during a time of shortage. The official industry association the Scotch Whisky Association fought hard to control the industry, and "bitterly resented the cowboys" who sought to work round the regulations and make a fast buck.[359] In February 1952, The People newspaper carried a story about Halsall Greenhill who made a fortune in less than four years by selling 'young' whisky (less than three years old) to South America, at a time when the big producers were short of supplies and restricting exports to that part of the world. On opening a wines and spirits business in Nottingham, Greenhill found there was a shortage of Scotch all over the world, and saw an opportunity to make some money "because the trade had forgotten that some countries would buy whisky of any age."[360] Greenhill had teamed up with a distiller in Scotland to supply his young whiskies – a distiller who turned out to be Joe Hobbs! Greenhill largely used spirit from Ben Nevis in his export trades. Joe made it clear that he was strictly following the law by only selling spirit three years or older to the UK market, but the unstated implication was that he did not object to selling younger spirit to overseas markets.

At the SWA's request, the government acted to protect the name and revenues of legitimate Scotch exports of spirits three years or older, which was Britain's biggest foreign exchange earner. Government action to enforce a ban on the export of young spirit less than 3 years old meant that the dealers and intermediaries in this trade saw their business terminated almost overnight. Joe was quoted saying the government's action "will mean that distillers have to lock up millions of capital to keep whisky until it is three years old."[361]

The following week, a group of distillers and traders who wanted to fight the government's ban on export of young whisky met in Glasgow to discuss the issue. They decided to form their own organisation, in opposition to the SWA, to fight for the right to sell younger spirit for export, and challenge the SWA's regulation of the industry. Halsall Greenhill was again an outspoken participant and member of the new Independent Scotch Whisky Association, which he said had been formed to "fight the monopoly" preventing export of young whisky. Joe was also present and was voted the association's first president.[362]

In retrospect, Joe's involvement with this Independent Scotch Whisky Association does not seem like his finest hour. Certainly, years of low production after WW2 meant there was a dearth of Scotch whisky, with the shortage of supply frustrating manufacturers and consumers alike. And Joe, with his entrepreneurial spirit and always wary of the dominance of the big players such as DCL in the established Scotch Whisky Association, clearly felt it he had a right to sell his products to whomever he wished. However, siding with the intermediaries and traders against the aims of pretty much the whole of the established whisky industry as well as the national government was perhaps not the smartest thing to do, and advocating for the right to sell poor-quality, immature spirit to overseas markets such as South America at a time of such shortage of whisky at home was not likely to win much public support either. Fortunately, with the easing of grain restrictions in 1953, and rapid normalisation of conditions in the industry, the black market disappeared, and the Independent Whisky Association quietly faded from view.

As the post-war restrictions eased after 1953, the industry really hit its stride, with production increasing by over 13% per year until 1963. With better supplies of malt and grains, and huge pent-up demand, the whisky industry entered a period of expansion and prosperity. Joe Hobbs was the first to react to this by commissioning and installing the new Coffey still at Ben Nevis distillery in 1955. With the new still installed, the completion of Joe's improvement works, and the frustrating shortages of barley now easing, Ben Nevis went back into full production and prospered during the remaining eight years of Joe's life. Joe was finally able to fulfil his vision of producing his own malt, grain and blends, and target lucrative export whisky markets, especially the USA. In fact, the whole industry boomed at this time, with the number of active distilleries in Scotland increasing from 80 in 1946 to 107 by 1963, and total Scottish whisky production rising to 94m gallons in 1963, more than 10 times what had been made in 1946–47. This was achieved partly by reactivating closed distilleries, but much more so by the expansion of existing distilleries and also by the construction of totally new distilleries for the first time since the 1890s.[363]

With Ben Nevis' challenges successfully resolved and the distillery prospering and operating at full capacity, Joe was able to begin looking for other ways to expand and take advantage of the booming industry conditions. From 1957 onwards, Joe focused on the last big entrepreneurial project of his life, in the form of Lochside, a new distillery he constructed from an old brewery in Montrose, on Scotland's east coast.

10

MacNab Distilleries and Lochside

After their return to the UK in 1933 following the disastrous end to Joe's property developments in Canada, Joe and Evelyn Hobbs initially went to live with Eve's mother, Flora, at her modest 1920s–30s era semi-detached home in London. Although it did not take Joe long to rebuild his business fortunes, living in a suburban semi-detached house with his mother-in-law must have been quite a contrast to the Laurier mansion and yachts of their Vancouver lifestyle.[al]

During this period, Joe set up a new company, MacNab Distilleries, which he intended to use as a vehicle to develop a new business in the whisky industry. He registered MacNab on 29th August 1933, with a nominal capital of just £100, and with himself and a hired Chartered Accountant, William Sharp, as the

---

al   Eve's mother, Flora Emily Snow, passed away on 5th February 1939 at
     the Lowther Road house. She left an estate of only £397, all of which
     she bequeathed to Eve. Eve had a younger sister, Vera, who married
     Kingsley Pearson Walker, an insurance broker. Vera was a regular visitor
     to Inverlochy in the 1950s. She died in 1987.

first directors. The address used on the company's Certificate of Incorporation was his mother-in-law's house at Lowther Road, Barnes – it is likely at this time that Joe was 'working from home' and could not afford his own office. After his return to the UK, it seems Joe harboured aspirations to acquire his own distilleries and move into the production side of the whisky business. Given his capital was so depleted, initially he did not have the resources to buy and operate his own distillery. Whilst the listed 'objects' (purposes) of MacNab Distilleries filed with Companies House allowed its operation as 'general distillers', it would take some time before Joe could fulfil his ambition to be a distillery owner. In the short term, MacNab was a 'good brand' for his established business of buying, selling and trading whiskies.

In establishing MacNab, Joe seems to have done his research on whisky history. In a press interview much later,[364] Joe showed he knew that the MacNab name had a long and "honoured"

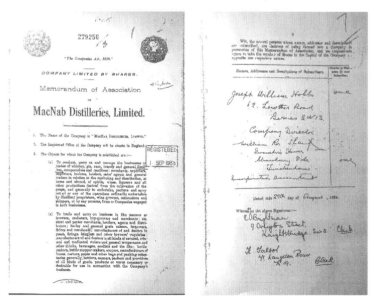

The original Memorandum of Association of MacNab Distilleries Limited, registered on 1st September 1933.

history in the whisky industry. Many of the ideas pioneered by John MacNab at the Glenmavis Distillery at Bathgate in Lothian in the second-half of the 19th century (for example making use of Coffey stills to distil malt whisky, and producing 'single blends' from malt and grain whiskies distilled on the same site) clearly influenced Joe's thinking and approach, and were to become 'trademarks' of Joe's own whisky career, repeated at ASD, Ben Nevis and Lochside. Whilst in the early 1930s he might have harboured plans to buy his own distillery and to revive Glenmavis, initially he lacked the resources to do so. Consequently, whilst Joe did pay in an additional £2,400 of share capital on 20th August 1936, taking the total to £2,500, he focused first on building up his whisky trading business, including commissioning his old friends at W.H. Holt & Sons to blend and bottle whisky branded as 'Sandy MacNab' for sale to the U.S. market, and sourcing whiskies for National Distillers. As

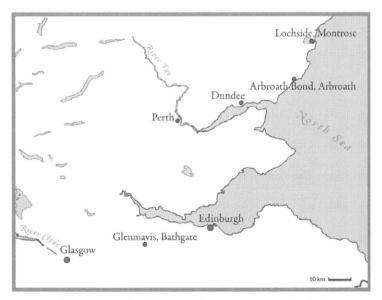

Map of Eastern Scotland showing the main sites involved when Joe developed his MacNab Distilleries business.

we have seen, in the latter part of the 1930s, this then developed into planning and implementing the extraordinary growth spurt of distillery acquisitions that were consolidated into Associated Scottish Distilleries.

As a result, while MacNab was initially used for his whisky trading business, Joe was not in a position to use the MacNab legal entity to progress his distilling aspirations for 15 years or so until after WW2. But, by the autumn of 1943, Joe clearly started thinking about and planning for post-war opportunities, investigating ways to move beyond simply trading whisky and achieve his ambitions as a whisky distiller and producer. He correctly anticipated that the outlook for the whisky industry was likely to improve considerably after the end of wartime restrictions, and began searching for distilleries available for a depressed price during the constrained wartime circumstances, planning to develop MacNab as a distilling company. In September 1943, the company share capital was increased by another £9,900, taking the total to £12,500 (2024: £0.7m), allowing Joe to move quickly once a suitable acquisition target was identified.

Joe's first move was to purchase the lease on Ben Nevis distillery in Fort William in December 1943, for which he set up a new company, 'Ben Nevis Distillery (Fort William) Ltd', to own the distillery lease and manage its operations. But in December 1945, he used MacNab Distilleries as the vehicle to acquire the Arbroath Bond at Arbroath in Angus, on Scotland's east coast. The property he acquired was the ex-'Baltic Works', a factory, mill buildings and warehouses, which for more than 50 years had been operated by the company Andrew Lowson Ltd. as a flax spinning business, but which had gone into liquidation. During the war, the site was occupied by the military who were still in occupation when Joe bought the premises.[365] Some writers have claimed Joe's intention was to convert the Arbroath site into a distillery.[366] It does seem that Joe indeed toyed with this idea during the later period he was struggling to get council approval to recommence distilling at Glenmavis distillery in Bathgate, but he did not promote this idea with local newspapers at the time, which was his usual modus operandi, and he did not raise the concept with the Arbroath council. Rather, Joe was initially mostly thinking about Arbroath as a site to store his maturing whisky, and in June 1948 obtained approval to convert the premises into a bonded warehouse with a capacity to store 4,000 casks.[367, 368] He subsequently used Arbroath Bond as both a storage facility for maturing whisky in casks, and a bottling plant for MacNab's and Ben Nevis whiskies.

Then, at some stage during 1948, Joe became aware that the Glenmavis distillery, long associated with the name of MacNab, was on the market, and he moved quickly to acquire it from the Edinburgh Merchant Company.

Originally constructed around 1783 in the town of Bathgate, Lothian, about 20 miles to the west of Edinburgh, Glenmavis had flourished in its early years, developing into a substantial operation with many buildings at its main site on Torphichen Road, as well as operating maltings and a bonded

Arbroath Bond (nee Baltic Works), Dens Road, Arbroath.

*The Arbroath Bond building today – it has been converted into flats,
with the adjacent warehouses all demolished.*

warehouse at a second site in Cochrane Street.[369] The distillery
had been bought in 1831 by John MacNab, who together with
his son (also John) owned and operated it until 1910 when
it was closed. In his excellent book 'Scotch Missed' on the
history of Scotland's many 'lost' and closed distilleries, Brian
Townsend provides a profile of the distillery, which uniquely
amongst malt distilleries after 1855 used a Coffey still to make
its malt whisky.[370] This technique for making grain whisky
differs markedly from the traditional approach to manufacture
more expensive and flavourful malt whisky, which uses smaller
'pot stills' to produce whisky in a succession of separate small
batches. It was – and still is today – very unusual to use a Coffey
or continuous still to make <u>malt</u> whisky, which is distilled with
expensive malted barley rather than cheaper corn, wheat or
rye grains, more typically used in Coffey stills, and indeed,
in Scotland today, Scotch Whisky Association rules prohibit
the use of Coffey stills for the production of whisky which is
labelled and sold as a 'single malt'.

MacNab's reasons for using a Coffey still are not clear. Townsend conjectures that possibly it was simply that MacNab had an opportunity to acquire this large still at a knock-down price from one of the other Lowland grain distilleries during a period when there was significant overcapacity amongst the big grain distillers in that part of Scotland. It could be that the price was less than the cost of buying two new small pot stills, but a large still such as this provided Glenmavis with much more capacity than it could use – the Glenmavis Coffey still was capable of turning out 2,000 gallons of new spirit a day, when it seems the distillery only ever produced a maximum of around 80,000 gallons over a full year at its peak in the mid-1880s. Townsend comments that the still "must have been the most underused item of plant in the whole Scotch whisky industry."[371]

Glenmavis was visited by Alfred Barnard during his famous 1886 tour of the whisky distilleries of Scotland. He reported Glenmavis to be "rustic" and somewhat old-fashioned, powered by waterwheel and using old methods and equipment at a time of considerable upgrading and expansion in the industry. The exception was the "handsome" Coffey still, the first Barnard had seen in use to make malt whisky. (As an aside, Barnard noted

Glenmavis Distillery, Bathgate, Lothian, c.1900.

Label from a bottle of MacNab's 'Celebrated Glenmavis Dew', a brand which inspired Joe Hobbs.

that John MacNab kept his own herd of 65 cattle, feeding them on the draff – the solid remains of the barley after mashing. This was another approach later adopted by Joe Hobbs, not just selling off the draff to local farmers, but using it to feed his own cattle on the Great Glen Cattle Ranch.) At the time of Barnard's visit, John MacNab bottled much of his production under his own brand, "MacNab's Celebrated Glenmavis Dew".[372] Unfortunately, production at Glenmavis ceased on the death of John MacNab's son in 1900, and after a ten-year period when it seems the company sold off its equipment and remaining stocks of whisky, the distillery closed down fully in 1910 and did not reopen.

Joe later explained that his primary reason for purchasing Glenmavis was to safeguard the MacNab name and prevent anyone else from using it – because by that time he had built a successful business selling the 'Sandy MacNab' brand of blended whisky.[373] But, in connection with the purchase of Glenmavis, he came to visit Bathgate, "liked the look of the district" and saw an opportunity to extend his business by rebuilding Glenmavis distillery. This is a repeat of his successful modus operandi with ASD in the late 1930s, bringing mothballed distilleries back to life. However, Glenmavis was more than just mothballed, it was largely derelict – most of the extensive original distillery buildings were in disrepair and unusable, and needed demolition and rebuilding. Joe brought in a Glasgow demolition firm to clear the old buildings, while he progressed his plans for a (supposedly) £300,000 investment to rebuild and re-equip the site.

However, right from the start of his Glenmavis project in 1948, Joe encountered obstacles and bureaucracy – he later complained in a 1956 press article about the red tape, saying he needed to get at least a dozen permits and "was still negotiating with the authorities after eight years". Whilst progressing the time-consuming task of obtaining all the necessary approvals, Joe turned his attention to rebuilding and completely modernising the "beautiful stone-built" Glenmavis House, the former home of the MacNabs, which he intended to make "one of the showplaces of the district", and several acres of landscape garden were laid out and planted with flowers and shrubs. Joe reasoned that this was also good for business, because "it impresses overseas buyers".[374]

A great deal of work was also required to restore the distillery's water source, MacNab's Pond, a well-known local landmark further up the hill to the north-east of the distillery, which had become choked and silted-up by debris and leaves accumulated over almost 50 years. Joe used modern equipment to clear it out, leading to the happy discovery that the pond

Glenmavis House, Bathgate, today.

sat atop several springs with good quality water bubbling up with surprising power – so the distillery still had a viable water source.

Things moved very slowly. Post-war restrictions meant Joe would not have been able to obtain supplies of barley to operate Glenmavis even had he rebuilt it, and so it was fully seven years after he acquired the distillery that Joe was given permission by the Board of Trade, in December 1955, to reopen.[375] On 20th January 1956, the West Lothian Courier reported that Glenmavis would soon restart.[376] Bathgate town Provost J.J. Shanks unofficially confirmed the news. A week later, the same paper ran a long story on broader efforts to promote industrial revival in the town, where again it was reported that the distillery had been renovated and would shortly go back into production – something the town council very much welcomed.[377] However, there was one big issue that remained to be dealt with – how to dispose of the effluent water from the distillery.

A month later, as part of a lengthy meeting to discuss redevelopment of Bathgate's water and sewage systems, the town council considered an application from Joe for permission to dispose of the Glenmavis distillery effluent through the borough sewers. Joe was quoted as saying he planned to spend £300,000 to re-equip and reopen the distillery, which would bring employment and income to the town, but he needed an immediate answer on the effluent issue before he could proceed to place the contracts for new equipment. The council had concerns that the acid nature of the effluent water might damage sewer pipes, and also that handling the Glenmavis discharge might result in a significant increase in the substantial expenditure already under consideration to upgrade the town's sewage works. Town Provost J.J. Shanks concluded that, while the council was positive about attracting new industry to the area, they could not give the immediate answer Joe had demanded and needed to understand the consequences in order better to safeguard ratepayers' interests. The council's consultant engineer would be asked for an opinion and the Public Health Committee would also look into the matter.[378]

The issue rumbled on for most of the rest of the year. Joe engaged in a charm and publicity offensive, taking every opportunity to talk up the size of the investments he would be making, and the benefits to the town and to local employment. He emphasised his policy to employ local labour and support local businesses, saying the distillery would employ 40 workers once established. He claimed that he already had orders for the whole first year of production from the new distillery – which, if true, must have been reservations from blenders, as it would take at least three years before the new production could legally be sold as whisky – more likely this was typical Joe Hobbs "sleight of hand" and any orders would have been from Joe's own blending and bottling operation. In a further interview in May 1956, on the issue of the effluent, Joe said the council had not yet reached a decision. The town's sewage works were old and needed to be rebuilt, and so there were concerns that, until the sewage works were upgraded, the distillery effluent would pass into local rivers unprocessed. Joe struck a typically positive note, saying if necessary he would "build our own purification plant".[379]

The article reported that Joe had taken the time to study the history and traditions of Glenmavis, saying it was the site of installation of the first Coffey still after Aeneas Coffey invented it 100 years earlier, and that Glenmavis had made "the first self-whisky". If by this he meant Glenmavis had been the first distillery to produce its own *blended whisky* from malt and grain whiskies both distilled at the same site, he could well have been right. The term "self-whisky" was, though, more commonly used at the time to refer to *malt whiskies* produced from a single distillery, of which there were many examples, and Glenmavis was far from the first. Joe was also quoted as having bought up many Glenmavis souvenirs and relics, although he was still searching for an old bottle to replicate. He explained that the whisky made at Glenmavis had once been famous in the trade and among connoisseurs for its quality, which he intended to revive and improve upon, saying "history was in fact made at Glenmavis". The whisky he intended to make at Glenmavis would be labelled 'Sandy MacNab' and be mostly for export.[380]

In an effort to work around the problem with the town's sewage works, Joe proposed an alternative plan to feed the waste water into the disused Balbardie Colliery on the other side of Waverley Road from the distillery. However, after evaluation, the National Coal Board refused to allow this, because the effluent water would have seeped through the old mine workings and entered another pit, Easton Colliery, that was still working.[381]

Joe seems to have been considering any and all options to solve the problem. He apparently considered a plan to use the two sites he owned at Glenmavis and Arbroath in combination, even though there was a distance of 80 miles between the two. He also at this time considered converting Arbroath for use as a distillery, and transporting casks of whisky made there for storage and maturation at the Glenmavis warehouses in Bathgate. But, without either site approved for distillation, all this proved unworkable.

Soon, another opportunity arose at Montrose, a little further up the east coast from Arbroath, at a brewery named Lochside. Brewing had taken place on the site for over 200 years, starting as the old Ross Brewery, then rebuilt and operated by the brewers James Deuchars Ltd. since 1898. Deuchars had been acquired by Newcastle Breweries Ltd. earlier that year in April 1956 (the combined firm going on to become the giant Scottish and Newcastle Breweries). However, with surplus capacity across their various plants, the newly enlarged company's management preferred to make use of their Duddingston brewery in Edinburgh. Joe heard that Lochside could be for sale in August, and came to see it as a better solution than persisting with Glenmavis.

Back in Bathgate, the Forth River Purification Board wrote to Bathgate Council on 7th November 1956 to inform them that the council needed to upgrade their sewage works (with Joe paying the cost for that part of the upgrade beyond what was required by the town for its own purposes); or alternatively, Joe had to spend £40,000 (2024: £1.25m) to install a new sewage system of his own, in order to prevent further pollution to the River Avon, a tributary of the River Forth. They refused Joe's request for a two-year grace period during which he be allowed to discharge into the river until Glenmavis was earning enough profit to either install his own purification plant or contribute to the council's costs to upgrade their sewage works.[382, 383]

In reporting this, the West Lothian Courier noted that Joe had "already spent a considerable amount of time and money acquiring and renovating the old distillery premises" and said they hoped Joe would still consider his alternative plan of installing the distillery's own water purification plant. The paper sympathised with him, but feared the Purification Board's decision would "have dealt a deadly blow to [his] scheme to revive Glenmavis distillery."[384] Perhaps justifiably Joe complained about the lack of 'joined up' thinking in government at that time: Bathgate was in a development zone and the Board of Trade had encouraged him to set up in the area; although the town's sewage system had been inadequate for years the government refused to give the town a grant to upgrade it, and the Purification Board then expected Joe to pay the full cost of making good the town's inadequate provision.

After eight years of work, the Purification Board's decision put the final nail in the coffin of Joe's efforts to rebuild Glenmavis and put it back into operation. Joe seemed to confirm he had spent less than he had implied getting the site ready for redevelopment, but indicated he had reached the end of the line with the project, saying "I spent £6,000 preparing the site... Eight men have been kept continuously employed on the site. Now they will have to be discharged." [385, am]

Up the coast at Montrose, Joe found a more supportive town council. The Lochside brewery in the town took its name from the nearby Mary's Loch on a site on the main road north. Brewing was thought to have taken place on the site for more than 200 years, taking advantage of good supplies of local barley and a reliable source of hard water from an artesian well. From 1842, William Ross, "brewer at Lochside of Newmanswalls", owned the land and operated the brewery with several partners before he was bought out by James Deuchar in the 1880s. Deuchars invested to upgrade the facilities, drilling new bore holes in 1888 to improve water supplies (which after subsequent upgrading were to enable the distillery to benefit from reliable supplies of 3,000 gallons of water an hour right up to the time of its eventual closure in 1992). At the same time, Deuchars commissioned the

---

am Bathgate Town Council eventually agreed in April 1959 to borrow £120,000 from the Home Office to finally upgrade its inadequate sewage facilities. The work took a further two years to complete, being finished in the early 1960s. Whilst the upgrade was to a standard that would satisfy the Forth River Purification Board and remove any danger to the council of liability arising from river pollution, it is interesting to note that even at that time the council were reluctant to commit resources beyond what was necessary to process the town's domestic water needs. A specific decision was taken not to upgrade to a level that could support any future whisky distillery in the town, such as had been proposed for Glenmavis – to do so would have doubled the cost of the scheme (West Lothian Courier, 17th April 1959, "New Sewage Works in Two Years").

famous distillery architect Charles Doig of Elgin to redesign and upgrade the buildings. Completed in 1889, the most striking feature of the design was a unique tower in the style of a German Brauhaus, which brought a Continental flavour to the small east coast town. In common with many of his other distillery and brewery designs, Doig used gravity wherever possible to assist operations, so that liquids flowed without the use of pumps from a tank at the top of the tower through all the later stages of production. Lochside was the only location outside Newcastle that the famous 'Newcastle Brown Ale' was brewed, with the output shipped from Montrose to Tyneside twice a week using the company's own ships.

Just a few weeks after Joe's plans at Glenmavis had ended, he successfully completed negotiations to acquire Lochside and announced his intention to convert it for use as a distillery. Joe said the conversion was subject to "the usual official permission"; however, the conversion itself would be relatively

The striking and unusual Charles Doig-designed brewery at Lochside, Montrose, which Joe Hobbs bought from Scottish & Newcastle Breweries in 1956 and converted into Lochside Distillery.

simple, the main work being the installation of the stills to make the whisky. Joe hoped to begin distillery operations as early as June or July 1957, and to employ about 25 men, most of whom would be former brewery employees. He explained that his plan was to mature whisky from Lochside at Arbroath prior to bottling, and that Lochside's output would supplement supplies from Ben Nevis. "Most of it will go to America after maturing. This has been done to meet the tremendous demand for whisky from America. The market there is absolutely crying out for it. We'll not be able to ship it for a few years, but right now I could distil three times as much as I'm doing," Joe said. He also made reference to the fact that this was the second time he was building a whisky distillery in Montrose, saying "I'm looking forward to renewing old acquaintances, for I built the Hillside Distillery in 1938-39. The Lochside Distillery will be similar to the one at Hillside."[386]

In an article the following day, the Bathgate newspaper bewailed that "Bathgate's loss is Montrose's gain," and that Joe and MacNab Distilleries had been "thwarted by the Forth River Purification Board," whose objections "are difficult to appreciate."[387]

At the time he took the decision to buy Lochside and finally give up on Glenmavis, Joe did not know for sure that he could avoid exactly the same problems disposing of the effluent from the distillery at Montrose that had stymied the efforts for eight years at Bathgate. Fortunately, the Montrose Town Council were to prove more pragmatic. At a meeting of the Council to discuss the issue of the new distillery's waste water, the Council stated that they did not know what effect the distillery effluent would have on the area's drainage system, and noted that as an element of the effluent was solid matter, it might lead to complaints. However, having obtained reports from the Medical Officer of Health and the Borough Surveyor, the Council agreed that

Joe could put the effluent into the town's sewers, although they reserved the right, in the event of any issue, to require Lochside to treat the effluent to clean it up before discharge.[388] With this important decision obtained in just a matter of weeks, Joe could move ahead with confidence at Lochside. He took the decision to move all remaining useful plant from Glenmavis to Lochside, and in parallel, began closing down and selling off assets at Glenmavis.[389]

Joe's approach at Lochside had many features in common with his earlier successful operations, for example buying mothballed and out-of-service assets on the cheap, refurbishing and reopening them, and using new technologies and methods to produce both malt and grain whiskies on the same site. At Lochside, the plan was to start operations as a grain whisky distillery, and then once that was established, to proceed to add malt whisky distilling capacity as a second phase, which would require only minor additional alterations. There was a short delay until February 1957 before Joe was able to gain access to the site, after which work began to convert some of the brewing plant into mashtuns and washbacks, and build a tower ready to install a 67-foot-high two-column Coffey still (which was manufactured in London) to produce grain whisky. Other work was done to convert the former maltings into storage space for 750,000 gallons of maturing spirit, upgrade the boilers from coal to oil power, and convert the former kiln into space to store up to 140 tons of grain. Water came from the artesian wells on the premises which was said to be of "highly satisfactory" quality. Whisky production was planned to commence in September 1957, at a very sizeable 14,000 gallons per week. Farmers in the district were expected to welcome the opportunity to sell their product locally and avoid substantial transport costs to get it to markets further away, and the grain distillery could operate with unmalted barley of a lower quality and higher moisture content than was required for malt whisky production, providing a market for more of the local area's barley production. Now aged 66, Joe spent about half his time during this period in Montrose, supervising the work.[390]

By the end of July 1957, Joe was able to show a reporter from the Montrose Review around the premises to see the progress of the £150,000 renovation (2024: £4.5m). The key features included installation of the Coffey still (one column weighed 14 tons, the other 6 tons) housed in its purpose-built tower; the two 2,500-gallon copper spirit receivers and a 7,500-gallon copper storage unit; and two one-ton cookers for preparing the barley and grains for distillation. Physical renovations had been quite extensive too, with the whole ground floor of Lochside House converted into offices. A new cafeteria had been built for the distillery workers, and the old brewery garden beautified. Subject to approval from the Customs and Excise officers (for whom special offices had been constructed), the new distillery was on track to commence operations around the end of September.[391] Joe recruited Mr. John Warren, formerly of Longmorn Distillery in Elgin, to be the new production manager.[392]

Later than originally planned, but still less than 10

months after concluding the purchase of the old brewery, on Monday, 7th October 1957, Joe formally opened the new Lochside Distillery, Montrose, after completion of the £150,000 refit. Joe hosted a delegation from the local

The Coffey still at Lochside distillery.

The unusual design of the washbacks Joe had constructed at Lochside.

council, proudly showing them around the premises prior to the start of first fermentation. The first distillation followed within 72 hours, with initial production set at 2,000 gallons per week, planned to increase to 9,000 gallons after six weeks, and then gradually to 14,000 gallons per week after that. The new distillery had storage capacity for 1–1.5 years of production, with more space for maturing casks also available at Arbroath. Initial interest and orders from the trade were said to be strong. Joe said "we are foresold to next April and orders are pouring in from all over the world", albeit most production was expected to be for the US market.[393] At the time, distilleries did not really produce whisky 'on spec'; rather they produced to fulfil orders from the blenders, who would typically combine multiple malt whiskies from different distilleries with at least one grain whisky in their blends. However, since Lochside's whisky was 'new', the blenders would not have been sure what it would actually taste like, especially since it would take three years of maturation before it could be legally included in any Scotch whisky blend. Joe and his team had done extremely well to secure strong advanced orders from the whisky trade for his new product, but it is quite likely a good proportion of those orders came from his own MacNab Distilleries blending arm, to be used for their Sandy MacNab blend.

Both of the town's newspapers covered the story, with the Montrose Standard using the opportunity to provide details about Joe's life and career, and celebrating that the new distillery "has brought back to Montrose one of the more colourful figures in Scotland today."[394] Much was made of the fact that most of the work to rebuild and fit out the new distillery had been done by local firms, many of whom contributed advertisements to a special feature on the new distillery in the following week's edition of the Standard. Employment was provided directly to 30 staff members working on a shift system, with office staff and lorry drivers bringing the total staff complement up to 40 people.[395]

Joe's bold move to develop Lochside also made the national news, with Scottish Television running a feature on Lochside on their news broadcast on 30th October 1957. Joe made arrangements for his workers to view the programme at the distillery, but apparently the reception was terrible and the programme almost unwatchable! [396]

At another press conference held only three weeks after the Lochside opening, Joe announced that he had bought 12 acres of land at Newmanswalls, nearby the distillery, in "one of the biggest private building schemes in Montrose since the war". 7.5 acres of land adjoining the main Aberdeen–Montrose road would be used to construct a large new warehouse, and the remaining 4.5 acres between the new warehouse and Panter Crescent would be used for construction of worker's houses and for private development. Joe said "We are looking to the future. At the moment, we only have storage capacity for 18 months. We have already shipped whisky to bonded warehouses in Glasgow, where it will be kept for a period of three years to mature. And once we are in full production we shall be turning out 14,000 gallons per week." Press articles also mentioned the benefits of the distillery to local farmers, both for selling their barley, as well as for recommencing supplies of cattle feed from the distillery draff, which had been in short supply since the brewery closed. Joe told the reporter from the Montrose Review that "the plant is giving entire satisfaction. It is one of the most up-to-date in the country."[397, 398]

The Review also carried a separate piece in their 'Round the Town' column, praising Joe as the "rancher millionaire... whose imagination and vision...has brought a new industry to the town" which was capable of further expansion and a welcome replacement for brewing, which was dying out. Joe was also praised for showing in various ways "his interest in the community. That interest is reciprocated and, we feel, will be productive and of lasting benefit to the town."[399] This was indeed a feature of the way Joe and Eve Hobbs conducted themselves, and throughout their time in the UK starting at Glenury in the late 1930s, during the war years in Leicestershire, at Fort William and Inverlochy after WW2, and then subsequently also at Montrose from the mid-1950s, the couple were active in support of the wider community and generous sponsors of its development. As an example, Eve visited the Dorward old people's home in Montrose in November, giving a slide show to residents and spending time talking to them afterwards. She was quoted as saying that she was "intensely interested in the welfare of old folk."[400] Joe was busy at the same time opening the annual bazaar for Montrose Football Club at the town's Drill and Recreation Hall.[401]

Later that month, Eve made the national press for her work supporting the elderly when, as a county councillor from Fort William, she attended and spoke at a conference in Edinburgh on services for the elderly. The Guardian published an article titled 'A Dram A Day' in which Eve is quoted as saying: "I am very keen on giving drams to old people. It helps to buck them up no end. Whenever I go visiting old folks in the Highlands I always carry a small bottle in my handbag. It works wonders. Not only old men need it; the old women need it too". Apparently Mrs Hobbs was cheered loudly by delegates, many of whom were pensioners.[402]

In the spring of the following year, Joe needed to put more money into MacNab to fund the distillery's operation and expansion. Whisky making is a costly and time-consuming business, with owners required to fund the cost of buildings and equipment upfront, pay for barley and grain, labour and running costs on an ongoing basis, and provide barrels and warehousing for storage for at least three years before the first whisky can be sold and revenues start to flow in. MacNabs had invested £150,000 to rebuild and equip Lochside, had to pay the substantial ongoing running costs, and now also needed to fund the land acquisition and construction costs for the new warehouses on the Newmanswalls site. MacNabs would certainly have had bank loans to help with all of this, but banks – as well as good corporate governance – would definitely have required Joe as the owner to contribute more of his own equity to the business. In April 1958, Joe paid in an additional £157,500 in cash to MacNabs, increasing the share capital from £12,500 to £170,000.[403] Joe often downplayed his personal wealth, but this is a sum equivalent to more than £4.6m in contemporary terms, and the fact Joe had the ability to contribute such a sum demonstrates (together with Ben Nevis, the Inverlochy Estate and Great Glen Cattle Ranch and his yacht Torlundy) that by this time Joe had substantially rebuilt the fortune he had lost in Canada.

Some of the additional funding was also used to proceed

Two of the four 'onion-shaped' stills Joe installed in 1958 to expand Lochside Distillery for malt whisky production.

with the planned second-phase expansion of Lochside as a malt whisky distillery, expanding from its grain whisky production capability which had been the first focus on reopening. Construction began in the spring of 1958 to build a second distillation plant at Lochside, with four new onion-shaped pot stills installed for the production of malt whisky. Once construction was completed in October 1958, the new unit added 2,000 gallons per week to the distillery's overall production capacity, which now totalled an impressive 16,000 gallons per week.[404]

Around this time in 1958, the distillery team was joined by Charles Sharpe, who originally had been employed by Joe to work on the refit of his yacht Ocean Mist, then redeployed to Lochside as the distillery maintenance engineer. In a nearly 40-year career with the distillery, Charles Sharpe was promoted to distillery manager in 1977, and oversaw its eventual closure for the last time in 1996.

The installation of the new pot stills for malt whisky production enabled Lochside to commence the practice – by now definitely something of a speciality of Joe Hobbs – of 'blending at birth', i.e. combining the new make malt and grain whiskies in casks to mature together. In an article on Montrose's industrial outlook, the Montrose Standard carried an extensive feature on Lochside, where the distillery was said to be unique in being able to produce both malt and grain whisky at the same site – actually, this was not true, as Joe's other distillery Ben Nevis could do it too! The article commented on the Lochside owner's practice to 'blend at birth', which they said "greatly enhances the quality of the blend" by allowing their flavours to harmonise together in the cask, as well as saving transportation and rehandling costs which would otherwise be incurred to mix the blend later. The blend was designed to remain in casks at the distillery warehouses until matured, ready to be bottled directly when it was three years old. This practice continued as a unique feature of the whiskies produced at Joe's distilleries up until his death in 1963.

The article also reported that plant capacity had now increased to 16,000 gallons per week due to the four new pot stills bringing a further 2,000 gallons of capacity on top of the 14,000 gallons that could be produced in the Coffey still. Warehouse capacity had increased to 1 million gallons, with a contract awarded to Burness & Sons to build the planned new warehouse at the Newmanswalls site opposite the distillery, which would be capable of storing a further 4,000 casks. As a result of the expansion, the directly employed labour force had increased from 30 to 45 persons.[405]

During the time Joe operated Lochside distillery, its produce was rarely bottled as a single malt, with almost all of the production, both malt whisky and grain whisky, destined to go into his blended whisky brands, the most famous of which was Sandy Macnab's. In commenting on Lochside's success in 1959, the Montrose Review highlighted that, at the time, whisky blenders had struggled to find sufficient stocks of grain whiskies to make up their blends, grain whisky production being dominated by a few major players such as the Distiller's Company Limited. This was a gap in the market that Joe had correctly diagnosed, and was behind his decisions to install Coffey stills for grain

'Sandy Macnab' blended whisky, bottled and marketed by Joe's 'MacNab Distilleries' company, using malt and grains whiskies distilled at Lochside distillery, Montrose.

whisky production at both Ben Nevis and Lochside, a key factor underpinning the financial success of both distilleries.[an]

With the strong demand for Lochside's whiskies, in February 1959, the Montrose Dean of Guild Court approved plans from MacNabs to build two more storage buildings at Lochside, at a cost of £17,000 each.[406] However, despite these strong signs of growth and expansion, after this two-year period of great activity and media coverage from the end of 1956 until early 1959, there were very few reports of Lochside or MacNabs until the time of Joe's death in 1963. From 1960 onwards, the normally very high-profile Joe Hobbs almost entirely disappeared from public view. Although there is a steady trickle of stories of Eve opening fetes,

---

an   This situation changed dramatically in the 1960s, with the construction of a huge amount of new grain whisky distilling capacity. This was driven by construction of 3 huge new grain distilleries – Invergordon in 1961 (with a capacity of 11m proof gallons by 1963); Girvan in 1963 (with a capacity of 5m proof gallons); and Moffat in 1965 (with an eventual capacity of 15m proof gallons). Together with expansion of existing grain distilleries such as those operated by DCL's Scottish Grain Distillers subsidiary, Hume & Moss have shown in their book 'The Making of Scotch Whisky' (1981) that total output of grain whisky in Scotland increased from 41m gallons in 1959 to nearly 90m gallons in 1966. Access to adequate supplies of grain whisky for blending became much less of a problem subsequently, and the Coffey stills Joe Hobbs installed at Ben Nevis and Lochside gradually became more of a disadvantage than an advantage.

A copy of a 1950s advert for Sandy MacNab's blended whisky painted by Margaret Hobbs, the wife of Joe's grandson Joseph Peter Hobbs.

supporting her successful teenage youth club in Inverlochy, and even, in July 1962, judging the Scottish Dairy Queen contest, she was alone in these engagements, and there is an almost complete absence of media coverage of Joe and his business interests. Joe was sighted in Montrose in February 1960 hosting the annual dinner of the Montrose and District Wild Fowler's Association, of which he was honorary president,[407] but, without Joe's active promotion, his business interests had far less media coverage after 1960. The reason was that Joe (who turned 69 in January 1960) began to suffer from ill health, which forced him to slow down considerably and withdraw substantially from his previously highly active 'hands-on' approach to management of his businesses.

For Lochside, without its owner's dynamic management, operations continued quietly through the early 1960s, until the time of Joe's death in August 1963.

11

The Inverlochy Estate and the Great Glen Cattle Ranch

Not long after he acquired the Ben Nevis distillery, Joe Hobbs made another big investment in the Fort William/Lochaber region when he bought the Inverlochy Estate, including the house that would become Joe's home for the rest of his life.

The area of Inverlochy just north-east of Fort William occupies a strategically important site to the south of the Lochy River at the entrance to the Great Glen, a natural thoroughfare to the Scottish Highlands and the route to Inverness. The area is home to Inverlochy Castle, a historic fortress built around 1270-80 AD. The castle's strategic location meant it featured in a number of notable battles over the years, including the First and Second Battles of Inverlochy.[ao] Inverlochy Castle was a

---

ao   The First Battle of Inverlochy took place in September 1431 when King James I was trying to break the power of Alexander Islay, Lord of the Isles, and bring the Highlands under his control. James imprisoned Alexander Islay, and in retaliation his kinsman Donald Balloch defeated a larger force loyal to King James commanded by Alexander Stewart, Earl of Mar, who were camped nearby Inverlochy Castle. The battle was

The ruins of Old Inverlochy Castle with Ben Nevis in the background.

formidable fortress, which has endured remarkably well into modern times, one of the most complete Scottish castles to survive largely intact from the 13th century.

The Inverlochy Estate, including the castle and its grounds, as well as the fishing rights on the River Lochy, one of Scotland's

---

influential in forcing a rethink by James I, subsequently reconciling with Alexander and establishing the Lord of the Isles as a key source of power and authority over the Highlands of Scotland.

The Second Battle of Inverlochy took place 200 years later in February 1645 when Scots Royalists were trying to engage 'Roundhead'-supporting forces in Scotland to prevent them from being deployed to England against King Charles I's Royalist forces during the English Civil War. The Royalist army of James Graham, the Marquess of Montrose, massacred the Covenanter (Parliamentarian or government army) forces of the Marquess of Argyle and Bute at Inverlochy after marching 36 miles in 36 hours over some of the toughest terrain in Britain in the middle of winter snows to surprise the larger Covenanter forces commanded by Sir Duncan Campbell of Auchinbreck.

best salmon rivers, was bought in 1837 by James Scarlett, the 1st Baron Abinger. Abinger was a lawyer, judge, MP and Privy Councillor. His successor William Scarlett, the 3rd Baron, had an imposing Scottish baronial-style mansion built out of granite in the grounds of Old Inverlochy Castle half a mile away, to replace an old shooting lodge. Sometimes referred to as New Inverlochy Castle, the house sits in a spectacular setting, in the vicinity of Ben Nevis, and with views over hills and glens in multiple directions. Improvements including restoration of ornate battlements were undertaken in advance of the visit of Queen Victoria, who stayed at the house for a week in September 1873, using it as a base for sightseeing in the Fort William area, and sketching and painting, before moving on to Glencoe and Oban. In her diaries, she wrote that she "never saw a lovelier or more romantic spot".[408]

The Abingers expanded the house between 1890 and 1893, increasing the number of bedrooms to 35. In 1939, the 7th Baron, Hugh Richard Scarlett, generously donated the house to the nation, with the intention that it would be used

Aerial photo of New Inverlochy Castle, viewed from the west, 6th June 1953, during the period that Joe Hobbs lived there.

for establishment of a Land Training Centre and agricultural college for the Highlands. However, the outbreak of WW2 soon after meant that the plan had to be abandoned, and as a result the government formally withdrew their acceptance of the offer to take over the house and grounds.

It was then requisitioned by the army for military training during the war. However, in July 1943, Hugh Scarlett died from a heart attack at the age of 64, whilst working on the estate. Inheritance passed to James Scarlett (8th Baron), who was serving in India. Despite having strong family ties to the area (he was a descendant of the Campbell of Auchinbreck, who was killed leading the fighting against Earl Montrose at the Second Battle of Inverlochy in 1645), the 8th Lord Abinger seemed to have had little interest in his Scottish estates, and agreed to sell a large part of the Inverlochy Estate and the Torlundy dairy farm to Joe Hobbs, retaining about half of the estate including some salmon fishing rights on the River Lochy.[ap]

Having established connections with the Fort William area when he purchased Glenlochy distillery back in 1937, which were further solidified following his acquisition of the lease on Ben Nevis distillery in December 1943, Joe was keen to find an appropriate home in the vicinity. He would have been well aware of the Inverlochy Estate, the pre-eminent estate in proximity to Ben Nevis distillery – in fact, the distillery had been built on land which had previously been part of the Inverlochy Estate. Joe was the son of a farmer and from a line of cattle-rearing farmers. It is not surprising that, with his fortunes re-established following his successful ventures with ASD and National Distillers of America, and with a new commitment at Ben Nevis distillery 'anchoring' him to the area around Fort William, Joe aspired like many before him

---

ap Lord Abinger bought a new home on the Essex/Suffolk borders to live in after his return from the war.

and many after to own a Scottish estate and assume the role of Scottish land owner and farmer.

In August 1945, The Scotsman newspaper announced that Joe had acquired the Inverlochy Estate from Lord Abinger.[409] By this time, after the war years when the house had been occupied as a military training centre and part of the estate used as a firing range, both New Inverlochy Castle house and the estate were in poor condition. As well as the house, Joe also bought the historic Old Castle, the Torlundy dairy farm with its herd of premium cattle, and the Achendaul sheep farm, together comprising a substantial estate in excess of 3,500 acres. To its further benefit, the estate enjoyed a free supply of electricity in perpetuity, which had been negotiated by Lord Abinger when the Lochaber Power Bill passed through Parliament in the 1920s, as part of the deal providing the land for the power station and as compensation for the power station's disruption to water rights on the River Lundy. It was later revealed that Joe paid £17,500 for the estate, and a further £2,500 for the pedigree dairy herd at Torlundy.[410] (In combination, approximately £1.1m today – something of a bargain, given the size of the estate, reflecting the poor condition of the house and estate at the time.)

In August 1945, Inverlochy Castle was reported in the Daily Record to be "in the process of de-requisitioning" after use by Allied soldiers during the war. The "magnificently panelled" rooms were awaiting repair and redecoration. The same article also reported that Ben Nevis distillery was slowly getting back into production, with staff and permit restrictions still in place hampering its return to full operation.[411]

In combination, the house and estate Joe had acquired comprised a sizeable property with some prestigious assets, and put Joe firmly on the map as a Highland landowner. However, both house and estate were substantially rundown and needed a lot of work done on them. Needless to say, Joe was not intending to live quietly on the estate and enjoy a life as a country gentleman. Later, Joe made some comments which give insight into his thinking at this time. He was asked how he decided on the idea to start the ranch, and in reply Joe said "I went up there to retire. I bought Ben Nevis distillery. I thought I had better buy a house. To get a house I had to buy an estate. I thought I had better put the estate to work."[412]

Typically, Joe quickly envisioned bold plans for the estate. An article in the People's Journal in August 1945 soon after the sale was completed noted "Mr Hobbs...has big plans for the fullest development of the estate. He means to reclaim wasteland so as to increase the head of cattle. Reforestation is to be undertaken to replace timber which was cut down during this war and the last war. He also intends to go ahead with the building of houses for his distillery and estate workers."[413] Between 1945 and 1947, Joe worked up substantial plans for developing the estate, leveraging his agricultural roots and knowledge of farming techniques from Canada. With his strategic mindset and flair for publicity, Joe wasted no time communicating his grand plans to transform large tracts of barren moorland into a productive 'Prairie-style' cattle ranch. Joe announced his intentions to reclaim wasteland, get rid of the sheep, substantially expand the cattle herd, engage in a programme of reforestation, and build new houses for the distillery and estate workers. Building on work begun by the 7th Lord Abinger to reopen the lime kilns and sawmills at Torlundy, Joe also had plans for the development of lime quarrying and timber processing, to supply lime to improve the farm soil and provide building materials for roads and housing in the area.

Seen in the context of Scotland's preceding agricultural history, Joe's ideas were new, unorthodox and, to some, controversial. Joe was right to say that Scotland had a long history of cattle rearing: from as far back as the 14th century, there was a well-organised trade involving the movement of large numbers of cattle from distant pastures across the Highlands to the big markets in Lowland Scotland (e.g. at Falkirk and Lanark), and on to England. However, following the forced break up and dispersal of the Highland Clans after the 1745 Jacobite Rebellion, and then the extensive impact of the Highland Clearances in the 18th and 19th centuries which forced thousands of small-holder farmers off land in the valleys and glens that were most suitable for cattle rearing and replaced them with large sheep farms, cattle rearing had declined considerably across the Highlands. The consolidation of landowning in a narrow cohort of extremely large estates, many of which were then used by their owners as 'sporting' estates predominantly for deer and grouse rather than commercial agriculture, compounded the issue. Gradually the practice of farmers across Scotland using drovers to send their cattle to market died out during the 18th century. Bracken and heather invaded the highland pasture lands, and cattle rearing substantially diminished. Now in post-war Britain, with rationing and food shortages, Joe saw a way to bring the barren uplands back into productive use, and stimulate cattle production in the Highlands again, using methods he understood from his experience in Canada for inspiration.[414, 415, 416]

Joe developed an evolving vision for how large-scale ranching using modern methods and equipment to reclaim and operate the uplands could change the face of farming in Scotland.[aq] In a 1951 article in the Vancouver Sun, Joe expressed the view

---

aq It was a characteristic of Joe's approach to farming that he deployed modern equipment. But the challenging environment took its toll on machinery, and Joe worked his equipment hard. Joe's grandson Joseph Peter Hobbs tells a story that having used a Zetor tractor (from the Czech Republic) for some years on the estate, he decided it had seen better days and made arrangements to sell it. A nearby farmer bought it, but 2 weeks later the irate farmer was back at Inverlochy Castle, angrily complaining to Joe that "that bloody tractor you sold me doesn't work!" To which Joe's reply was "Why do you think I wanted to sell it?"

that "with the proper methods, Scotland's beef production can be doubled in 5 years. The land isn't worn out. Difficulties in winter and heavy rain can be overcome. In proper ranching, you make nature work for you." Joe genuinely believed that if his ranching ideas were adopted at scale across Scotland "we could make this Britain's larder."[417] With his strategic vision, Joe saw this as connected to efforts that needed to be made to develop lime quarries, build roads, address depopulation, progress electrification, and systematically develop the Highlands. Joe's thinking was aligned with the post-war Labour government's approach to economic planning for the Highlands, with Joe articulating a vision to build "a new Scotland with useless acres reclaimed, the land resettled and production of all foods increased".[418] Government leaders invited Joe to participate in a number of commissions and initiatives to assist their efforts to develop the Highlands.

Joe's plans were both ambitious and novel – many people thought his ideas eccentric and many farming observers doubted his chances of success, mainly because it was thought that the Highland moorland was not rich enough to provide sufficient feed to keep a herd of cattle alive. The core of Joe's plan for developing the estate was what became 'The Great Glen Cattle Ranch'. Inspired by what he had seen and learned in Canada, Joe planned a programme to recover barren moorland and turn it into good-quality cattle grazing land, to be operated 'Prairie-style', allowing the cattle to roam and graze over large tracts of open land. Joe believed ranching had huge potential across the Scottish Highlands, and that the Highland land could be made much more productive, contribute to higher living standards and sustain a larger population. As with his earlier plans for the development of Vancouver, Joe's emerging vision once again demonstrates his 'big picture thinking' and ability to act boldly and with great energy and determination to realise his ideas. In this case, Joe's vision was not just for his own land at Inverlochy, but also for the development of wider Highland Scotland and of many other areas of upland Britain, helping to solve Britain's post-war meat shortages, contribute to the national economy and reduce reliance on imported foods. At this time, Britain's currency was under sustained pressure, and producing more food at home and reducing expensive imports became a priority for a succession of post-war governments. In a later interview with the Liverpool Echo, Joe was said to be "ploughing fortune back into undiscovered Scotland", and to have calmly poured £100,000 into cattle ranching over 21 square miles of the Highlands and made it pay. Joe said, "This is the most undeveloped part of the Empire, close to markets. What we've got to do is level the ground, roll off the rocks, fill up the holes and get rid of the heather all over Lochaber."[419]

Joe developed his own approach to making the estate productive again, which he described as "more of an engineering problem than a farming problem."[420] The approach was comprehensive, taking advantage of modern techniques across the whole range of farming practices on the ranch, and, typically for Joe, often applying knowledge from other fields of activity to the specific farming problems in Highland Scotland for the first time. This was further evidence of Joe's engineering and technical mindset. It took years and great persistence for Joe's vision to transform the estate into a productive and profitable ranch, but, with his usual determination, hard work and willingness to lead by example and get his hands dirty, Joe was able to prove his methods worked and make the ranch highly successful over the coming years.

In putting all of this together, Joe worked closely with the Inverlochy estate factor – the estate manager. Joe's first factor at Inverlochy was a man called Henderson. He and Joe did not get on because Henderson was an 'old school' factor who expected the laird to keep at 'arm's length' and not get involved in day-to-day management of the estate – which was never going to work with Joe Hobbs. So, in March 1948, not long after he moved to implement his ranching vision, Joe appointed Charlie Palmer as his new factor. Palmer had previously been assistant factor on John Gilbert Ramsay's estate at Kinlochlaggan, 25 miles away at Newtonmore. Palmer was one of many who were at first sceptical about the ranching approach, but, from experience in practice, Palmer became an enthusiastic convert. Palmer was quoted in the News Chronicle later that year (1948) as saying: "It's beef we are after, and that's why we are using methods which have been found effective in Canada, the U.S. and the Argentine."[421]

Charlie Palmer's son Ralph remembers moving into the Factor's House at Inverlochy as a boy, and is one of the few people still alive who had close contact with Joe Hobbs at that time. Ralph has lots of memories of Joe, whom he would see often because Joe and his father were in regular contact over all aspects of running the estate. Ralph lived in the Factor's House, and Joe and many of the estate workers and visitors came through the house every day. Joe was very 'down to earth' and made time to talk to Ralph and his younger brother Charles. This was in stark contrast to Ralph's memories of the 'Laird' at the Palmer's previous estate at Kinlochlaggan, John Ramsay, whose aloofness and arrogance left Ralph with the implacable opinion that he was "an absolute bastard." At Inverlochy, Joe was clearly the boss, but Charlie Palmer won Joe's confidence and together they developed an effective working partnership. Charlie became one of those that was closest to Joe up until the time of his death.

Charlie analysed the activities on the estate – his son Ralph describes him as being "a 'spreadsheet' man long before the era of personal computing" – using logbooks to keep detailed records so that he could calculate exactly what worked and what did not. He was Joe's "numbers man" for the estate, and owner and factor talked about everything together. In combination, they were a good team – whilst Charlie was not afraid of innovation, he was useful to Joe in helping him quantify risks and potential returns, and rein in some of Joe's more unusual ideas. Together, they developed a scheme of practical innovation for the ranch, with components including out-wintering the cattle on the open moorland, digging the silage pits to provide feed to keep the cattle alive during winter, improving the best land on the lower elevations of the ranch to grow grasses and legumes to make winter silage, etc. Like all good entrepreneurs, some of Joe's ideas worked; others were less successful. But, overall, Joe and Charlie got a lot more right than wrong.[422]

Joe's comprehensive approach to ranching on the estate had a number of different components. Firstly, Joe was clear that, unlike the majority of stockbreeders in the UK at that time, there was no place for sheep on his estate; he was concentrating 100% on cattle. "Sheep and cattle raising don't go together, at least not in this part of the world."[423] Joe also decided that his ranch would focus specifically on the breeding and initial rearing of the cattle, after which the young cattle would be sold to be fattened on more productive land in Lowland Scotland or northern England. Joe liked to emphasise this difference from prevailing wisdom elsewhere in the Highlands, that he operated a *ranch* (where the focus is on raising livestock), not a farm (where the focus is on growing crops and using livestock to produce dairy products). The same article quoted Joe saying the main difference between a ranch and a farm was that 'On a ranch, nature does the work. On a farm, you do the work.'[424] This was a nice quote for the newspapers, but the reality was that Joe and his team had to engage in a massive amount of work over many years to reclaim the land on the estate and bring it back into productive use as a ranch.[ar]

A second element of Joe's comprehensive plan for his estate was that, arising from his understanding of how ranching cattle was managed successfully in Canada, Joe determined to have his cattle live out on the open moorlands throughout the year, in all but the most extreme weather. To be able to use the estate for raising cattle like these, Joe needed to transform the land to provide good quality grazing pasture on the open hill and mountainsides, while converting the better-quality lowland areas to grow feed for the cattle during winter.

When he took over the estate in 1945, large tracts of the upland parts were covered with bracken and heather, while much of the lower level land that could be used for arable purposes (comprising about 20% of the total land area) had deteriorated into waterlogged peat bogs. To develop the uplands so that they could provide grazing land, Joe adopted a 2-to-3-year programme where the cattle were used to help progressively trample down the bracken, which was the main vegetation on the moorland, and expose their roots to winter frost. Joe's men moved the cattle around the upland areas so that their trampling, or 'poaching' as they called it, was evenly spread over the areas to be cleared. At the same time, cattle manure helped fertilise the soil. Joe also extensively limed the ground, which helped to

---

ar   Ralph Palmer confirms that his father, Charlie, was won round to Joe's approach to managing the ranch, and in most issues of management the pair were closely aligned. However, Charlie had one major disagreement with Joe on farming, and that was in relation to keeping sheep. Charlie thought the ranch should have sheep as well, that they would be complementary to the cattle. Joe was quite "religious" about only having cattle, partly because of his North American ranching background, but also because big subsidies were available for cattle, and Joe wanted to maximise that. But Charlie thought Joe missed the point that they could have put sheep on the same land for no extra cost and little extra effort, and this would have contributed a valuable additional revenue stream.

kill off the heather and bracken. Once this was done, on all the upland areas, caterpillar tractors were used with new specialised machines bought in for the purpose, consisting of heavy rollers with blades protruding. These squashed the bracken flat and severed their stems, where after 2-3 years of cutting and rolling by machines and trampling by the cattle the bracken was progressively eradicated. Thereafter the moorland grazing areas were ploughed by heavy duty 'Prairie busting' ploughs similar to those used in Canada, and reseeded for grasses to provide upland pasture for the cattle.[425, 426]

This was supported by a programme to reclaim the land with the best arable potential, mostly on the lower areas of the estate. Much of this land was waterlogged bog. Joe had the soil tested and found that the majority of the lower level land consisted of underlying clay with 18–24 inches of rotting vegetable matter on top, which retained water like blotting paper. So, the first task was drainage, cutting wide drainage ditches with tractors and bulldozers. The benefit was immediate with wild clover and grasses regenerating naturally within a year. Joe and his team spent years using heavy equipment to dig miles of drainage ditches to drain the boggy land, which was then ploughed with tractors and fenced.

The next problem was winter feed. Bringing in hay from the south was uneconomic and contributed to the failure of many previous Highland cattle farms. Joe's solution was to plough up the best of the reclaimed land and apply a 5-year programme sowing different seed each spring, using rotations of oats, vetch, peas, rye grass and clover, interspersed with a few years growing grass.[427] The crops grown were used as silage to provide supplementary feed for the cattle during winter. By the early 1950s this was yielding 10–12 tons of silage per acre, in total producing over 3,000 tons of silage per annum. Joe introduced to Scotland the method of using silage pits dug by bulldozers

A silage pit on the Great Glen Cattle Ranch in use in the 1950s.

to store the silage: five pits were dug, each one 7 feet deep and capable of holding 600 tons, providing more than enough nutritious feed to get the herds through the winter.

At the Great Glen Ranch, Joe also added the draff from Ben Nevis distillery, as well as experimenting by adding molasses and fish oil (and also waste pot ale from the distillery), to improve the vitamin composition and make the silage more nutritious for the cattle.[as] The silage produced was better quality than hay,

---

[as] Hobbs saw the opportunity to obtain more fish oil (which was high in vitamin D, in which most Highland cattle were deficient due to lack of sunshine) from the expansion of fish meal factories around the Scottish coast. At the time using vitamin supplements in cattle feed was little understood, and this innovation is another example both of Joe's constant experimentation and striving to apply scientific principles to make improvements; but also of his 'joined up' thinking seeing a way to develop Scotland's wider economy by expanding the fish processing whilst using one of it by-products (fish oil) to improve livestock rearing.

One of the silage pits close to the home farmhouse at Achendaul today.

with a protein content above 14%, and Joe's later experiments to grow lupins and Russian comfrey could produce silage with up to 30% protein content. Many observers commented positively on the benefits of this approach. R.P. Winfrey in his article 'Beef from Barren Acres' commented, "Anyone who has seen the pathetic efforts at haymaking in the Highlands will see the wisdom of this."[428] During the winter months, tractors fitted with caterpillar tracks carried the silage up to mobile feeding boxes distributed across the upland grazing areas, often having to traverse deep snow to get there. However, despite the difficulties, this system of winter feeding proved very effective in providing the cattle with what they needed to survive well through the harsh Scottish winters.

In combination, this improvement of the pastoral land for year-round grazing, and ability to upgrade the most fertile land to grow silage to feed to the cattle in winter, meant that Joe was able to leave his cattle out on the ranch all year round. Unlike

The silage Joe was able to produce on the ranch was a key factor enabling his cattle to remain out in the open all year round.

some others experimenting with cattle rearing on the Highland uplands at the same time, who brought their cattle in off the high ground during winter, Joe left his cattle out on the open range summer and winter alike. This enabled Joe to claim with some justification that "Great Glen is the only *real* ranch in Scotland."[429]

Joe also had strong opinions on the type of cattle to rear on the ranch. Despite the upland nature of his land at Inverlochy, bordering on Britain's highest mountain Ben Nevis, which was snow-capped for most of each year, Joe knew from his Canadian experience that cold would not to be a problem for cattle rearing at the western end of the Great Glen due to the moderating influence of the Gulf Stream currents on the western coastline. However, the heavy rainfall of 84 inches per annum on average, and over 100 inches in wet years, was an issue for the cattle. Joe was not a fan of the traditional longhaired Highland cattle, which, despite their hardiness, he thought "unsuitable" for the very rainy Lochaber climate,[430] and also too slow to mature and not producing enough meat.[431] These Highland cattle also tended to lose their fertility after their third or fourth calf.[432] Instead, Joe went to Ireland with his factor Charlie Palmer and bought shorthaired Irish heifers which were a cross of Aberdeen Angus cows and Hereford bulls, which had shown they could thrive in a wet climate. He introduced another cross, using White Shorthorn bulls, resulting in blue-grey calves that came to be typical on his ranch. With this focus on Shorthorn cross-breeds, Joe built an excellent track record of selling high-quality young livestock for fattening that achieved good prices at auction in the years ahead.[433]

With Joe's typical zest for modern methods and science, all the cattle on the ranch were vaccinated against common cattle diseases, which resulted in negligible mortality rates amongst his herds. In particular, Joe's beef and dairy herds were vaccinated against bovine tuberculosis, a disease which as late as the 1930s was estimated to afflict more than 40% of Britain's cattle, with TB-infected milk and beef contributing to widespread TB infections in the UK's human population.[434] Joe was a strong advocate of vaccination, and signed up for the regular inspections and testing regime organised by the government under the 'Attested Herds Scheme' so that his herds could achieve official "Attested" status, i.e. certified free from TB. TB was also more prevalent in herds which spent a large part of their lives in poorly ventilated cattle sheds, whereas Joe's cattle, which spent their entire lives outdoors, were arguably amongst the healthiest in the country.

After taking ownership of the estate soon after the war, and still subject initially to wartime restrictions (e.g. on fuel and equipment), Joe began to use modern methods, tractors and bulldozers to remodel and develop the land on the estate. In his first two years between 1945 and 1947, he invested £20,000 on improvements to the estate – the same amount he had spent to buy it in the first place – including £6,900 on buildings and more than £6,000 on draining, fencing and road-making.[435] In March 1947, the lease of a tenant farmer on the Achendaul Farm part of Joe's estate expired, and Joe took back the land for his own operation. With a sizeable acreage now available for open grazing of his herd, Joe took the step to formally begin ranching in March 1947, increasing the size of his herd and allowing them to roam free on the unfenced upland areas of the estate all year round, supplementing the natural grazing during winter with silage grown on the estate's best plots. Between 1947 and 1949, Joe reclaimed 75 acres of land, put up 14 miles of fencing, and built 10 miles of drainage. In subsequent years, Joe maintained constant efforts to reclaim more land both for grazing and arable purposes, his success in increasing the amount of silage produced each year providing enough winter feed to expand progressively the size of the herd that could be carried through the winter.

In doing this, he had to overcome a lot of cynicism from unconvinced locals. Working closely with Charlie Palmer, Joe persuaded crofters on the estate to come and work for him building ranch-style cattle shelters at intervals over the estate. These structures, built from poured concrete and originally painted in Joe's 'trademark' yellow (he used the same colour on his yacht, Torlundy, and on Lochside Distillery in Montrose), are still landmarks visible at regular intervals to anyone driving along the A82 from Fort William towards Inverness. Shelter No. 1 was used for Joe's herd of Ayrshire dairy cattle on Achendaul farm, where he installed a new milk parlour in the early 1950s; Shelters No. 2 and 3 were intended for the beef herd.[436] The idea was that the shelters provided somewhere for the cattle to come in out of the cold and rain in bad weather, and get a feed of silage and turnips. The shelters were deliberately built near the main road to make it easier to keep them supplied with fodder.

The shelters were also used as a place for the pregnant cows to give birth, with head cowhand during the 1940s–50s John Cameron and his no. 2 John McCallum visiting by lantern-light on winter nights to check on their charges, and occasionally act as 'midwives' in difficult cases.[437]

All these efforts in combination started to achieve positive results, with the estate producing 170 calves from its 220 head of cattle in the 18 months to September 1949, enabling Joe to

Hobbs built cattle shelters on the Great Glen Cattle Ranch as part of the strategy to have the cattle live out all year round.

Cattle shelters built by Joe Hobbs on the Great Glen Cattle Ranch are still in use today.

increase the size of the herd to 400 head. He publicly stated his intention to grow the herd to 1000 head within the next five years, an ambition he was able to realise in full.

In September 1949, Scottish Secretary Arthur Woodburn and a senior official from the Department of Agriculture for Scotland, Mr Isbister, had been invited by Joe to witness the round-up of 400 black Irish cattle on the GGCR. Initially sceptical of this approach, officials were gradually won over to the potential of the idea. Woodburn was "favourably impressed" by the large-scale cattle-rearing project, which the government of the day clearly saw as having the potential to make an important contribution to food production in the country (at a time when shortages and rationing after WW2 were still a major problem). Pictures in the press coverage particularly focused on the 'cowboys' Joe used to round up the cattle, but Joe and Secretary Woodburn did their best to emphasise the project had a serious purpose: Joe said the western Highlands were "particularly suitable" for raising large herds of cattle, whilst Woodburn commented that the Highlands "are the one part of Britain that has room for any extensive increase in the cattle population," and that the GGCR was making "a very important contribution to the food production of this country". The papers noted that "the experiment is arousing much interest in the Highlands" and covered the story many times in the years ahead.[438, 439, 440]

By no means everyone agreed, however, with leading farming and breeding figures amongst the many to voice scepticism and doubt. At the annual dinner of the Scottish Shorthorn Breeders Association in Perth in 1950, 'one of Scotland's leading cattle breeders' J.A. Cameron specifically referenced Joe's Great Glen operation when speaking against ranching, saying "I do not agree there can be cattle extension on ranching lines anywhere in Scotland, and particularly in the North of Scotland." Cameron

The proprietor enjoyed helping with the round-ups.

was of the opinion that traditional farms, now supported by a "soundly conceived and fairly administered" government cattle policy, was the way to go.[441]

Through much of the early years of his ownership of the Inverlochy Estate, Joe was embroiled in his long legal battle with the North British Aluminium company. Particulate fluorine, a by-product from the nearby aluminium works, was ingested by the dairy cattle and beef herd on Joe's estates, weakening them and giving rise to a problem with their teeth that prevented them from chewing properly. The fluorine also damaged a lot of the trees on the estate. After Joe's settlement with British Aluminium in January 1950, old smelters at the plant were replaced, which reduced emissions substantially. However, the effects of the poisoning were undoubtedly a major impediment to Joe's efforts to develop the ranch, significantly hindering the healthy development of the cattle, dairy herd and forestry on the estate, as well as sucking up a huge amount of time, energy and resources as Joe battled for five years to force a resolution. But, with that problem resolved early in 1950, the way was clear for sustained and healthy expansion of the ranch.

In June 1950, the Dundee Courier carried a story 'Scots Cowboys in Unusual Roundup', where Joe had deployed some of the 'cowboys' from the ranch to assist the local police in rounding up alleged salmon poachers on the River Lochy. Nine men were arrested and nets, oars and other equipment seized.[442] This was classic Joe, using his resources to solve a business problem, whilst at the same time maximising the opportunity for positive publicity. Joe didn't always win these battles. Locals still tell the tale of how Doxie Cameron, a big man and stalwart of the Fort William shinty club, was walking from Braes of Lochaber to Fort William one day when a "huge American car" drew up beside him. The Lochaber News tell the story that "At the wheel was Joseph W. Hobbs, owner of the Great Glen Cattle Ranch, and the policies, parks and fishing rights all around it. Joe bade Doxie hop in, after putting his bag in the trunk. [They had a] good crack all the way to Inverlochy Castle. From where Joe insisted on taking Doxie on into the Fort. The farewells were made at the west end after Doxie had retrieved his bag. Whereupon, had Joe tarried a little, he would have observed Doxie heading for the kitchens of a town hotel with three large salmon, borne there by courtesy of a lift in Joe Hobbs' 'huge big American car'. And poached from Joe's stretch of the River Lochy."[443]

In the spring of 1951, with the dispute with British Aluminium behind him, Joe had more time to promote his activities and success on the ranch. In March, he addressed the Chamber of Commerce at Inverness, and gave an update on the progress of the ranch, which by this time was carrying 570 head of cattle, with the amount of reclaimed land now up to 100 acres.[444]

As well as putting significant energy into the work required

Doxie Cameron, 5th from left, back row, a member of the 1946–47 Fort William shinty team, and sometime poacher of Joe Hobbs' salmon.

to turn the "derelict" moorland he had acquired into a highly productive cattle-rearing ranch, Joe also worked hard to try to change the opinions of officials, other farmers and investors, as well as the general public about the potential of the Highlands for rearing cattle. Continuing the steady stream of publicity for the ranch, in April 1951 The Sphere published a two-page photo story on the GGCR called 'Cattle Ranching Amidst the Glens of Lochaber'. Joe was persisting with the work to reclaim unused land, and by this time had successfully recovered 150 acres of arable land over the preceding 4 years which had previously been unusable. Joe commented that ranching on this scale required capital, equipment/machinery, and the ability to wait several years for a return. But he was hopeful that more private companies and syndicates would see the potential and start to fund the wider application of the ranching method across the Highlands. Amongst the many other visitors who came to see what Joe was up to, the article reported that Argentine Ambassador Senor Hogan and a party of Argentinians had paid

Joe Hobbs and Charlie Palmer won the visiting Secretary of State for Scotland over to their methods during his visit to the Great Glen Cattle Ranch in May 1951.

a visit. The implication was that even the Argentinians with their very extensive cattle ranching experience were coming to see what they could learn from Joe Hobbs.[445]

In May 1951, Joe invited the new Secretary of State for Scotland, Hector McNeil, to stay at Inverlochy for three nights during the period in which that year's crop of young cattle were rounded up and sent to market. Once rounded up, the cattle were separated and driven to Spean Bridge, where they were loaded for transport by train to the stock markets at Stirling or Lanark in Lowland Scotland. Joe invested time and effort to show McNeil the ranch's operations. The Dundee Courier reported that the 200 GGCR Angus Shorthorns had been sold at prices "in excess of seller's expectations" at auction in Lanark.[446] The Gazette covered the same story the following day, advising that the herd had together raised £6,710 (2024: £260,000). Joe said "It is not a hobby. The ranch is a paying proposition. It has to be – I have not so much money as people say. There is a big capital outlay."[447] The visit concluded with Secretary McNeil telling the Dundee Courier he was "won over" to the project of rearing cattle in the Highlands, and that the approach "can be successfully applied to many other parts of the impoverished West Highlands."[448]

As evidence of the positive results he was achieving, as well as his continued ambition and commitment to the project, in July 1951 Joe took the step of purchasing the remaining 4,500 acres of the Inverlochy Estate that he had not acquired initially, doubling the size of his estate to more than 9,000 acres. No price was cited in the press. Joe was quoted as saying that he planned to use the additional land to expand the ranch, continuing the process of reclaiming barren land that had proven successful with the first 4,500 acres. The purchase also included – seemingly at Charlie Palmer's suggestion – extending Joe's fishing rights on the River Lochy in the upper reaches bordering the ranch which he had not purchased in 1945, making him the owner of the fishing rights on almost 10 miles of the river all the way from the sea up to Mucomir.[449] This was to prove a very sound investment, the fishing rights eventually proving more valuable than the estate.

Joe's mounting success with the ranch, as well as his efforts to persuade officialdom of the potential of his ideas, resulted in him being consulted on various government-sponsored efforts to develop the Highlands. In October 1951, Joe was among nine hill farmers and leading agriculturalists who were invited by the Secretary of State for Scotland to serve on the 'Hill Lands (North of Scotland) Commission', which was then being set up, designed to stimulate more rapid expansion of cattle breeding and rearing in the Highlands. Under the chairmanship of Lord Balfour of Burleigh, the new Commission drew on a strong array of talented personnel, including what the Arbroath Herald called "doughty pioneers in this field," Joe Hobbs and Duncan M. Stewart of Millhills, Crieff.[450] The Commission specifically aimed at delivering a 50% increase in the cattle population in the Highlands, which at that time numbered 80,000. A 50% increase would contribute an additional 6 ounces of meat a week to the British ration book – persistent shortages meant that meat was still rationed in Britain at that time, more than six years after the end of WW2.[451] It was explained in various newspaper articles that the Commission differed from previous efforts on this topic in that it was intended to be "of a more executive and continuing nature – to select those areas where schemes of cattle-rearing development could most profitably be promoted and advise on the best methods of promoting them." Improvement schemes would be funded by grants under the Hill Farming and Livestock Rearing Acts.[452] Joe was an active and energetic contributor to the Commission, which later also submitted a comprehensive report to Parliament on the issue in July 1956, and contributed to the Hill Farming and Livestock Rearing Acts of the same year.[453]

In similar fashion, on 9th September 1953, Joe was appointed Chairman of the Scottish Board for Industry's Highlands and Islands Committee, and gave a press announcement for a bizarre-sounding plan to build mobile fish meal and fish oil production plants to "follow the fishing fleet" in much the same way mobile sawmills were used to support timber felling.[454] Unsurprisingly, not much came of this particular plan, which seems to have been motivated by Joe's earlier experiments using fish oil to supplement cattle feed. Nonetheless, his appointment to the Board was further evidence of Joe's rising stature, whilst this particular story also shows that, as a true risk-taking entrepreneur, not all Joe's ideas were successful. Joe continued to do good work as Chairman of this committee, for example, getting the Highlands equipped with improved rotary-type snowploughs of the type used in Canada. Later, Joe's committee developed plans for a new wood-pulp and chipboard factory on a site on the north side of the Caledonian Canal which was ideally situated to make use of timber extracted from forestry thinning operations and take advantage of local hydro-electric power and cheap transport by water.[455]

In the spring of 1952, another photo article in The Sphere maintained national newspaper coverage for Joe's ranching activities, this time reporting wooden houses being assembled in "the fastest housing project in Britain" on the Great Glen Cattle Ranch. Joe is quoted as having seen the innovative timber kit houses on a visit to Kristiansand, Norway, and got permission to import 10 of them, which were being assembled for estate workers on the Great Glen at a rate of one per day. Joe had ambitious plans to accommodate 100 workers and their families in a "prosperous...composite community."[456] In his book on the history of Inverlochy Castle, Dominic A. Sargent tells us that the wooden kit houses came from a very costly sailing expedition Joe made to Norway on his yacht 'Torlundy'. First, the yacht ran aground, requiring replacement of both its propellers. Then, while Joe thought he had secured a bargain due to the low cost of buying the wooden houses, the cost of shipping, transporting and then assembling them on the GGCR provide to be far higher than Joe had reckoned for, resulting in the final cost being multiple times more than the price of the houses themselves.[457]

Despite the cost, this initiative was fully aligned with Joe and Eve's overall approach to business, where providing employment and supporting local development were an intrinsic element. Sargent explains that, in addition to all the direct employment opportunities Joe and Eve created in their house, on their estate and in the distilleries, Joe also provided housing for many workers, for example via the Norwegian kit houses, and by building two hostels at Torlundy and Achendaul to accommodate teams of Irish labourers on the estate and dairy farm. Sargent comments that "As an employer and a boss, Hobbs was well-liked and highly regarded. A stocky man with a colourful character and a listening ear, he soon became known affectionately as Old Joe."[458] Joe and Eve also built a lot of goodwill in the community through their charitable and benevolent activities. In Joe's case, this was achieved through initiatives such as using his farm equipment to improve the drainage of the local sports fields. In Eve's case, it was through a wide range of activities in support of the youth and the elderly in the Inverlochy and Fort William communities. Whilst Eve was not directly involved in running Joe's businesses, she was very influential in ensuring the results of Joe's successful entrepreneurship also benefitted the employees and the wider community. Throughout their marriage, Eve built relationships with important stakeholders in the community. She went on to become a county councillor and actively served the Lochaber community for many years after Joe's death.

By October 1953, Joe had put 650 acres of reclaimed land back into permanent pasture, sufficient to enable him to build up the cattle herd to 600 head, the aim still being to reach 1000 head eventually. Joe also ran a dairy herd of 100 Ayrshires at Torlundy. On the main ranch, calves were born each spring from January to April, and were sold in late October as weaned calves ready for fattening on stations further south. In the autumn of

The Caol Shinty Cup, donated by Joe Hobbs as a prize for one of the local shinty clubs in Fort William. Shinty was a sport that was a 'religion' for some in the Highlands.

1953, an article in the Fresno Bee (a Californian newspaper) titled "Bagpipes and Beef Return in Scotch Highlands to Tune of US Pasture Methods" explained Joe's methods on the Great Glen, and commented that Joe had successfully adopted US cattle rearing and land reclamation methods to bring beef back into the economy of highland Scotland, in the process "transforming…beautiful but worthless hillsides of heather and bracken into highly productive pasture land". Next to pictures of kilted herdsmen and a 'cowboy' rounding up cattle on his horse with a dog, Joe is quoted as saying the large-scale approach was working: "This is no longer an experiment. We've proved the economic sense of it. It's paying off now."[459]

Certainly, by this time, the years of hard work and investment were starting to deliver impressive results. In a 1955 article in the Dundee Courier, Joe talked about the returns he had been getting, explaining that he had been "in the red a year or two at the start. But then it showed 5 and 10 per cent… and last year a 13 per cent profit."[460] By the early 1950s, the ranch was on a sustainable business footing. However, it must be said that Joe benefitted from post-war subsidies designed to support Britain's efforts to ramp up domestic food production. The Hill Farming Act of 1946 (which provided support for farm improvement in Britain's hill and upland areas) and the Agriculture Act of 1947 (which undertook to provide "proper remuneration" for farmers and introduced a system of price guarantees for agricultural output) provided substantial financial support. Among other things, grants were available for the number of hill cows a farm had, for bringing pasture under the plough, and eradicating bracken – all of which were directly applicable to the GGCR and provided substantial assistance to Joe Hobbs.[461] Writing in the 1970s, David Turnock of Nottingham University's Geographical Field Group noted Hobbs would have benefitted from 50% contributions from

Rancher Hobbs on horseback.

the government for many of the improvement initiatives he took.[462]

It is interesting to speculate whether without these subsidies Joe's ranching experiments could have been sustainably profitable, and also whether availability of these subsidies was a factor in Joe taking on the ranching project in the first place. Joe acknowledged the impact of subsidies in a 1955 interview in The Province newspaper, Vancouver, where he was fondly remembered from his work to construct the Marine Building. Joe said he had long wondered why some canny Scot had not previously tried the ranching approach in Scotland, "for here you have a ready market at the door, generous subsidies from the government, a temperate climate, civilised living conditions, good roads, etc. In fact, everything appeared to be favourable except high taxation. But in Britain you do get something for your taxes...I decided that the subsidies offered by the government would go a long way to off-set high taxes. And in any case, Britain needed beef!"[463] In addition to government support and subsidies, Turnock showed Joe was unusual because he had sufficient capital to match the government's 50% with his own money, enabling him to invest in the modern equipment and machinery to implement his scheme successfully. Having his own source of lime from the Torlundy quarries to improve the soil and draff from his own distillery to feed the cattle were valuable contributors as well. But, whilst all these tail winds for Joe's initiatives were important, none of this would have mattered without Joe's own 'improving' mindset and strong determination to make the ranch a success, drawing on his experience from Canada, his technical knowledge, his capacity for hard work and willingness to lead by example. Ralph Palmer, the son of Joe's estate manager Charlie Palmer, who grew up living on the Great Glen Cattle Ranch and saw a great deal of Joe Hobbs as a child, credits Joe's huge energy and determination as a key factor in his success with the ranch. Joe Hobbs was a man "who made a lot of things happen which otherwise would never even have been started." [464]

Joe clearly relished the challenge and loved to supervise the work personally. Sargent tells us when he brought in a big 'prairie buster' plough similar to those used in Canada and modern bulldozers to dig trenches and flatten hillocks, "in all weathers, he would be out supervising and directing the earth-moving operations."[465] Horses were used extensively by the ranch staff for getting around the estate and for rounding up and driving the cattle. The cattle round-ups took up to a week using the 'cowboys' and horses, which Joe saw as a very efficient way of covering the large area which would have taken too long on foot, and often required navigating terrain which was inaccessible to motor vehicles. Round-ups took place three times a year: once in the spring at weaning time when the calves were separated from their mothers; a second round-up in June was for a veterinary check-up and removal of sick or weak animals; and the important third round-up of the year in the autumn was to select the animals for the annual sales – Joe's practice was to sell most of the stock as yearlings.[466] Sheepdogs had been trained to work with the cowboys to assist in rounding up the cattle. Joe himself was acknowledged to be a first-rate horseman, although apparently he was a terrible driver of motor cars. Joe was known for his use of big, blue American Hudson cars, and would think nothing of using them in the fields as he went about his work on the ranch. Eve also had an eye for stylish vehicles, being known for her glamorous white Jaguar with personalised "EVE953" number plate.[467]

The following table provides a summary of how Joe's efforts at land reclamation and expanding the ranch developed over time:

Table 4: Development of the Great Glen Cattle Ranch, 1945–1957

Year	Estate Size (Acres)	Cattle (head)	Arable (acres)	Fencing (miles)	Drainage (miles)
1945		75	36		
1946	3500				
1947		220			
1948		300			
1949	4000	400	75	14	10
1950		400	100		100
1951		570	150		
1952			300		
1953		600	650		
1954	9000			50	
1955		900	760		180
1956		1200		58	
1957		1286	1250		

The first 70 head of cattle were bought from Ireland. When Joe started ranching properly in March 1947, he had 220 head, having by then recovered and prepared enough grazing and arable land to grow winter feed to support a larger herd. Those 220 cattle produced 170 calves the following year.[468] From then on, every year Joe and his men maintained the pace of reclamation, drainage and fencing, making more pastoral land available for grazing, and more arable land for production of silage to support the herd through the winters. This enabled the size of the herd that the ranch could sustain to be increased year-by-year, while also allowing a steady increase in the number of young cattle which could be sold at auction for fattening elsewhere. Joe sold his 2000th calf at the auctions in October 1954.[469] In 1955, Joe emphasised in a talk that it had taken seven years of constant toil and effort to drain and reclaim land, plant silage, and build shelters and homes for workers. He thought "a great many more cattle could be bred in the Highlands," although he accepted many glens were too small for ranching and the quality of herbage became poorer the further you went inland from the west coast, which benefitted from the moderating influence of the Gulf Stream. By this time the ranch had 760 acres of arable production, compared with just 36 acres when he took over. Joe said they did not have a specific blueprint for the drainage work, and just followed the natural watercourses, but by this point had constructed 180 miles of drains. In addition, thousands of trees had been planted to make good years of deforestation.[470] By 1955, Joe was sending 400 head of young cattle to market each year at Lanark.[471] And by 1958, Joe was able to report he had sold 4,000 head of cattle in total at the auctions since he started, equivalent to 2,000 tons of beef.[472]

His efforts garnered a lot of interest, boosted as always by Joe's penchant for publicity, with a constant stream of visitors and reporters coming to witness his progress. In a letter to his niece Barbara Barran in May 1954, Joe explained: "The back road round behind the Ranch is now paved, and when parties of people come we are able to send the buses right round the place. Last year we had over 2,000 visitors."[473] Elspeth Berardelli, wife of Paolo Berardelli, the current owner of Achendaul Farm, a core part of what used to be Joe's Great Glen Ranch, comes from farming stock and recalls that, in her youth, Joe's efforts to promote his initiatives in raising cattle meant that almost every farmer in Scotland was aware of his story.[474] Among the general public, stories about the Scottish 'cowboys' that Joe used to round up the cattle seemed to grab the public's imagination, with many newspaper articles on the subject in Scotland, but also in England and internationally. In a dreary post-war environment of shortages and rationing, and at a time when American culture and "Western" films were all the rage in the UK, the image of cowboys working the Scottish glens seemed alluring. In North America, the story also resonated perhaps because it told of American skills and capabilities being adopted to improve the 'old country'. Neil King in his blog about Joe's ranching activities quotes from the Greensburg Daily Tribune in Pennsylvania, which reported in 1951 that Joe was employing "four Gaelic-speaking cattle hands. From dawn to dusk they range this Scottish ranch on horseback and carry 12 foot whips."[475] The popular newsreels of the day also made the Great Glen a regular topic for their stories, with both Pathé and British Movietone News running features showing a very solid-looking Joseph Hobbs and his cowboys on horseback rounding up cattle on the windswept high moors.

Joe was a master of self-promotion, but he was not alone in his efforts to develop cattle rearing as a viable way of developing the Highlands agriculturally. 80 miles to the north at Braulen near Loch Monar, Lord Lovat (famous for his work as a Commando leader during WW2) was undertaking similar experiments. Lovat had travelled in North and South America where he learned about ranching, and applied the approach to his estates west of Beauly, Inverness-shire, after his return, building up a herd of cattle from 40 head in 1946, to over 650 head by September 1949.[476] Not as flamboyant as Joe, Lovat used Land Rovers and dogs to round up his cattle rather than cowboys. Like Joe, however, Lovat also stressed that Scotland actually had a history of raising cattle in this way on open moorland, and that for many years prior to the 20th century the Highlands had been a major exporter of cattle to the Lowlands and England. The article in the Fresno Bee from 1953 reported that at that time there were around 12 similar experiments taking place across the Highlands, following slightly different approaches.[477] The Daily Record reported in October 1953 on a sale of hill calves at Fort William, where 600 calves from West Highland farms were sold. Two hundred of them came from Joe's Great Glen Cattle Ranch, but over 400 others came from Major Anthony Wills' ranch at Glenelg; Mrs McLintock's Locheil Estate at Appin; Major Taibor's farm at Onich; and Mr E. Heyman's farm at Fasnacloich. The Record commented that "This growth in development is a tribute to the pioneering enthusiasm of Mr. J.W.Hobbs and his staff at Inverlochy, who have been tireless in persuading all who would listen to them to have a go at filling the empty glens with cattle and new life."[478] With support and subsidies from government, this was part of a major initiative to improve Britain's meat production and solve its food problem. But of all these efforts, Joe's ranch was the best known. The University of Nottingham's David Turnock concluded in his 1977 study that, while Joe Hobbs did not do everything right (Turnock thought Joe should have made better use of forestry as 'wind breaks' and used surface treatment methods rather than ploughing to get rid of the bracken), overall Joe had been a "particularly influential innovator" whose "results were impressive...no other farmer [in Lochaber] achieved the same level of intensification" of production.[479]

Having achieved his goal to build the ranch to sustain more

than 1000 head of cattle reliably, from about 1957 – and at a time when Lochside Distillery was taking much of his attention – Joe seems to have ceased the constant reclamation work to expand the usable area of the ranch, and was content just to run it each year at that level in a 'steady state'. However, Joe continued to work consistently to promote the thinking behind the Great Glen Ranch in the subsequent years. In 1957, The Times reported a dinner held to celebrate Joe's achievements over 10 years as a rancher. Joe was guest of honour at the dinner in Fort William on 15th September of that year, organised by the Scottish Peat and Land Development Association in recognition of his land reclamation work in the Highlands. By that time, more than 1,250 acres of waste land had been brought into production, and the ranch supported a herd of 1,286 head of cattle, up from 200 in 1947 when the project began.[480]

Joe addressed 70 participants at the dinner including farmers, crofters and agricultural experts from across a wide area of Scotland, and explained how large tracts of land on the Inverlochy Estate had been successfully cleared of bog, heather and bracken by drainage, fertilising and ploughing. "If we live long enough," he said, "we shall make these barren hills of Lochaber look like the Downs of England." Asked by a guest if he considered the whole project to be economically viable, Joe said "I would not be in it for six months if there were no dividends."

In a later interview in the Daily Herald, Joe again emphasised the potential of his approach to help address Britain's beef shortage. Lack of land was an issue across the UK, but his ranching methods had been shown to work and could be applied to unused uplands in many different parts of the country. Joe said that when he started, many of Britain's cattlemen regarded him as an eccentric idiot, but "I reckon I've proved I can teach other beef producers a lot, and perhaps even solve Britain's beef shortage – if other guys copy what I've done." Joe explained that he had always been interested in the way Canadians ran prairie ranches, so when after WW2 he saw a large stretch of Highland hill lands available for a low price he decided to give ranching a go in Scotland. Now, 10 years later, he had bred over 4,000 head of cattle on his ranch – that was 2,000 tons of beef. Joe diagnosed Britain's beef problems to be due to a shortage of cattle breeders on a large scale. "I can see no reason why other guys in the Pennines, Dartmoor, Exmoor, the Welsh Highlands and other places in the Scottish Highlands shouldn't do what I do." Joe agreed that this required resources (he himself had spent £20,000 on machinery and £50,000 to stock up with cattle). But he got out of the red after five years and had since been making money, saying "Dammit, I wouldn't be doing it if I wasn't!"[481]

From around the middle of 1959, when Joe was aged 68, health concerns started to impact on this most active of men. The normally very high-profile personality disappeared from view, and the flow of media stories diminished to a trickle. In August 1961, the Scottish Daily Mail carried an 'exclusive' story that "Anglo-Canadian millionaire Mr. J.W. Hobbs is selling the major part of his ranch for health reasons."[482] Sargent says with Joe's failing health in the early 1960s, "having successfully achieved his ranching ambitions, he decided to sell the Great Glen Cattle Ranch."[483] However, irrespective of the success of the ranch, it seems that it was his declining health, and the apparent unwillingness or inability of his son Joe Junior or daughter Patricia to take it over, that drove Joe's decision to sell up.

Another article in The Scottish Daily Express titled "Hobb's Choice: Rugged Ranch Boss Says I Have to Slow Down," helps explain both Joe's absence from public view as well as the background to the sale of the Great Glen Ranch. Alongside a photo of a gaunt-looking Joe smoking a cigarette, the article explains that "nothing would ever stop this burly, white-haired farmer's son born in Hampshire 70 years ago from bulldozing his way towards whatever his next goal happened to be," and goes on to ask "Why then is this…stubborn, determined man… slowing down, to the extent that he is now prepared to sell most of his 10,500 acres and 1,100 head of cattle?" Joe explained his situation: "I am not really well. I have angina, which I always realised was a serious thing. But what really showed me the red light was the recent deaths of my two pals, Charlie Palmer, my factor for many years, and Sandy Carroll.[at] Both died from similar complaints, and both were younger than I. When they died…I made up my mind, I had gone far enough. It seems I chose the wrong motto, I always said 'Up and At It.' Now I have to forget all that."[484]

Angina is a condition whereby the coronary arteries have narrowed, stopping the heart getting enough oxygen, which would have caused Joe considerable pain especially when undertaking physical activity, certainly sufficient to force him to stop exerting himself. It was a warning that if he continued to push himself, he would likely have a heart attack. Illness was to dog Joe's remaining life, and was clearly instrumental in his decision to sell the ranch. Even though he had made the decision to sell up, The Scottish Daily Express article speculated that Joe was probably hoping nobody would actually make him an offer, quoting Joe as saying, because the ranch meant so much to him,

---

at   Joe's pal Alexander Carroll passed away aged 60 in July 1961 after battling a huge 20lb salmon for more than half an hour on the River Lochy. Having landed the salmon, he then fell down dead. Another angler found him face down in the water. Although doubtless of no consolation, it was the largest salmon caught in the river that year.

      Charlie Palmer, Joe's long-term estate manager and collaborator on the Great Glen Cattle Ranch, died suddenly at the age of just 53 in the Inverlochy Estate Office from diabetes and coronary artery disease causing heart failure, on the morning of 6th May 1961.

"I insist that whoever may take over the ranch must continue on similar lines to what I have been doing."

In August 1961, The Observer carried a story that a syndicate of 12 "prosperous businessmen bent on stockbreeding on a big scale" were planning to bid for the GGCR.[485] The syndicate was headed by H.R. Hood Barrs, an English industrialist and stockbreeder with a 12,000 acre estate on the Isle of Mull, with negotiations led by Gordon Thomson, a landowner and stockbreeder with 2,000 acres and 600 breeding cows on his farm at Craigellachie in Speyside. Hood Barrs told The Observer that the proposal was at a very early stage, but "what we are anxious to achieve is a large cattle-breeding organisation in which stock can be moved to the best advantage between one place and another, a sort of merger with my interests here, the Great Glen ranch, and Mr. Thomson's interests on Speyside." The Scottish Daily Mail also covered the story, explaining that the syndicate were seeking to exploit the opportunity to supply top-grade beef to Europe once the UK joined the European Union.[486, au] They planned to combine a chain of ranches stretching from Mull to Speyside, and build up an amalgamated herd of more than 3,000 cattle. Hood Barrs said "We anticipate that the sale of Scotch beef will be one of the most profitable developments from our entry into the Common Market. Our object is to produce cattle for distribution over the huge European market…The purchase of the Great Glen is under our consideration and it is quite likely it will go through." The article said the syndicate's plan could enable them to earn £1–2m p.a. in revenue from export

---

au   It seems the syndicate were way too optimistic on this front: in practice, French President Charles de Gaulle twice vetoed the UK's applications to join the European Union in 1963 and 1967, and it was to take until 1972 before Prime Minister Ted Heath was finally successful in negotiating Britain's entry to the "common market".

of prime beef to Europe, and the Great Glen would clearly have been a critical and valuable component of their plan.

However, Joe rather pooh-poo'd the approach, telling The Observer "I have not had any offer yet", although he was aware of the syndicate's interest and understood the logic of their business proposition. Joe said that he was "not very keen" to sell the ranch and commented that if he did agree to a deal he might not sell all of it. However, given that Joe had already publicly stated the ranch was for sale, and very soon afterwards sold to another buyer, it seems he was just playing 'hard to get' in order to push the price up.[487] The fact that all this was reported in some of the leading national papers of the day indicates how high the profile of Joe Hobbs and his Great Glen Cattle Ranch had become.

Around a month later, on 13th September 1961, multiple newspapers reported that the Great Glen Cattle Ranch had been sold. No price was disclosed at the time, but in his obituary in 1963 The Guardian reported the price to have been £123,000 (2024: £3.4m).[488] The Aberdeen Evening Express stated that the buyer was the Hon. Alan Mackay, son of the 2nd Earl of Inchcape and member of the famous 'shipping family' (his uncle, the First Lord Inchcape, had been Chairman of P&O), who already had extensive farming interests in Ayrshire and in Australia. The estate was said to extend to nearly 10,000 acres and at the time of the sale, was carrying 1,200 head of cattle. During the period Joe owned and operated the ranch, it was said to have reared 4,500 cattle.[489] The Birmingham Post carried the same story on 14th September, commenting that it was one of the biggest land deals in the UK in recent years.[490]

The following month, on 30th October 1961, the Aberdeen Evening Express carried a story titled 'The Last Round Up', reporting how Joe supervised his final round-up of cattle on the Great Glen Cattle Ranch over the preceding weekend. The cattle were sent by special train for the annual sales at Stirling, commencing the following week, bringing the curtain down on Joe's extraordinary Scottish ranching venture.[491] The last of Joe's cattle raised £27,000 at the Stirling stock auction (2024: £750,000).[492] After the sale, Joe retired to the 300+ acres he retained at Inverlochy Castle.[493]

However, that was not quite the end of the story. Dominic Sargent tells us that, despite his failing health, Joe continued to "conduct business from his castle bed." Having sold the bulk of the estate and all the cattle, Joe retained the castle, Ben Nevis distillery and the land in between. On this smaller piece of land, he restarted his ranch on a smaller scale, creating Inverlochy Castle Farm by clearing the trees, re-seeding the ground, building a cattle shelter and introducing 50 new Irish cattle. He also built the original petrol station at Inverlochy, with a house, shop and café.[494] In a letter to his niece Barbara Barran in Canada, Joe explained "When I sold the ranch I kept the parks and meadows round the Castle, and 370 acres and 50 head of cattle, so I am still a farmer and have plenty to take up my time and interest. What I need now is some health and strength."[495] Whilst his health was a major obstacle to his continued activity, Joe retained his vision, drive and love for cattle rearing to the end of his days.

12

Yachting

A part from his business activities, Joe's main passion in his later years was yachting. Yachts and yachting were a central part of Joe's life in Vancouver in the 1920s, when he was compiling his first fortune. After the lean times of the 1930s and the years of WW2, when he had neither the resources nor the opportunity for sailing, it is no surprise that Joe took up his preferred hobby again as soon as he was able to do so after the war. Fort William is a great location for yachting, with access both to Scotland's beautiful west coast and islands heading west down Loch Linnhe, and also, by transiting eastwards through the Caledonian Canal which starts at Fort William, to the East Coast and North Sea. Joe's yachts – first 'Torlundy', and subsequently 'Ocean Mist' – with their funnels painted in his trademark pale yellow, remained a central part of his life throughout his later years. Moored in Loch Linnhe, they were a familiar part of the scenery for local residents and tourists visiting the area – in fact the 'Torlundy' featured in a famous postcard of Fort William, which sold well to tourists, and epitomised the town for many visitors.

Joe had an enduring interest in the yachts themselves, and devoted a lot of time and effort, and took great pride, in restoring and refitting them to very high standards both functionally and in terms of comfort. Yachting is a rich man's hobby, and Joe's boating activities were his biggest indulgence. But, throughout his life, Joe's boats and yachts were also a very practical part of his business life, used extensively for entertaining important dignitaries and society figures, customers, and the media. The yachts were a key tool for Joe to build his social and business relationships.

The first post-war yacht was 'Torlundy'. As always with Joe's yachts, it was an ex-naval craft with some history and character, which actually started life as a naval landing craft. Built in 1945 at the Alexander Findlay & Co. Ltd. shipyard at Old Kilpatrick on the River Clyde west of Glasgow, as "LCG.125", she was one of many similar 'LCG' vessels built towards the end of the war to enable transport of men and equipment for waterborne invasions. Vessels of this type were used extensively in the D-Day Normandy landings, as well as in the Sicily-Salerno-Anzio campaigns in Italy. The 'LCG' of the name stood for 'Landing Craft Gun'. The design was an evolution of the original and more numerous 'LCT' or 'Landing Craft Tank' vessels developed by military shipbuilder Thorneycrofts, which had an open loading bay for the carriage of men, tanks and equipment, and were designed to be run straight onto a beach, with the men and tanks driving off from a loading ramp at the front. In the LCG variant, the loading ramp at the front was replaced by a closed bow, with the open cargo area of the original covered by a welded-on steel deck, to which were affixed 2 British Army 25-pound guns or 2 x 4.7in diameter naval guns. The LCG's purpose was to provide direct fire against beach positions in support of infantry and equipment landing operations – packing a formidable punch for vessels of their size, they were described by the BBC as 'mini-destroyers.'

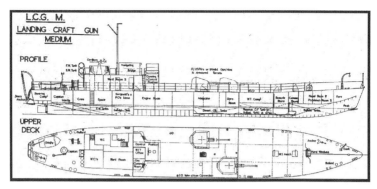

Design of 'Landing Craft Gun' vessel, as 'Torlundy' was prior to conversion.

Surplus to requirements after the war, Joe was able to acquire her, stripped of her guns and military equipment, sometime in 1946–47, and undertook a major conversion to make her into a luxuriously outfitted motor-yacht. This was no mean achievement: the conversion from basic military hardware into luxury yacht really would have been an extreme makeover, requiring design and fitting out of totally new superstructure, cabins and accommodation. With strict control of essential commodities in post-war Britain, it is not clear how Joe obtained the materials for this. However, Joe was highly resourceful and driven, and found a way to obtain the materials he needed, using his own men to undertake the conversion work. Joe's grandson Joseph Peter Hobbs tells that there was a near disaster when Joe's men used gas cutting equipment to remove the old gun platform – only to discover some previously unknown wartime live ammunition still stored beneath![496] However, typically for Joe, he went to an enormous amount of trouble to manage the conversion extremely well, resulting in the creation of a sleek, low-profile motor-yacht fitted out to the highest standards, although still with a flat bottom, which was to be a bit of a problem for passenger comfort when used on open seas.

The new vessel, renamed 'Torlundy' after a village on Joe's estate at Inverlochy, was 154 feet long, 22 feet wide, of 316 gross tons, and powered by 2 x 12-cylinder diesel engines with an output of 1,000 horsepower, capable of driving the yacht through her twin propellers at a maximum speed of 10.5 knots. Joe kept 'Torlundy' moored at Camusnagaul, on the far side of Loch Linnhe, opposite Fort William, where she became a familiar part of the waterline to residents and visitors. Operated with a crew of eight, Joe used the 'Torlundy' as a hospitality suite to entertain friends and guests on Loch Linnhe, with longer summer sailing expeditions to the West Coast of the Highlands, Ireland, and as far as Scandinavia. 'Torlundy' was the longest size of vessel able to pass through the Caledonian Canal locks, and required the full length of the locks to do so – as usual, clearly Joe had done his homework! But, with typical vision, determination, and quite some effort and cost, Joe created for himself a luxury craft enabling him to indulge his passion for sailing, as well as a high-quality resource to support his business and social networking. In a post-war Britain characterised by shortages and an absence of glamour, 'Torlundy' was an impressive and luxurious status symbol.

Once completed, Joe made extensive used of 'Torlundy'. In the summer of 1949, The Scotsman reported in an article on West Highland Week that "Mr. J.W.Hobbs has placed his yacht 'Torlundy' at the disposal of the regattas at Oban as Commodore's ship".[497]

In 1953, Joe had the honour to participate on 'Torlundy' in the Coronation Review of the Fleet by Queen Elizabeth II at Spithead, off Portsmouth on England's south coast. This was the first post-war review of the fleet, the most recent edition of a periodic historic event that dated back to 1346 when Edward III reviewed his fleet before sailing off to war in France. The 1953 Review took place on 15th June, just two weeks after the

Joe's yacht 'Torlundy', 1950s.

Coronation itself, as part of the extensive celebrations across the country marking the new Queen's ascension to the throne. Over 200 ships – including five aircraft carriers – of the Royal Navy and Commonwealth Navies, 16 vessels from foreign navies, and 50 vessels of the merchant and fishing fleets (281 vessels in total) lined up in an area 8 miles long by 2 miles wide for review by the new Queen, who passed through the fleet on HMS Surprise, deployed as Royal Yacht for the event. This was a real 'feather in the cap' for Joe – many private yachts came to Spithead to watch the review as spectators, and there must have been dozens of well-connected wealthy yacht owners in the UK that would have leaped at the chance to be involved, but 'Torlundy' was one of very few non-military vessels participating in the review itself. Joe's inclusion was a result of his service and excellent relations with the Navy, and his appointment with 'Torlundy' as the head of one of four new 'mine-watching' commands around Britain's coast.

The event was extensively reported in newspapers and TV newsreels, with the Dundee Courier providing Scottish colour to the event when they reported that "the ships gathered for review will range in size from the massive battleship Vanguard to the yacht 'Torlundy', belonging to Mr. J.W. Hobbs of Inverlochy Castle, Fort William. This lovely yacht is a familiar sight to visitors to Fort William".[498]

On 21st June 1953, the shipping movements section of the Western Mail reported 'Torlundy' was sighted off Lizard Head in Cornwall, on its homeward voyage back to Scotland after the Spithead review, although we do not know if its proud owner was still aboard.[499]

In a letter to Barbara Barran in Canada in 1954, Joe wrote extensively about his yacht. "The 'Torlundy' is still my great love. Yesterday (Sunday) Eve and I and her sister, Mrs Walker from London, went out for the day and although there was a gale blowing we had a most enjoyable time. I am planning to do a Spring Cruise round the Irish coast shortly but I fear that I have had to give up my idea of a yachting trip to Scandinavia this year as business compels me to remain close to Fort William."[500]

Later in the same letter, he provides evidence of the lengths he went to – and obvious pride he obtained from – maintaining his connections with the Royal Navy: "In March I went to Portsmouth for a few days doing a Naval Training Course and had an opportunity of seeing some of the warships and looking through a submarine, meeting many old friends, and really enjoyed the holiday, with the result that I have been made Chief Mine Watcher in the Hebrides. This is a new branch of the Naval Service which spots mines which may be dropped from aircraft and plots them on a chart for the mine sweepers to clear. It is quite interesting because 'Torlundy' now flies the flag of the Royal Naval Mine Watching Service and all my crew have been sworn in as mine watchers."[501]

Tragedy struck in 1957 when wealthy US oilman Armor Archbold (48) died after collapsing on 'Torlundy'. He was on a cruise of the Hebrides with friends after announcing his plans to wed the Countess of Seafield, "one of Britain's wealthiest women" – Joe had lent them use of the yacht for a celebration cruise. 'Torlundy' immediately brought Archbold to hospital at Oban, but he died two days later as a result of a 'stomach haemorrhage'. Countess Seafield had recently divorced her elaborately named first husband Derek Ogilvie-Grand-Studley-Herbert.[502] Joe was not mentioned in the extensive news coverage of the incident and may well not have been on the yacht at the time. However, despite the tragedy, just a few days later, Joe used 'Torlundy' when he officiated as Commodore of the Royal Highland Yacht Club at the Oban Regatta. The annual regatta at Oban on Scotland's west coast was a regular feature of Joe's summer calendar, and he was an active member of the Yacht Club there. [503]

The ship's bell from 'Torlundy' still hangs at the entrance to the Malt House in Ben Nevis distillery to this day.

Joe's reasons for eventually deciding to sell 'Torlundy', which had clearly given him so much pleasure, have not been documented conclusively. However, one possibly apocryphal story is told by Hugh Dan MacLennan, the Gaelic-speaking writer and broadcaster who has researched Joe Hobbs' life and given talks about him on several occasions over the years. Hugh Dan relates that one of the ship's crew in the 1950s, Alec MacDiarmid, told him that on one occasion leaving Peterhead on a windy day, the 'Torlundy' was making heavy weather of the sea conditions when they were smoothly overtaken by a large sea-going steam trawler that they could not keep up with. Being a converted ex-navy landing craft with a relatively flat bottom, 'Torlundy' did not weather well in open seas. Apparently, Joe was impressed by the trawler's seaworthiness, and vowed to the crew that his next boat would be a steam trawler.[504] Given Joe's naval connections and interest in minesweeping, it is likely that he knew all about the fleet of minesweeper trawlers built by the Royal Navy based on the proven design of steam trawlers then commonly in use. Given it was Joe Hobbs, the 'trawler' he subsequently found to replace 'Torlundy' was a pretty exceptional vessel. But, in 1959, having found a new yacht, Joe sold 'Torlundy' to the Canadian government, who renamed it 'Le St. Barnabe' and made use of it as a training boat on the St. Lawrence river at Quebec for the remainder of its life.[505]

The vessel Joe found as a replacement for 'Torlundy' was 'Ocean Mist', which, being another historic ex-Navy vessel that had been converted with luxurious accommodation (similar to Mabel Dell, Stadacona/Lady Stimson, and Torlundy previously), clearly 'ticked all his boxes'.

We know the history of the 'Ocean Mist', which dates back to just after the First World War, from the work done by Capt. Walter Hume, who worked as Chief Officer on the vessel during her later life. During WW1, many steam fishing trawlers were requisitioned by the Admiralty and set to work as minesweepers, locating and clearing marine mines set by the Germans in the key shipping channels. To meet the need for more minesweepers and replace the many ships lost in service, the Admiralty developed a large programme, which extended to over 500 vessels, to purpose-build simple minesweepers to designs based on steam fishing trawlers then in common use. 'Ocean Mist' is the only known steam trawler from this programme to have survived into the 21st century. The ship was originally given the name Samuel Green, in a sequence of ships named for crew members on HMS Victory and HMS Royal Sovereign at the Battle of Trafalgar in 1815. Built by George Brown & Co. at Greenock, it was not completed until 30th April 1919, by which time the War was over, and it was equipped to operate as a standard fishing trawler. Later the same year Kenelm Guinness, a member of the famous Irish brewing family, bought the ship and renamed it 'Ocean Rover'. Guinness remodelled the ship, removing its fishing gear and installing comfortable accommodation for the owner and his guests. Guinness was an avid motor racer (who had set a new land speed record in 1922 and was the inventor of the famous KLG engine spark plug which was the industry leader between the world wars),[506] so he had the fish hold and ice room of 'Ocean Rover' converted to allow him to transport his racing cars from the UK to competitions in Europe.

Passing through a succession of wealthy owners during the 1930s, at the outbreak of WW2 in 1939, 'Ocean Rover' was requisitioned by the Admiralty and redeployed to her originally designed purpose as a mine sweeping and coastal patrol ship. Given the elaborate accommodation and absence of fishing winching gear, 'Ocean Rover' was not really suitable for practical minesweeping work, and so very sensibly was used instead as a Commander's Head Quarters ship.[507]

After the end of WW2, most other similar vessels went back to work as trawlers, but once again 'Ocean Rover's customised fit-out made her unsuitable for fishing. Consequently, she remained laid-up at Portsmouth until 1949, when she was acquired by Mr F.D. Fenston of London for use as a yacht. By 1954, with most of the war-time restrictions on materials and equipment eased, 'Ocean Rover' was bought by the multi-millionaire owner of one of the UK's largest construction companies F.G. Mitchell. A keen racing yachtsman, Mitchell renamed the yacht 'Ocean Mist', and refitted and refurbished her again for use as an accommodation ship, also replacing the old coal-fired boilers with modern oil-fired equipment. When Frederick Mitchell died in 1957, his widow Blackie Mitchell kept the ship for a few years but apparently never sailed in her.[508]

This was the background to Joe's purchase of 'Ocean Mist' in 1959. His new yacht was a similar size to 'Torlundy', being 125 feet long, 23 feet wide, and weighing 280 gross tons; but as a purpose-designed sea-going vessel, her seaworthiness and

'Ocean Mist', early 1960s.

comfort was a big step up from 'Torlundy'. In April 1959, Joe brought his new acquisition with its crew of 12 up from the south coast to Montrose on Scotland's east coast, where he was busy working on his Lochside distillery project, so that 'Ocean Mist' could have repairs and upgrading work done at one of the Montrose boatyards. A crowd of locals turned out to witness the arrival, with Joe again winning plaudits from the local newspaper for "following his usual practice of employing local tradesmen" for the refit work.[509] Thereafter, he took the vessel through the Caledonian Canal to Corpach, close by Fort William, on the northern side of Loch Linnhe, near where the loch meets the entrance to the Caledonian Canal. Repainted in Joe's beloved yellow, 'Ocean Mist' was based at Corpach for the rest of Joe's life, although, sadly, Joe's declining health during his later years meant he was unable to use her as much as he doubtless would have liked, mainly restricted to voyages around Loch Linnhe and along the Caledonian Canal.

Since his early years in Sault Ste Marie, Joe Hobbs was always a keen sailor, and in addition to his motor yachts, his resources after he moved to Fort William were sufficient that he

Joe's sailing yacht 'Panther', seen here at Oban.

could also indulge himself with an elegant and fast sailing yacht, the 'Panther.' Joe raced the 'Panther' in regattas around Scotland, and especially at the annual regatta at Oban each summer. For a time in the 1950s, Joe was Commodore of the Royal Highland Yacht Club at Oban.

Joe's passion for yachts and sailing was something which gave him great satisfaction, whilst simultaneously providing him with practical tools to progress his business interests, used to entertain and impress customers and influential stakeholders. His yachting activities contributed substantially to making Joe Hobbs the man he was.

13

Awards and Recognition

R eflecting his achievements, high profile and good standing, Joe received multiple honours and recognition in the UK in the latter part of his life.

The first award came very soon after the war, when in 1946 Joe was admitted to the Worshipful Company of Shipwrights, and made a Freeman of the City of London. This award was largely in recognition of the work he did with Oxy Ferrolene Ltd during World War 2, and the selfless way he provided his steel welding and cutting patents and technologies to support the war effort. Historically, being made a Freeman of the City of London was both honorific and of considerable practical relevance, providing rights to vote in elections, exemptions from many business taxes and duties, and conferring other privileges helpful to successfully conducting business in the world's most important commercial capital. By the time he was admitted in 1946, the trading privileges of membership were less helpful to Joe, but being granted the Freedom of the City of London was still a notable and prestigious recognition of his standing and contribution.[av]

---

av   Unfortunately, because of data protection rules it is not possible to get access to the citation nominating Joe for this award.

The majority of City of London Freemen are admitted by being members of one of the 110 London Livery Companies, the historic associations of traders (for example drapers, goldsmiths, stonemasons) that arranged training and ensured quality standards and organisation for the many trades and occupations in the City. Joe was admitted to the Worshipful Company of Shipwrights, whose origins date back to the 12th century, and membership of which was only open to those with a professional maritime background (military or commercial) – so, of all the Livery Companies, this was the one most appropriate for Joe. The Shipwrights have a special connection to the Royal Navy and to the Royal Family, and both of these connections were attractive and useful to Joe. For example, in a letter to Barbara Barran in 1954, Joe wrote "I am a member of the Shipwrights Guild of London and the Duke of Edinburgh takes over as Master or what we call Prime Warden this Summer, so I will be dining with him on the occasion of his installation and will have an opportunity of a chat. He has already told some of my friends that he wants to come and see the Ranch."[510]

Some years later, in the New Year's Honours list of 1950, Joe was awarded the rank of Commander of the Order of St John of Jerusalem by the King. The order of St John is a royal order of chivalry, an order of knights inspired by the Crusades, named after St John the Baptist. The order traces its roots back to the Knights Hospitaller in the Middle Ages, who founded a hospital dedicated to St John in Jerusalem in 1099 to care for sick, poor and injured pilgrims coming to the Holy Land. It was reconstituted in the UK in 1888 by a Royal Charter issued by Queen Victoria. The order has 25,000 members, with the aim "to prevent and relieve sickness and injury, and to act to enhance the health and well-being of people anywhere in the world." In the UK, it is best known for the work it did founding and developing the volunteer St John's Ambulance Brigade and

Cross of the Order of St. John, as awarded to Joe Hobbs on 21ˢᵗ June 1950.

the St John's Eye Hospital Group. At the investiture ceremony held at the City Chambers in Glasgow on 21st June 1950, the organisation's head in Scotland, the Lord Prior of Scotland, the Earl of Lindsay, invested Joe as a commander of the organisation, one of three so awarded in Scotland that year.[511]

Later in 1950, Joe was also presented with the Freedom of Fort William, his adopted home in Scotland. The Scotsman newspaper brought the news in April that Fort William town clerk Robert Dow had announced that Joe and Sir Donald W. Cameron of Lochiel (Head of the Clan Cameron and Lord Lieutenant of Inverness-shire) were to be conferred the Freedom of the Burgh of Fort William at a ceremony to be arranged in the summer. Joe was described as the proprietor of Ben Nevis distillery, but also of Highland Lime Quarries and the Great Glen Cattle Ranch – indicating the lime quarries were seen to be important locally, although the distillery and ranch were what Joe was known for outside Scotland. The honour was "in recognition of his public-spirited generosity to the burgh and district". That he was honoured together with Cameron of Lochiel, an old aristocrat and Lord Lieutenant of the county, also clearly demonstrates that Joe was a valued and established leader of the community. This was only the third time Fort William had granted a freedom award since the burgh was formed in 1875, showing that the local people had really taken Joe into their hearts and recognised his contribution to the area.[512]

The actual investiture took place on 27th October at a ceremony attended by 400 people at Fort William Town Hall, including many local leaders and dignitaries. The citation for the award was read out by the town clerk, explaining that it was given "in recognition of his tireless achievements in industry, agriculture, and stockbreeding, unprecedented in the history of the local economy, and of his unstinted and spontaneous munificence to the Burgh of Fort William for the advancement of the recreational and social facilities of its people, and in testimony of the esteem in which he is held by its citizens." Provost MacFarlane amplified on the many positive things Joe had done for the district, including providing accommodation for nurses at Belford Hospital, his work improving Ben Nevis distillery, creating jobs at the lime quarries, and reclaiming previously barren land and putting it into productive use. MacFarlane commented on Joe's remarkable "energy and industry" and his "inventive genius."[513]

In his acceptance speech, Joe was quoted as saying "100 years ago, the hills of Lochaber were covered with cattle". He saw no reason why this should not happen again. "Britain was built on beef and beer and not on lettuce" he said, stressing the ability of the Highlands to contribute more to Britain's meat production problem. Joe also spoke about how promotion of industry could contribute more to Highland development, urging that all potential sources of primary wealth in the area should be actively developed.[514]

Newspaper articles at the time also comment that Joe's "energy and enterprise have brought new life to Lochaber" and

Joe Hobbs was awarded the 'Freedom of the Burgh' of Fort William in October 1950.

commended him for finding time to work out a new drainage scheme for local playing fields so that sports events were no longer cancelled by flooding. The Dundee Courier said this was the sort of thing that "made proud Lochaber take this Englishman to its heart".[515] The media in Canada also picked up the news, sharing in Joe's reflected glory, and commenting that Joe "had taken the Highlands to his heart and was determined to stay for good."[516]

In combination, these three major awards and recognitions for Joe's achievements are impressive. However, it is interesting to speculate, given Joe's selfless contribution in two world wars; his achievements in the whisky industry, buying, refurbishing and putting back into operation no less than eight major distilleries; his role in transforming a barren Highland estate into a highly productive cattle ranch, helping to address Britain's meat shortage and providing a lot of positive publicity for the government's campaign to get farmers to produce more meat; as well as his service on a number of government committees and philanthropy in the communities in which he operated;

why Joe Hobbs did not receive any more formal, high-profile and national award or recognition, such as a knighthood or being made an OBE, MBE or CBE. Others with arguably less impressive contributions to Britain's development were so-rewarded, so why not Joe?

Given the lack of transparency in Britain's antiquated public honours system, it is difficult to be sure about the reasons for this. Part of the explanation probably comes from the fact that Joe himself, always pragmatic and down-to-earth, did not spend time and effort lobbying or positioning himself for such awards. Neither was he politically active, and therefore did not receive support from the political organisations which are often conduits promoting worthy individuals to be recognised.

But it could also be that there was some legacy of Joe's reputation as a rum runner in Canada in the 1920s, and association with some decidedly dodgy business dealings from his partners in Stimsons over the construction of the Marine Building in Canada. Certainly in Canada, there is rumour to this day that there was hesitation in confirming Joe's appointment as the first commander of the Royal Canadian Navy Volunteer Reserve in Vancouver in 1924 because of the way he earned his money. Joe took care not to break any Canadian laws, but it seems there was some doubt about the appropriateness of appointing someone who was clearly involved in smuggling alcohol into the USA to a high-profile leadership role in the Canadian navy. Eventually the naval authorities did confirm Joe's appointment, but there were voices questioning his character and values.

After his return to the UK in the early 1930s, Joe's career was solidly legitimate, and there were no scandals or reputational issues to damage his good standing. Joe was adept at demonstrating how his businesses created employment and benefitted the communities in which he operated, as well as involving himself in various government committees working to improve different aspects of the Highlands economy. However, over the course of his career, Joe had plenty of battles with authority (e.g. with British Aluminium at Ben Nevis; his criticisms of government over his distillery proposals at Glen Mavis; and his dispute with the government and the Scotch Whisky Association over selling 'young whisky' overseas in the shortage years after WW2). Joe was not breaking any laws or regulations in these disputes, and arguably deserves credit for doggedly pursuing the best interest of his business in the face of bureaucratic muddle and indecision. But these actions conceivably did not endear Joe Hobbs to some sections of the 'establishment', including possibly some individuals that might have been asked to comment or endorse his consideration for awards. We shall never know, but it seems the guardians of the UK's rather opaque mechanisms for awarding good public service concluded Joe's efforts were more to the benefit of his own business than contributing to the wider public good.

14

The Great Man of the Great Glen – Later Years and Legacy

On the family front, although Joe and Eve never had children together, Joe's son Joe Junior delivered him three grandchildren. Joe Junior first married Dilys Ann Davies, who had been born in Barry, Wales, at Blaby, Leicestershire, in January 1944. The couple had a daughter, Joe's first grandchild, Susan Ann Hobbs, a short time later in July 1944 at Market Bosworth, Leicestershire.

The marriage did not last, and the couple divorced in 1948. In 1950, Joe Junior married a second time to Grete Fogh. Grete was Danish, and she and Joe Junior had met in 1948 when they were both travelling on the same ship, taking Grete to Los Angeles and Joe Junior to Vancouver. The couple had two children together, both of whom were born in Copenhagen. Joe's second grandchild, Annemarie Hobbs, was born on 28th March 1953, with Joe's third and final grandchild, and first grandson, Joseph Peter Oscar Hobbs, born in November 1955.[517, aw]

---

aw   After Joe's death, Annemarie helped her mother run Inverlochy Castle

Three generations of Joseph Hobbs – Joe, son Joe Junior, and grandson Joseph Peter Hobbs, at Inverlochy Castle towards the end of Joe's life.

With declining health from the late 1950s, Joe Hobbs had been forced to slow down the hectic pace of his business and social commitments, and in September 1961 had sold his beloved Great Glen Cattle Ranch to the Hon. Alan Mackay. After the sale in the late autumn of 1961, Joe 'retired' to the 370 acres he had retained at Inverlochy Castle.[518] In early December 1961, Joe took ill during a business visit to Montrose, and had to be admitted to Stracathro Hospital, at Brechin, 10 miles to the west of Lochside Distillery at Montrose. In one of his last letters

Hotel, but did not get involved as a director of the family businesses. She subsequently relocated to Tuscany in Italy, where for many years she has operated a successful agro-tourism business. Joseph Peter went to Uppingham School Rutland between 1969 and 1975, then studied at the Ecole Hoteliere de Glion hotel school at Montreux, Switzerland, between 1975 and 77. After that, from 1978 to 1998 he was part-owner and also director (from 31/8/1993 to 20/12/1996) of Inverlochy Castle Ltd hotel. Joseph Peter was responsible for the successful conversion of the old "Factor's House" on the estate into an offshoot of the main hotel. From January 1998 until retiring in 2021, together with his wife Margaret, he owned and operated La Bastide Toscane at Correns, Provence, a farmhouse with large pool and grounds which he rented out to tourists.

to his niece Barbara Barran, Joe explains he had been suffering with angina and bronchitis, which required his hospitalisation for the best part of a month from early December until he was discharged on Christmas Eve. The Aberdeen Evening Express reported on 27th December: "Well Again: Mr Joseph W. Hobbs (70), who has been a patient in Stracathro Hospital, has been discharged and has returned to his home Inverlochy Castle."[519] He told Barbara he had to remain in bed at home for several weeks after his discharge; however, by the time he wrote to his niece on 1st March 1962 he was upbeat, saying "with the parks and meadows round the Castle, 370 acres and 50 head of cattle…I am still a farmer, and have plenty to take up my time and interest. What I need now is some health and strength."[520]

The reality of Joe's condition was that heart failure kills someone slowly, and, however upbeat he tried to be around friends and relatives, he probably knew it was unlikely he would get better. Joe lived on for another 16 months, but for much of this period he was not well enough to go out or actively manage his business, and spent his days mostly at Inverlochy – Dominic Sargent in his history of Inverlochy Castle says that during this period Joe "conducted business from his castle bed".[521] He spent some time putting his affairs in order. In 1962 he sold 12 miles of fishing rights on the River Lochy to Lord Dulverton for £127,000 (£2.7m today).[522] Whilst Joe knew full well the high value of quality salmon fishing rights in Scotland, it must have caused at least a small pang of disappointment in the old rancher that these fishing rights earned him almost exactly the same amount of money at the time of their sale as had the whole of his Great Glen Cattle Ranch when he had sold that a year earlier.

Despite his poor health, Joe did not lose his "up and at it" spirit. His grandson Joseph Peter Hobbs tells the story that Joe had his staff clearing hedges and bushes in the vicinity of the house, so that they did not impede Joe's efforts to shoot rabbits from his bedroom window![523]

Joe spent most of April and part of May 1962 getting treatment in London. The Aberdeen Evening Express reported in a story entitled "Rancher Heads for Home" that after spending the previous six weeks in a London nursing home Joe was well enough to return to Inverlochy Castle on the overnight sleeper train to Fort William.[524]

After that, for more than a year, very little was heard from the previously high-profile Joe Hobbs, until in August 1963 a number of local newspapers reported that Eve had to cancel public engagements because Joe was ill. These were the last days, and Joe Hobbs died quietly at home at Inverlochy Castle just after midnight on Monday, 19th August 1963. He was 72 years old.

Joe had been quite seriously ill for more than three years, severe enough to curtail his business activities and social life, and keep him at home with long periods in bed. Four serious conditions were listed on Joe's death certificate: Aortic Stenosis (a narrowing of the main artery as it comes out of the heart); Cardiac Hypertrophy (enlargement of the heart muscle, which could have been secondary to the aortic stenosis, or to high blood pressure); Myocardial degeneration and failure (the heart muscle not working properly, heart failure); and Cirrhosis of the Liver. This is quite a list, but in summary Joe had been progressively dying from heart failure. There could be a congenital or inherited aspect to this as several other family members suffered from heart disease and angina, but there was quite likely also a degenerative dimension linked to Joe's lifestyle and behaviour. The best guess from this range of problems is that Joe died from a combination of the effects of alcohol and narrowing of his aortic artery, which forced his heart to work harder to pump the blood through the narrower arteries, leading eventually to heart failure. In combination, he would have felt and looked dreadful. Together with the inability to make any physical effort, this combination of factors conspired to keep him out of the public eye over the last years of his life.

Joe was buried on 21st August 1963 in a quiet ceremony at Innis na Birlinn Cemetery, five miles out of Fort William, on the hillside overlooking his favourite loch, Loch Linnhe, where his yacht Ocean Mist lay at anchor.[525] His wife Eve was later buried in the same plot. Their grave is marked by a simple headstone, very much in keeping with the ambience of this quiet Highland graveyard, which is noticeably lacking in elaborate or ornate grave furniture.

Obituaries to Joe Hobbs appeared in the UK and Canadian national media, as well as in a multitude of local and regional newspapers, especially in Scotland. The UK nationals, including The Times and The Guardian, eulogised Joe as making a fortune

The plain and now rather weather-worn gravestone at Innis na Birlinn Cemetery near Onich which marks Joe and Eve Hobbs' final resting place. The simple inscription on the stone reads "In loving memory of J.W.Hobbs and his wife Eve F. Hobbs of Inverlochy Castle, Fort William."

in shipping and property, and then after losing it all following the Great Crash of 1929, having the capability to rebuild his fortunes as a whisky distiller and cattle rancher in Scotland.[526] The Canadian media emphasised Joe's ability to make fortunes on both sides of the Atlantic, and his innovation in successfully applying Canadian/North American ranching techniques to make his Scottish estates fertile and productive. The Canadians also stressed Joe's role in WW1 and success with the Marine Building in Vancouver.[527, 528] Perhaps understandably, though, it was the Scottish papers that provided the most comprehensive reviews of Joe's life, although here too it was the Great Glen ranching activities that seem to be given 'pride of place' in the long list of Joe's achievements. The Aberdeen Press and Journal summed it up best when they described Joe as "The Great Man of The Great Glen," a worthy epithet and one of which Joe would doubtless have been extremely proud. The hard-won respect of the tough and not-easily-impressed locals of Lochaber meant a great deal to Joe in his later life, and he definitely considered himself an 'adopted son' of that part of Highland Scotland.[529]

In a little more than 70 years, Joe Hobbs had certainly lived life to the full, packing more into each decade of existence than most people achieve in a lifetime. Throughout his life, Joe's ability to think strategically and act decisively enabled him to exploit opportunities, gain experiences and earn rewards quickly and at scale, even if sometimes his willingness to take risk led him to operate in areas which were not helpful to his long-term reputation.

Having had a solid education and established a good technical knowledge through his early years with the Clergue businesses and in government service in Sault Ste Marie, Joe opted for the glamorous but highly risky arena of military aviation during WW1. Joe excelled as a military pilot, and, although his even more talented younger brother Basil outshone him in terms of awards and decorations, merely surviving four years of active service as a military aviator during a conflict in which one-third of airmen died demonstrates Joe's skill, determination and endurance. Joe also acquired important experience as a leader, in project management, and was trusted with important consultations and liaison work with Canada's US allies.

After WW1, the phenomenal speed with which Joe acquired his first fortune in whisky trading, shipping and rum running was extraordinary. His natural aptitudes and capabilities, honed and refined by his testing wartime experience, equipped Joe to become one of the leading entrepreneurs of his generation in post-WW1 Canada. The unique situation of Vancouver with its proximity to Prohibition-era America presented the opportunities for Joe to give full rein to his entrepreneurial talent. He was remarkably successful, accumulating a sizeable fortune in just a few years, enabling him to build a mansion in the most fashionable part of Vancouver and own the largest yacht (and play a leading role) at the Royal Vancouver Yacht Club. Physical, financial and reputational risks inclined Joe to give up rum running in the latter part of the 1920s and reposition his businesses to focus on entirely legitimate areas of activity which still offered the potential of very high returns, especially shipping and property development.

While Joe's shipping fleet was actually relatively modest compared with the larger ship owners of his day, his legitimate shipping business was certainly lucrative, and enabled him to indulge his lifelong passion for ships and yachts. His communication and people skills propelled him during this period into the heart of Vancouver and British Columbia's business and social elite. Moving away from rum running and turning his attention to property development was an entirely natural and sensible progression, which enabled Joe to fully leverage his excellent social standing and connections to contribute something, in the form of the Marine Building, of lasting value to his adopted home of Vancouver.

Joe was visionary in seeing the opportunity to build Vancouver's first skyscraper, and provide a home for all of Vancouver's maritime and trade-related businesses close to the waterfront, in the heart of what became the city's Central Business District. Joe provided incredible energy, drive and persistence to see the Marine Building project through to a conclusion, putting substantial effort and seemingly quite some of his personal fortune into negotiating the refinancing arrangements that were required to finish construction after the Great Crash in 1929. The truth is that the Marine Building was not just Vancouver's first skyscraper; it was an outstanding and iconic building whose design and construction were top class, with hundreds of interesting and thoughtful design features, as well as (for the time) state-of-the-art technology. For a long time the tallest building in Canada, Joe oversaw the design and construction of a seriously impressive art deco building, one which UK Poet Laureate Sir John Betjeman (a knowledgeable and passionate advocate for good architecture) later described as "the best Art Deco office building in the world." After the challenging period following its construction, with the bankruptcy of Stimsons and a very weak property market in the early years of the Great Depression, Marine Building went on to have a very successful later history as one of the leading commercial buildings in Vancouver, and a stand-out feature of its skyline and building stock to this day. It would not have been completed at all were it not for Joe's work to refinance the construction after the Great Crash of 1929 and Stimson's bankruptcy.

In his property development career in Canada, Joe had become a Vice President of G.A. Stimson & Co. Ltd. Initially a well-run and respectable business, under F.G. Johnston's leadership Stimsons evolved into a company that operated with some very suspect business practices which ultimately ended in a messy and high-profile bankruptcy, with three of the Stimsons senior leaders sentenced to jail time for their actions. Joe was not personally responsible for the mismanagement by Stimsons, but the consequences were still severe for him, causing him to lose almost all of his hard-earned fortune, making it ultimately impossible for him to rebuild his business empire in Vancouver. For once Joe's timing was not good. It is an interesting thought, what Joe Hobbs might have achieved in property and construction had it not been for the Stimsons collapse and the Great Depression.

As it was, Joe was made of stern stuff, and had the courage and determination to pick himself up and rebuild his career even more successfully in the UK. With his new wife Eve by his side for the rest of his life, after his return to the land of his birth in the early 1930s, Joe focused first on building up his whisky trading business, working closely with National Distillers Products Corporation, and then acquiring six Scottish distilleries in less than three years, refurbishing and rebuilding all of them and putting them back into operation. Joe's Associated Scottish Distilleries became the second-largest whisky company in the industry, behind only the mighty DCL in terms of scale. Joe's contacts, know-how and negotiating skills were instrumental in making this possible, and his technical and engineering knowledge enabled him to supervise modernisation and refurbishment of the plant and bring them back into effective operation. The decision to construct a grain distillery at Hillside/Montrose meant ASD were perfectly positioned to produce high-quality blended whiskies for the booming US market. In the process, Joe was able to make a lot of money for himself, netting around £5m at 2024 price levels, and substantially rebuilding his fortune in the process.

But as the architect and main executor of the plan to acquire and operate the distilleries, Joe also created a lot of value for his partners, especially for T&M and its ultimate parent National Distillers. Although WW2 intervened to prevent National reaping their reward immediately, when the ASD distilleries and T&M were sold on after the war, National earned £3.25m in 1953 (over £93m today), enabling them to make a return of around 15 times their initial investments. Seton Porter's decision to back Joe Hobbs in this project (and to allow Joe a fair share of the spoils) was an inspired decision and an outstanding financial investment.

Post-WW2, Joe continued his whisky innovation at Ben Nevis and Lochside. During Joe's ownership of these distilleries, both were highly unusual in operating with traditional pot stills and also with Continuous/Coffey stills, enabling them to make both malt whisky and grain whisky at the same site, in order to be able to make all the components of his blends himself. While Joe was not technically the first to go down this route, it is quite possible that in taking this course he did inspire and influence other industry players, as several major operators later adopted a similar approach.

While some of Joe's innovation at Ben Nevis has not stood the test of time, Joe was undeniably a good and improving owner of the distillery who spent a lot of time and money upgrading and refurbishing it after years of neglect, nursing it through the difficult years after WW2. Fundamentally, Joe secured the long-term future of the distillery by winning the legal case with British Aluminium which provided security of tenure of the distillery's lease for 99 years. As a result, whisky lovers everywhere have reason to be grateful to Joe Hobbs in securing the survival of a distillery that only more recently has started to be appreciated for its true quality.

At Lochside distillery in Montrose, Joe designed and created a modern distillery out of the remnants of the old Deuchars brewery. Although very little of its production was ever released as a single malt, in its 35-year history as a working distillery Lochside achieved a very high reputation for the quality of its whisky. Joe died before the trend towards single malt whisky production and sales really took off, and the subsequent owners (DYC of Spain) preferred to use most of the production for blends, or sold it in bulk to improve the quality of their Spanish-distilled whiskies. The absence of a well-known profile and 'brand' for Lochside was almost certainly the main factor that contributed to Allied Distillers' decision to close the distillery after they took it over from DYC in 1992. Given the high regard in which rare bottles of Lochside single malt whisky are held by whisky aficionados, unfortunately in doing so Allied also deprived consumers of an opportunity to enjoy what could have become one of Scotland's great whiskies.

Although Joe was a highly colourful character in the whisky industry we should not over-romanticise his role. Joe was fundamentally a seriously talented entrepreneur who made a fortune in whisky, rather than someone who focused mainly on whisky as his life's passion. David Daiches in 'Scotch Whisky: Its Past and Present' said something similar of some of the late 19th/early 20th century whisky barons such as James Buchanan, Alexander Walker, Tommy Dewar and Peter Mackie: "some of them were entrepreneurs who happened to have chosen whisky as their product and could have done just as well with anything else."[530] This was also true of Joe Hobbs, who did just as well with property development, ship owning and cattle ranching. Joe himself was rather dispassionate about his whisky activities: in the 'Modern Millionaires' article in the Liverpool Echo in January 1954, Joe said "I've made millions of gallons of whisky since then (ASD). It isn't very difficult. But personally, I prefer a glass of milk."[531] Even allowing for a bit of hyperbole in an article from a series which pitted Joe up against other well-known millionaires, Joe does not give the impression he was passionate about whisky. He understood the industry, was good at making money from it, but he did not labour from morning to night to make the best whisky he could, in a way that some other successful whisky firms have done. In any case, it is not impossible Joe quite literally preferred drinking milk over whisky by the time of the 1954 article because of his developing health problems!

The other great passion of Joe Hobbs in his later years in Scotland was the Inverlochy Estate and, in particular, the Great Glen Cattle Ranch. After labouring for years to reclaim land and prove his model for ranching could be profitable and successful in Scotland, Joe had somewhat surprisingly sold the ranch in 1961. In his book on the Inverlochy Castle Hotel, Dominic Sargent conjectures that with Joe's health failing in the early 1960s, "having successfully achieved his ranching ambitions, he decided to sell the Great Glen Cattle Ranch".[532] However, Joe had expressly stated that his hope was to pass on Inverlochy Estate to his son.[533] In a TV interview with Fyfe Robertson on BBC's 'Tonight' programme on Monday, 27th July 1959 (just two years before he sold the ranch) Joe explained that up till that point he had reclaimed 1,100 acres of land on the estate, and intended to continue until he had 3,500 acres of grassland. The clear implication is that Joe had not yet completed all that he planned to achieve with the ranch, and would have carried on if ill health had not intervened.[534] It was probably the unexpected death of Charlie Palmer, Joe's long-term factor on the estate and right-hand-man, in May 1961, that triggered a rethink for Joe about the estate. With Joe's own health failing, and with his son Joe Junior unwilling to take over responsibility for the estate and the ranch, it seems Joe decided it was not realistic to hire a new factor and try to soldier on. But, knowing what we do about Joe's

"Up and at it!" mentality, this cannot have been an easy decision.

Hobbs supporters, in both the UK and in Canada, were convinced that his ranching approach worked, and sang Joe's praises. The Province newspaper in Vancouver concluded that "Mr Hobbs is a man who has pioneered in reverse, coming from Canada to Scotland to find fortune…. The 'Canadian' has made good and brought new prosperity to the Highlands."[535] In Scotland, there were doubters and cynics initially, but at least some of these were likely to have been conservatives reacting to Joe's perceived brashness, uncomfortable with his willingness to try something new in a rather insular and traditional Highland environment. Joe was able to win a lot of people round, locally, nationally, and also in government. Other pioneers were undertaking similar experiments at the same time, as Britain made a concerted effort to increase meat production and land under cultivation in the shortage years after WW2, and many others were inspired by Joe's efforts to take up cattle rearing. Joe was able to make money from the ranch, and successfully produced a lot of beef from land which had been barren and idle. His success with the ranch and benevolence to his community in Lochaber were amongst the main reasons Joe was recognised and awarded with the Freedom of Fort William and Commander of the Order of St John. He proved his point, and showed his method was economically viable, but he himself admitted that the approach required a lot of capital and the means to wait a number of years for a return.[536] Government subsidies also played an important role in the financial equation, and the ranch would not have been profitable without them.

The sale price achieved on disposal of the estate at £123,000 (2024: £3.4m) looks disappointing given the size of the estate and the huge amount of work that had gone into making it productive. Joe received almost exactly the same price for selling his fishing rights on the Inverlochy River as for the whole of the Great Glen

Ranch when he sold it, although The Scotsman were correct in pointing out in their obituary that Joe had successfully turned land worth 10 shillings an acre when he bought it into land worth £40 an acre, which he achieved through "determination, know-how, imagination, boldness, even obstinacy and the personal knowledge and skill which he held personally or delegated."[537] However, relatively few of his innovations sustained, e.g. Joe introduced the sileage pit to Scotland, and the practice of adding molasses and fish oil to sileage to make up vitamin deficiencies, neither of which caught on. At the end of the day, Joe's grand ranching experiment did not even survive his own lifetime, with the bulk of the estate being sold in 1961 before he died. After the estate was sold, the new owner reintroduced sheep to the ranch in place of some of the cattle and reverted to more 'traditional' ways of hill farming on the land.

The EU's Common Agricultural Policy had a huge impact on the profitability of cattle rearing in the Highlands, contributing to a protracted decline in cattle rearing under the Single Farm Payment system, with livestock numbers across Scotland falling successively in recent years. The trend began at the turn of the millennium in the case of pigs and sheep, but dates from the mid-1970s in the case of cattle. In 2020, there were 1.7 million cattle in Scotland, down from a peak of 2.8m in 1974, with livestock numbers across Scotland the lowest since the 1940 and 1950s. Moreover, current agricultural policy is evolving towards preserving the natural state of the environment, probably antithetical to Joe Hobbs' idea to raise beef production figures and make the glens "look like the Downs of England".[538]

The economic reality of farming in the hills and remote parts of Scotland always has been a very challenging proposition, and even today most hill farm production is financially uneconomic. Government support payments do help keep people on the land, but, with modern subsidies no longer linked to the number of animals produced, stock levels have gradually dropped. Whilst rising stock prices in recent years have helped, the beneficial impact has been negated by the fact that costs have also been rising, with the result that many hill farmers continue to struggle to ensure viability of their businesses.[539] Joe Hobbs proved his point that ranching in the Highlands could be made profitable, successfully return barren lands to productive use, and generate jobs and income for the local economy. Although Joe contributed to an upturn in cattle rearing and beef production in the Highlands for a time, and exhorted others to follow his lead, his innovations were not substantially taken up by others or replicated at scale elsewhere. The Great Glen Cattle Ranch was something of a one-off, and did not go on to fulfil the potential Joe identified for ranching across the upland areas of Britain to make a meaningful improvement to the country's meat production. Although the land on his ranch is farmed much less intensively today, aiming for sustainability and environmental balance rather than to maximise production, Joe would probably be pleased to see that cattle still roam free over the open uplands that he reclaimed, and still survive the winters fed from silage produced on the farm – innovations which Joe introduced, and which have successfully stood the test of time.

After Joe's death, Eve moved out of Inverlochy Castle to a new home at The White House, Onich, south-west of Fort William.[540] The house had an outstanding location with views right down beautiful Loch Linnhe, a place she loved, and close to where she and Joe were both buried. Eve remained active as a county councillor and social worker, representing the district of Caol from 1955 and 1967, and served as Vice Chairman of the County Health and Welfare Committee, and Chairman of the Children's Committee. Amongst other things, Eve was instrumental in setting up a number of residential homes for the elderly in the Highlands. After 1967, she moved for a period of time to London, and then to an elder care home in Berwick. In later life, she suffered from Parkinson's Disease, and, having expressed a desire to return to Fort William, in 1980 two local councillors helped her move back to be nursed at Invernevis House in Fort William, on the site of the old Nevis Distillery that Joe had bought in 1944.[541, 542] She passed away in Fort William in 1983 at the age of 83, having outlived her husband by more than 20 years.

Joe Junior brought his mother, Joe's first wife, Mabel Dell, over to live out her final years in the UK as well. She lived with Joe Junior at Oadby, Leicester, before passing away less than a year after Joe, on 26th April 1964. Although she was not a wealthy woman, Joe had supported her directly and indirectly throughout her life. Mabel took annual holidays together with her daughter Patricia, usually by sea and invariably travelling first class. Since Patricia never married and only worked intermittently, it seems Joe continued to provide for Mabel and Patricia for the remainder of their lives. Patricia became a naturalised US citizen in 1942 and lived most of her life in the USA, but she also came to live in the UK for the final years of her life, living at the apartment at 55 Park Lane in London that she had inherited from Joe, and passing away there in July 1987 at the age of 65.

Joe's last will and testament has proved hard to track down. The family did not retain a copy, and the official file that contained it seems to have gone missing when records were transferred from Fort William to the National Registers of Scotland in Edinburgh. Joe was always secretive about his fortune, and it does not seem out-of-keeping that information about his wealth and estate has been hard to establish even at his death. However, with excellent help from the Scotland's People archivist, it has been possible to obtain a transcript of Joe's will, filed as a 'Deed in Court' with Fort William Sheriff's

Court, which was sometimes the practice for larger estates and more prominent individuals. From this, it has been possible to establish that Joe left the entirety of his estate and responsibility for managing his legacy business interests to his son Joe Junior, without making any specific bequests to other family members or individuals.

For reasons known only to himself, Joe did not make specific provision for Eve, Mabel or Patricia. This must have left Joe Junior in quite a difficult situation to navigate. On the domestic front, it seems Joe Junior provided for Mabel and Patricia, both of whom lived out their remaining years in England. However, Eve is believed to have had to contest the will before obtaining a provision from the estate. There is some suggestion that Joe and Eve had become estranged in Joe's final years, and even that Eve had an affair. She was said to be close to a high-profile public figure in Fort William, although the person concerned had moved away from the town in the 1950s and was living in Edinburgh for some time before Joe's death in 1963, which raises doubts about this story. At 60 years' remove from events, it is difficult to establish with any certainty what may have transpired, but it does seem a pity after more than 30 years of marriage, during which Eve contributed substantially to a partnership in which the couple achieved a great deal together, that Joe and Eve's final years were perhaps less happy.

After the disposal of Ben Nevis in 1981, all of Joe Hobbs' main assets apart from Inverlochy Castle Hotel had been liquidated. Joe Junior passed away not long afterwards on 30th May 1984 at Inverlochy, where he spent the last few months of his life, at the relatively young age of 65. Joe Junior's children Annemarie and Joseph Peter Hobbs believe the strain of trying to find good buyers for Lochside and Ben Nevis in a very challenging financial environment contributed to Joe Junior's early demise from cancer of the oesophagus.

Joe Hobbs lived an extraordinary and colourful life. In each phase, he faced different challenges and opportunities, but, throughout his life, his quiet determination and capacity for hard work was the bedrock that enabled him to achieve substantial success in business, as well as in civic and social life. His background and upbringing equipped him well for the opportunities ahead. Coming from yeoman farmer stock, he had a practical, hands-on mentality, but also an expectation that hard work and persistence could enable a person to achieve wealth and good standing in the community. Certainly, the highly entrepreneurial examples set by his father and grandfather provided both inspiration and lessons for the young Joe, whilst also raising an expectation that he should get on and make something of his life. Joe saw himself as being of 'pioneering stock', a phrase he applied to himself a lot. Asked in later life to account for his success, Joe attributed his progress to "close application to business. If you're of pioneering stock you can make a success in Canada, Australia, or even in Scotland. But you've got to be of pioneering stock."[543] This was something he learned from his grandfather and father, and from his childhood experience as part of a migrant family struggling to carve out a new life in Canada.

His education and early career in Sault Ste Marie equipped him with a technical and engineering knowledge that would prove highly valuable in his subsequent career operating ships, constructing buildings, and managing distilleries. His constant inventiveness and efforts to apply new technologies to improve businesses and activities repeatedly created value for Joe and his business partners. Like all successful entrepreneurs, not every idea was a winner, but he was never afraid to try. His second wife, Eve, said he was "forever trying out something new, learning from his failures, and starting afresh."[544]

Joe's strategic vision, his ability to see clearly how things fitted together, and how to obtain value from a process or opportunity, were constant themes throughout his life. He coupled this with a willingness to act quickly and decisively, which often enabled him to seize and profit from opportunities, but which sometimes got him into trouble or put him into situations which bordered on unethical.

Joe combined all this with a gift for effective communication, an ability and understanding for how to deal effectively with the media, and a talent for self-promotion which enabled him to publicise his ideas and gain understanding and support for what he was trying to achieve. One newspaper asked in 1955, "What sort of man is Joseph Hobbs? In the first place, he is a man with a message."[545] Throughout his life, Joe was adept at obtaining coverage for his ideas, and skilful in conveying them in ways which resonated with his audience. Joe also realised that sharing information and investing in goodwill with the media and important influencers proved valuable when things did not turn out well.

In combination with his stubbornness, determination, and refusal to give up – John Bull magazine said Joe Hobbs had "a forceful, driving personality, about as easy to check as a bulldozer in low gear"[546] – these traits enabled Joe to succeed where others would have failed. When he coupled this with his belief in the need to create employment, provide housing and benefits for his workers, and contribute generally to the communities in which he operated, Joe proved very effective in convincing doubters and sceptics, enabling him to win the support, approval and friendship of even the hard-bitten and charm-resistant Highland Scots. Joe himself always said that his motto in life was "Up and At It," and this certainly characterised his fast-moving, determined, energetic, and driven approach to life, and helps explain how he managed to get so much done.

Joe was also adept at making the most out of his assets and opportunities, squeezing every dollar of value for his businesses.

Conceivably, this was something Joe had learned from F.H. Clergue during his formative years in Sault Ste Marie. Clergue's approach of using one of his businesses to support another led to the phenomenal expansion of the Consolidated Great Lakes Corporation business empire. Joe frequently adopted similar thinking. With the Great Glen Cattle Ranch, for example, Joe used the draff and spent pot ale from Ben Nevis distillery to help feed the cattle on his ranch during winter, and used the lime from his Torlundy Lime Quarries to improve the quality of the soil to sustain crop production for silage. He was able to benefit from government subsidies for improving his land in this way, effectively getting the government to pay him to use one of his assets to improve another.[547]

Throughout his life, Joe was very business-focused and pragmatic, perhaps not the most emotional man. Joe was decent to those he cared for, and was seen as a good employer who earned the respect and loyalty of his employees.[548] Joe enjoyed life's luxuries, especially his yachts, but also living in good houses, travelling first class, and the smart cars he bought for Eve and himself, even though he was not a good driver. Whilst perhaps a little reticent and reserved,[549] he knew how to be sociable, and was an adept host who entertained regularly at home and on his yachts, and used this to good effect to progress his businesses. Joe was generous in sharing his wealth and lifestyle with close family and friends, but had definite blind spots, for example not providing financial support for his less-well-off sisters in Canada.

Joe was passionate about his hobbies, especially yachting, and always maintained an interest in all things naval. He put great effort into maintaining his naval contacts long after he ceased active service with the navy. Despite being a solid figure, Joe was a very capable horseman, which was of considerable practical advantage during his years running the Great Glen

Joe Hobbs was a good shot, and a lifelong hunting enthusiast.

Ranch.[550] He enjoyed country pursuits, was a good shot, and regularly organised shoots of his own.[ax] He was patriotic and more than willing to contribute his considerable energies and abilities during the two world wars.

An Englishman who grew up and spent many years in Canada, Joe adopted Scotland as his home, and to a large extent Scotland adopted him in return. Joe seemed to feel at home in Scotland; he had big ambitions for the Highlands, and did a lot to contribute to its development. Through his efforts and his clearly authentic love for the country and its people, he came to win the respect of the tough and hard-to-impress locals in Lochaber. It is fitting that he died at Inverlochy, on his estate in his adopted homeland. In his last months, a TV crew from the Canadian Broadcasting Corporation came to Inverlochy to make a documentary about Joe and his activities, titled 'The Laird of Inverlochy', imagery with which Joe (in his final letter to his niece Barbara) seemed very taken.[551, 552]

Over the course of his eventful and entrepreneurial business life, Joe moved progressively towards legitimacy, but never

---

ax   Joe purchased a 25-year shooting lease on the estate at Meallmoor near Daviot, south of Inverness, and every 12th August invited family, business partners and long-term employees to join for the annual grouse shoot.

orthodoxy. In the 1920s he steered away from rum running and towards property development; but he only narrowly avoided being implicated in the dubious business practices of his chosen partners in Stimsons. He escaped bankruptcy by a whisker, but his situation was bad enough that he had to leave Canada and returned to the UK to start again. In the UK, he rebuilt his fortune and reputation with ASD, but still employed some sharp business practices in 'flipping' the distillery assets he acquired on to his partners at significantly inflated prices. After WW2, he demonstrated he could still play hardball in the dispute with British Aluminium over the Ben Nevis lease, but in his war work with Oxy Ferrolene, and his continued efforts to contribute to the economic and community development of the Highlands, he progressively transitioned to a highly respected member of the community, albeit one who still often went about things in unusual ways. Joe was justifiably proud of his achievements, pleased to be invited to contribute to government committees, and always keen to maintain his naval connections. Whilst he lived life well and in a grand style with his castle, yachts and estate, Joe obtained the most satisfaction from doing something worthwhile, and earning the respect of others. In the mid-1950s, when asked what pleasure he got from his fortune, Joe's reply was "The pleasure of using it to make two blades of grass grow where one grew before." [553]

In all of this, it can very much be seen that Joe Hobbs lived a colourful and eventful life, throughout which he repeatedly demonstrated he was anything but an average Joe.

15

Postscript

At the conclusion of this review of Joe Hobbs' varied and most active life, it is interesting to extend the timeline a little, investigating what happened to some elements of his business empire after his passing.

1. Whisky
A) Associated Scottish Distilleries
Although Joe Hobbs' involvement with ASD came to an end in early 1940 when he sold his shareholding back to his partners Train & MacIntyre, Joe's departure was not the end of the story for ASD or its distilleries.

The onset of the Second World War led to tough restrictions on the whisky industry, and strict rationing of supplies of barley and grains, which were largely prioritised for use as a foodstuff. Whilst some distilling did continue, most distilleries closed for extended periods during the war years, and many of them were commandeered for military and other purposes in support of the war effort.

ASD was heavily impacted by this, and was not able to

make very much whisky after 1940. Glenury Royal, Glenlochy, Benromach and Fettercairn were closed during most of World War 2; Bruichladdich was mothballed again between 1941 and 1945; whilst Hillside/Montrose had hardly been in production for a year as a grain distillery before distilling ceased, and the premises were used as a barracks for the duration of the war. Benromach's situation was typical, with production ceasing in 1939 and the distillery used to garrison initially British and subsequently Polish troops, right through until 1946. [554]

After WW2, ASD attempted to restart operations at its portfolio of Scottish distilleries. However, shortages and restrictions remained in place for quite some years after the end of the war, and this prevented ASD from realising the potential of its Scottish assets. With cash flows tight, and not much whisky being made, the decision was taken to dispose of National Distillers' Scottish assets. Two of the distilleries were sold separately: Bruichladdich distillery and its whisky stocks were purchased by Glasgow whisky brokers Ross & Coulter in 1951/52 for £205,000 (a sum which appears to be close to the value of whisky stocks alone),[555] whilst Fettercairn was sold to Aberdonian businessman Tom Scott Sutherland for £100,000 in 1953.[556] Both of these sales realised markedly more for ASD than it had originally paid for the assets (only £23,000 and £5,000 respectively). As such, Joe's vision and ability to negotiate great deals still delivered real value to National, selling the assets for more than six times what they had cost to buy, enabling them to make a profit on the sale of these two distilleries of £187,000 (2024: £6.5m).

The remaining assets of Train & McIntyre (Glenury Royal, Glenlochy, Benromach, Hillside/Montrose, Strathdee, and T&M's bottling and blending businesses) were sold en bloc to the Distillers Company Ltd, the industry leader, and predecessor to Diageo, in October 1953. DCL paid £2.75m for

T&M (2024: £96m). DCL paid for the transaction by giving T&M a combination of 2 million of its shares (valued at 17 shillings each, i.e. £1.7m) with the remaining £1.05m paid in cash. As well as the physical infrastructure of the distilleries and T&M's offices and bottling plant, the deal also included "a substantial stock of mature whisky". DCL commented that they had no intention of expanding the T&M whisky brands after the acquisition, but would use the whisky stocks to augment their existing well-known brands such as, at that time, Johnnie Walker, Haig, and Dewar's, which had been in such short supply during and after WW2.[557, 558] Whilst the market was initially cool to the news, DCL's stocks easing down slightly on the day of the announcement, DCL was in the middle of a very good year, with significantly improved profits, which saw the shares rise to over 22 shillings once the annual profits were announced later in the year.[559] This provided National with a further £0.5m profit (at 1953 prices) from the rise in value of the DCL shares they now owned. The sale of T&M made sense for both parties: National realised a sizeable profit on the assets Joe Hobbs had helped them buy cheaply before the war. For DCL, the purchase enabled them to acquire substantial stocks of whisky at a time where shortage of supply continued to be the biggest drag on the company's growth, and further consolidated their dominant position as by far the largest owner of whisky production facilities in the industry. Moreover, the deal with T&M would definitely have strengthened DCL's ability to market its products in North America and boosted future US dollar sales going forward, very likely a factor in the UK government approving the deal at a time when foreign exchange movements were strictly controlled to protect the UK's balance of payment position.

So, although National's vision of controlling its own portfolio of Scottish distilleries to supply demands for its blended whiskies in North America came to an end in the early 1950s, the association with Joe Hobbs and the whole plan to buy up mothballed distilleries on the cheap had been extremely successful for them. National was able to sell on its distillery assets after the war for more than 15 times what they had paid to acquire those assets in the late 1930s. Clearly, they had incurred running costs in the interim period, and some of the value of T&M came from business which was nothing to do with Joe Hobbs and ASD. But, even if the ASD businesses are conservatively assumed only to have broken even from operations in the years they owned these distilleries, the return on National's initial investment was massive, and would have fully justified their involvement and decision to back Joe Hobbs to build the business in the first place.

Ironically, National Distiller's foray in Scotland came to an end just before post-WW2 demand for Scotch whisky in the American market really started to take off in the 1950s-60s. The strong demand for Scotch whisky in North America was not lost on Joe Hobbs, and this drove his continued efforts to find opportunities to exploit American demand in the final phase of his whisky career after WW2, with Ben Nevis and Lochside distilleries.

Of the ASD distilleries themselves, today, Benromach (under the ownership of Gordon & Macphail), Fettercairn (under the ownership of Whyte & Mackay) and Bruichladdich (under the ownership of Remy Cointreau) are all prospering as successful distilleries during the long 21st-century whisky boom.

Unfortunately, the other four ASD distilleries fared less well. Strathdee in Aberdeen never reopened after the WW2 closure, and was demolished afterwards to make way first for a garage and car showroom; later, the site was converted into apartments.

Glenury Royal was actually expanded by DCL after the acquisition from T&M, increasing from two to four stills and undergoing an extensive renovation in 1965. However, it was mothballed in 1983, before the last casks were sent away and it closed for good as part of DCL's rigorous cost-cutting in response to the 1980s 'whisky loch'. The site was demolished and redeveloped as a housing estate in 1993.

Glenlochy went the same way, closed in 1983, its equipment dismantled and removed. An application to demolish the buildings was rejected by Lochaber District Council in 1986, and it took until 1992 before West Coast Inns Ltd bought the site and redeveloped it into apartments and a guest house, now operating as the 'Distillery Guest House' bed & breakfast. The pagoda-roofed maltings and kilns and one of the warehouses have been retained as part of the design for some of the flats.

Montrose was operated on-and-off as a grain distillery by DCL post-acquisition in 1953, until in 1964 they removed the Coffey stills and reinstalled pot stills, renaming it as Hillside. Alongside it, a huge new barley maltings plant was constructed in 1968. DCL successfully operated Hillside as a malt distillery until 1980, when they renamed the whole site (both the whisky distillery and the maltings) Glenesk. In 1996, the entire operation was sold to specialist maltsters Paul's Malt Ltd. Distillation finally ceased at this point, with most of the old Montrose distillery buildings demolished. The maltings, one of the largest in the UK, continues to this day, however, now under the ownership of Boortmalt of Belgium, with some of the old Montrose warehouses still used for storage on the site.

Rare bottles of Glenury, Glenlochy and Hillside are still highly desirable among collectors and sell for premium prices at whisky auctions.

B) Ben Nevis, Lochside and Glenmavis

After Joe Hobbs' death, the Scotch whisky industry continued to expand overall, but increased competition with a wave of new distillery openings and expansions made operating their distillery business more difficult for the Hobbs family. Joe's son Joe Junior worked hard to make a success of Ben Nevis and Lochside, but the reality was that without Joe's leadership and know-how, and with increased competition from the major players, the family struggled with their distilling business, and consequently, the distilleries were eventually sold off.

Ben Nevis did the better of the two Hobbs distilleries: although the Coffey still was removed in 1971, the distillery continued operations for 15 years after Joe's death, before being mothballed in 1978. Joe Junior then sold the distillery to the Whitbread brewery group in the spring of 1981. With a nice irony, prior to acquiring Ben Nevis distillery, Whitbread had also bought the 'Long John' brand, named for the original founder of Ben Nevis distillery Long John MacDonald. It was thus Whitbread subsidiary Long John International that acquired Ben Nevis, bringing the distillery and the name of its founder back together again. In an article titled "The Long John name returns to Ben Nevis" in the Aberdeen Press and Journal, it was explained that initially Long John/Whitbread wanted Ben Nevis distillery to help meet their need for more warehousing – having not distilled for more than two years at the time of the takeover, Ben Nevis' empty warehouses provided Long John with immediate access to storage for around 2.5m gallons of whisky. [560]

Not long afterwards however, the company spent £2m refurbishing the distillery, including replacing Joe's experimental concrete washbacks, and the old cast iron mash tun. Whitbread recommenced operations in 1986 and operated reasonably successfully for a few years before they, too, sold the distillery on. The new buyers in 1989 were Nikka, one of Japan's leading whisky manufacturers, who had been a major customer for Ben Nevis whisky for years. Nikka refurbished again before recommencing operations in 1991, including opening a visitor centre. Under Nikka's management, Ben Nevis has been in continuous operation, in part driven by a strong demand for Ben Nevis' malt whisky as a constituent element in Nikka's blended whiskies in Japan. Large quantities of Ben Nevis are shipped each year to Japan, meaning less Ben Nevis is sold as a single malt than its many fans would like to see, because the quality of the whisky is certainly very high.

Following Joe's death, his son Joe Junior repeatedly tried to sell Lochside distillery, but it took nearly ten years before a buyer could be found. Before then, things got tough for Lochside, which from the late 1960s suffered periodic closures before reopening at only 25% of normal production in January 1968.[561] In 1970, the large Coffey still was mothballed, and then in 1971 all production was suspended indefinitely. The distillery remained closed for two years until finally, ten years after Joe Hobbs' death, a somewhat surprising buyer was found in the form of the Spanish company Distillerias Y Crianzas (DYC or "Deek"), who took over in November 1973. They paid £240,000 (2024: £3.6m) to acquire MacNab Distilleries Limited, including both Lochside distillery and the Sandy MacNab brand on 5th November of that year.[562]

With strong demand from their native Spanish market, which was growing 20–25% per annum in the mid-1970s, and a desire to obtain better malt to improve the quality of their blends, DYC recommenced production of malt whisky with the pot stills, but, although the Coffey still was not removed until later, grain whisky production at Lochside had ended permanently. DYC installed a new bottling plant at Lochside at an investment of £250,000, creating an additional 15 jobs, which was operational from June 1975. Prior to this, most production had gone to blending and bulk exports to Spain, with only a small proportion bottled as Lochside single malt.[563] DYC board member Carlos Sagrero was responsible for Lochside, and lived three weeks a month at an apartment in the distillery, returning to Barcelona for the other week each month. In an interview in June 1975, Sagrero said Lochside was now focusing on malt whisky production, with production of 600,000 gallons per annum. In Spain, whisky needs to mature for five years in cask before it can be sold, so Sandy MacNab was matured for at least five years before bottling.

Macnab's blend was bottled on site from 1975, as was the Lochside single malt 10-year-old from 1987. The malt was available at 8, 10 (until 1991) and 12 years old while the blend was bottled in standard, 5- and 8-year-old variants. The practice of 'blending at birth' seems to have died out with Joe Hobbs, and after the DYC acquisition Sandy MacNab was a more traditional blend with a relatively generous 35% malt content, with between 15 and 20 different malts contributing to the recipe. From the mid-1970s there was a period of around 10 years where production at Lochside was at maximum output. However, by the mid-1980s, with general industry overcapacity contributing to the build-up of the 'whisky loch', production dropped back to around 60% of capacity. During the period of DYC's ownership, the majority of Lochside's production was destined for export to Spain.

Lochside Distillery, Montrose, derelict in the year 2000.

The site converted to flats today.

The Lochside Bar opposite the site of the distillery is all that's left as a reminder of Lochside distillery today.

In 1990, the sherry firm Pedro Domecq acquired DYC, before in May 1992 Domecq merged with Allied Distillers to form Allied Domecq. The end for Lochside came quickly after the Allied Domecq merger, the new Allied management deciding at a time of low demand and high stocks that they did not have the need for a relatively small and unfashionable brand. Lochside's equipment, which was new in the late 1950s, was obsolete by the early 1990s and would have required replacement and upgrading. Production ceased in the same month of May 1992, with the decision to close permanently following in September 1992, with all the distillery production staff made redundant. It took four more years to sell off the remaining whisky stocks, at which point, in 1996, the warehouses were also closed and all remaining staff made redundant, with Charlie Sharpe, the distillery manager originally hired by Joe Hobbs in the 1950s and who had been present throughout almost all of Lochside's years of operation as a distillery, literally turning off the lights and locking the doors for the last time. Despite an effort by conservationists to have the Brauhaus tower listed and saved, the distillery buildings were dismantled in 1997, with the warehousing following suit in 1999. After a fire in January 2005, the remaining buildings were cleared from the site. Today, an unimpressive block of flats sits on the distillery site, while the area previously used for the distillery's warehouses is now being used by a supermarket.[564, 565, 566] Across the street on the other side of North Esk Road, a local hostelry is named the Lochside Bar, the only nod to the memory of the location's earlier, illustrious history as a brewery and distillery.

Joe Hobbs' efforts to revive Glenmavis distillery at Bathgate in Lothian in the 1950s was pretty much the final word in the story of that distillery. 'Glenmavis Dew' is one of the many once-famous whisky brands that are no longer produced, although the Inver House company (owner of five modern-day distilleries)

Glenmavis House today.

The Glenmavis Tavern, Gideon Street, Bathgate.

'John MacNab' mirror and photo of Glenmavis distillery workforce in the main bar of the Glenmavis Tavern.

retain the rights to the brand, having used it previously to market a blended whisky called Glen Mavis. Today, most of the Glenmavis buildings at Bathgate have been torn down and replaced by housing, although the historic Glenmavis House still survives. A mile or so away in the Glenmavis Tavern in Gideon Street, Bathgate, a mirror extolling the virtues of MacNab's whiskies and a photo of the distillery workforce still has pride of place in the main bar.

Whisky Innovation

Joe Hobbs initiated a number of new innovations and experiments during his years as a distiller, and was constantly trying out new ideas, techniques, processes and materials. During his ASD days in the late 1930s, he set up a testing laboratory at Glenury Royal, equipped with two small stills, which was used to experiment in the search for improvements and greater efficiency. Throughout his whisky career, Joe had a 'trademark' of operating both traditional pot stills for the production of malt whisky and Coffey or continuous stills for the production of grain whisky within his portfolio – indeed, at Ben Nevis and Lochside distilleries, Joe installed both types of stills at the same site.

Joe took advantage of being able to produce malt and grain whiskies on the same site to pioneer two particular innovations: 'single blends', combining malt and grain whiskies produced at the same distillery to produce a blended whisky from the same origin, and 'blending at birth', putting both malt and grain whiskies in the same barrel to mature directly after distillation.

In both cases, Joe was breaking with established industry practice. Joe had two main reasons for doing this. Firstly, he aimed to innovate and make his blended whisky products distinctive – he claimed that by blending his whiskies on site, and allowing them to marry for long periods 'in the wood' in his warehouses, he was able to produce blended Scotches superior to those of his competitors. Secondly, in the search for efficiency, Joe argued blending at birth could avoid a lot of cost to rehandle and transport malt and grain whiskies later when they were mature and would need to be moved, emptied into blending vats and mixed together to produce blends prior to bottling. However, in Scotland at least, these innovations did not take off, and were not really replicated by other industry players.

There are a number of reasons for this. For the 'blending at birth' idea, most successful scotch whisky blends have complex recipes combining multiple malt and grain whiskies of various flavour profiles and ages – some have over 40 different constituents, which are scrupulously managed to ensure precisely the flavour combination required. A Ben Nevis 'single blended whisky' solely comprising malt and grain whisky from the same distillery would not have been able to match the famous blends such as Johnnie Walker, White Horse and Cutty Sark, which contained a much more extensive 'menu' of whiskies in their mix, for complexity and balance of flavours. Moreover, since every cask of whisky made is subtly different from every other cask, and with each cask maturing at slightly different rates, the blended whisky produced from 'blended at birth' casks would be subject to a lot of variation in aroma and taste from barrel to barrel. The Scotch Malt Whisky Society are of the opinion that Joe's 'blended at birth' product "had varied results and proved to be inconsistent", and as a result the practice was not adopted by other large players.[567] The big blended whisky brands go to great lengths to ensure consistency of their whisky from bottle to bottle, batch to batch, year to year, so that consumers can rely on getting the same taste every time they open a bottle. Cask variation would have been a fundamental disadvantage of Joe's 'blended at birth' whiskies, and the only way to get around it would have been to pour multiple casks into blending vats to allow the whiskies to fully combine – thereby undermining the specific aim of avoiding rehandling and transport costs that was the reason for 'blending at birth' in the first place.

The second main reason Joe had for installing Coffey stills at Ben Nevis and Lochside was to secure reliable supplies of grain whisky. That was certainly a key issue in the 1950s-60s when Joe owned these distilleries, when a small number of large players dominated by DCL controlled almost all the grain whisky supplies in Scotland. Other industry players had experienced the same challenge of obtaining reliable supplies of grain whisky previously, opting to build their own grain distilleries as a solution. Today, most of the big producers of blended whisky have taken steps to ensure access to their own supplies of grain whisky. Joe's concerns about getting access to the grain whiskies he needed for blending, and doing so reliably and at a fair price, were very real.[ay] So Joe was not

---

ay   Diageo have their own grain distillery at Cameronbridge in Fife; Chivas Pernod have Strathclyde distillery in Glasgow; Edrington have a share in the ownership of North British distillery, Edinburgh; Whyte & Mackay have ownership of the Invergordon distillery in the town of the same name on the Cromarty Firth north of Inverness; and La Martiniquaise own and operate their Starlaw grain distillery in Edinburgh.

wrong to see the strategic need to secure his own supplies of grain whisky.

However, the nature of the Scotch whisky industry has changed considerably since Joe's time. Whilst blended whiskies are still the biggest selling whiskies by volume, since the 1960s there has been a consistent rise in sales of single malt whiskies, which, although they only make up around 10% of whisky sales by volume, contribute substantially more as a share of the value of whisky sold. This means that, for high-quality distilleries like Ben Nevis, it is economically more valuable to concentrate on maximising the amount of its output as single malt, rather than 'wasting' capacity in producing grain whisky, which can be done more cheaply and efficiently at huge, specialised grain whisky distilleries. At the same time, the evolution of modern competition laws mean non-producing blenders can more reliably obtain supplies of grain whiskies without the need to make it themselves. Today, at least one major blender, Dewars, part of the Bacardi group of companies, and many smaller ones are able to compete effectively in the blended whisky market without the need to operate their own grain whisky production facility.

What was a problem for Joe Hobbs in the 1950s and early 1960s is much less of a problem today, which likely explains why currently very few distilleries operate pot stills for malt whisky production and continuous stills for grain whisky production on the same site. In Scotland, the Loch Lomond distillery west of Glasgow is the most famous exception. At Ben Nevis, after Joe died in 1963, production continued in much the same way for a few years, but the Coffey still was removed in 1971, and since then the distillery has reverted to production solely of malt whisky. Consequently, there was no more 'blending at birth' either – although a famous bottling of 40-year-old 'single distillery blend' Ben Nevis distilled in 1962 was released in

2002, fetching high prices – the few bottles remaining are highly desired by collectors.

A willingness to experiment with malt and grain whisky production on the same site has actually been more prevalent outside Scotland – in Canada, it has been a common practice for years. In Japan, one of the two largest whisky makers, Nikka, a subsidiary of the Asahi brewing company, distil malt and grain whisky on the same site at their Miyagikyo distillery in northern Japan. In fact, since Nikka were for many years a major buyer of Ben Nevis whiskies and went on to acquire the whole distillery, it is tempting to speculate whether Nikka's management may have been influenced by Joe's use of Coffey and pot stills in same distillery at Ben Nevis, when constructing their distillery at Miyagikyo.

2. The Ranch

It is interesting to trace the development of the Great Glen Cattle Ranch's land after Joe disposed of it in 1961, albeit some information is a little anecdotal. The new owner in 1961, Alan Mackay, was already a substantial landowner and farmer in his own right, with estates in Ayrshire and Australia, and he had his own views on how best to use the land, which were not entirely aligned with the way Joe had operated the ranch. Mackay brought in Alex Kerr to manage the estate from 1961 until 1982. One of the first things they did was to reintroduce sheep, with initially 400 Newton Stewart-type black-faced sheep, later increased to 600. These are hardy sheep well-suited to hilly upland areas, capable of converting low-quality grazing into high-quality protein. As a result of introducing the sheep, the cattle herd was reduced from 1200 head at the end of Joe's tenure, to around 600 under Mackay.[568] A consequence of this was that some areas of the ranch that Joe had started to use to grow crops for winter fodder reverted to rough pasture. Rather than growing his own hay and silage, Mackay also brought in all his winter feed from outside (it is thought this was partly to make use of surpluses available at his other farms in the Lowlands), although he still used the draff from Ben Nevis distillery. Mackay also changed the cattle, switching to use of Hereford bulls and Galloway cows. The sheep flock seems to have done well, with Mackay at least following part of Joe's approach by sending the lambs off to his other farm in Ayrshire each spring to be fattened. Sargent reports that all this resulted in considerable job losses, with the ranch under Mackay's ownership employing fewer than half the farm and ranch workers that Joe had used.[569]

During the 1970s and beyond, following the UK's entry into the European Union and the application of the Common Agricultural Policy, significant changes impacted the UK's agricultural economy, which are largely beyond the scope of this book. However, whilst subsidies offered to farmers under the CAP, based on production and the numbers of cattle or sheep they produced, gave some support to hill farmers in the Scottish Highlands, studies have shown that the only Scottish farms to maintain their real incomes in the 1970s were cereal and crop farms, mostly in the Lowland south.[570] At the same time, a sustained move towards reforestation in Scotland resulted in a sizeable part of the ex-GGCR lands being sold off by the Mackays to the Forestry Commission.

Then in the 1980s-1990s, the large production surpluses created by the CAP led to pressure for reform, so that the various subsidy schemes were replaced by the Single Farm Payment system, which was not linked to production or the number of animals kept, removing an important incentive to cattle farmers to maintain high stock numbers. With rising costs and cheap imports, the reality from the 1970s onwards was that farming in the hills and remote uplands of Scotland was challenging, and most hill farms were not economic without government subsidies and support payments. Since the advent of the Single Farm Payment (SFP), although the beef industry remains an important contributor to Scotland's economy and food and tourism value chains, cattle rearing has become more difficult and less profitable, so that livestock numbers in Scotland of all types have fallen consistently in recent years. For cattle, the declining trend began from the mid-1970s, with cattle numbers in Scotland falling from their peak of 2.78m in 1974 to only 1.71 million in 2020, the lowest number since the 1940s.[571]

Against this background, it is perhaps not surprising that Alan Mackay sold some areas of rough ground for forestry, and then eventually in the 1980s sold off all his remaining land in the Great Glen to concentrate on his Ayrshire farms. Today the owners of the land at Achendaul on the site of what was once the great Glen ranch are Paolo and Elspeth Berardelli, who operate a farm that extends to 2000 acres and supports around 100 breeding cows and 400 breeding ewes.

In Joe Hobbs' day, the estate ran all the way from the Spean River at Spean Bridge in the north-east, down through Torlundy, up to the edge of Fort William at Old Inverlochy Castle. It was bounded by the River Lochy to the west and by the Fort William to Inverness railway line to the east, with a narrow strip of land to the east of the A82 and to the west of the railway included in the estate. Land sales by the Mackays to the Forestry Commission and other private landowners since the 1970s saw the bulk of the north and eastern end of the old GGCR sold off. The Berardelli's bought the central core of the old ranch in the form of Achendaul Farm in 1982.

When Paolo's father bought the farm from the Mackays in 1982, it had once again become quite run down, with a number of the pastures reverting back to bracken and thistle. Interestingly, Paolo and his father have reintroduced a number of Joe's innovations with considerable success. They began by

Achendaul Farm today still has some of the most ruggedly beautiful farm land in Scotland, just as it did when it was part of the Great Glen Cattle Ranch.

re-clearing the pastures that were falling back into bracken and thistle, and removing many fences on the upland parts that had been used to segregate sheep, cattle and arable land. Some of the better land in the lower parts of the farm is again used to produce silage and hay, just as it was in Joe's time.

The silage pits dug over various parts of the estate when Joe ran it were used for a time by the Berardellis for storage of draff from the Ben Nevis distillery, prior to feeding it to their own livestock or selling it on to other farmers. While silage in Joe's day included peas, clover and other tall grasses which grew to quite a height, to which Joe added pot ale from the distillery and fish oil, today Paolo just uses grass from the most productive low lying land to grow silage for the winter.

Paolo took a conscious decision a few years ago to go organic in his management of the farm. He scaled back the numbers of sheep and livestock on the farm to a level that can be environmentally sustained without fertilisers and chemicals on land which is fairly low in terms of its natural productive capacity. This is a very different approach from that adopted by Joe Hobbs, who aimed to increase productivity, maximise the volume of outputs, and manage a high-intensity operation. Joe's approach has to be seen in the context of the times in which he was operating, when the priorities were raising production from previously barren land, contributing to solving Britain's meat shortage, and providing jobs to help develop and repopulate the Highlands. Similarly, Paolo's approach today has to be seen in the context of contemporary drivers of farming methods. Recent years have seen a consistent movement towards sustainability and encouragement of good stewardship and husbandry of the land, aiming for quality over quantity, and optimising the whole ecosystem. This means that, whilst in Joe's day subsidies were paid by the government for the number of cattle carried on the land and the amount of new arable land brought into production, today subsidies and incentives are paid to switch away from use of fertilisers and pesticides, instead managing through crop rotation and good husbandry techniques to improve soil fertility, and achieve balanced, sustainable management of the land. Paolo's approach is an appropriate and successful evolution of farm management on the ex-GGCR lands, fit for the modern context, but he still lets his cattle roam across the estate, and still sells each year's calves every October for fattening on more productive lands further south, just as Joe did.

Paolo is not using the same cattle as Joe; rather, he has stuck with the change made by the Mackays to use black-haired Galloways, which prosper in the wet conditions. This type of cattle are good grazers, keeping the grasses fairly evenly eaten back across the whole farm, and able to take nourishment even from some of the tougher heather- and gorse-infested slopes. Whilst Paolo puts food out for them every other day in winter, all but the young ones remain out in the fields all year round. They are tough and robust, and there are few stock losses. Four

Cattle still graze in the open over the unfenced upland parts of Achendaul Farm today, just as they did in Joe Hobbs' time.

bulls serve the herd, and around 90% of the cows produce calves each year. The cattle shelters are still used for the sheep and cattle in cold or wet weather.

So, whilst operation of the farmland at Inverlochy, which used to be the Great Glen Cattle Ranch, has evolved since Joe's death 60 years ago, some of the innovations he introduced have endured and stood the test of time. Joe Hobbs' ranching experiment has left a positive legacy. Most importantly, the exposed ridge of Highland land from Inverlochy, through Achendaul, up to Spean Bridge might not even be in use as active farmland today if it were not for Joe Hobbs.

3.   The Hotel

The challenge of farming profitably in Highland Scotland also manifested itself in the subsequent history of Joe's home at Inverlochy Castle after his death. The bulk of the Inverlochy Estate had already been sold before Joe's passing, and, while Joe had retained 370 acres of farmland around the house when he sold the rest of the estate, this was more of a 'hobby farm' that could not make enough profit to pay for the increasingly high costs of maintaining the house. After Joe's death, Joe Junior and Grete continued to use Inverlochy Castle as a holiday home for a few years.

However, deprived of its estate, the house could not pay for itself, and this situation was instrumental in the decision to convert the house into the Inverlochy Castle Hotel in 1969. Grete credits her husband Joe Junior with coming up with the idea of making the castle into a hotel, and managing all the construction work to equip it initially (e.g. fitting a lot of new bathrooms, so that every bedroom had a high-quality en-suite bathroom). However, Grete became more and more involved in running the hotel, and most of the credit for making it the success it became belongs to her. In 1989, shortly after being made "Hotelier of the Year" – the first woman to win this prestigious award – Grete gave an interview to The Scotsman where she explained, "Obviously we were not hoteliers. My husband certainly didn't want to have anything to do with it himself. He had set it up, but someone else could run it."[572]

Ralph Palmer, Charlie Palmer's son, explains that the hotel's chef Mary Shaw had actually been hired by Charlie Palmer as the family's cook before Joe Hobbs died. Mary had been training as a cook at the Imperial Hotel in Fort William town when Charlie offered her the role of cook to the Hobbs family at Inverlochy Castle – free accommodation thrown in with the package was apparently a large part of the attraction. Joe's grandson Joseph Peter Hobbs tells a slightly different version of Mary's hiring. The story handed down through the Hobbs family is that Joe went to stay at the Imperial Hotel in Fort William town for a period while renovations were done at the castle. He soon realised that Mary was far better than any of the various cooks that had been employed at the castle, and promptly offered her a job. Whichever version is correct, Mary moved up to Inverlochy, where she was highly appreciated and respected by the family, who always referred to her as 'Miss Shaw.' When the castle was converted into a hotel, Mary, along with a number of other staff, agreed to stay on and became the hotel's chef. Her skill as a cook became a central part of the hotel's success. Mary was a Gaelic speaker who came from the island of Harris in the Outer Hebrides, off Scotland's far north-west coast. She was an intuitive cook who could not pronounce the fancy names of the dishes she was cooking. She formed a close working relationship with Grete Hobbs, and the two developed the habit of having a glass of wine together at the end of each day, over which they would plan the menu and approach for the following day, depending on who was coming to stay, and making best use of whatever local ingredients were then in season. Grete was a talented cook in her own right and was good at giving feedback, and guided Mary on how to present her cooking to best effect. Grete gradually assumed the role of hotel manager, and steered it through years of success.

It was one of the first luxury Scottish country house hotels. It opened with 16 bedrooms, but as Grete advised a news reporter, in the early months of operation, if two rooms were booked it was a busy week. However, the hotel immediately won critical acclaim and was awarded 'Hotel of the Year' by Egon Ronay in 1970, at that time the leading hotel guidebook in the country.[573] It went on to win multiple decorations and awards as one of Scotland's best country house hotels. Mary Shaw was awarded an MBE for her culinary work, and the hotel became a favourite holiday destination for film stars (including Charlie Chaplin, Charlton Heston and Robert Redford), millionaires and royalty.[az]

During the 1970s-80s, Grete led the hotel to many years of sustained success. Grete had help from her children – Joe's granddaughter Annemarie helped her mother run the hotel in the 1970s, with a focus on exclusivity and service. Annemarie explained that the hotel deliberately restricted the number of guests, with the aim to treat them "as friends of the family rather than paying customers".[574] Joe's grandson, Joseph Peter Hobbs, was also involved in managing the hotel. After attending Uppingham School in Rutland from 1969 to 1975, Joseph Peter learned to speak fluent French in order to attend the

---

az   There is a good family story about the award of Mary Shaw's MBE, where Mary invited Grete to accompany her to Buckingham Palace to receive her award. Mary wanted to treat herself to a fur coat, so Grete took her to Harrods, and they found a mink coat which Mary liked, selling for £3,000. When asked "how would you like to pay?", Mary replied "Cash" and opened her bag and proceeded to count out 3,000 individual £1 notes which she had accumulated from her weekly wage packets, saved up in a brown bag under her bed at the castle.

Queen Elizabeth II was one of many important and influential people to visit Inverlochy Castle Hotel after the Hobbs family converted it to a hotel in 1969. During this visit in the early 1970s she is introduced to Joe Hobbs' grandson Joseph Peter. Grete Hobbs stands on Joseph Peter's left, and Inverlochy Castle Hotel MD Michael Leonard to his right.

prestigious 'Ecole Hoteliere de Glion' hotel school at Montreux in Switzerland between 1975 and 1977. Thereafter, he played an active role helping to manage Inverlochy Castle Hotel and was a director of the company in the 1990s. He also proposed and implemented a successful conversion of the old Factor's House at the end of the drive into a smaller, simpler offshoot of the main hotel. The family appointed Michael Leonard as manager and eventually Managing Director of Inverlochy Castle Hotel, and he continued to run the business very successfully before it was sold at the end of 1996.[ba]

---

ba   Today the hotel is still thriving. The Hobbs family sold it to Dr Chai

Joe's home at Inverlochy is still flourishing today as the Inverlochy Castle Hotel.

For some years after it was taken over by the new owners and managers, Grete Hobbs would return periodically to dine at Inverlochy Castle Hotel. The current hotel manager, Jane Watson, told me that, shortly before she died in 2020, Grete visited one last time, and spent a happy evening after dinner talking to the other hotel guests and reminiscing, effortlessly reprising, in her 91st year, her role as an outstanding host for this most celebrated of country house hotels. Grete Hobbs is buried in a private cemetery on the Inverlochy Castle Hotel grounds.

King Chong (a Malaysian businessman) at the end of 1996, and Inverlochy Castle Hotel is now part of the Chai family's ICMI hotel management company, which manages a chain of exclusive luxury hotels in the UK and the Caribbean. The hotel now has a restaurant managed by Michel Roux, and continues to win awards regularly as one of Europe's finest country house hotels.

4. Yachts

After Joe Hobbs passed away, the family initially kept Joe's yacht Ocean Mist for a number of years, using it whenever they came to Inverlochy, and sometimes for business entertaining purposes.

However, the yacht was used less and less over time, and so, when Joe Junior negotiated the sale of Ben Nevis Distillery to Long John International/Whitbread in 1981, Ocean Mist – technically an asset owned by Ben Nevis distillery, and on the books of the distillery company when it was sold – was disposed along with the distillery. Joe's grandson Joseph Peter says that he was pained at the thought of losing his grandfather's treasured yacht, and asked his father to sell Ocean Mist to him separately. However, by this time Ben Nevis had become something of a noose round the family's neck, and Joe Junior asked him in reply, "Are you going to pay the yacht's mooring fees? The

Joe Junior and Grete Hobbs making use of Ocean Mist, Corpach, September 1966. Joe's granddaughter Annemarie Hobbs is just visible between her parents.

maintenance costs? For a certified captain and crew?" With much-constrained financial circumstances by the early 1980s, Joseph Peter saw he had no choice but to reluctantly withdraw his request.

However, Whitbread really had no interest in the ship and sold it on again in 1982 to two businessmen who saw an opportunity to turn it into a family holiday home. Due to the high cost of the restoration work, two other partners were brought in as well, and together they formed The Leith Steamship Company. The vessel was moved down the Caledonian Canal to Leith in Edinburgh, where after six years' effort and £0.5 million restoration costs, she was put to work as a floating restaurant from August 1988. Since then, she has been moored alongside the 'Kings Wark' quay in the Old Harbour at Leith Docks, beside Bernard Street Bridge. Ocean Mist served as a floating restaurant before closing in 2000, and then reopened in 2007 as Cruz Bar

Ocean Mist moored at Leith today. It now operates as an exclusive floating hotel.

and Restaurant.[575, 576] Post-COVID, she was refurbished again, and, with a second tier added to her superstructure, Ocean Mist is now operating as an exclusive floating hotel.

Image Credits

Before Title Page : Joe Hobbs at his desk. Source : Courtesy of Joseph Peter Hobbs

Page 5 : Manor Farm, Thatcham, as it looks today. Source : Author's Photograph

Page 7 : The Broadway, Thatcham, Berkshire, in the early 20th century. Source : Public Domain

Page 8 : Heatherwold Farm, Burghclere. Source : Author's Photograph

Page 9 : Highclere Castle, Hampshire, in the late 19th century. Source : Public Domain

Page 12 : Snelsmore Farm, near Chieveley, Berkshire. Source : Author's Photograph

Page 22 : 17 Russell Street, Reading. Source : Author's Photograph

Page 25 : Joe and his younger brother Basil Hobbs, c.1900. Source: Courtesy of Joseph Peter Hobbs

Page 28 : The S.S. Tunisian, c. 1900. Source : Public Domain

Page 36 : F. H. Clergue. Source : www.CanadianHeritage.org, Public Domain

Page 37 : The Hobbs family, c.1904. Source : Courtesy of Alexandra Anthony

Page 38 : Formal photo of the young Joe Hobbs. Source : Courtesy of Joseph Peter Hobbs

Page 39 : Joe repairing telephones for the Lake Superior Corporation. Source : Courtesy of Joseph Peter Hobbs

Labrador and Newfoundland. Source : Courtesy of Joseph Peter Hobbs

Page 66 : HMS Pegasus in WW1 'dazzle' camouflage. Source : Public Domain

Page 67 : Joe, Mabel, Helen (Basil's wife), and Basil Hobbs together after the end of WW1. Source : Courtesy of Alexandra Anthony

Page 81 : RVYC Point Grey Clubhouse Vancouver under construction 1927. Source : Public Domain

Page 82 : Joe's first yacht, Mabel Dell (2 images) and Joe and Mabel at the helm of the Mabel Dell. Source : Courtesy of Joseph Peter Hobbs

Page 83 : Vancouver Board of Trade delegation to Great Britain 23rd May–15th June 1923. Source : Public Domain

Page 86 : Joe Hobbs supervising Royal Canadian Navy Volunteer Reserve training. Source : Courtesy of Joseph Peter Hobbs

Page 87 : Stadacona, Joe's first commercial ship. Source : Courtesy of Joseph Peter Hobbs

Page 88 : 1656 Laurier Avenue, Shaughnessy Heights, Vancouver under construction in 1925. Source : Courtesy of Joseph Peter Hobbs

Page 89 : 1656 Laurier Avenue, Vancouver today. Source: Courtesy of Man Yee Lui

Page 93 : John Gilbert's "Two Homes" – his house in Beverly Hills and his yacht The Temptress – ex-Mabel Dell. Source : Public Domain

Page 94 : Joe's second luxury yacht, Vencedor. Source : Courtesy of Joseph Peter Hobbs

Page 97 : Andrew Volstead. Source : Public Domain

Page 98 : Cartoon "By Jing! The old ceiling leaks." Source : Public Domain

Page 103 : The Rum Runner 'Malahat'. Source : City of Vancouver Archives, Public Domain

Page 110 : Stadacona in the 1920s. Source : Courtesy of Joseph Peter Hobbs

Page 110 : US Coast Guard cutter Snohomish. Source : US Coast Guard, Public Domain

Page 115 : The motor-freighter 'Lillehorn'. Source : Walter E Frost fonds, City of Vancouver Archives, Public Domain

Page 117 : The motor-freighter 'Hurry On'. Source : Public Domain

Page 121 : HMS Harebell, a sister ship to Oaxaca. Source : Public Domain

Page 128 : The Commerce and Transportation Building in Toronto. Source : Toronto Public Library, Public Domain

Page 129 : Joe Hobbs late 1920s. Source : Courtesy of Joseph Peter Hobbs

Page 130 : The Merchants Exchange Building, Vancouver. Source: Vancouver City Archives, Public Domain

Page 139 : Start of construction work on the Marine Building, 1929. Source : Vancouver City Archives, Public Domain

Page 141 : Marine Building under construction, Vancouver, 1930. Source : Vancouver City Archives, Public Domain

Page 143 : William A. Starrett, Jr. Source: Public Domain

Page 147 : Marine Building shortly after its opening. Source : Vancouver City Archives, Public Domain

Page 148 : The completed Marine Building. Source : Vancouver City Archives, Public Domain

Page 149 : 3 images of Marine Building. Source : Courtesy of Col. John Orr

Page 169 : The end of Prohibition, 5th December 1933. Source : Public Domain

Page 170 : Seton Porter. Source : Public Domain

Page 175 : Baltic Chambers, 60 Wellington Street, Glasgow. Source : Author's Photograph

Page 177 : John H. Suter, Swiss engine inventor and designer. Source : Courtesy of Joseph Peter Hobbs

Page 183 : John Baird, 3rd Laird of Ury and 1st Viscount Stonehaven. Source : Public Domain

Page 184 : Glenury Royal distillery, Stonehaven, in the early 1900s. Source : Courtesy of Martin Sim

Page 184 : The Glenury distillery workforce in 1939. Source : Courtesy of Joseph Peter Hobbs

Page 185 : 2 images of the Glenury distillery site today. Source : Author's Photographs

Page 187 : Benromach distillery in the 1930s. Source : Public Domain

Page 187 : Benromach distillery today. Source : Author's Photograph

Page 189 : 2 images of the Glenlochy distillery site today. Source : Author's Photographs

Page 193 : Fettercairn distillery in the late 1930s. Source : Courtesy of Joseph Peter Hobbs

Page 193 : Fettercairn distillery today. Source : Author's Photograph

Page 196 : Hillside distillery site Montrose today. Source : Author's Photograph

Page 199 : 33 Gordon Street, Glasgow. Source : Author's Photograph

Page 200 : The Strathdee distillery site today. Source : Author's Photograph

Page 202 : Advertisement for Old Angus blended whisky. Source : Public Domain

Page 211 : The freighter Konprinsen. Source: Public Domain

Page 212 : Horry calcium carbide furnaces. Source : Public Domain

Page 217 : Oxy Ferrolene Gaz compressors. Source : Courtesy of Joseph Peter Hobbs

Page 217 : Oxy Ferrolene manufacturing brass nozzles. Source : Courtesy of Joseph Peter Hobbs

Page 219 : Manor Farm House, Carlton Curlieu, Leicestershire. Source : Author's Photograph

Page 220 : Oxy Ferrolene House today. Source : Author's Photograph

Page 224 : Ben Nevis Distillery, Fort William. Source : Author's Photograph

Page 227 : Advertising Hoarding for Long John's Dew of Ben Nevis. Source : Author's Photograph

Page 228 : Ben Nevis distillery c.1900. Source : Public Domain

Page 230 : 2 images of Ben Nevis distillery, Fort William. Source :

Copyright Historic Environment Scotland, © © HES. Reproduced courtesy of J R Hume.

Page 231 : 2 images of Nevis distillery, Fort William. Source : Copyright Historic Environment Scotland, © © HES. Reproduced courtesy of J R Hume.

Page 231 : 2 images of the old gates of Nevis distillery. Source: Courtesy of Paolo Berardelli.

Page 237 : Joe Hobbs at Fort William in May 1946. Source : Source: Vancouver Archives, Public Domain

Page 242 : Aerial photograph of the North British Aluminium plant at Lochaber. Source : Copyright Historic Environment Scotland, © © HES. Reproduced courtesy of J R Hume.

Page 243 : Commodore R.G.H. Linzee, C.B., C.B.E., R.N. (Retd). Source : Public Domain

Page 246 : Construction of the new still-house at Ben Nevis distillery 1954–55. Source : Courtesy of Ben Nevis Distillery

Page 247 : 2 images of Ben Nevis distillery today. Source : Author's Photographs

Page 249 : New electrical equipment installed at Ben Nevis distillery in 1955. Source : Courtesy of Ben Nevis Distillery

Page 253 : A very rare bottle of Ben Nevis 1962 'blended at birth' whisky. Source : Courtesy of Whisky Auctioneer, www.whiskyauctioneer.com

Page 259 : Memorandum of Association of MacNab Distilleries Limited, 1st September 1933. Source : Public Domain

Page 262 : 2 images of Arbroath Bond, Dens Road, Arbroath. Source : Copyright Historic Environment Scotland, © © HES. Reproduced courtesy of J R Hume.

Page 263 : The Arbroath Bond building today. Source : Author's Photograph

Page 264 : Glenmavis Distillery, Bathgate, Lothian, c.1900. Source : Public Domain

Page 266 : Glenmavis House, Bathgate, today. Source : Author's Photograph

Page 272 : Lochside distillery, Montrose. Source : Copyright Historic Environment Scotland, © RCAHMS. Reproduced with permission.

Page 275 : The Coffey still at Lochside distillery. Source : Copyright Historic Environment Scotland, © RCAHMS. Reproduced with permission.

Page 276 : The unusual washbacks at Lochside distillery. Source : Copyright Historic Environment Scotland, © RCAHMS. Reproduced with permission.

Page 280 : Two of the four 'onion-shaped' stills installed at Lochside Distillery in 1958. Source : Copyright Historic Environment Scotland, © RCAHMS. Reproduced with permission.

Page 283 : A copy of a 1950s advert for Sandy MacNab's blended whisky painted by Margaret Hobbs. Source : Courtesy of Margaret Hobbs.

Page 285 : The ruins of Old Inverlochy Castle with Ben Nevis in the background. Source : Author's Photograph.

Page 286 : Aerial photo of New Inverlochy Castle, 1953. Source : Copyright Historic Environment Scotland, © Courtesy of HES (Aero Pictorial Collection)

Page 197 : A silage pit on the Great Glen Cattle Ranch in use in the 1950s. Source: Courtesy of Hugh Dan MacLennan

Page 298 : One of the silage pits close to the home farmhouse at Achendaul today. Source : Author's Photograph

Page 299 : Silage was a key factor enabling cattle to remain out in the open all year round. Source: Courtesy of Hugh Dan MacLennan

Page 302 : Hobbs built cattle shelters on the Great Glen Cattle Ranch. Source: Courtesy of Joseph Peter Hobbs

Page 302 : Cattle shelters built by Joe Hobbs on the Great Glen Cattle Ranch are still in use today. Source : Author's Photograph

Page 304 : The proprietor enjoyed helping with the round-ups. Source: Courtesy of Hugh Dan MacLennan

Page 306 : 1946–47 Fort William shinty team. Source: Courtesy of Hugh Dan MacLennan

Page 385 : 2 images of Achendaul Farm today. Source : Author's Photographs

Page 387 : Cattle grazing on Achendaul Farm today. Source : Author's Photograph

Page 391 : Queen Elizabeth II visiting Inverlochy Castle Hotel in 1969. Source : Courtesy of Joseph Peter Hobbs

Page 392 : The Inverlochy Castle Hotel today. Source : Author's Photograph

Page 393 : Joe Junior and Grete Hobbs making use of Ocean Mist, Corpach, September 1966. Source : Courtesy of Joseph Peter Hobbs

Page 394 : Ocean Mist moored at Leith today. Source : Author's Photograph.

All Maps used in the text are the author's own copyright.

References

Chapter 1: Pioneering Stock

1. 1871 Census, Public Record Office, ref. RG 10 1247.
2. T.W. Fletcher, "The Great Depression of English Agriculture, 1873-1896," Economic History Review, April 1961.
3. Arthur Marwick, "The Deluge: British Society and the First World War," 2nd Edition, London: Macmillan, 1991, p.58.
4. The Berkshire Chronicle, 7th August 1897, "Jos. Hobbs v Overseers of Thatcham."
5. Newbury Weekly News, 2nd June 1892, "The Chievely Estate."
6. The Berkshire Chronicle, 1st July 1876, "Ward v Hobbs."
7. Reading Mercury, 23rd November 1895, "The Bankruptcy of Mr. J.W.Hobbs of Snelsmore Farm."
8. Old Bailey Court Records, 1881.
9. Leighton Buzzard Gazette, 25th June 1889, "Marriages: Hobbs – Morgan."
10. Berkshire Chronicle, 22nd June 1889, "Marriages: Hobbs – Morgan."
11. Reading Mercury, 23rd November 1895, op.cit.
12. Reading Mercury, 23rd November 1895, op. cit.
13. Reading Mercury, 23rd November 1895, op. cit.
14. The Hampshire Chronicle, 5th April 1890, "Kingsclere: Overseers."
15. Birth Registrations: England and Wales Civil Registration Birth Index 1891 Q1 Kingsclere.
16. 1891 Census, UK Public Record Office, ref: RG12/966.
17. Newbury Weekly News, 14th September 1892, "Agricultural Horses."

18. Birth Registrations, General Register Office. England and Wales Civil Registration Indexes.
19. Reading Mercury, 23rd February 1895, "The Earl of Carnarvon v Hobbs: an Umpire's Award Remitted."
20. Berkshire Chronicle, 3rd November 1894, "The Game Laws: Important to Farmers".
21. West Somerset Free Press, 24th November 1894, "Lord Carnarvon and His Tenant".
22. Birth Registration, General Register Office. England and Wales Civil Registration Indexes.
23. Reading Mercury, 23rd February 1895, "The Earl of Carnarvon v Hobbs".
24. Newbury Weekly News, 4th April 1895, "The Highclere Estate: Lord Carnarvon v J.W.Hobbs, Important Arbitration Case."
25. Reading Mercury 6th April 1895, "A Hampshire Farm Arbitration, Lord Carnarvon v Hobbs."
26. The Reading Mercury, 23rd November 1895, "The Bankruptcy of Mr. J.W.Hobbs of Snelsmore Farm."
27. Newbury Weekly News, 19th December 1895, "A Farmer's Bankruptcy: £10,000 Gone in 10 Years."
28. Last Will and Testament of Joseph Hobbs, 16th June 1910. From Hobbs Family papers.
29. Newbury Weekly News, 2nd January 1896, "Sales by Auction. In Bankruptcy – J.W.Hobbs, Snelsmore Farm."
30. Newbury Weekly News, 17th June 1897, "Pigs for Sale – Apply J.W.Hobbs, 17 Russell Street, Reading."
31. The Berkshire Chronicle, 14th May 1898. "Newbury County Court. Re-Joseph William Hobbs."
32. The Faringdon Advertiser, 14th May 1898, "Bankruptcy of a Chieveley Farmer and Cattle Dealer."
33. Joseph William Hobbs, Curriculum Vitae for Canadian Air Force application, 1919.
34. Hobbs, Joseph William, in "Who's Who in Canada 1930-31", p.1687.

Chapter 2: Formative Years – Canada
35. Canadian Council for Refugees, "100 Years of Immigration to Canada 1900-99", www.ccrweb.ca

36. Canadian Council for Refugees, op. cit.
37. Library and Archives Canada. Census of Canada, 1901. Ottawa, Ontario, Canada: Library and Archives Canada, 2004.
38. Library and Archives Canada. Census of Canada, 1901, op.cit.
39. Parks Canada Agency, Government of Canada, "History of the Sault Ste Marie Canal", www.Parkscanadahistory.com
40. The Burlington Free Press, 1st December 1902, "Wonders at Sault Ste. Marie."
41. L'Anse Michigan Sentinel, 27th January 1900, "The Importation of Livestock a New and Successful Feature".
42. Cited in Seskatchawan Leader Post, 21st August 1963 in their obituary to Joe Hobbs, "Canadian Cowboy Made Two Fortunes".
43. Personal letter from Joe Hobbs to Barbara Barran, 3rd May 1954. Hobbs family papers.
44. Sault Ste. Marie City Directory, 1907 (Courtesy of John Orr).
45. Library and Archives Canada. Census of Canada, 1911. Ottawa, Ontario, Canada: Library and Archives Canada, 2007.
46. Library and Archives Canada. Census of Canada, 1911. Ottawa, Ontario, Canada: Library and Archives Canada, 2007, op.cit.
47. The Sault Star, Spring 1912, "Builds Fine Launch".
48. John Orr, date unknown, "Joseph William Hobbs – Short Biographical Sketch."
49. Sault Ste Marie Evening News, 1st October 1913, "Three Soo Men Weather Gale."
50. Sault Star, unknown date in 1913, "Soo Man's Launch Crashed into Ice on Lake St. George."
51. The Globe, Sault-Ste-Marie, 23rd June 1913, "Jumped Into River to Save Their Lives."
52. Sault Daily Star, 7th August 1913, "Joe Hobbs Again in the Limelight."
53. State of Michigan, Marriage Registration, 30th June 1914.

Chapter 3: A Splendid War

54. 49th Field Artillery Regiment, Royal Canadian Artillery: Our History, at www.canada.ca
55. Hobbs, Joseph William, in "Who's Who in Canada 1930-31", p.1687.
56. Chris Sharpe, "Enlistment in the Canadian Expeditionary Force

1914-1918", in Canadian Military History, Volume 24, Issue 1, 2015.

57. Liwen Chen, 2009, "Canada's First Aerodrome, Long Branch Curtiss Aviation School", Heritage Mississauga.

58. S.F. Wise, 1980, "Canadian Airmen & the First World War: The Official History of the Royal Canadian Air Force". University of Toronto Press: Toronto, Ontario.

59. Royal Air Force, "Our Organisation, Our History" on www.raf.mod.uk

60. Liwen Chen, 2009, op. cit.

61. John M. MacFarlane, "Lieutenant Joseph William Hobbs (RCNVR) – Entrepreneur and 'Exporter,'" www.nauticapedia.ca, 2013.

62. New York State Census, 1st June 1915

63. John M. MacFarlane, op. cit.

64. History Revealed Magazine, www.historyrevealed.com

65. Royal Air Force Benevolent Fund, www.rafbf.org

66. Sault Star, 9th January 2019, "Sault's Basil Hobbs downed Zeppelin."

67. Nauticapedia Canada, www.nauticapedia.ca, "Hobbs, Basil Deacon, Group Captain (RCAF)."

68. Victoria Daily Times, 3rd December 1919, "Capt. J.W.Hobbs Arrives to Represent Canadian Air Board."

69. Joseph William Hobbs, military service records, ADM 273/7/217, The National Archives, Kew, United Kingdom.

70. 'S.S. Baltic' Ship Manifest, 16th August 1916.

71. 'S.S. Scotian' Ship Manifest, 16th January 1917.

72. The Vancouver Sun, 28th November 1919, "Flying Gets a Boost."

73. Victoria Daily Times, 3rd December 1919, op.cit.

74. Joseph William Hobbs, military service records, ADM 273/7/217, op.cit.

75. The Province, 5th October 1930, op.cit.

76. Joseph William Hobbs, Curriculum Vitae for Canadian Air Force application, 1919.

77. 'S.S. Melita' Ship Manifest, 25th June 1918; 'S.S. Olympic' Ship Manifest, 3rd August 1918.

78. Victoria Daily Times, 3rd Dec 1919, op.cit.

79. J.D.F. Kealy and E.C. Russell, "A History of Canadian Naval

Aviation 1918-1962", The Naval Historical Section, Canadian Forces Headquarters, Department of National Defence, Ottawa 1965.

80. Peter E Lawson, 2008, "Naval Air Station North Sidney 1918", https://cgaviationhistory.org/wp-content/uploads/Narratives/NAS_North_Sidney_Master.pdf

81. J.D.F. Kealy and E.C. Russell, op.cit.

82. J.D.F. Kealy and E.C. Russell, op.cit.

83. Victoria Daily Times, 3rd December 1919, op.cit.

84. Vancouver Sun, 28th November 1919, op.cit

85. Vancouver Sun, 28th November 1919, op.cit.

86. Joseph William Hobbs, Curriculum Vitae for Canadian Air Force application, 1919, op.cit.

87. Victoria Daily Times, 3rd December 1919, op.cit.

88. Benjamin D. Rhodes, "The Anglo-American Intervention at Archangel, 1918-1919: The Role of the 339th Infantry", in The International History Review, Vol. 8, No. 3 (August 1986).

89. Yvonne McEwan, "When British forces invaded Russia to fight a campaign like no other", The Scotsman, 23rd April 2019.

90. The National Archives, Spotlights on History, "The Allied intervention in Russia 1918-19", http://www.nationalarchives.gov.uk

91. Rear-Adm. Kemp Tolley, USN, U.S. Naval Institute, "Our Russian War of 1918-1919", 1969.

92. 'S.S. Baltic' Ship Manifest, 8th November 1919.

93. The Vancouver Sun, 28th November 1919, op.cit.

94. Victoria Daily Times, 3rd December 1919, op.cit.

95. Calgary Herald, 17th December 1919, "Seaplane Base at Vancouver Favored."

96. Calgary Herald, 17th December 1919, op.cit.

97. The Vancouver Sun, 11th July 1929, "J.W.Hobbs is Surveyor of Aircraft Here."

98 The Province, 30th June 1930, "Promoted: Capt. J.W.Hobbs."

Chapter 4: Boom Years

99. Vancouver Daily World, 15th April 1920, "Capt. Hobbs to Live Here."

100. Vancouver Daily World, 15th May 1920, "New Vice President."

101. Vancouver Daily World, 15th June 1920, "Appointment to Air Board."
102. Vancouver Daily World, 22nd January 1921, "Auditorium is Scene of Dance by Flying Club."
103. Liverpool Echo, 11th January 1954, "The Modern Millionaires."
104. S.S. 'Minnedosa' ship manifest, 13th August 1921.
105. S.S. 'Matagama' ship manifest, 30th September 1921.
106. Mark Davidson, "The Tall Tale of Ben Nevis Distillery", article on www.WhiskyIntelligence.com, 6th January 2013.
107. 'Peter Dawson's Special' article on 'Whiskypedia' @ www.Scotchwhisky.com
108. The Gazette (Montreal), 7th July 1908, "Peter Dawson for the United States."
109. The Gazette (Montreal), 7th December 1908, "Peter Dawson Liqueur Scotch was supplied to H.R.H. The Prince of Wales."
110. The Times Colonist, 28th April 1927, "Gauthier in Box Tells of Alleged Deals in Liquor: No Agent in B.C."
111. Mark Davidson, "Lochside Distillery 1957 – 1992 R.I.P", Whisky Intelligence, 5th January 2014.
112. Hobbs, Joseph William, "Who's Who in Canada, 1930-31", p.1687
113. Dominion Bureau of Statistics, Sixth Census of Canada, 1921.
114. Vancouver Sun, 13th June 1922, "Auto Club Gets New Members."
115. Vancouver Sun, 26th August 1922, "Speeders Fined."
116. The Nauticapedia, Ship Details: H.M.C.S. Naden, www.nauticapedia.ca.
117. The Gazette, Montreal, 9th May 1923, "Delegates Coming from Vancouver."
118. The Province, 20th May 1947, "Board of Trade Diamond Jubilee Year."
119. Canada Passenger Arrival Declaration, 17th July 1923.
120. Gilbert Norman Tucker, "The Naval Service of Canada: Official History", Ministry of National Defence, Ottawa 1962.
121. The Province, 29th September 1924, "Five Residences and Cosy Bungalows Commenced in Point Grey."
122. S.S. 'Montcalm' Ship Manifest, 7th February 1925.
123. S.S. 'Letitia' Ship Manifest, 25th April 1925.
124. S.S. 'Montnairn' Ship Manifest, 3rd April 1926.
125. S.S. 'Montroyal' Ship Manifest, 4th June 1926.

126. Vancouver Sun, 20th January 1927, "Yachting Officials Selected."
127. The Province, 28th Apr 1927, "Yacht Mabel Dell Sails to New Owner in the South."
128. The Province, 28th June 1956, "Ship and Shore."
129. Times Colonist, 14th August 1928, "Handsome Yacht Now In Drydock."
130. The Nauticapedia, Ship Details: Vencedor, www.Nauticapedia.ca
131. Royal Vancouver Yacht Club, Annals Section 1, "History of the Club, Part 1."
132. S.S. 'Montrose' Ship Manifest, 17th June 1927.
133. S.S. 'Montroyal' Ship Manifest, 2nd August 1927.
134. S.S. 'Empress of France' Ship Manifest, 8th October 1927.

Chapter 5: Rum Runner

135. History.com, "Prohibition," www.history.com
136. Letter to Senator William Borah (Republican, Idaho), 24th February 1928. Sen. Borah had requested the views of all the Republican Presidential candidates on the subject of Prohibition. It was quoted in many newspapers at the time.
137. Victoria Daily Times, 16th June 1923, "Caution Shown by Rum Runners."
138. The Times Colonist, 9th October 1924, "Liquor Runners Agree to Shoot on Sight."
139. The Province, 20th June 1925, "B-C Rum Runners May be Hard Hit by Competition."
140. United States Treaties and Other International Agreements (UST), U.S. Library of Congress, "The Convention between the United States and Great Britain – Prevention of Smuggling of Intoxicating Liquors, 1924."
141. James B. McDonough, Virginia Law Review Vol. 12, No. 3 (January 1926), "The International Liquor Treaties and The Eighteenth Amendment."
142. The Province, 13th June 1925, "Seized Papers May Show How Rum Ring Works."
143. Victoria Daily Times, 17th December 1926, "Move to Collect $75,807 as Tax."
144. The Gazette, 14th October 1924, "Big Ship Seized on Pacific Coast."

145. The Province, 16th March 1925, "U.S. Ships Escort B.C.Rum-Runners."
146. Times Colonist, 25th November 1925, "Customs Allege Vessel Made False Clearance."
147. The Province, 5th June 1925, "Stadacona Has Changed Her Name to Kuyakuzmt."
148. The Province, 23rd June 1925, "Seizure of B.C. Ship Reported."
149. The Calgary Herald, 31st December 1988, "Some of the Best Were Rum Runners."
150. Jason Fagone, "The Woman Who Smashed Codes," Dey Street Books, 2017.
151. The Calgary Herald, 31st December 1988, op.cit.
152. Victoria Daily Times, 18th March 1926, "Seventeen New Firms Ready to Start Business."
153. The Province, 20th January 1927, "Export Houses Printed Own Labels."
154. The Province, 20th January 1927, op.cit.
155. The Province, 22nd May 1928, "Freight Vessel is Chartered by CN Steamships."
156. The Province, 12th November 1927, "Hobbs Bros Sell MS 'Lillehorn.'"
157. The Province, 18th November 1927, "Plan to Erect New Exchange Building."
158. The Nauticapedia, Ship Details: Oaxaca, www.nauticapedia.ca
159. The Province, 13th July 1928, "Millionaires Yacht Piles of Reef in Wrangell Narrows."
160. The Province, 16th October 1928, "S.S.Oaxaca Goes to Esquimault Dock."
161. Times Colonist, 15th October 1928, "Oaxaca Now in Esquimault for General Repairs."
162. The Province, 22nd May 1928, op.cit.
163. Vancouver Sun, 25th April 1929, "Famous Ship to be Used as Yacht Here."
164. The Province, 6th August 1929, "Col. F.G.Johnson of Toronto Guest on Fishing Cruise."
165. The Vancouver Sun, 16th September 1929, "Journalists are Guests of Capt. Hobbs."
166. The Province, 30th October 1929, "Vancouver Yacht is Sold."

167. The Province, 11th December 1982, "Smuggling Spirits: Tales of the Rum Runners."

168. Vancouver Sun, 19th July 1971, "From Out of the Drought Came High Adventure."

169. Vancouver Sun, 19th July 1971, op.cit.

Chapter 6: The Best Art Deco Office Building in the World

170. The Province, 5th October 1930, "Canada's Oldest Bond House Improves Skyline of Leading Cities."

171. Letter from JWH to Barbara Barran, 3rd May 1954.

172. The Province, 5th October 1930, op.cit.

173. The Ottawa Citizen, 5th May 1928, "The Merchants Exchange Building Vancouver 6% Gold Bonds."

174. Vancouver Sun, 4th November 1927, "Capt. J.W.Hobbs has bought the Vancouver Merchant Exchange Building."

175. The Province, 18th November 1927, "Plan to Erect New Exchange Building."

176. Vancouver Sun, 22nd December 1927, "Canada's Oldest Bond Firm, Stimson & Co, Establish Office Here."

177. S.S. 'Scythia' Ship Manifest.

178. Advertisement in The Ottawa Citizen, 5th May 1928, op. cit.

179. Ontario, Canada, Death Registration 16th May 1928.

180. Vancouver Sun, 5th May 1928, "Capt. J.W.Hobbs Joins Bond House."

181. The Province, 11th November 1928, "Developing Property Business."

182. For example, The Vancouver Sun, 23rd November 1928, "To Rush Tallest Building."

183. Vancouver Sun, 30th April 1930, "Worldwide Firms Locate in the City."

184. Cited in "The Marine Building", by Elizabeth Newton, Creators Vancouver Magazine, 2nd October 2020, www.creatorsvancouver.com

185. Murray Foster, article in "The Greater Vancouver Book: An Urban Encyclopedia", edited by Chuck Davis, Linkman Press, Canada 1997.

186. The Province, 6th December 1928, "RCNVR Company Makes Presentation to Capt.J.W.Hobbs."

187. S.S. 'Majestic' and S.S. 'Montroyal' Ship Manifests.
188. Vancouver Sun, 21st January 1929, "Start Work on Skyscraper for Stimson Co."
189. The Province, 13th March 1929, "Work Starts on Marine Skyscraper."
190. Vancouver Sun, 13th March 1929, "Work Starts on Erection of 18 Storey Skyscraper costing $1,500,000."
191. The Vancouver Sun, 27th April 1929, "Sand For Marine Building."
192. The Vancouver Sun, 11th July 1929, "J.W.Hobbs is Surveyor of Aircraft Here."
193. The Vancouver Sun, 5th August 1929, "Handsome Trophies Offered for First B.C. School Games."
194. The Vancouver Sun, 17th August 1929, "Port's Destiny Emphasised by Stimson & Co."
195. The Vancouver Sun, 16th September 1929, op.cit.
196. The Vancouver Sun, 17th October 1929, "Marine Building Interior Work Contracts Let."
197. The Province, 30th October 1929, "Vancouver Yacht Is Sold."
198. S.S. 'Berengaria' and S.S. 'Duchess of Richmond' Ship Manifests.
199. Stephanie Ben-Ishai, 'Bank Bankruptcy in Canada: A Comparative Perspective', in Banking and Finance Law Review, 2008.
200. The Province, 13th January 1930, "Home from London. Rush Work on Marine Block."
201. The Vancouver Sun, 25th February 1930, "Skyscraper to be Rushed as Cold Ends."
202. The Vancouver Sun, 9th April 1930, "N.Y.Firm to Finance Skyscraper."
203. The Province, 9th April 1930, "Marine Building Financing Complete."
204. Vancouver Sun, 30th April 1930, "Worldwide Firms Locate in City."
205. Vancouver Sun, 12th May 1930, "Land Owners Nominate."
206. Vancouver Sun, 2nd July 1930, "Admiralty Honors Local Yachtsman."
207. The Province, 30th June 1930, "Promoted."
208. The Province, 29th June 1930, "When our business man turns explorer – yachting in B.C.waters."
209. The National Post Toronto, 4th September 1930, "Stimson's

Enterprises Not in a Strong Condition as Public Stops Buying."

210. The Province, 7th September 1930, "Austin Sells Five Houses in the City."

211. The Sunday Province, 5th October 1930, "Canada's Oldest Bond House Improves Skyline of Canada's Leading Cities."

212. The Vancouver Sun, 7th October 1930, "Marine Building Centralises Trade of the Port of Vancouver."

213. The Province, 9th October 1930, "Marine Building Opened."

214. Cited in Harold Kalman, "Exploring Vancouver: Ten Tours of the City and its Buildings." Vancouver: University of British Columbia Press, 1974, p.101.

215. The National Post, Toronto, 20th November 1930, "Stimson offer 20% interest to defer claims."

216. The National Post, Toronto, 11th December 1930, "Grants Injunction Restraining Stimson."

217. The Vancouver Sun, 24th December 1930, "The Oldest Bond House in Canada Extends to You the Old, Old Wish: A Merry Christmas and A Happy New Year."

218. The Ottawa Citizen, 14th January 1931, "Stimson Firms in Assignment."

219. The Ottawa Citizen, 14th January 1931, op.cit.

220. The Vancouver Sun, 14th January 1931, "Four Stimson Subsidiaries Have Assigned."

221. The National Post, 15th January 1931, "Four Projects of Stimson Now Bankrupt."

222. The Gazette, Montreal, 15th January 1931, "Large Bond House in Liquidation."

223. Vancouver Sun, 19th January 1931, "Officers Raid Local Offices of Stimson Co."

224. Vancouver Sun, 21st January 1931, "Marine Bldg Out of Stimson Probe."

225. The National Post, 22nd January 1931, "Self-Styled Oldest Bond House in Canada Chiefs Face Charges."

226. The National Post, 22nd January 1931, op. cit.

227. Victoria Daily Times, 23rd January 1931, "Stimson Hearing in Toronto Court."

228. The Vancouver Sun, 2nd February 1931, "Stimson Manager Surrenders Self."

229. The Vancouver Sun, 6th February 1931, "Stimson Assets Called Small."

230. Supreme Court of British Columbia court records, 23rd February 1931.

231. The Province, 8th January 1932, "Marine Block is Redeemed."

232. The National Post, 30th April 1931, "Little to Salvage for Stimson Shareholders."

233. Windsor Star, 2nd June 1931, "F.G.Johnston Sentenced to 3 Years and L.E.Clark to 2½. False Prospectus."

234. Times Colonist, 28th September 1931, "Appeal of Three Ontario Brokers Fails."

235. Vancouver Marriage Certification, 27th May 1931, reg. no. 1931-09-387203.

236. General Register Office, Uxbridge, Middlesex, 4th March 1929.

237. 'S.S. Empress of Scotland' Ship Manifest, 17th May 1930.

238. U.S. Immigration Service declaration, Blaine, Washington, 15th November 1930.

239. Hobbs, Joseph William, "Who's Who in Canada, 1930-31", p.1687, op. cit.

240. Joseph Peter Hobbs, personal discussion with the author, 1st July 2022.

241. Vancouver Sun, 20th July 1933, "Marine Building Changes Hands."

242. Chuck Davis, "History of Metropolitan Vancouver," Harbour Publishing, 2011. Quoted at https://vancouverhistory.ca/chronology/chronology-1930/

243. Murray Foster, article in "The Greater Vancouver Book: An Urban Encyclopedia", 1997, op. cit.

Chapter 7: Whisky Baron: Associated Scottish Distilleries

244. Vancouver Sun, 29th November 1935, "G.W.Dawson Dead."

245. The Province, 4th February 1932, "Riding Enthusiasts Enjoy Team Jumping."

246. The Province, 19th August 1932, "Prepare Plans for Studios: Capt. J.W.Hobbs Announces Work on Preliminaries for Industry."

247. The Vancouver Sun, 19th August 1932, op.cit.

248. Ted Magder, Piers Handling and Peter Morris, "Canadian Film

History 1896-1938", The Canadian Encyclopedia, 2012. www.thecanadianencyclopaedia.ca

249. The Leader Post Canada, 21st August 1963, "Canadian Cowboy Made Two Fortunes."

250. Liverpool Echo, 11th January 1954, "The Modern Millionaires."

251. Encyclopedia.com, "National Distillers and Chemicals Corporation," International Directory of Company Histories, 17th June 2021. https://www.encyclopedia.com.

252. Encyclopedia.com, "National Distillers and Chemicals Corporation," op.cit.

253. Edinburgh Evening News, 3rd September 1932, "Too Much Whisky: 79 Scots Distilleries to Close."

254. Dundee Courier, 5th September 1932, "Scots Whisky Stoppage: Biggest Slump in Trade's History."

255. Belfast Newsletter, 28th August 1933, "Scottish Distilleries: Anticipation of Demand from America."

256. The Leader Post, 21st August 1963, "Canadian Cowboy Made Two Fortunes."

257. Jim Allen, 24th May 2019, "First in Flight: The Packard DR-980 Radial Aircraft Design", www.dieselworldmag.com.

258. Lawrence Ward, op. cit.

259. Letter from W.S. Noblitt, Secretary of Aviation Diesel Engine Company Ltd to Joe Hobbs, dated 3rd December 1934.

260. Letter from W.S. Noblitt, Secretary of Aviation Diesel Engine Company Ltd to Joe Hobbs, dated 14th March 1935.

261. S.S. 'Bremen', Ship Manifest, 26th January 1934.

262. S.S. 'Bremen', Ship Manifest, 26th January 1934, op.cit.

263. The Tatler, 9th July 1947, "Her Social Journal."

264. Victoria Daily Times, 17th May 1924, "Tolmie is Man Responsible for Canadian Exhibit."

265. Calgary Daily Herald, 14th June 1924, "No Extravagant Compliments When Tis said That Canada has Beaten Everybody."

266. R.B. Weir, "The History of the Distillers Company 1877-1939", Clarendon Press, Oxford, 1993, p.276.

267. S.S. 'Bremen', Ship Manifest, 7th August 1936.

268. Whisky Fun, 25th September 2006, "Glenury Royal".

269. Aberdeen Press and Journal, 11th January 1928 and others.

270. Whisky.com, Distilleries, Glenury Royal. https://www.whisky. com/whisky-database/distilleries/details/glenury-royal.html.

271. Aberdeen Press and Journal, 31st December 1938, "Distillery for Angus."

272. The Scotsman, 31st December 1936, "Benromach Distillery Let to American Firm."

273. The Scotsman, 26th November 1934, "Glenlochy Distillery Sold to Contracting Firm: Future Uncertain."

274. Louis Reps, The History of Glenlochy Distillery, www.glenlochy. com.

275. Daily Record, 18th February 1937, "Distillery to Reopen After Ten Years."

276. The Scotsman, 24th March 1937, "Lochaber Industrial Expansion."

277. Difford's Guide, Distilleries and Producers: Bruichladdich Distillery. https://www.diffordsguide.com

278. Quoted in "Goodness Nose", by Richard Paterson and Gavin D. Smith, Neil Wilson Publishing Ltd, 2008.

279. The Scotsman, 3rd March 1938, "Reopening of Distillery."

280. The Dundee Courier, 3rd March 1938, "Distillery Closed Ten Years Reopens."

281. Aberdeen Press and Journal, 10th August 1938, "Whisky Trade's Busy Time."

282. Aberdeen Press and Journal, 10th August 1938, op.cit.

283. Brechin Advertiser, 16th August 1938, "District News: Hillside."

284. Montrose Review, 19th August 1938, "Round the Town – Topics of the Week: Distillery Sold."

285. Montrose Standard, 21st October 1938, "Distillery Reopened."

286. Aberdeen Press and Journal, 31st December 1938, "Distillery for Angus: Operations to Start in June."

287. The Aberdeen Evening Express, 4th January 1939, "New Distillery."

288. Montrose Review, 6th January 1939, "1939 Brings Good News to Montrose: Hillside Distillery to Resume Production."

289. Brechin Advertiser, 10th January 1939, "Hillside Distillery to Make Whisky Again."

290. Montrose Review, 17th February 1939, "£50,000 Hillside Scheme: Effluent Disposal Problem."

291. Montrose Standard, 3rd March 1939, "Montrose Distillery Question."
292. The Scotsman, 22nd July 1939, "Associated Scottish Distilleries Limited: Wanted."
293. The Dundee Courier, 25th June 1938, "New Scottish Companies: Associated Scottish Distillers."
294. The Liverpool Echo, 11th January 1954, "The Modern Millionaires."
295. Brechin Advertiser, 6th February 1940, "District News: Stonehaven."

Chapter 8: Duty Calls Again

296. Commercial Motor, 14th June 1935, "Importance of Oxy Ferrolene method of cutting and welding."
297. Manchester Guardian, 27th September 1937, "Increasing uses of gas in industry."
298. Vancouver Sun, 13th May 1946, "Financier Gains Honor as Inventor."
299. David White, "Bitter Ocean: The Battle of the Atlantic, 1939–1945." New York, 2008.
300. Quoted in David Edgerton, 2011, "Britain's War Machine: Weapons, Resources, and Experts in the Second World War."
301. Daily Express, 22nd November 1943, "6-inch Steel Bar Cut in 4 Seconds: new process used in war factories."
302. Mechanical World and Engineering Record, 10th March 1944, "Metal Cutting with Ferrogas: the Use of Enriched Coal Gas."
303. Sunday Dispatch, 11th July 1943, "Big Game Hunter's Invention is Aiding Nazi Defeat."
304. Mechanical World and Engineering Record, op.cit.
305. Leicester Evening Mail, 28th December 1943, "Inventor's Secret Tests in Leicestershire."
306. The Winnipeg Tribune, 31st October 1942, "British Women do the Building."
307. Personal letter from Joe Hobbs to A.S. Seggie, 18th February 1944 (in the possession of Peter Hobbs).
308. Coventry Evening Telegraph, 15th September 1944, "Brighter Homes of the Future."
309. Leicester Evening Mail, 28th December 1943, op.cit.
310. Rowly Wilkes, recorded memoir, op.cit.

311. Joseph Peter Hobbs, correspondence with the author, 11th June 2022.
312. Brechin Advertiser, 6th February 1940, "District News: Stonehaven."
313. Leicester Evening Mail, 28th December 1943, op.cit.
314. Aberdeen Press and Journal, 14th August 1939, "Lord Stonehaven and his house party at Ury House, Stonehaven," and others.

Chapter 9: Ben Nevis

315. Brechin Advertiser, 6th February 1940, op. cit.
316. Montrose Standard, 15th March 1940, "Council Shorts."
317. Montrose Standard, 5th April 1940. "Hitch in Council's Plans for Kinnaber Mill: No Negotiations with Distillery, says Chairman."
318. The Scotsman, 20th July 1940, "Wills and Estates."
319. Johannes van den Heuval, quoted on Malt Madness, Ben Nevis Distillery Profile, www.malt-whisky-madness.com
320. Alfred Barnard, The Whisky Distilleries of the United Kingdom, 'Ben Nevis Distillery, Fort William, Invernesshire,' 1886.
321. The Elgin Courier, 29th October 1847, "The Prince of Wales's Whisky."
322. Alfred Barnard, 1886, op.cit.
323. Alfred Barnard, 1886, op.cit.
324. Mark Davidson, "The Tall Tale of Ben Nevis Distillery," Jolly Toper Tastings, Distillery Profiles, www.jollytopertastings.co.uk
325. Ingvar Ronde, The Malt Whisky Yearbook, 2021.
326. Mark Davidson, op. cit.
327. Aberdeen Press and Journal, 14th February 1944, "Ben Nevis Distillery Bought."
328. Glasgow Herald, 15th February 1944, "Scottish Whisky Deal".
329. Personal letter from Joe Hobbs to A.S. Seggie, 18th February 1944 (in the possession of Peter Hobbs).
330. Scotch Malt Whisky Society, Distillery Profile: Ben Nevis, on https://smws.com, 2021.
331. Personal letter from Joe Hobbs to A.S. Seggie, 18th February 1944, op.cit.
332. Time Magazine, 18th February 1946, "Sir Ben's Battle."
333. Daily Record, 25th August 1945, "Highland Distillery Speeds Production."

334. Aberdeen Press and Journal, 23th August 1945, "8 Years of Whisky Shortage."

335. The Scotsman, 13th January 1945, "Whisky Production: Ben Nevis Distillery to Resume."

336. The Scotsman, 23rd August 1945, "Ben Nevis Distillery Resumes."

337. The Liverpool Echo, 11th January 1954, op. cit.

338. The Scotsman, 16th February 1946, "Ben Nevis Distillery Closed Down."

339. The Scotsman, 10th February 1947, "Scottish Distillery Resumes, Barley for Six Weeks Only."

340. The Scotsman, 17th June 1947, "Ben Nevis Distillery Close, Barley Quota Exhausted."

341. The Scotsman, 5th January 1949, "A Fort William Distillery to Close, No Permit for More Barley."

342. Dundee Evening Telegraph, 18th November 1948, "Professor Says Cows Were 'Pitiable Wrecks.'"

343. The Scotsman, 17th March 1948, "Fluorine Fumes: Ben Nevis Distillery's Interdict Action – Damage Alleged."

344. The Scotsman, 2nd December 1948, "Fort William Action: Aluminium and the Export Trade."

345. The Scotsman, 20th May 1948, "Noxious Fumes: Interdict Proceedings Against Aluminium Company."

346. The Scotsman, 17th November 1948, "Noxious Fumes: Highland Estate Owner's Complaint."

347. The Scotsman, 18th November 1948, "Fort William Action: Cattle Affected by Toxic Fumes."

348. The Dundee Courier, 26th November 1948, "Witness Critic of Estate."

349. The Dundee Evening Telegraph, 11th March 1949, "Factory Fumes Complaint Was Justified."

350. Aberdeen Press and Journal, 12th March 1949, "Judge Continues Fumes Action."

351. The People's Journal, 20th November 1948, "Witness in Fort William Allege Fumes Poison Cattle and Blight Trees."

352. The Scotsman, 18th November 1948, op. cit.

353. Dundee Evening Telegraph, 11th January 1950, "Moves to End Fumes Nuisance Satisfy Castle Owner."

354. Ralph Palmer, 2nd June 2022, Personal correspondence with the author.

355. David Daiches, 'Scotch Whisky: Its Past and Present', 1969, Andre Deutsch, p.111.
356. Personal letter from Joe Hobbs to Barbara Barran, 3rd May 1954.
357. John R. Hume and Michael S. Moss, "The Making of Scotch Whisky", Canongate Books, Edinburgh, 2000. Chapter 2, 'Scotch Triumphant: 1945-80.'
358. Hume and Moss, 2000, op.cit.
359. Hume and Moss, 2000, op. cit.
360. The People, 10th February 1952, "Whisky Battle."
361. The People, 3rd February 1952, "Whisky Gave Them Double Quick Riches."
362. The People, 3rd February 1952, "Whisky Gave Them Double Quick Riches", op.cit.
363. Hume and Moss, 2000, op.cit.

Chapter 10: MacNab Distilleries and Lochside

364. West Lothian Courier, 18th May 1956, "Glenmavis Distillery Preparations."
365. Aberdeen Press and Journal, 7th December 1945, "Fort William Buyer of Arbroath Works."
366. Mark Davidson, Whisky Intelligence, 5th January 2014, Lochside Distillery 1957 – 1992 R.I.P."
367. Dundee Evening Telegraph, 14th June 1948, "Arbroath Works to be Bonded Warehouse."
368. Montrose Standard, 22nd November 1956, "Lochside Brewery to be Re-opened as a Distillery."
369. Alfred Barnard, The Whisky Distilleries of the United Kingdom, 1887, 3rd Edition 2018, pp.337–338.
370. Brian Townsend, Scotch Missed, The Angels Share publishing, 2017, pp.122-123.
371. Brian Townsend, 2017, op.cit, p.122.
372. Alfred Barnard, op.cit.
373. West Lothian Courier, 18th May 1956, op.cit.
374. West Lothian Courier, 18th May 1956, op.cit.
375. Montrose Standard, 22nd November 1956, op.cit.
376. West Lothian Courier, 20th January 1956, "Bathgate Brevities."
377. West Lothian Courier, 27th January 1956, "Search for New Industry for West Lothian."

378. West Lothian Courier, 17th February 1956, "New Distillery Snags."
379. West Lothian Courier, 18th May 1956, "Glenmavis Distillery Preparations: First Year's Output Already Booked."
380. West Lothian Courier, 18th May 1956, op.cit.
381. West Lothian Courier, 9th November 1956, "Bathgate Brevities."
382. Montrose Standard, 22nd November 1956, op.cit.
383. West Lothian Courier, 18th September 1959, "Rates up 2/10 in the £: Sewage Scheme Debate."
384. West Lothian Courier, 9th November 1956, op.cit.
385. Montrose Standard, 22nd November 1956, op.cit.
386. Montrose Standard, 22nd November 1956, "Lochside Brewery to be Re-Opened as a Distillery", op.cit.
387. West Lothian Courier, 23rd November 1956, "Bathgate Brevities."
388. Montrose Standard, 17th January 1957, "Lochside Distillery."
389. West Lothian Courier, 28th December 1956, "Property For Sale: Upstairs Flat"
390. Montrose Review, 6th June 1957, "Lochside Distillery Progress."
391. Montrose Review, 1st August 1957, "Lochside £150,000 Transformation Scene."
392. Montrose Review, 29th August 1957, "Mr. Hobbs Disagrees."
393. Montrose Review, 10th October 1957, "Orders Pour In To Distillery."
394. Montrose Standard, 10th October 1957, "Whisky Galore."
395. Montrose Standard, 17th October 1957, "Montrose's Newest Industry Begins Production."
396. Montrose Review, 31st October 1957, "Montrose Distillery Development."
397. Montrose Standard, 31st October 1957, "Major Building Scheme Planned for Nemanswalls."
398. Montrose Review, 31st October 1957, op.cit.
399. Montrose Review, 31st October 1957, "Round The Town."
400. Montrose Review, 14th November 1957, "A Lovely Home – Mrs. Hobbs."
401. Montrose Review, 14th November 1957, "Montrose Football Club Bazaar."
402. The Guardian, 25th November 1957, "A Dram A Day."

403. Companies House records.
404. Montrose Standard, 8th January 1959, "Montrose Industrial Outlook."
405. Montrose Standard, 8th January 1959, "Lochside Distillery, Montrose."
406. West Lothian Courier, 20th February 1959, "Bathgate Brevities."
407. Aberdeen Evening Express, 6th February 1960, "News in Brief."

Chapter 11: The Inverlochy Estate and the Great Glen Cattle Ranch

408. Quoted in Inverlochy Castle Hotel brochure, http://inverlochycastlehotel.com/about.html
409. The Scotsman, 8th August 1945, "Inverlochy Estate Bought By Distillery Proprietor."
410. The People's Journal, 20th November 1948, "Witness in Fort William Allege Fumes Poison Cattle and Blight Trees."
411. The Daily Record, 25th August 1945, "Highland Distillery Speeds Production."
412. Dundee Courier, 9th March 1955, "Mr Hobbs Makes a Highland Ranch Pay."
413. The People's Journal, 11th August 1945, "New Owner of Inverlochy."
414. William Thompson, Cattle Droving Between Scotland and England, Journal of the British Archaeological Association, 1932, 37:2, 172–183
415. A.R.B. Haldane, The Drove Roads of Scotland, 1952
416. David Watson Hood (ed), The Highland Drovers, at www.scotshistoryonline.co.uk
417. Vancouver Sun, 30th October 1951, "Ex-Vancouverite in Scotland Launches Big-scale Ranching."
418. Vancouver Sun, 30th October 1951, op.cit.
419. Liverpool Echo, 11th January 1954, "The Modern Millionaires."
420. The Sphere, 10th December 1955, "Britain's Only Cattle Ranch."
421. News Chronicle, 7th October 1948, "Story of the Highland Cowboys."
422. Ralph Palmer, 26th May 2022, personal discussion with the author.
423. The Sphere, 10th December 1955, op.cit.

424. The Sphere, 10th December 1955, op.cit.

425. The Sphere, 21st April 1951, Cattle Ranching Amid the Glens of Lochaber.

426. The Sphere, 10th December 1955, Britain's Only Cattle Ranch.

427. The Sphere, 10th December 1955, op.cit.

428. Peterborough Citizen and Advertiser, 23rd November 1951, "Beef From Barren Acres."

429. John Bull Magazine, 12th November 1949, "Cowboys in the Highlands."

430. Vancouver Sun, 30th October 1951, op.cit.

431. The Sphere, 21st April 1951, "Cattle Ranching Amid the Glens of Lochaber."

432. The Peterborough Citizen and Advertiser, 23rd November 1951, op.cit.

433. The Sphere, 21st April 1951, op.cit.

434. Keir Waddington, 2004, "To stamp out 'so terrible a malady': bovine tuberculosis and tuberculin testing in Britain, 1890-1939." Medical History, 48(1), 29–48. https://doi.org/10.1017/s0025727300007043

435. The People's Journal, 20th November 1948, "Witness in Fort William Allege Fumes Poison Cattle and Blight Trees."

436. Dominic A. Sargent, "Inverlochy Castle: A History", 1998, p.13.

437. John Bull Magazine, 12th November 1949, "Cowboys in the Highlands", op.cit.

438. The Scotsman, 9th September 1949, "Cattle Rounded Up: Canadian Ranching Methods in Great Glen."

439. Dundee Courier, 9th September 1949, "Highland Cowboys in Round-up."

440. Aberdeen Press and Journal, 9th September 1949, "It Was Not Texas – But a Scottish Hillside."

441. The Scotsman, 14th February 1950, "Cattle Extension by Ranching: Leading Breeder Is Not In Agreement."

442. Dundee Courier, 5th June 1950, "Scots Cowboys in Unusual Roundup."

443. Lochaber News, 12th May 2001, "Roamer Column."

444. Dundee Courier, 12th March 1951, "Rain is Bad for the Reindeer."

445. The Sphere, 21st April 1951, "Cattle Ranching Amidst the Glens of Lochaber."

446. Dundee Courier, 17th May 1951, "Farmers Impressed by Ranch Cattle."

447. The Gazette, 18th May 1951, "Rancher Hobbs' Herd Fetches £6,710."

448. Dundee Courier, 17th May 1951, "Farmers Impressed by Ranch Cattle", op.cit.

449. Dundee Courier, 26th July 1951, "Great Glen Ranch Grows."

450. Arbroath Herald, 12th October 1950, "Scottish Commentary: Hill Lands Commission."

451. Windsor Star, 20th May 1952, "Cattle Ranches in Highlands to Provide Meat for Britons."

452. Dundee Courier, 3rd October 1950, "Beef From the Hills is Their Aim."

453. Hansard, 24th July 1956, Written Answers, Scotland: Hill Lands (North Of Scotland) Commission (Report), https://hansard.parliament.uk/Commons/1956-07-24/debates

454. Dundee Courier, 9th September 1953, "Factories to Follow Fishing Fleets."

455. Dundee Courier, 3rd March 1955, "Highlands Want Better Snowploughs."

456. The Sphere, 1st March 1952, "In Scotland's Great Glen The Fastest Housing Project in Britain is Being Pushed Ahead."

457. Dominic A. Sargent, "Inverlochy Castle: A History", 1998, op.cit

458. Dominic A. Sargent, "Inverlochy Castle: A History", 1998, op.cit

459. Fresno Bee, 4th October 1953, "Bagpipes and Beef Return in Scotch Highlands to Tune of US Pasture Methods."

460. Dundee Courier, 9th March 1955, "Mr. Hobbs Makes A Highland Ranch Pay", op.cit.

461. Duncan Campbell, "The Real Crisis of Scottish Agriculture", in 'The Scottish Government Yearbook 1985', edited by David McCrone, Unit for the Study of Government in Scotland, University of Edinburgh.

462. David Turnock, 1977, Nottingham University Geographical Field Group, "Geographical Field Group Regional Studies No. 20: The Lochaber Area."

463. The Province, 13th April 1955, "Ex-Cariboo Rancher at Home on the Range", op.cit.

464. Ralph Palmer, conversation with the author, 26th May 2022.

465. Dominic A. Sargent, 1998, op.cit.
466. Edmonton Journal, 9th May 1952, "Ex-Albertan Operates Highlands Cattle Ranch."
467. Dominic A. Sargent, 1998, op.cit.
468. News Chronicle, 7th October 1948, "Story of the Highland Cowboys", op.cit.
469. Calgary Herald, 25th November 1954, "Cattle Ranch in North of Scotland is Prospering."
470. Dundee Courier, 9th March 1955, "Mr. Hobbs Makes Highland Ranch Pay", op. cit.
471. The Sphere, 10th December 1955, "Britain's Only Cattle Ranch", op.cit.
472. The Daily Herald, 20th September 1958, "Yippee! It's the Way to Cheaper Beef."
473. Personal letter from Joe Hobbs to Barbara Barran, 4th May 1954, op.cit.
474. Paolo and Elspeth Berardelli, 24th May 2022, personal conversation with the author.
475. Neil King, "The Great Glen Cattle Ranch", Exceptthekylesandwesternisles.blogspot.com, 20th February, 2011.
476. The Scotsman, 16th September 1949, "Round Up of Hill Cattle."
477. Fresno Bee, 4th October 1953, "Bagpipes and Beef Return in Scotch Highlands to Tune of US Pasture Methods", op.cit.
478. The Daily Record, 30th October 1953, "The Battle for Beef."
479. David Turnock, 1977, op.cit.
480. The Times, 16th September 1957, "Rancher's Achievement in 10 Years."
481. Daily Herald, 20th September 1958, "Yippee, it's the way to cheaper beef!"
482. Scottish Daily Mail, 10th August 1961, "Syndicate May Buy Great Glen."
483. Dominic A. Sargent, 1998, op.cit.
484. The Scottish Daily Express, 3rd August 1961, "Hobb's Choice: Rugged Ranch Boss Says I Have to Slow Down."
485. The Observer, 13th August 1961, "The Big Ranch Mystery."
486. Scottish Daily Mail, 10th August 1961, op.cit.
487. The Observer, 13th August 1961, op.cit.

488. The Guardian, 20th August 1963, "Obituary: Joseph W. Hobbs."
489. Aberdeen Evening Express, 13th September 1961, "Great Glen Cattle Ranch Sold."
490. Birmingham Post, 14th September 1961, "10,000-acre Land Deal in Scotland."
491. Aberdeen Evening Express, 30th October 1961, "The Last Round Up."
492. Hugh Barron (ed), 1985, "The Third Statistical Account of Scotland: The County of Inverness."
493. The Guardian, 20th August 1963, op.cit.
494. Dominic A. Sargent, 1998, op.cit.
495. Personal letter from Joe Hobbs to Barbara Barran, 1st March 1962, op. cit.

Chapter 12: Yachting

496. Joseph Peter Hobbs, 1st June 2022, Personal discussion with the author.
497. The Scotsman, 2nd August 1949, "West Highland Week."
498. Dundee Courier, 15th June 1953, "Queen Elizabeth to Meet New Armada."
499. Western Mail, 21st June 1953, "Shipping Movements: Signalled off the Lizard."
500. Personal letter from Joe Hobbs to Barbara Barran, 3rd May 1954.
501. Personal letter from Joe Hobbs to Barbara Barran, op. cit., pp.3–4.
502. Rochester Democrat and Chronicle, 22nd July 1957, "Archibold Passes, Wealthy Oil Man."
503. Montrose Review, 1st August 1957, "Regatta Commodore."
504. Hugh Dan Maclennan, undated, "Hobbs' Yachts."
505. Scottish Built Ships: The History of Shipbuilding in Scotland, 'LCG125', http://www.clydeships.co.uk
506. www.HistoricRacing.com, accessed 9th June 2022, "Kenelm Lee Guinness, 14/8/1887 – 10/4/1937."
507. Scottish Built Ships: The History of Shipbuilding in Scotland, 'Samuel Green', http://www.clydeships.co.uk
508. Capt. Walter Lyle Hume, "Edinburgh Today: 'Ocean Mist'", 10th February 2007, http://www.edinphoto.org.uk
509. Montrose Review, 2nd April 1959, "Crowds Watch Arrival of Luxury Yacht."

Chapter 13: Awards and Recognition

510. Personal letter from Joe Hobbs to Barbara Barran, 3rd May 1954, op. cit.
511. The Scotsman, 22nd June 1950, "Order of St. John of Jerusalem: Glasgow Festival."
512. The Scotsman, 19th April 1950, "Benefactors to be Honoured."
513. The Northern Chronicle, 1st November 1950, "Lochaber Freedom Ceremony."
514. The Dundee Courier, 28th October 1950, "Clan Chief and Rancher Honoured."
515. The Dundee Courier, 28th October 1950, "Clan Chief and Rancher Honoured", op.cit.
516. Vancouver Sun, 25th August 1950, "British Vancouverite Wins Scottish Honors."

Chapter 14: The Great Man of the Great Glen – Later Years and Legacy

517. Companies House records for Inverlochy Castle Ltd.
518. The Guardian, 20th August 1963, "Obituary: Joseph W. Hobbs."
519. The Aberdeen Evening Express, 27th December 1961, "Well Again."
520. Personal Letter from Joe Hobbs to Barbara Barran, 1st March 1963, op. cit.
521. Dominic A. Sargent, "Inverlochy Castle: A History", 1998, op. cit.
522. The Times, 20th August 1963, "Obituary: Joseph William Hobbs."
523. Joseph Peter Hobbs, personal conversation with the author, 1st July 2022.
524. Aberdeen Evening Express, 11th May 1962, "Rancher Heads for Home."
525. Aberdeen Press and Journal, 20th August 1963, "Hillside Grave for Rancher Hobbs."
526. The Guardian, 20th August 1963, "Obituary: Joseph W. Hobbs", op.cit.
527. Vancouver Sun, 20th August 1963, "Wild West Rancher Dies."
528. The Leader Post, 21st August 1963, "Canadian Cowboy Made Two Fortunes."
529. Aberdeen Press and Journal, 20th August 1963, "Hillside Grave for Rancher Hobbs", op.cit.

530. David Daiches, "Scotch Whisky: Its Past and Present", 1969.

531. The Liverpool Echo, 11th January 1954, "The Modern Millionaires."

532. Dominic Sargent, "Inverlochy Castle: A History", 1998, op. cit.

533. The Scotsman, 17th November 1948, "Noxious Fumes: Highland Estate Owner's Complaint."

534. The Montrose Review, 30th July 1959, "Mr Hobbs on TV."

535. The Province, 13th April 1955, "Ex-Cariboo Rancher Home on Scotland's Range."

536. The Daily Herald, 20th September 1958, "Yippee! It's the way to cheaper beef."

537. The Scotsman, 20th August 1963, "Great Glen Ranching Pioneer."

538. The Times, 16th September 1957, "Rancher's Achievement in 10 Years."

539. Scottish Agricultural College Rural Policy Centre, "Farming's Retreat from the Hills", 2008.

540. Aberdeen Press and Journal, 15th June 1964, "Children's Gala Day Damper Annoys Village."

541. Aberdeen Press and Journal, 21st March 1980, "Hobbs Widow Wants Back."

542. The Scottish Banner, 22nd November 1984, "Scottish Castles: Inverlochy."

543. The Liverpool Echo, 11th January 1954, "The Modern Millionaires", op.cit.

544. Leicester Evening Mail, 28th December 1943, "Inventors Secret Tests in Leicestershire."

545. The Sphere, 10th December 1955, "Britain's Only Cattle Ranch."

546. John Bull Magazine, 12th November 1949, "Cowboys in the Highlands."

547. News Chronicle, 30th May 1952, "Meet the Amazing Mr. Hobbs."

548. The Scottish Banner, 22nd November 1984, "Scottish Castles: Inverlochy", op.cit.

549. The Sphere, 10th December 1955, "Britain's Only Cattle Ranch", op.cit.

550. British Pathé, "Highland Cattle Ranch", 1952, www.britishpathe.com

551. Canadian Broadcasting Company, "The Laird of Inverlochy", from the TV series 'Close Up' first released 29th April 1962.

552. Personal letter from Joe Hobbs to Barbara Barran, 1st March 1962.

553. The Liverpool Echo, 11th January 1954, "The Modern Millionaires", op.cit.

Chapter 15: Postscript

554. Gordon & Macphail: booklet accompanying bottles of Benromach 1977 39 Year Old Heritage Whisky.

555. Difford's Guide, Distilleries and Producers: Bruichladdich Distillery, op.cit. https://www.diffordsguide.com

556. The Scotsman, 3rd April 1947, "District News: Sale of a Distillery."

557. The Guardian, 10th October 1953, "Distillers Buys Whisky."

558. The Western Mail, 10th October 1953, "Distillers U.S. Deal."

559. The Guardian, 19th August 1954, "The Distillers Company Limited: Sir Henry J Ross Reviews the Year's Activities."

560. Aberdeen Press and Journal, 11th March 1981, "The Long John name returns to Ben Nevis."

561. Aberdeen Press and Journal, 12th January 1968, "Distillery Producing Again."

562. Companies House records, 5th November 1973, MacNab Distilleries.

563. Aberdeen Press and Journal, 23rd May 1975, "Spanish Boost: Montrose distillery plan means more jobs."

564. Mark Davidsen, "Lochside Distillery RIP", Whisky Intelligence, op.cit.

565. Brian Townsend, Scotch Missed: The Original Guide to the Lost Distilleries of Scotland, 2017, pp.96–98

566. Perth Courier and Advertiser, 8th October 2016, "Lasting legacy of whisky industry pioneers."

567. Scotch Malt Whisky Society, Distillery Profiles: Ben Nevis, https://smws.com

568. Neil King, "The Great Glen Cattle Ranch", Exceptthekylesandwesternisles.blogspot.com, 20th February, 2011, op.cit.

569. Dominic A. Sargent, 1988, op.cit.

570. Duncan Campbell, Scottish Government Yearbook 1985, op.cit.

571. Scottish Agricultural Census 2020, 15th December 2020, "Steady decline of total cattle numbers," www.gov.scot

572. The Scotsman, 12th May 1989, "The First Lady of Scotland."
573. The New York Times, 21st July 1985, "Storming the Ramparts."
574. The Calgary Herald, 11th September 1976, "Castle guests treated as friends."
575. Mark Davidson, Whisky Intelligence, 5th January 2014, "Lochside Distillery 1957 – 1992 R.I.P."
576. Edinburgh Today, 10th February 2007, "Ocean Mist."